PUBLIC SECTOR MANAGEMENT

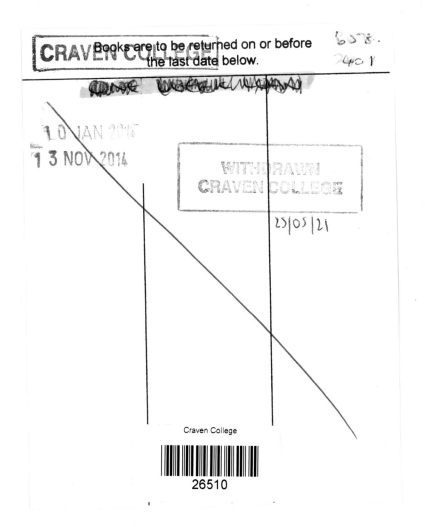

Public Sector Management

Mission Impossible?

Ian Chaston

Visiting Professor of Marketing and Entrepreneurship,
CENTRUM Catolica Business School, Peru

palgrave
macmillan

First published 2011 by
PALGRAVE MACMILLAN

Palgrave Macmillan in the UK is an imprint of Macmillan Publishers Limited,
registered in England, company number 785998, of Houndmills, Basingstoke,
Hampshire RG21 6XS.

Palgrave Macmillan in the US is a division of St Martin's Press LLC,
175 Fifth Avenue, New York, NY 10010.

Palgrave Macmillan is the global academic imprint of the above companies
and has companies and representatives throughout the world.

Palgrave® and Macmillan® are registered trademarks in the United States,
the United Kingdom, Europe and other countries.

ISBN 978–0–230–29279–6

This book is printed on paper suitable for recycling and made from fully
managed and sustained forest sources. Logging, pulping and manufacturing
processes are expected to conform to the environmental regulations of the
country of origin.

A catalogue record for this book is available from the British Library.

A catalog record for this book is available from the Library of Congress.

10   9   8   7   6   5   4   3   2   1
20   19   18   17   16   15   14   13   12   11

Printed and bound in Great Britain by
CPI Antony Rowe, Chippenham and Eastbourne

Contents

List of Figures and Tables

Figures

Tables

Preface

Since the mid-1970s many of the Governments in developed nations have been facing increasing problems funding the provision of public sector services. The core of attempts to reduce the balance demand for services relative to available funds led to various actions collectively known as New Public Management (NPM). Although the aim of NPM was to improve economics, effectiveness, and efficiency within the public sector, many of these initiatives had no real significant impact, and public sector spending continued to rise. In 2007/8, the crisis in global banking forced some developed nation Governments to intervene in the financial services industry to rescue failing institutions. These actions led to a massive rise in public sector deficits in some countries. Concurrently, the situation was made worsen because some countries such as Greece had made inappropriate decisions in their approach to borrowing money to fund public sector expenditure. As a consequence of these events, some Governments are now being forced to implement major cutbacks in public sector spending as the only realistic strategy to reducing their country's financial deficit. The outcome of these actions is that public sector managers are now entering an extended period of financial constraint. This will require some fundamental changes in the way public sector organizations are managed in the future. The purpose of this text, therefore, is to review public sector management practices as the basis for proposing actions that realistically do have the potential to improve economics, effectiveness, and efficiency within these organizations.

To understand why the public sector is facing growing problems over the imbalance between service delivery responsibilities and available resources, there is a need to understand how the welfare state has evolved over time. Hence, Chapter 1 examines the factors influencing the role of Governments to become more involved in the provision of social services to their countries' inhabitants. Following the emergence of problems such as rising inflation, economic downturn, and labour union inflexibility in the 1980s attempts were made by some Governments to reform the public sector. Chapter 2 reviews what has become known as the NPM approach and identifies some of the weaknesses of this philosophy when used to alter public sector processes.

Joseph Schumpeter and the Austrian School of Economics, on the basis of the analysis of economic cycles and the Great Depression, posited that long-term survival is dependent upon organizations recognizing and responding to meta-events. The twenty-first-century public sector manager will be facing an unprecedented combination of meta-events. Chapter 3 examines the meta-event threats created by population ageing, globalization, and the impact on public sector deficits following the need for Governments to respond to the global banking crisis.

One of the problems facing public sector managers is the complexity of the needs of different stakeholders. Chapter 4 examines the issue of stakeholder management and the adoption of appropriate values to assist the survival of public sector bodies in the face of severely constrained financial resources. Given that survival in the face of meta-events is dependent upon developing a clear understanding of how to manage the future direction of the organization, Chapter 5 examines the relevance of strategic planning in public sector organizations and the need for these organizations to develop a more innovative and creative orientation. Chapter 6 presents the perspective that adopting an innovative, entrepreneurial orientation demands identification of an appropriate vision and an ability to embed this vision into all aspects of an organization's operation. This typically requires the organization is led by a visionary leader. Hence the chapter reviews the key role of these individuals and the managerial attributes which they exhibit.

In recent years there has been a diversity of opinions expressed for and against the continued utilization of positivist, linear sequential business planning models which have dominated the management literature for the last 50 years. The strongest critics of such paradigms argue their total inapplicability in volatile or rapidly changing market conditions. Despite these criticisms, many of these analysis tools that have been developed over the years still have relevance in today's organizations. The purpose of Chapter 7 is to present some of these tools and to illustrate their ongoing role, sometimes in an updated version, in the business analysis process.

Highly entrepreneurial leaders may adopt an intuitive style during early phases of opportunity identification. This can be contrasted to other leaders who exhibit a more rational, problem-solving orientation. In both cases, however, the greater the knowledge accumulated about conditions external to the organization, the more likely is opportunity for understanding will be enhanced and potential risks more clearly identified. Chapter 8 examines the importance of understanding external environmental change, customer behaviour, and associated strategic implications. Many of the successes associated with private sector organizations achieving national or global market dominance and the ability of some of their organizations to combat competitive pressures can be attributed to the identification and introduction of a new or alternative technology. Chapter 9 reviews the implications of technological change and the degree to which this is critical in enhancing performance of public sector organizations.

The success of private sector organizations is often attributed to an organization which identifies and develops core competences which are superior to those of competition. Known as the resource-based view (RBV) of the firm, this theory clearly underlines the role that organizational capability can play in achieving long-term, sustainable growth. Chapter 10 covers the issues associated with identifying and exploiting core competences and examines how superior capability such as organizations structure or appropriate operational processes can assist public sector organizations achieve their performance goals in relation to the provision of services. Having covered the issues of external and internal analysis, Chapters 11 and 12 utilize the knowledge generated from these activities as the basis for identifying potential opportunities and how to select the most appropriate strategies through which to convert innovation and entrepreneurial thinking into a viable proposition for use by public sector agencies.

Merely developing a new plan which provides a more appropriate strategy is no guarantee of actual operational success. Chapter 13 covers issues of effectively managing the processes associated with implementing a strategy based on innovation and change. Rarely, however, is implementation of a revised business strategy a totally problem-free process. Hence, Chapter 14 examines how barriers to successful implementation can arise and how these can be overcome.

There are clear signs that events such as the collapse of Enron and recent excesses which have occurred within the world's financial community will require greater effort by commercial organizations to demonstrate to stakeholders that a higher level of responsible governance now underpins their business activities. Chapter 15 reviews how the behaviour of managers in the public sector and how the adoption of principles associated with corporate governance and corporate social responsibility (CSR) can be utilized to achieve this goal.

Fundamental shifts in the political and economic fortunes of nations, new global problems, and the advent of major technological change all have implications for almost every organization over time. Although their actual impact is often difficult to accurately forecast, the certainty is that such meta-events will occur. Hence, the final chapter examines some of the key environmental and technological changes that may occur over the balance of the twenty-first century in relation to how these may demand further fundamental revisions in future organizational strategies of public sector organizations.

Sector Evolution

The aims of this chapter are to cover the issues of:

(1) The evolution of the concept of Government intervention in the provision of services to a nation's population

(2) Evolution of the welfare state model during the twentieth century

(3) Emerging problems over funding public sector services in the 1980s

(4) Keynesian versus monetarist economic theories and the emergence of 'New Public Management' (NPM)

(5) Allocation of funds across different areas of public sector service provision

(6) The limited ability of NPM as a mechanism to control public sector spending

(7) The relevance of strategic planning for managing the current public sector financial crisis.

Sector emergence

From the early days of the creation of the first nation states, rulers and Governments have raised monies through direct and indirect taxation to fund public sector expenditure. For thousands of years the primary use of these funds was to support the armies which countries' leaders considered necessary to protect their citizens or alternatively, implement acts of aggression against other nations. Social support such as caring for the sick, the elderly, or the unemployed tended not to be considered a state responsibility. Provision of services to the disadvantaged was usually undertaken by charitable and religious bodies.

Prior to the Industrial Revolution, people primarily worked on small family-owned rural farms. This provided regular employment to all who were able and a social structure that supplied most of their needs. This self-sufficiency and family-oriented social structure were supported through bartering to acquire needed goods with the consequent result of there being only a limited need for money. Businesses were generally small operations with their owners only occasionally employing people from outside their immediate families. Craftsmen were skilled in specific trades and provided employment through a system of apprentices and journeymen, again often recruiting these individuals from within their own families. The advent of large factories during the Industrial Revolution employing thousands of unskilled workers led to increased demand for labour which prompted a mass exodus from rural to urban areas.

The Industrial Revolution induced many social, economic, and political changes in Western democracies. One of these changes was the shift towards Governments accepting greater responsibility for caring for the aged, unemployed, ill, or injured workers. This occurred because the urbanization of society that accompanied the Industrial Revolution gave rise to significant problems in relation to the health and welfare of inhabitants living, packed together, in poor housing with inadequate water supplies or sewage disposal. Recognition of the relationship between infrastructure failings and the outbreak of diseases such as cholera and typhoid led Governments to allocate an increasing proportion of tax income to supporting the general health care of their respective populations (Pollitt and Bouckaert 2004).

One of the first Governments to become more involved in the welfare needs beyond that of merely public health issues was Germany. In the nineteenth century Bismark created a 'state corporatist' model based upon the introduction of insurance schemes for people in work. These schemes provided a certain degree of protection from poverty in old age and income reduction caused by becoming unemployed (Pollitt and Bouckaert 2004). This 'statist approach' to funding such services has remains in place in Germany to the present day as is demonstrated by the policy that those in employment being mandated to purchase an insurance policy to cover their health care needs. In the nineteenth century in most other countries, however, Governments were unwilling to adopt the German model. As a consequence access to free or subsidized welfare service was only made possible by the intervention of charitable bodies and socially aware, rich industrialists who were prepared on a somewhat limited basis to fund schools and hospitals for the most socially disadvantaged in society.

Twentieth-century events

The expansion of the electoral franchise in many Western democracies to include the majority of the population in the late nineteenth and early twentieth centuries led to the emergence of new political parties seeking to represent the rights of the workers. There was also pressure from the increasingly well-organized labour unions to demand the state make greater provision for the elderly and the unemployed. Although men returning from World War I were promised a 'nations fit for heroes', this benefit remained undelivered. This was due to the parlous financial state of many of the Allied powers which had been caused by huge borrowings to fund their wartime expenditures. An example of the scale of Government deficits created by wartime borrowing is provided by the United Kingdom, where the national debt had risen from £677 million in 1910 to £7.81 billion by 1920 (Wallop 2010). In 1921 the Prime Minster David Lloyd George appointed Sir Eric Geddes to advise on reducing this deficit. He recommended annual cuts in public sector expenditure of £87 million. Although the Cabinet only approved £58 million in cuts, these were achieved by a huge reduction in the size of the British Armed Forces, a 35 per cent reduction in the size of the civil service, salary cuts, and reductions in social benefits such as subsidized secondary education. In Germany the situation was greatly exacerbated by the massive reparations that were imposed on the country by the Allied powers following the cessation of hostilities. The social unrest this caused in Germany would eventually lead to the rise of fascism and only 20 years later, the outbreak of World War II.

In addition to the public sector financial deficit problems of the 1920s, further financial pain faced by the peoples of the Western democracies as the Great Depression of the 1930s led to mass unemployment and declining standards of living. In the United States, the country most impacted by the downturn, recognition of the worsening living conditions of the average family saw the introduction of Roosevelt's New Deal, a component of which social security provided a more secure pension for the elderly and welfare payments to the unemployed.

During World War II, the more astute politicians in the Western democracies began to consider new approaches to provide free or subsidized education, unemployment, pensions, and health care in preparation for the returning members of the armed forces and their families. From these deliberations emerged the welfare state which now absorbs the vast majority of Western democracies' public sector spending (Lindbeck 1995). One of the key factors influencing the scale of public sector spending was the degree to which various Governments across the world adopted a 'universalist' model of the type proposed by William Beveridge in the United Kingdom. His model was based upon a philosophy that access to welfare services should be offered 'free at point of delivery to all' with no restrictions in relation to either an individual's financial position or level of income.

Overtime, however, the high costs associated with a universalist model have caused many Governments to move towards an 'encompassing' model. Under this alternative system some welfare services are made available free at point of provision (e.g. education), whereas others require financial contributions from the recipient when in work (e.g. earnings-related sickness benefits). The scale of the public sector spending in some countries after World War II has also been increased by retention of ownership within the public sector of services such as utilities, broadcasting, and telecommunication. In some cases this was accompanied by the subsequent nationalization of certain industries such as rail, coal mining, and steel. The motive behind these latter actions usually reflected a nation's leadership deciding that more secure, safer working environments could be created for workers by the state becoming their employer.

The problem for many Western Governments in 1945 was how to fund these new social welfare programmes because their wartime borrowings had left most of the democracies with massive national debts. Foresight over the desire to avoid the political unrest that led to the rise of fascism in Europe in the 1930s and concerns over the further expansion of communism caused the US Government to announce the Marshall Plan. This provided a huge injection of overseas aid equivalent to over $100 billion in today's money. These funds supported the rebuilding of war-torn infrastructure across the Western economies and paid for new forms of social welfare.

The economic growth enjoyed by the Western democracies during the 1950s and 1960s generated rapidly rising GNP and increasing revenue flows from taxation. Rising level of tax receipts supported an ever-increasing expansion of the public sector. This, in turn, resulted in some cases of Governments becoming the largest employers. In the United Kingdom, for example, the National Health Service (NHS) reached the point of having the largest workforce of any organization within Western Europe (Salamon and Anheier 1998).

A key aim of welfare spending after World War II in Western Europe was the achievement of full employment. Returning members of the United States' armed services, however, encountered few problems in obtaining employment in a rapidly expanding, consumer-led, post-war economy. As a result, in the United States the post-war social contract did not include the welfare provision target of achieving full employment as had occurred in Europe.

Different Priorties

Case Aims: To illustrate the differences which exist between the American welfare model and the systems elsewhere in the world.

Many in the American private sector would argue that their country's economic model represents the highest, most advanced form of capitalism. The principles underlying the model include

> *deregulation, privatisation, and the free setting of prices and especially wages in competitive markets, without interference from unions or concern for the shape of the resulting distribution of wealth. To this model, right wing politicians and their supporters would add the reduction of public subsidies, public transfer payments including pensions and keeping public enterprise to the minimum. This is accompanied by the desire for "sound" fiscal and monetary policies, with the former dedicated to budget balance and the latter exclusively to price stability.*
>
> (Galbraith 2007, p. 3)

Galbraith also suggests that the American model is repellent both to left-wing politicians and for most people in Europe because the modern Americanism is

(cont'd)

perceived to be opposed to the social democratic values of fairness, solidarity, and tolerance.

These differences in social and political attitudes between nations are critical factors in explaining the variation in the welfare service model found in the United States versus other developed nation economies elsewhere in the world. Key aspects of the American model are reflected in the provision of social amenities available to the middle class, namely, health care, education, housing, and pensions. Health care, in the United States, consumes some 15 per cent of GDP compared to 8–11 per cent in Europe. However, direct expenditure on health expenditures by the US Government consumes only 6.8 per cent of GDP. This is because until 2010 in the United States the direct public commitment to the provision of free or subsidies health care was limited to the elderly, disabled, poor families, and military veterans. For the rest of the population, medical care was covered by private insurance schemes. Overall in the United States, the tax-financed share of health care spending is approximately only 60 per cent of the country's total health care expenditure.

College education in the United States consumes about 3 per cent of GDP, whereas in Europe what Governments typically spend is about half this level. This difference reflects the greater importance that the United States places on funding a system to generate a high proportion of knowledge workers and a perception that college is a more effective alternative to paying young people unemployment benefits. The other alternative to welfare for young people in the United States is via the retention of a large military constituted of several million members which consumes 4.5 per cent of GDP. In relation to housing, expenditure on social housing in the United States is lower as a proportion of GDP than in most European countries. This reflects the fact that many Americans own their home and to ensure this ability is widely available, the Government has created various financial institutions and financial systems to enable lower paid workers to afford a mortgage.

In relation to pensions, social security payments to the elderly represent 8 per cent of GDP in the United States. The American elderly tend to live in their own paid-off homes and although via Medicare they pay only a fraction of their own medical expenses, they remain responsible for the bulk of their expenditure on pharmaceuticals. Social Security benefits provide the major source of disposable income of 65 per cent of American elderly and are the only source of income for 20 per cent of the elderly.

The American welfare model is clearly different from many other developed nations'. In these latter countries, health, college education, housing, and pensions remain substantially more within the public sector domain than in the United States. As a consequence, public spending represents a much higher share of GDP in these other countries. Galbraith posits that the American model requires lower funding as a per cent of GDP because due to relatively high levels

(cont'd)

of employment, there is less need to fund benefit programmes for the unemployed. In his view, Europe's inability to reduce unemployment reflects weaker economies, Governments' unwillingness to resolve structural unemployment problems, the payment of benefits well in excess of prevailing wage in lower level service economy jobs, and restrictive employment laws that reduce job mobility. He does admit, however, high employment in the United States over the last 20 years has been made possible by excessively liberal private sector lending practices by the financial institutions. This has resulted in both high price inflation and consumers' willingness to borrow and spend money on the basis of the perceived value of their houses.

An issue not covered by Galbraith in terms of the ability of private citizens to self-fund certain social services is the employer/employee relationships negotiated by the American labour unions during the country's rapid period of economic expansion in the 1950s. The shortage of skilled labour in certain industries and high profitability being enjoyed by major companies permitted workers to successfully negotiate additional fringe benefits, the most significant of which were employer-funded private pensions and medical insurance schemes. Employee benefits, which were a miniscule part of the average company budget in 1900, had risen to 20 per cent of total payroll by halfway through the twentieth century. Although potentially a small proportion of the private sector's total wage bill, the social ramifications reflect a significant shift of responsibility for providing higher worker standards of living from individuals to employers, with the US government only required to act as a safety net in the provision of health care and pensions for the elderly. In the twenty-first century, however, the business, social, and economic climates are much different than they were in 1950s. As noted by Jerrell (1997) by the late 1990s, corporate restructuring, technological advances, the declining power of the unions, and the poor performance of many major US corporations in world markets have meant that employee benefits are a logical area of re-evaluation by organizations seeking to survive in an increasingly competitive world. Jerrell posits that although the magnitude and long-term effects of change in employee benefits are uncertain, either employees will be required to self-fund a greater proportion of pensions and health care, or alternatively the American electorate will be more supportive of political parties willing to offer an expansion in the country's welfare state provisions.

Emerging storm clouds

In the 1970s developed nation economies were hit by the OPEC nations imposing export embargoes on their oil which they followed by the introduction of very significantly higher oil prices. Concurrently major manufacturers were beginning to encounter problems as the new Tiger Nations such as Japan and Taiwan began to make inroads into world markets for both industrial and consumer goods. To survive, major firms in the Western world were forced to reduce the size of their domestic workforce and relocate manufacturing operations to lower labour cost countries elsewhere across the globe. These actions led to a fall in corporate tax flows and rising unemployment.

By the mid-1970s, rising inflation, union unrest, and an inability to generate sufficient tax revenues to support Government spending gave rise to a reconsideration of the purpose, scope, and scale of many countries' public sector services and the management of public sector deficits. From the 1950s onwards, Governments had been supportive of what they perceived as the philosophy known as 'Keynesian economics'. Their perspective was that the theories of the economist John Maynard Keynes provided justification for the legitimacy of Government policies designed to avoid high unemployment by using public sector spending to stimulate demand during periods of adverse economic conditions, even though the inevitable outcome was an ever larger public sector deficit.

It is true that John Maynard Keynes had concluded there would be insufficient saving to finance much-needed investment following the end of World War II in order to rebuild war-torn, shattered economies (Brown-Collier and Collier 1995). This view reflected his concerns that a lack of investment in the early years of a peace-time economy would lead to high levels of unemployment. His proposal was the implementation of social investment by Governments would complement private investment, thereby leading to the creation of a more stable economic condition. However, what Governments failed to understand, or possibly decided to ignore, was that Keynes was strongly opposed to long periods of deficit spending on social programmes as a means of stimulating consumption. In his view deficits in social programme expenditure should only occur during an economic downturn with these deficits being funded by the accumulation of public sector financial surpluses from taxes raised during periods of economic growth. Consistent with this emphasis on counter-cyclical public investment, Keynes was generally opposed to policies aimed at varying incomes via tax policy in order to stimulate consumption. In his view the outcome of such policies would be rising inflation, which in turn would eventually lead to even higher unemployment.

Keynes accepted that long-term deficits should be created by Government borrowing to fund capital investment such as the building of roads or construction of hospitals. Even in these scenarios, which he referred to as 'productive debt', Keynes felt that borrowing was only justified where there was evidence of a return on the investment over the longer term. This return could be in the savings in welfare payments from the creation of jobs associated with the capital spending and from the revenue flows from services generated once a capital project had been completed.

Neoclassical economists, as well being disturbed by the way Keynesian economic theory had come to dominate political thinking, were also concerned that the inevitable outcome of prolonged deficit spending would be inflation and collapsing economies (Jordan et al. 1993). One of the leading opponents of Governments continuing to expand the size of public sector deficits through borrowing was the University of Chicago Professor Milton Friedman. Referred to as a 'monetarist', Friedman produced a number of academic papers and the hugely successful book entitled *Capitalism and Freedom* that demonstrated the abuses which can be created by a misapplication of Keynsian economic theories. His perspective on monetary theory was that in order to defeat inflation Governments should use Central Banks to establish stable monetary policies. Concurrently the emphasis should be on creating an affordable welfare state by focusing on promoting the wealth generation activities of capitalism that via taxation created a non-inflationary supply of public sector funds.

There have been wide variations in the way Governments have accepted or sought to adopt monetarist policies. In the United Kingdom where by the late 1970s the economy was moving towards meltdown, the leading proponent of a monetarist solution was the new prime minister, Margaret Thatcher. She came to power following the election of a Conservative Government. As an ardent supporter of monetarist theory Margaret Thatcher held the view that in addition to stronger monetary controls, the public sector was significantly less efficient in the provision of services than private industry. She concurred with Friedman's views that Governments involvement in any provision of services should be minimized. This led to a raft of privatizations across industries such as electricity, gas, railways, water, and telecommunications.

The degree to which public sector reform was deemed necessary in other Western nations in the 1970s and 1980s was influenced both by the health of their respective economies and the degree to which political parties in power were supportive of the importance of the public sector's involvement in the provision of services. Thus, for example, within the European Union, because countries such as Germany and France were owners of more robust economies and political parties in power were using more socialist manifestos, there was less interest in reducing the size of the public sector through privatization. Nevertheless by the mid-1980s, inflation and rising unemployment were problems confronting virtually every Western democracy. Where reduction in the size of the public sector was deemed either inappropriate or unacceptable, Governments focused on initiatives designed to upgrade the ability of their public sector entities to be more effective managers of increasingly scarce resources (Kim and Hong 2006).

Moving the Goal Posts

Case Aims: To illustrate how differing political views can frustrate the introduction of new public sector policies.

The role of politicians as stakeholders influencing the performance of public sector bodies can be illustrated by a review of the national health insurance

(cont'd)

debate in America. In 1965, the US Government enacted the Medicare and Medicaid Act which led to health expenditures growing from 4.4 per cent of the federal budget in 1965 to 11.3 per cent in 1973. The existence of Medicare and Medicaid provided evidence of the benefits of government-financed health care, but did nothing for those under 65, a large proportion of whom were without any health care coverage because they could not afford the premiums charged by private sector insurance providers. In 1974, the US Congress and US Senate attempted to introduce changes whereby national health provision might be extended to those who could not afford private health cover. Southern Democrats who held key committee chairs had previously been an obstacle to reform began to be influenced by the pressures of the non-Southern, liberal majority in the Democratic caucus. Previously in 1971, the Nixon administration had proposed a subsidized health insurance programme for the poor but this was rejected by Republicans senators. The HEW Secretary, Caspar Weinberger drafted a new health policy bill and was able to overcome the objections of others in the administration. The insurance industry worried that reform would eliminate their role in health financing pushed for a more modest bill, whilst Republican legislators were divided, some thought change would avoid introduction of socialized medicine and others wanted to be seen to support a Republican President. In the face of concerns about how reforms could be funded, the Kennedy–Mills bill was introduced which proposed mandatory employee participation in any new system. This was to stop employers who would be required to contribute to insurance premiums putting pressure on their employees to opt out of the proposed system. Eventually a compromise Act was presented to the critically important Ways and Means Committee where it failed to receive sufficient support and hence this attempt at health care reform was unsuccessful.

With the continuing upward rise in the cost of health care, President Clinton in the 1990s also attempted to introduce reforms (Ratajczak 1994). The debate was again influenced by both differing party political thinking and also the views of bodies outside the legislator. Some economists, for example, concluded that the only way to control health care costs would be to impose price controls. This idea was vehemently rejected by the medical profession and the pharmaceutical industry. Clinton attempted to draft legislation that would support concepts such as medical service purchasing alliances, community budgets schemes, and revising the training of physicians. Clinton was unable to obtain the bi-partisan support he required in either the Congress or the Senate due to widely differing views inside the US legislature. Hence, his attempt, similar to Nixon's, ended without any real progress being made.

As part of his presidential election campaign, in recognition of the continuing upward spiral causing health care costs to be some 16 per cent of total GDP and approximately 40 million American people to be without any form of

---

(cont'd)

health care cover, Barak Obama announced his plan for a Healthy America (Anon 2009a). His stated objective was to tackle needless waste and spiralling costs. Specific proposals included (a) an independent institute to conduct comparative effectiveness studies on drugs, devices, and procedures, (b) to allow Americans to buy their medicines from other developed countries if the drugs are deemed safe and prices are lower outside the United States, (c) to increase the use of generic drugs within Medicare and Medicaid, and (d) prohibit large drug companies from keeping generics out of markets.

Following his election, President Obama faced massive resistance to his plans from both inside and outside of the legislature. Opponents embarked on a large-scale public relations campaign, some of which was a distortion of the facts about what was being proposed by Obama. Pro-lifers, for example, believed that reforms would mean taxpayer-funded abortions. Older people on Medicare feared their benefits would be cut in order to fund the new programme. The Republican legislators vowed to outlaw the rationing of care by age. Few Americans had a clear idea how 'Obamacare' would affect them. A problem for the Democrats is many Americans have health insurance but have no real idea of how much it costs. Taxpayers foot the bill for the old. The uninsured have the most to gain from the proposed reforms, but they are only 15 per cent of the population. As a consequence those in employment and paying for their own insurance cover can expect that it will be they who will be paying for any reforms in whatever form they are finally agreed.

Sustaining a difficult, often bruising, battle, 12 months after his election, Obama was finally able to persuade Congress to pass his Patient Protection and Affordable Care Act. The scheme includes a number of elements with possibly the most important element being the extension of health care insurance to low-income families. The long-term costs of the Bill are claimed to be less than $1 billion. However, whatever the costs finally prove to be, the view of many in the health care industry and those in employment already paying for their own insurance cover is they expect that through higher taxation they will eventually end up paying for any reforms in whatever form they are finally agreed (Leavitt 2010).

Factors of influence

Tanzi and Schuknecht (2000) used International Monetary Fund (IMF) data to estimate that on average, real total public sector spending in the developed nations has increased from 12.6 per cent of GDP in 1960 to 17.3 per cent in 1995. In addition to extended welfare benefits to a greater proportion of the socially disadvantaged, the other factor influencing higher spending has been many Governments providing support for an increasing number of unemployed persons. Another area where spending has risen is in education. Initially this was due to the rising number of school children as a result of the post-1945 baby boom. More recently, Governments, however, have also been spending more money on tertiary education reflecting a policy of seeking to increase the skills and capabilities required in today's knowledge-based economies.

Jackson's (2009) analysis of OECD data shows that the continuing expansion of the public sector showed no sign of abating in the early years of the twenty-first century. In the United Kingdom, for example, Government expenditure as a per cent of GDP rose from 33.5 per cent in 1965 to 49.7 per cent in 2004, from 33.1 per cent to 46.8 per cent in the European Union, and from 25.6 per cent to 31.3 per cent in the United States. This reflects these countries' Governments seeking to provide greater access to 'positive freedom goods', that is goods that expand individuals' access to services such as education, health care, pensions, and unemployment benefits that widens their opportunities to enjoy a better lifestyle. As well as passing legislation providing greater access to freedom goods to a larger proportion of the population, Governments have also faced in some sectors, especially health care, the problem of a huge rise in the cost of providing these services. This has been caused by technological advances increasing the cost of equipment, treatments, and the consumables being utilized by health care providers.

One of the earliest predictions of future trends in the scale of public expenditure was produced in the nineteenth century by Adolph Wagner (Florio and Colauti 2005). In what subsequently has become known as 'Wagner's Law' this individual posited that there was an exponential relationship in the ratio between public expenditures and national income (known as the 'G/Y ratio'). The nature of the relationship is that as national income increases this is accompanied by an ever-larger proportion of funds being expended on the public sector. Wagner's justification for this outcome was that Governments were able to better fulfil the provision of certain goods (e.g. education) more effectively which were superior to that available from any private sector suppliers. Although certain questions exist concerning validity of this perspective, support for Wagner's theory is provided by the fact that the G/Y ratio was between 5 per cent and 10 per cent in the second half of the nineteenth century in the United States, the United Kingdom, France, Germany, Italy, and Sweden, but by the end of the twentieth century the ratio was risen to a level of between 35 per cent and 55 per cent.

Wagner's analysis reflected a Malthusian orientation of the world where exponential growth curves are of an infinite nature. Similar to other examples of Malthusian growth models, analysis suggests that in fact the actual data are more likely to exhibit a sigmoid shape. Thus, the rate of growth of G/Y increases over time until at a certain point the process is reversed with G/Y still increasing but at a much lower rate. Eventually, this growth rate will approach zero which leads to a plateau in total spending. As noted by Florio and Colauti, this is the outcome that has now occurred because by the end of the twentieth century G/Y growth rate curves are beginning to move towards zero in most developed economies, probably indicating the emergence of a steady state scenario.

These authors posit that this outcome is caused by the burden of ever-increasing taxation eventually acting as a brake on Governments' ability to persuade the electorate of the need to sustain further increases in expenditure on publicly provided goods.

The volume of data that developed nation Governments now publish on issues such as population size, population age profiles, unemployment, and spending levels has for many years provided economists and sociologists with a wealth of information. This has led to numerous research studies seeking to determine which other factors might influence the absolute size of the public sector budgets in different countries. One widely debated issue within the litera-ture is the degree to which the manifestos of political parties influence the nature and scale of public expenditure. Known as the 'partisan politics' model, this theory posits that left- and right-wing parties adopt different macro-economic policies in relation to the trade-off between inflation and unemployment. This, in turn, affects the level of public expenditure and the size of budget deficits. The typical hypothesis associated with the model is that political parties compete for votes by promising to implement programmes that best serve those mem-bers of the electorate which they claim to represent. Lower income voters are generally in favour of a large, active, and market-regulating state. They tend to be more inclined to support socialist or social democratic parties who promise lower unemployment which can only be achieved by increased levels of public sector spending and higher budget deficits (Brauninger 2005).

Although the partisan model is intuitively appealing, the degree to which empirical evidence exists to support the theory is limited and also tends to be somewhat contradictory. In an attempt to assess model validity, Brauninger anal-ysed the size of government expenditure and distribution in relation to two major budget categories, social security and economic affairs, using data from 19 OECD countries over the time period 1971–1999. The data utilized for the analysis came from Australia, Austria, Belgium, Canada, Denmark, Finland, France, Germany, Iceland, Ireland, Italy, Luxembourg, the Netherlands, New Zealand, Norway, Portugal, Spain, Sweden, and the United Kingdom. In all of these countries stated manifestos were found to have directly impacted on total government expenditure following an election. Hence, if a manifesto promised spending cuts, public sector expenditure is likely to decrease. Where a higher spending level is promised, subsequent government expenditure is likely to increase. The analysis further appears to support the view that the potential for policy change towards either social security or economic support spending as defined in political manifestos will influence the distribution of expenditure between these two budget categories. A promise of higher social security spend-ing does indeed result in higher expenditure for this area, as does a promise in relation to expenditure on seeking to influence a nation's economic perfor-mance. However, his analysis was unable to support the prevailing view that socialist or social democratic parties are more likely to increase total public sec-tor expenditure. Instead, actual spending tended to be influenced by prevailing economic conditions, namely as GNP increased, whichever political party was in power the usual outcome would be an increase in public sector spending. Conversely, in most cases, a downturn in an economy can be expected to be reflected in a reduction in public sector spending no matter which political party is in power.

Keefer and Vlaicu's (2007) study of the relationship between the election of politicians and public sector spending also confirmed the perspective that manifesto promises made to attract voters will usually determine the public expenditure pattern of the next Government. They concluded, however, that expenditure patterns are also influenced by the way in which politicians have generated support from voters. The authors posit that in those democracies which are endowed with political competitors having a well-known policy position, politicians are more able to make credible promises to the entire electorate. Once elected, these politicians can immediately pursue policies which they perceive as in the best interests of the general public. In some democracies, usually those which are relatively new, politicians may have fewer resources, their party will still be engaged in building credibility, and, hence, they are often less able to effectively communicate their manifesto to the electorate. Under these circumstances, the politicians may rely upon intermediaries such as wealthy landowners or owners of large factories to persuade their employees and their families of the need to vote in a certain way. Once elected, these politicians are expected to fulfil the promises made to gain the support of the key intermediaries. As a result, policies in relation to expenditure will be biased towards meeting these promises. This will usually be to the detriment of the provision of adequate welfare services for the general population. In some of the newer democracies, politicians prefer to invest in their own ability to make credible commitments to voters rather than to channel their appeals through intermediaries. In these democracies, public policy and expenditure over time tend to be increasingly directed towards delivery of services that meet the needs of the majority of the country's inhabitants.

Although the scale of public sector spending is heavily determined by a nation's GNP, the sociology literature, especially in relation to the European democracies, provides evidence that differing views between socio-economic classes will influence the way in which expenditure is distributed across the welfare state. Known as the 'power resources approach' model this concept is concerned with the ways that different actors within a society can use their influence over politicians to ensure their interests are fulfilled when Governments are setting budgets for different areas of public sector expenditure. Although democracy annulled the traditional correlation between wealth, the right to vote, and socio-economic class, the distribution of economic resources in most countries has remained unequal with the upper classes enjoying a much higher standard of living than members of the lowest social classes. Class members who enjoy an above average standard of living can be expected to favour Government allocation of public sector economic resources that support market-related expenditure policies, whereas citizens from relatively disadvantaged social classes are likely to utilize activities such as joining together in a union in an attempt to strengthen their ability to influence Government spending decisions. To a substantial degree the evolution of the welfare states in the twentieth century can be seen as outcomes of such efforts.

Following the end of World War II, the ability of the lower social classes to exert their power by voting for their preferred political manifesto has led to a greater proportion of public sector spending being directed at decreasing inequality and poverty within society. Achievement of this goal has been greatly assisted by those individuals desiring for greater social equality having their views being represented by strong unions. These organizations can be expected to oppose employers who they perceive as seeking to limit the abilities of politicians to fund social programmes through the imposition of new corporate taxes. In contrast, it is somewhat difficult to identify the exact actual role of employers in directly influencing welfare state policies. However, it is apparent that in the absence of major left-wing parties of the type found in Europe and without strong and centralized trade unions, the United States is a country where the views of business can be expected to have had the greatest chance of opposing greater allocation of public sector spending towards the expansion of welfare services for the unemployed or socially disadvantaged.

The advent of the welfare state has been accompanied by an expansion of public sector agencies responsible for managing activities such as education and benefit payments. These organizations are constituted of both middle- and working-class employees. Their shared preference to minimize unemployment has led to reduction in differences of opinion (or 'class divide') concerning which political party can be expected to best represent their interests. This shift in attitudes has become very apparent since the mid-1980s when Governments of very different political standing in the face of rising inflation and declining economic performance have been forced to cap or even reduce sector spending, whilst concurrently diverting more resources to supporting the unemployed. In countries such as France, Germany, and Italy, for example, Government proposals for spending cuts and the redistribution of public sector spending often lead to strikes and demonstrations by individuals from different social classes. These events are usually organized by the unions representing both white- and blue-collar members who work in the public sector.

The convergence of social attitudes has caused some sociologists to conclude that in most democracies the growing need for Governments to implement austerity measures in relation to public sector spending has virtually abolished the social divide in relation to political loyalties across different social classes. It is argued that supporting evidence is the way virtually all political parties have apparently moved away from representing the needs of specific social classes and instead positioned themselves as offering more universalist manifestos in relation to their policies over public sector spending. However, universalist manifestos can lead to the electorate being unable to identify any evidence of 'clear blue waters' between the different parties and, as a consequence, voter apathy can emerge, thereby increasing the probability of no one single party achieving a majority with the consequent emergence of coalition governments.

During the 1990s, although there has been general acceptance of the need for greater austerity in public sector spending, there has been a tendency for some Governments to continue to increase the size of their public sector deficits. In an attempt to determine what factors influence this trait Harrinvirta and Mattila (2001) undertook a detailed empirical study of Government expenditure in OECD countries in relation to the spending decision made by the political parties who are in power. They concluded that even in periods of economic austerity, public sector spending can be expected to increase more rapidly in those countries run by coalition governments. In their view this outcome reflects the fact that in multi-party governments, the tendency of each party is to support the needs of the voters who brought them to power. This means that for a decision to be reached within a coalition, compromises are required that have the consequence of preventing significant budget reductions ever being achieved. Additionally none of the parties will support any new tax proposals that would adversely impact the voter group(s) who brought them to power. As a result, during an economic downturn in countries run by coalition governments, public spending often continues to increase and because tax inflows are reduced, the size of the public debt is much larger than in countries where a single party has been voted into power. Furthermore, even when economic conditions start to improve, countries run by coalition governments require many more years before any real reduction in the public sector deficit is achieved.

Regression of Progression

Case Aims: To illustrate the changing nature of the policy of relying upon progressive taxation to fund the public sector.

By the late 1970s, many Governments were beginning to face rising discontent from both industry and their electorates over progressive taxation. This situation forced politicians to reconsider the ongoing acceptability of a public sector funding model based upon steeply rising progressive taxes. There were a number of factors influencing this discontent. In the corporate sector the globalization of the world economy has led many major manufacturers in developed nation economies to relocate their operations to elsewhere in the world. Key attractions of relocation included lower labour costs, lower corporate funding of employee welfare taxes, Government grants, and in many cases, the further incentive of not having the requirement to pay corporation taxes during the early years following their arrival in a new country. Additionally, those firms which feel unable to relocate overseas, who previously were content with tax incentive policies that released them from paying taxes as long as they invested

(cont'd)

in new plant and equipment, no longer found these incentives sufficient to protect them from paying higher taxes. Additionally, many of the tax incentives that Western democratic Governments had introduced to stimulate private sector investment led to the creation of tax loopholes which permitted large corporations to dramatically reduce their domestic tax liabilities. At the same time, the general public was becoming increasingly dissatisfied with tax systems. The average citizen were presented with stories in the media of huge corporations who paid little or no taxes, whilst at the same time the amount of tax being deducted from their wages was growing. Increasingly, the general public came to feel their tax system was unfair, corporations and the wealthy seem to be paying too little in taxes, whilst they were now paying too much. In some countries, such as Sweden, where personal tax rates were very high, it became to appear that entrepreneurs were being discouraged from creating new, high growth businesses and the average citizen perceived little benefit is exhibiting a work ethic because this did not lead to increased spending power, merely a larger tax bill.

By the mid-1990s in the Western democracies, as the general public observed major employers relocating overseas with the resultant reduction in the number of domestic jobs, arguments for social justice were increasingly being overwhelmed by the claims in support of tax regimes being more orientated towards stimulating economic growth. Governments responded to cutting corporation taxes and marginal tax rates for higher incomes earners. The revenues lost in these rate reductions have usually been replaced by increases in indirect consumption taxes or social insurance premiums. These moves represent a significant reduction in the use of taxation policy as an instrument of economic management. Instead of a philosophy of letting markets shape the future economy, intervention by Governments has begun to appear in many more political manifestos. Accompanying this shift has been increasing support for the idea that by reducing the use of progressive taxation, this would increase consumer disposable spending power which, in turn, would lead to economic growth and the creation of additional jobs. The United States reduced the top individual tax rate from 70 to 33 per cent and top corporate tax rate from 46 to 34 per cent; the United Kingdom reduced its top individual tax rate from 93 to 40 per cent and top corporate rate from 52 to 35 per cent. Opining upon this trend in taxation policy, Steinmo (1994, p. 18) comments that

> Business has always enjoyed a privileged position. Still, the victory of the interests of average citizens over capital has been a hallmark of the success of modern democracy throughout the world. But as the power resources available to capital increase with its growing internationalism, it may be that the difficult battle will become a futile one.

Seeking savings

The growing pressure in the 1980s on nations such as the United Kingdom and the United States to find ways of controlling ever-rising public sector spending led to more emphasis on the introduction of 'managerialism' as a mechanism through which to achieve greater efficiency and effectiveness within public sector organizations. Reform of the public sector, implemented under the banner of 'New Public Management' (NPM), was seen as increasingly necessary in order to reduce the public sector's share of GDP (UN/DESA 2005). These policies were adopted by some Governments for ideological reasons. In other countries changes in public policy reflected the increasing vulnerability of national economies in the face of increased competition due the globalization of economies. From the outset, NPM was often characterized as involving the introduction of private sector management models into public sector organizations. Politicians who favoured such moves considered this strategy as the most effective way of improving efficiency and levels of service provision (Osborne 2010).

From the outset one of the obstacles confronting the new philosophy was the problem that delivery of services in many areas of the public sector (e.g. education and health care) is the responsibility of professionals who were resistant to the idea that utilization of resources would become the domain of managers. These latter individuals were perceived as bureaucrats more interested in gaining control over all decision-making than in meeting the needs of the general public to whom services are delivered (De Bruijin 2005). The perspective of the professionals was re-enforced by the fact that underlying the NPM doctrine was the foundation stone of seeking new ways to measuring performance as the basis for determining opportunities to achieve cost savings in public sector expenditure (Hood 1991).

As the appeal of the NPM doctrine led to the adoption of the concept in additional countries such as Australia, Canada, and New Zealand, an increasingly debated issue was the effectiveness and validity of the performance management systems being utilized by public sector managers. Academics such as Beryl Radin (2006) argued that measures only concerned with efficiency and effectiveness represented a narrow perspective about the nature, role, and purpose of public sector organizations (PSOs). In her view, there is a need to also include measures assessing 'process' using the variables of openness, integrity, and participation and 'regime' using the variables of robustness, reliance, and innovation. Added support for the validity of this view was provided by the media publicizing situations of managers implementing organizational reforms more aimed at ensuring 'all the boxes have ticked' whilst ignoring how changes in organizational process might provide the basis for developing new and more productive approaches to service provision. In commenting on this situation, Van Dooren et al. (2010, p. 31) concluded that although the concept of performance management has existed long before the emergence of NPM, many PSOs have continued to ignore the need 'to make a clear distinction between performance measurement and performance management which is needed for a better insight in the functioning of performance management systems'.

Some countries, such as those in mainland Europe, decided that most NPM solutions were unacceptable. In some cases, this is because their welfare service tradition is perceived as philosophically incompatible with the idea of introducing private sector practices into public sector organizations. These countries reject NPM on the grounds that privatization would introduce a profit motive which breaches a long-established, social conscience-based obligation to support the needs of the disadvantaged within society. Furthermore, in countries with well-embedded bureaucracies and extremely well-paid public sector workers, civil servants usually have sufficient power and influence to successfully resist a change towards greater emphasis on managerialism.

Despite strong support in some texts dedicated to presenting the philosophy (Hughes 2002), even during the early years of NPM some academics were questioning the potential of the philosophy to achieve fundamental reforms. Hood and Jackson (1992) concluded that NPM was a 'disaster waiting to happen' and Farnham and Horton (1996) perceived NPM as a failed paradigm. In their analysis of the benefits claimed for NPM, Pollitt and Bouckaert (2004) determined that claims made for positive outcomes were at best partial and in some cases, even somewhat questionable. Fredickson and Smith (2003) concluded that in reality NPM was simply a sub-school of Public Administration (PA) theory which lacked any genuine theoretical validity and conceptually was insufficiently rigorous.

Public sector managers will tend to argue there are grounds to question the validity of such criticisms by pointing to achievements such as establishing a stronger customer orientation in the provision of services and the impact of the Internet in the provision of more cost-effective 24/7 service provision in areas such as tax returns, the provision of information, and the capability to accept online applications for welfare claims. Nevertheless, a key objective of NPM was to stop the ever-increasing rise in public sector expenditure. OECD data indicated that expansion of the public sector showed no sign of being brought under control in the early years of the twenty-first century. In the United Kingdom, for example, Government expenditure as a per cent of GDP has risen from 33.5 per cent in 1965 to 49.7 per cent in 2004, from 33.1 per cent to 46.8 per cent in the European Union, and from 25.6 per cent to 31.3 per cent in the USA. Hence, if judged against the criteria of permitting nations to either cap or even reduce public sector spending, then it is difficult to conclude that NPM has been overwhelming success.

Strategic planning

By the beginning of the twentieth century the increasing complexity of organizations in the private sector prompted the emergence of a managerial philosophy based upon the use of business planning as a system through which to define and achieve future performance objectives. After World War II, the addition of new management theories and real-world managerial practices led to the evolution of more sophisticated approach which ultimately emerged as a new paradigm known as 'strategic planning'. By the 1960s, the accepted components of this process were all in place; namely organizations understand required actions involve determining relevant internal strengths and weaknesses, specifying distinctive competences and developing strategies which are aligned with the opportunities and threats which exist in the external environment (Learned et al. 1965).

The applicability of strategic planning in the public sector was widely accepted in the early years of NPM as an effective process through which to define and implement actions for improving the performance of PSOs. Unfortunately, factors such as poor leadership skills and weaknesses among middle and lower managers often resulted in strategic planning failing to deliver the promised benefits of providing a platform for successfully defining future organizational activities. In his assessment of failure Bunning (1992) concluded that many managers had not been trained to understand what is strategic and what is not. Managers who are for many years had focused on the effective implementation of standard administrative processes were often unable to think imaginatively about alternative ways their organizations might operate and how internal processes might be changed to more effectively respond to environmental change. Bunning also perceived that within many PSOs, a serious problem was that strategic planning was often introduced by mandate without any attempt to persuade the workforce of the relevance of the philosophy or fundamental aspects of process. Furthermore, some senior managers, when importing the philosophy from the private sector, totally failed to appreciate that a different set of assumptions are required when utilizing strategic planning in the context of a public sector scenario. Not surprisingly the outcome of such failings was strategic planning was frequently perceived as a ritual to be performed involving the production of a highly detailed document which only had the purpose of keeping the politicians and external stakeholders happy. As a consequence, once the annual strategic plan had been written typically, there was a marked fall-off of attention and interest paid to anything actually contained within the plan.

Even in those cases where the original intent was to utilize the strategic plan to guide future operations, there was a common tendency to adopt a consensus-seeking process to identify a strategy which is not objectionable to any of the major internal stakeholders. Political bargaining to achieve agreement inside the PSO and with relevant Government funding sources usually results in a sub-optimal strategy in relation to the effective future provision of public sector services. As a consequence, within a very short period of time, many public sector managers began to perceive strategic planning as a non-functional aspect of NPM. This caused them and their external advisors to turn to other, apparently more appealing alternative concepts such as Total Quality Management, Customer Care, and workforce empowerment to guide future organizational activities.

The rejection of strategic planning in the public sector was also assisted by the emergence of the debate in the academic literature concerning the relevance of the concept even in private sector organizations when managers face turbulent or rapidly changing external environments. One of the leading proponents of this perspective was the Canadian academic Professor Henry Mintzberg (1990). He argued that the specification of a deliberate, detailed strategy cannot be achieved with any real degree of absolute confidence in today's increasingly uncertain world.

Crisis management

The history books will describe the early twenty-first century as a period when consumers, businesses, and Governments all became enamoured with low interest rates and limited intervention of Central Bank providing opportunities to support greater spending through higher borrowing. The first indication of trouble with this economic model was the emergence of problems in the United States' sub-prime mortgage market. This was followed by banks in both the United States and Europe due to their involvement in complex financial derivative products being forced to admit their balance sheets contained high levels of toxic debt. In order to avoid a banking collapse of the scale previously seen in the 1930s, Governments were forced to intervene. This resulted in a massive increase in public sector deficits. The scale of these deficits was further exacerbated in some Mediterranean countries because Governments had been making the mistake of sustaining economic growth through excessive borrowing. By 2009, the only solution for many developed nation economies has been to implement massive cuts in public spending.

The problem now confronting public sector managers and students expecting to enter the public sector following graduation is given the apparent failure of concepts such as strategic planning and other aspects of NPM, what alternative managerial concept can be used to sustain the delivery of services in the face of the fundamental financial funding crisis now facing most PSOs. The fundamental perspective upon which this text is based is to provide this managerial solution by proposing that academics and practitioners were wrong in rejecting strategic planning as an effective model through which to determine and guide the future activities of PSOs. The justification for this viewpoint is provided by Bryson's (1981) seminal article in which he examines why strategic planning is an effective paradigm through which to resolve public sector crises. In the article, Bryson draws upon the earlier writings of Thompson (1967) who proposed that when there is environmental stability and no widely accepted perceptions of emerging threats, individuals who are advocates of seeking new approaches or alternative solutions are perceived as pursuing their own personal agendas. As a consequence, it is only when a major crisis occurs that such individuals are no longer considered to be a source of organizational instability but instead are now recognized as the source of effective ideas and appropriate solutions. However, in order to identify and implement effective solutions, there is a fundamental requirement that everybody comes together with a common aim of developing a comprehensive, systems-wide solution. Bryson posits that this activity is precisely the purpose and philosophy underlying the concept of strategic planning. In his view, the reason that some academics and practitioners have continued to reject this managerial philosophy is they have not understood that examples of failure in the use of strategic planning are not caused by flaws in the fundamental concept, but instead stem from management errors during process implementation.

Further support for the benefits of utilizing strategic planning in the response to significant change is provided by Pullen (1993). He proposed that during periods of discontinuous change in the public sector, such as major reduction in financial resources, managers need to focus on organizational and managerial processes that can permit reconstitution into new, often significantly different operational entities. In his view, managers who spend their time worrying about where the boxes should be on the organization chart are liable to create a losing proposition. Pullen believes that strategic planning will provide the basis for an organizational re-creation by focusing on creating, building, and hoarding strategic resources that can support a rapid adaptation to sustaining the delivery of core services in a very different external environment.

In his assessment of the benefits of strategic planning in the face of discontinuous change in public sector organizations, Pullen (1993, p. 38) concludes that

> Vision is not enough to sustain an organization during the potential chaos of the transition period. A key challenge is to learn how to manage transitions effectively; how to disengage from the old state and engage with the new environment in a way that minimizes the human and organizational costs of change. It requires not only charismatic skills like envisioning, enabling, and energizing, but also substantive people skills in structuring, controlling and motivating, and institutional skills in diffusing leadership throughout the organization by leveraging skills and building management ability.

In terms of explaining why strategic planning may have fallen out of favour in the public sector, Plant (2009) has recently presented the perspective that practitioners have become so focused on meeting performance measures that a complete disconnect has emerged between a PSO's strategic plan and the key performance targets that have been imposed by a funding source or Government department. Plant suggests that in the currently highly problematic world facing PSOs there is a fundamental requirement to understand the relationship which exists between the strategic plan and the organization's performance measurement framework. This requires that performance measurement must be positioned as one element of the strategic plan. This permits an effective plan to be created in which all stakeholders will comprehend the degree to which available resources will permit partial or complete attainment of the organization's future goals and objectives. Furthermore, once the strategic plan is implemented, the performance management system by being linked into the strategic plan (i) defines objectives against which progress is measured, (ii) tracks inputs, outcomes, and efficiencies, (iii) establishes benchmarks for setting targets and undertaking performance comparisons, and (v) permits the evaluation of service provision effectiveness.

Troubled Reformation

2

The aims of this chapter are to cover the issues of:

(1) The aims of NPM in relation to efficiency, effectiveness, and economy in public service provision

(2) The desire to reduce neutrality in the behaviour of public sector employees

(3) The role of privatization as an element of the NPM model

(4) Utilizing performance indicators to assess the effectiveness of public sector service delivery

(5) The role of quality in relation to the delivery of services

(6) Introducing the concept of customer orientation into the provision of services

Political purpose

Faced with delivering manifestos of seeking to meet the needs of society in the face of increasingly inadequate public sector funds, in the late 1980s politicians became enamoured with the idea that reforming public sector practices could close the gap between service supply and demand. Referred to as the NPM model the emphasis was on achievement of the '3 Es' of economy, efficiency, and effectiveness. The focus on economy related to minimizing the cost of inputs and ensuring their most economic use in the provision of services. Efficiency is concerned with optimizing the cost of outputs. Effectiveness involves maximizing outputs.

As politicians sought to explain the growing problem of funding the welfare state, an early target to divert attention away from the electorate blaming the political system for any errors having been made was to claim huge inefficiencies and ineffectiveness existed due to poor working practices within the public sector

(Denhardt et al. 1989). In presenting this perspective, politicians were prepared to infer that public sector employees were the primary obstacle standing in the way of change. What actually was occurring was that public servants were seeking to retain the role of exhibiting neutrality over public policy whilst concurrently providing politicians with guidance on what should be considered when determining whether proposed changes met the fundamental criteria of 'being in the public interest'. In the face of such behaviour politicians espoused the need to introduce private sector-inspired management models on the grounds that this would remove the lethargy and resistance to change which they felt they faced when working with civil servants. The new employment model sought to remove job protection for civil servants and to substitute tenured employees with contract workers who are obliged to provide specific outputs with few job security guarantees if they fail to fulfil objectives specified by politicians. The view of those demanding this public reform justified their proposals on the grounds that productivity will increase when governments are run on more 'business-like lines'. Unfortunately, to date, there is little evidence that the new employment model leads to significant improvements in efficiency or effectiveness. In fact, available data suggest that changes made in working practices in the public sector under the banner of 'modernization' can actually lead to a decline in productivity, morale, and organizational loyalty.

In reaching the conclusion of a need to fundamentally restructure the public sector, it appears politicians had forgotten the reforms their predecessors had been forced to introduce into the civil service in the nineteenth century. These were deemed necessary to eradicate favouritism, cronyism, intimidation, and corruption involving a system that encouraged mediocre governance caused by the highest priority being given to rewarding friends and to granting political favours in return for favours received. The replacement model which was introduced involved the creation of a merit-based civil service. The role of civil servants was seen as acting as the moral guardian of democracy by accepting rule-based and virtue-based codes of behaviour (Bowman and West 2007). Public servants were now expected to be loyal to the system of government, not to any particular political party. They could allow civil servants to give free and candid advice because their positions were safeguarded by both legislation and the prevailing values of political parties. In return, civil servants were expected to be responsive and efficient in their delivery of services. Competence was the foundation of ethical public management with response to Government requests for action being led by highly professional managers guiding the activities of non-partisan employees and ensuring individuals were shielded from unscrupulous politicians. As noted by Bowman and West (2007, p. 177),

> When choices are guided by benevolence, creativity, an ethic of compromise and social integration – a moral tenet of democracy – there is at least the satisfaction that the problem has been fully examined and that the decision can be rationally defended. Those who remain in the more politicized workplace may displace their loyalties from serving the public to obeying political masters. Manipulating public servants as disposable commodities or interchangeable parts is demeaning and misguided.

In his studies of effective organizational structures that influenced the success of organizations, Max Weber described bureaucracy as an organizational form involving a hierarchy of authority, impersonal rules to define tasks, standardized procedures, promotion based on achievement, and the employment of specialized labour. Weber expressed the view that bureaucracy was capable of attaining the highest degree of efficiency and the most rationally known means of exercising authority over human beings. More recently, it has become popular amongst politicians to use the term 'bureaucrats' as a derogatory description of public sector employees. One of the potential weaknesses of a bureaucracy is the organization may evolve into a multi-layered hierarchical management structure where there is an excessive reliance upon rules and rigid control of permitted behaviours. This, however, is not an attribute which is confined to public sector organizations. The same behaviour traits can also emerge in major private sector organizations (Weymes 2004).

What critics of bureaucracies seem to forget is one of the strengths of the public sector version of the Weberian model is that the organizational form is extremely effective for building shared values among employees concerning the fair treatment of citizens and strong defence of the public good. Within this system the bureaucrat is expected to act as the transfer agent of the ethics of public interest. Codification of processes through the use of clearly defined regulations usually ensures actions are suitable and appropriate. In their review of NPM, Caron and Giauque (2006) note this new managerial philosophy was claimed by politicians to remove ineffectiveness and inefficiency within public organizations. In reality the usual outcome is the introduction of new values by which the performance of today's civil servants is judged using variables such as productivity, efficiency, risk-taking, and exhibiting initiative. These authors posit that this new orientation means civil servants are confronted with conflicting values that may lead to paradoxes that call into question their long-established professional values in relation to their capacity for ethical and critical deliberation. Caron and Giauque posit that there is evidence of the emergence of new professional values based upon achieving whatever results are demanded by their political masters, thereby leading to civil servants exhibiting self-interest and personal opportunism. Such an eventuality would be in complete opposition to traditional Weberian public ethics values and ultimately could lead to total erosion of the fundamental purpose of public servants, namely acting as the defenders of public interest.

Frederick W. Taylor argued at the beginning of the twentieth century that his philosophy of scientific management could be applied to both industry and government in the United States. His view was supported by government reformers who were seeking to create an impartial, merit-based civil service. This aim was reflected by the opinion that inefficiency could be closely identified with public sector corruption that was prevalent at that time in many US cities. World War II introduced the need for new approaches to more effective planning and action execution in the country's Federal administration. This requirement included the need for administrators to become more heavily involved in policy making. Taylorism and Weberian managerial models are associated with the norms of hierarchy, impartiality, and neutrality which means public servants are expected to ensure that their own personal, social, or political values do not influence fulfilment of their assigned job roles. This behavioural trait has been labelled as the 'morally mute manager' who does not voice or act on their own sense of morality while holding public office (Menzel 1999). The emergence of the NPM model has led to questions being raised about the validity of sustaining the 'morally mute manager' concept. This is because NPM is seen as requiring public sector managers to become responsible for defining strategy for their organization, utilize empowerment, expand participation in decision-making, promote competition, put customers first, and foster the concept of 'market-oriented government'.

Caron and Giauque utilized case materials to examine the introduction of NPM into Canada and Switzerland. In both countries there was evidence that civil servants perceived opportunities to adopt a more flexible approach to decision-making that could lead to innovative behaviour in terms of identifying more effective approaches to managing service delivery. A more negative outcome was that the frontiers that traditionally separated the world of political decision-making from administrative decision-making have been breached. Some administrators began to start making political decisions and some politicians have become involved in administrative decisions. Also of concern were the rules for respecting anonymity and neutrality in the provision of advice between administrators and politicians have been broken repeatedly, with both groups using the public arena to accuse the other of making errors. In some cases, a culture of fear has been created in which civil servants worried about their careers now avoid expressing concern or disagreement with their political masters over matters of policy. Identification of these negative outcomes caused Caron and Giauque to suggest that new public ethics concerned with a results-orientated approach to management is now the dominant feature within public sector organizations. Their concern is that in judging the effectiveness of civil servants' performance, employees' commitment to upholding public interest is no longer considered to be important. Under these circumstances, NPM would appear to favour the development of a greater allegiance of civil servants to undertaking whatever task their employer organizations has been assigned and that any allegiance to the protection of the common good has ceased to have any relevance.

Privatization

Evidence of the benefits of centralized planning in World War II and concerns about the lack of concern for employee welfare in industries such as coal mining and ship building caused politicians in countries such as the United Kingdom to perceive strong economic and social benefits in nationalizing key industries. The outcome was that by the 1970s, nationalized industries in some countries often represented approximately 50 per cent of total GDP and employed a significant proportion of the total workforce. In the face of increasing problems over sustaining economic growth, right-wing politicians concluded there was a strong case to adopt a philosophy of privatization involving the return of many nationalized entities back to the private sector. The articulated justification for such actions was that nationalized industries had become bureaucratic structures and that the only solution for achieving greater efficiency was to inject the discipline of private sector management practices (Manning et al. 1992).

Politicians' justification for implementing privatization was consistent with the view that this action provided the means of introducing 'market discipline' into the economy, thereby leading to greater organizational efficiency. For some political parties it is an article of faith that state-owned corporations are less efficient, less competent, and less profitable than their private sector counterparts. This was even considered to be the case where both operates in the same competitive environment with the public sector enjoying advantages such as protective legislation or being in receipt of Government subsidies. The assumption of these politicians is that private sector firms will automatically respond to market signals in a competitive market and introduce strategies to optimize the allocation of resources to reflect customer demand. It was felt that capital markets encourage private corporate efficiency through the threats of possible loss of market share, takeover, or even bankruptcy.

Subsequent longitudinal studies of various industries following privatization reveal little evidence of any productivity gains, thereby raising questions about the fundamental assumption that private sector managers are able to create more efficient organizations. Furthermore, in those cases where the privatized operation has appeared more efficient, it was often due to the new owners reducing or withdrawing the provision of services to the socially disadvantaged or implementing employment practices which greatly decreased average wages or involved removal of employee benefits (Letza et al. 2004). These authors concluded that a more realistic approach to assessing the benefits of privatization is to recognize that in increasingly complex and rapidly changing world, neither private nor public ownership alone can decide an organization's future performance. This is because there are numerous economic, political, technological, social, and cultural factors which determine long-term success. As demonstrated by the failure of the UK car manufacturer British Leyland following return to the private sector, merely being more efficient is unlikely to provide the basis for ensuring organizational survival.

Assessing Outcomes

Case Aims: To illustrate that in some cases there is little or no evidence that privatization leads to gains in efficiency or effectiveness.

As long as politicians seek to deliver higher quality services at a lower cost, privatization will remain on the policy makers' agendas. Privatization usually means increasing the role of the private sector in the production and distribution of

(cont'd)

public goods. One form of privatization is 'contracting out' in which a Government body defines service standards, but permits companies the freedom to choose how they wish to deliver services. In the United States in the 1980s, one area where privatization was observed to be an effective strategy for achieving greater efficiencies was public transportation. Implementation of this philosophy varied across the country and as a result service delivery was split across private sector firms, managed transit systems, and government-owned agencies. Since the 1980s the number of private sector operators has declined over time, in many cases being replaced by a contracted out transit system.

A number of research studies generated data on operational costs in the early years of transit privatization. These data permitted Leland and Smirnova (2009) to undertake a comparative assessment of performance change after 25 years that these different types of organization achieved based upon using the same influencing variables that had been identified as critical in earlier studies. Labour efficiency is represented by revenue vehicle hours per operating employee and revenue vehicle hours per total employee. Revenue vehicle hours (RVH) and revenue vehicle miles (RVM) represent the time spent on actual operations. Vehicle efficiency is assessed in terms of vehicle miles per peak vehicle and vehicle hours per peak vehicle. Maintenance efficiency is assessed in terms of vehicle miles per maintenance employee. Consumption of transportation service is assessed by passenger trips in relation to operating expense. The safety factor is reflected by revenue vehicle miles and revenue vehicle hours between failures. Revenue generation includes passenger miles per operating expense and operating revenue per revenue vehicle hour. Finally, the public assistance component is represented by the operating subsidy vehicle hour and the total subsidy per vehicle hour.

Leland and Smirnova's analysis caused them to conclude that after 25 years privately owned and managed transit systems are no longer more efficient and effective than government-owned agencies. Their perspective is that this may have occurred for several reasons. Firstly, the lack of competition in the industry could be one reason. Without any serious competition, private sector transit services usually remain a monopoly and operate under the same conditions as public providers. Secondly, the number of private firms has significantly decreased possibly because rising operating costs over time have outweighed any initial cost savings achieved by using private sector organization. Thus, as service provision ceases to be profitable, many private companies will decide to leave the market. The study also concluded that transit agencies that contract out services are no more efficient and effective as they were 25 years ago. The researchers propose this outcome reflects costs arising from the contracting out system. In their view, this has arisen because payments made to the transit authority by the provider have remained unchanged. Hence, there is no incentive for the supplier to focus on efficiency or introduce cost-cutting

---

(cont'd)

measures. Also, once a contract is awarded, then there is no real competition. This is because the contractor usually is granted a monopoly over service delivery in a specific geographic area. The data also indicated that general-purpose government agencies that contract out services have remained more efficient and effective than special-purpose agencies over the 25-years period. This may reflect the case, however, that general-purpose governments also may not fully report the true costs of delivering transit service because these costs may be shared by other departments.

Leland and Smirnova's overall conclusion from their study is that the available empirical evidence is unable to demonstrate that privatization of service delivery arrangements is any more cost-effective or efficient than ongoing provision of services by public sector agencies. Hence, in the case of bus transit systems, it would appear that none of the efficiency or effectiveness gains which politicians claimed would occur following the transfer of services to external providers has actually emerged. Furthermore, the researchers believe this conclusion is probably also applicable to other public sector scenario involving the transfer of assets to a new provider, especially when the new organization is granted a geographic monopoly over service delivery.

Market forces

A frequent justification of privatization is the process exposes organizations to 'market forces' and the pressures of competition will lead to increased efficiencies. In some cases, such as the privatization of British Airways, the new entity was required to introduce fundamental strategic changes in operations in order to survive in the increasingly competitive world of international air travel. However, the legislation that accompanied other privatizations in areas such as utilities and telecommunications ensured that the new private firms remained as monopolist entities within their sector of industry. Additionally, concerns among politicians that the new companies might introduce much higher prices that would cause dissent among the electorate can lead to the creation of sector regulators able to define key operational variables such as pricing and levels of capital expenditure (Willman et al. 2003). For example, the privatization of the water industry in the United Kingdom defined that ten companies were to become responsible for supplying water and sewerage services to most of England and Wales. The industry is regulated by the Office of Water Services (OFWAT), whose primary duties are to ensure the proper provision of water and sewerage services, to see companies are adequately funded, and to protect customers' interests with respect to charges. OFWATs developed a formula based upon the Retail Price Index and an adjusting 'K factor' which prevented companies from increasing prices beyond a ceiling specified by the regulator. This regulation, accompanied by a ruling that the water companies were not permitted to operate within the market area of any other water company, has ensured that the concept of competition being utilized to improve efficiency has little relevance in this sector of UK industry.

It is also usually the case that politicians would propose that privatization would require the new organizations to be more customer-orientated. In fact, in those cases where a regulator is appointed, it is the decisions of this individual which become the primary concern of management within the privatized companies. There is little point in being worried about the needs of the final customer in this situation because it is the regulator, and not any form of competitive market forces, that determine key decisions such as the pricing and service performance. Given this observation, the question may arise as to whether there were other, more opaque motives behind politicians' support for privatization. One clear benefit was that in the sale of public sector assets the Government of the day usually obtained a significant inflow of funds and a removal of operating deficits and liabilities from the public sector balance sheet. Possibly of even greater benefit is that privatization can be an effective tool through which to limit the power of the unions. Certainly the perspective of reducing the power of the public sector unions during the privatization process was central to UK Prime Minster, Margaret Thatcher's manifesto for economic change. This was because a primary aim was to destroy the ability of unions to demand more employment rights and benefits for their members (Foster and Taylor 1994). As part of the public sector, unified actions by employees in sectors such as the utilities, mining, and transportation have the potential to disrupt entire economies. Privatization disaggregates the power of unions because there is a tendency for the unions to now focus their attention on the needs of employees in their specific industrial sector whilst concurrently being less interested in the needs of employees working in other industries.

Culture Shock

Case Aims: To illustrate some of the problems a private sector manager may encounter upon being recruited into a public sector organization.

In certain cases, the option of privatization is not available to the politicians. This can be due to potential for major adverse reaction from the electorate (e.g. privatizing public sector health care provision) or because the entity in question could not be recreated as a financially viable, private sector business. Politicians seeking to introduce what they perceive as the superior managerial expertise of business people may, therefore, opt to recruit new senior managers from the private sector. The issue then arises over whether these new recruits are able to exploit their expertise to achieve the efficiency and effectiveness gains desired by their new public sector masters.

(cont'd)

In his examination of this issue, Ross (1988) has identified a number of barriers that even highly qualified and experienced individuals from the private sector can expect to encounter in seeking to improve management processes in public sector organizations. He suggests the first problem to be encountered is the approach to decision-making. Private sector managers are used to identifying a problem, implementing an analysis, selecting the most effective solution, and then implementing appropriate actions. In the public sector this outcome is often unlikely to occur. This is because numerous bodies and political influences will seek to determine which solution best meets their own individual needs. As consensus is rarely an option, compromise and modifications to the proposed solution will occur to gain wide agreement over an acceptable resolution of the identified problem. Consequently the typical outcome is that the recommending manager is confronted with a final decision which represents a less than optimal solution.

In the private sector managers are used to defining and then operating against relatively precise, usually quantifiable targets such as revenue or profitability. This level of preciseness is rarely present in the goals specified in new legislation which defines the politicians' requirements concerning the future performance of public agencies. Instead of clearly defined targets the legislation will often contain vague or ambiguous terms and qualitative statements such as 'excellent', 'adequate', or 'reasonable' to define what is required in the provision of a specific welfare service. In many cases, these definitions have emerged in order for politicians to achieve sufficient consensus to get the new legislation passed. Unfortunately, this does not help the senior manager in the affected agency because they are left being required to achieve goals which are not quantitative and hence it is difficult to define objectives against which to effectively assess actually achieved outcomes.

A related issue is when a private sector manager recognizes an error in a current strategy it is usually acceptable that the individual should be permitted to immediately implement a change in operational policy. This behaviour trait in the private sector will typically be seen as the act of a decisive manager aware of the need to respond to new environmental challenges. Unfortunately, a similar view rarely exists in the public sector. This is because politicians or the politically appointed head of a public sector agency are/is typically concerned that a decision to revise operational activities may result in criticism from the media. Hence, it is perceived as much safer to reject any proposal for fundamental change because there is the risk that acceptance could result in these individuals being criticized for their actions.

The other dilemma facing the individual from the private sector is the management of poorly performing employees. Private sector organizations usually have effective HRM systems which (a) can identify poor performance and

---

(cont'd)

(b) have mechanisms for either re-training, redeploying, or terminating poor performers. Although the public sector in recent years has sought to introduce such HRM practices into their organizations, actual systems have often proved to be inadequate. Hence, the individual from the private sector may encounter situations where although certain employees' inadequate skills are severely damaging overall organizational performance, it proves impossible to terminate these individuals or move them into more appropriate job roles.

Performance indicators

The need for commercial organizations to be profitable in order to remain in existence means that the private sector has always used financial data as basis for assessing performance. As large organizations began to be increasingly dependent on external equity to fund growth in the nineteenth century, the importance of financial data has become even more important in terms of providing information to their shareholders and the financial markets. In those industrial sectors where companies provide very similar products to customers such as retailing or production of commodity goods, financial data on sales and profits can provide the bulk of the information needed to permit management to assess performance. Such situations are relatively rare, however, because in many industrial sectors managers need other additional data to acquire a meaningful understanding of how their organization is performing in relation to the strategic plan. The nature of this additional information will vary by sector with certain performance indicators being perceived as critical to understanding company performance. Examples of key performance indicators (or 'KPIs') are the number of new drugs successfully patented in the pharmaceutical industry, scale of identified, owned reserves in the oil industry, and brand shares in consumer goods companies.

In the past, politicians and civil servants have sought to avoid the use of KPIs as a mechanism for assessing performance in the public sector. The advent of activities, such as privatization, market orientation, and outsourcing, has resulted in a major shift in opinion over this critical issue. Hence, accompanying politicians' desire to implement NPM has come the acceptance of the perspective that the management of change will require performance indicators to assess the degree to which new policies within the public sector are proving to be successful.

By the early 1990s, performance measurement and performance reviews became the vogue among senior civil servants seeking to satisfy pressures being applied by their political masters. In the United Kingdom, for example, primary reasons for this outcome include:

(1) Pressure from the politicians seeking to justify the benefits of NPM;

(2) Greater public expectation and consumerism;

(3) Compulsory introduction of competitive tendering;

(4) Changing culture and attitudes among public sector managers;

(5) Loss of confidence among politicians that public sector managers were able to implement NPM policies.

In many democracies, actual delivery of public services is delegated to state-level or regional bodies. Within the United Kingdom, for example, much of this role is assigned to Local Government Authorities who employ over 2 million people engaged in delivery of a wide range of services. These services include education, training, housing, environmental services, roads and transport, leisure and recreational facilities, social services, police, and other emergency services. In terms of effective implementation of an NPM philosophy in the delivery of services, these local authorities face a number of additional operational complexities (Ghobadian and Ashworth 1994). These include:

(1) Lack of alternative supplier in many cases.

(2) Absence or low risk of bankruptcy.

(3) Large, long-life asset base.

(4) Continuous Government pressures.

(5) Lack of apparent direct connection between services and cost to the electorate.

(6) Wide range of services with varying degree of tangibility.

(7) The powerful role of staff, backed by the support of strong public sector unions, in relation to their ability to frustrate the aims of their line managers. As noted by Van Peursem et al. (1995), the performance indicators which have been developed for the public sector during the introduction of NPM are aimed at assessing one or more of the three variables of economy efficiency and effectiveness.

Economy is usually concerned with examining the use of resources by providing data on the relationship between input costs and their application to a number of situations. The empirical relationship between number of patients seen and the number of nurses in post or total expenditure on programmes for the unemployed in relation to the total number of unemployed persons enrolled on Government programmes provides examples of economy measures. The attraction of this type of performance indicator is the data are readily accessible and hence generation of a measurement is an extremely simple process. The drawback, however, is the knowledge generated is very limited in terms of guiding decision-makers on how to improve future services because the data only provide insights on inputs utilized in the service delivery process.

As the limitations of economy measures became apparent, a preference emerged among politicians for data which provided information concerning the outputs associated with expenditure on service provision. This can be achieved by the use of indicators which focus on assessing efficiency. Efficiency may be associated with a wide range of activities. These are usually under the control of management and, therefore, this type of indicator is of assistance to both the service provider and those seeking to evaluate the effectiveness of the organizations delivering a specific service. The empirical relationship between number of patients receiving dental treatments and the number of dentists in post or total expenditure on start of your own business programmes for the unemployed in relation to the number of individuals who successfully launch a new small business provides examples of efficiency measures.

Behaviour Traits of Politicians

Case Aims: To illustrate the possible outcome of politicians' response to an emerging public sector problem.

There is a tendency for politicians when confronted with a major public sector problem to introduce new legislation followed by the imposition of new performance indicators to ensure their demands for action are being implemented. This behaviour trait usually has the outcome of imposing even more performance indicators on the public servant. This results in a further diversion of scarce resources away from front-line services into administrative activity. As noted by Kane (1989), an even more adverse outcome is the new legislation often does little to resolve the identified problem. In his view, this is due to the following very damaging reflexes that are often exhibited by politicians, namely:

(1) *The Ostrich Reflex*, which involves remaining uninformed about the problem which has arisen and therefore being incapable of defining an effective solution.

(2) *The Trust-me Reflex*, which involves using the power of office to reassure doubters who seek to express concern about the viability of the proposed solution.

(3) *The Cover-up Reflex*, which involves concealing any mistakes in public sector policy which emerge as a result of excessive speed in passing the new legislation. This is usually accompanied by actions to discredit those who express concerns about the potential effectiveness of politicians' proposed solutions.

(4) *The Weasel Reflex* of seeking out a convenient, credible scapegoat, such as public sector employees, when the errors in the legislation become apparent to the general public.

Efficiency

Measures of efficiency are more informative than economy measures because the former provide knowledge about the scale of outputs being achieved relative to the resources being allocated to the activity. What efficiency measures do not provide in sufficient details is the knowledge to permit diagnosis of the effectiveness of the service being delivered. 'Assessment of effectiveness' is usually a concept which seeks to assess the quality of outcomes being delivered by the service provider. For example, in the case of the health care sector, effectiveness is often linked to the quality of care which patients have received. The problem is that assessment of effectiveness typically demands some form of multi-dimensional measurement process which involves generation of both quantitative and qualitative date. In relation to health care, for example, it is usually the case that measurement concerning the quality of care requires assessment of the structure and process of health care delivery. Donabedian (1980, p. 80), for example, suggests that process is 'a set of activities that go on within and between practitioners and patients'. Determination of effectiveness will need to focus on patient satisfaction and on medical, social, and psychological interactions between the patient and the provider. In contrast, structure is concerned with the scale of resources available to the provider such as number of staff, diagnostic equipment, and treatment capacity.

On the basis of a case-based analysis of the experience of using performance indicators in UK Local Authorities, Ghobadian and Ashworth concluded that the requirements of an effective performance measurement system include:

(1) Being a series of measures designed to meet the requirements of different organizational levels;

(2) The capability to capture the essence of both the efficiency and effectiveness dimension of performance;

(3) Provide the means of identifying trade-offs between various dimensions of performance;

(4) Include qualitative measures as well as quantitative measures;

(5) Be based on a philosophy which regards the measurement as an ongoing and evolving process;

(6) Recognition of the need to define measures which cannot be manipulated by managers utilizing the data;

(7) Recognition of the need to avoid performance measures becoming ends in themselves;

(8) Provides managers with tools to assist planning and decision-making as well as control;

(9) Offer clear links between the measurements being made, corporate objectives, and annual plans.

A widely recognized problem with performance indicator control systems is that managers may place excessive emphasis on ensuring their organization is meeting the criteria defined by imposed indicators and cease to be concerned about effective implementation of actual strategy. In commenting upon this phenomenon, Cassidy (2003) concluded that compliance with defined indicators has led to a managerial philosophy of 'box ticking' accompanied by a failure to be concerned about the needs of employees, customers, suppliers, and the wider general community. Unfortunately, the advent of NPM has been followed by a shift towards box ticking in the public sector. In order to undertake the box ticking task, public sector organizations have shifted resources away from the delivery of front-line services into funding a major expansion in administrative staff and systems. Of even greater concern is the willingness of some public sector managers to manipulate events to the detriment of the general public in order to remain able to tick the 'right boxes'. One example in the United Kingdom of this practice is that which occurred following Government legislation demanding that all out patients arriving at hospital A&E departments must be seen in 2 hours. When administrators decided this target could not be achieved, some resorted to the practice of leaving patients outside in ambulances for some hours because this permitted deferment of acknowledging the patients had arrived at their hospital.

In reviewing the numerous reported failures of performance indicators to assist in enhancing the management of service delivery in the public sector, Kravenuck and Schack (1996) noted that most of these indicators were only suitable for completely unambiguous situations. Unfortunately, most public sector service provision systems are highly ambiguous which renders the performance indicators being utilized as failing to provide the data required to identify appropriate actions for change. Van Dooren et al. (2010) in commenting upon this conclusion have proposed that the performance management systems need to be 'ambiguity proof'. In their view this can only be achieved by taking into account the complexities of public service provision and creation of systems which can monitor highly ambiguous environments. They propose this aim can be achieved by listening to the professionals engaged in service delivery and recognizing that the design of performance indicators must be based upon an understanding of 'real-world' experiences.

The Balanced Scorecard Approach

Case Aims: To illustrate some of the problems of using multi-dimensional performance indicators in the public sector.

Concerns within the private sector of the limitations of single dimension performance indicators led to the proposal of the 'balanced scorecard' approach by Kaplan and Norton (1992a). Their performance measurement system includes financial measures and drivers of future financial outcomes in relation to

(cont'd)

delivering strategic aims concerned with customers, internal processes, organizational learning, and business growth. The framework involves consideration of both outcome and process, and internal and external perspectives of different stakeholders' interests. Even in the private sector, there have been some concerns about the effectiveness of the technique in terms of supporting strategic management processes. Norreklit (2000), for example, argued that to be applied as an effective strategic management mechanism, the scorecard should be embedded in the management practice of the organization. In his view, scorecard systems do not always fulfil this requirement. This can occur because the dimensions assessed by the technique may be different from the strategic model being utilized by the organization.

With a tendency for NPM performance indicators to move towards multi-dimensional assessments to determine the effectiveness of public sector strategies, attempts have been made by various public sector bodies to introduce the balanced scorecard system into their organizations. In the United Kingdom one example is that of the National Health Service where the system was introduced with the aim of determining effectiveness in relation to the six dimensions of health improvement, fair access, effective service delivery, efficiency, patient experience of care, and health outcomes. To permit evaluation of these six dimensions, a set of performance indicators were developed, called the High Level Performance Indicators (HLPIs). Indicators for each dimension were chosen for assessing delivery of long-term objectives and targets.

To assess the effectiveness of the new NHS system, Chang (2007) used interviews with managers to determine whether HLPIs assisted these individuals achieve the goal of integrating central government's performance targets into their local operations. His conclusion was that managers found the process indicators chosen were unable to reflect their local health authority's attempt to improve health care standards and that a balanced scorecard approach is problematic for strategic management within a decentralized public service delivery system. Of greater concern was that the balanced scorecard technique, which is more expensive to implement because of the greater complexity of the system, achieved the same outcomes as simpler performance indicators and that local managers continued to attempt to prioritize central government's targets even at the price of skewing delivery of identified, more important, local health care priorities. This behaviour trait indicated whatever system is used public sector managers often feel they face pressures associated with ongoing personal job security which cause them to acquiesce to whatever is demanded of them by central government. In commenting on this situation Chang (2007, p. 117) concluded that in relation to the benefits of adopting a balanced scorecard in the public sector 'that such a claim is based on rational instrumentalism and does not consider the political context that a public sector organization faces'.

Service quality

A key dimension of NPM is the concept that public sector bodies should pay more attention to the needs of their customers, which in most cases are the general public. This perspective gave rise to new performance indicators including measurements of customer satisfaction. In the case of services, satisfaction reflects an interaction between what the customer hopes will occur (i.e. their 'expectations') and the 'perceptions' which are created as the result of their actual service experience. Satisfaction occurs when perceptions are equal or exceeded by expectations. In those cases where expectations are much greater than perceptions, this means the provider will need to consider actions aimed at improving the quality of the service experience currently being delivered.

The growing importance of service sector businesses as a proportion of GDP in development economies over the last 30 years has resulted in major service organizations investing in techniques for understanding and managing their customers' service experience. This had led to acceptance of the perspective that merely measuring the difference between expectations and perceptions is of limited benefit. This is because such data do not provide an understanding of the causes of customer dissatisfaction or identify the factors within the organization which are the source of customer dissatisfaction. Recognition of the need to go beyond merely measuring dissatisfaction led to the development of the SERVQUAL model by Parasuraman et al. (1988, 1985). This model proposes there are five sources of dissatisfaction or 'gaps' that together will determine the level of service quality being delivered by an organization. In relation to public sector organizations these gaps are as follows:

Gap 1 caused by legislators or managers of public sector organizations not comprehending the actual expectations of customers.

Gap 2 caused by a failure to translate perceptions of customer expectations into service quality standards by which employees can assess actual performance.

Gap 3 in which a lack of resources or inadequately skilled employees results in an inability to deliver services which meet performance standards that have been defined.

Gap 4 caused by the organization communicating information to customers which causes them to be misled or misunderstand the services that actually would be made available.

Gap 5, which is a combination of Gaps 1–4, determines customers overall assessment of how their expectations have been met by the services received.

Research undertaken by Pitt et al. (1998) on the reasons why gaps emerge, although not specific to public sector providers, is very useful in terms of revealing factors that cause organizations to fail in delivering customer satisfaction. In relation to Gap 1 these researchers concluded there are three key factors.

Firstly, is the lack of a marketing research orientation. This reflects an inadequate level of interaction between management and customers. Secondly, an inadequate level of upward communication between customer contact personnel and management. Thirdly, too many levels of management separating contact personnel from top management. In relation to Gap 2 key factors include a lack of commitment to service quality by senior executives and an absence of realistic goal setting. Assessment of Gap 3 issues caused the researchers to conclude influencing variables included ambiguity in the definition of staff roles, conflict over who is responsible for roles which have been defined, a poor fit between the skills of employees and their assigned tasks, conflict over employees concerning task responsibilities, and poor teamwork. As far as Gap 4 is concerned, contributing factors include poor co-ordination of communication between team members and an organizational propensity to overpromise about the quality of delivery.

As with any new paradigm, some academics can be expected to question the validity of the concept relative to other existing, widely utilized research approaches. Such has been the case with the Parasuraman et al.'s original SERVQUAL model. These researchers concluded the key five variables influencing customer perceptions were responsiveness, empathy, reliability, tangibility, and assurance. Other academics questioned the universal applicability of these 5 variables on the grounds that the SERVQUAL model had been evolved by mainly focusing on consumer behaviour in relation to service expectations in retail and financial services environments. Hence, in terms of utilizing the SERVQUAL model to study public sector scenarios, instead of just duplicating the original survey tool, some researchers have adopted the approach of firstly determining which variables influenced customer perceptions in relation to a specific public service. Yusoff et al. (2008), for example, adopted this methodology in their study of service quality provision by a Local Authority in Malaysia. In this case, factor analysis identified 40 elements which included a human capital component, property, technology and ICT, and working processes. The researchers concluded there were seven variables that dominated customer perceptions, namely responsiveness, professionalism, empathy, reliability, type 1 asset tangibles, type 2 asset tangibles, and assurance. Utilization of these variables then permitted an assessment of what factors were influencing any service gaps which existed between customer expectations and perceptions in a public sector scenario. This knowledge provided the basis for identifying which areas of activity within the Local Authority required modification in order for management to achieve the objective of improving service quality.

Significantly more important than pedagogic debates over the most appropriate methodology for analysing factors influencing service quality are the issues of whether (a) an expensive market research technique provides knowledge greater than that which an observant manager could have identified through discussions with staff and (b) the research is used to justify the imposition of new operational process that further damage the morale of employees who are struggling to cope with inadequate resources. The critical nature of these issues was highlighted in a study of social care in Australia (Stack 2003). This researcher noted that a paradox exists for service providers. This is because although NPM principles purport to liberate staff from oppressive bureaucracies, in reality health care providers in Australia are now confronted with an increase in regulatory and performance management systems aimed at enhancing the quality of care. Key issues which care providers are now required to consider include management systems, staffing, delivered personal care resident lifestyle, physical environments, and patient safety. Government legislation covering these variables has been introduced involving performance indicators which focus on a 'need to show continuous improvement'.

Stack's study revealed that the introduction of performance indicators for service quality has resulted in care assistants now spending approximately 15 per cent of their time filling in forms. Registered nurses spend an even greater proportion of their time on administrative tasks. She also concluded that NPM economic imperatives have led to trends in management that de-personalize the care process in the interest of reducing costs. Community nurses are required to significantly increase the number of clients they visit each day, while they no longer have control over which patients they work with. This means the continuous, time-consuming relationships which medical staff and their patients perceive as an essential aspect of caring are no longer permissible under the new Government-mandated performance targets. As a consequence, even greater performance indicator gaps between expected and actual outcomes have emerged. A primary reason for this outcome is that residential care practice is now focused on technology and tasks, with residents often being left completely alone for almost 50 per cent of the day. Accreditation standards for residential care homes now define specific targets for things such as car parks, number of *en suites* bathrooms in new homes, and kitchen and laundry facilities. At the same time, there is no definition of the required ratio of patients to staff or any requirement concerning staff qualifications. Not surprisingly this had led to a reduction in staffing in care homes and a move to replace nurses with untrained care assistants.

This perspective of how imposed control systems will usually lead to a failure to deliver adequate service quality is echoed by Freyens (2008). In his review of NPM in OECD countries he concluded that experiments with new modes of service delivery are driven by a changing economic context but as a consequence any efficiency gains from changes in organizational processes usually are achieved at the expense of a reduction in service quality. In his view, managers of service delivery systems in the public sector need understand the practical implications of using economic principles as the basis for justifying organizational change. This is because economics and service delivery are profoundly interlinked in such a way that gains achieved by change in dimension can often result in a decline in outcomes in the other dimension. A similar conclusion was reached by Freeman (2002) in his review of the literature concerning the impact of performance indicators in the provision of healthcare in the United Kingdom. He concluded that the use of performance indicators in assurance and performance has created fundamental problems which have the potential to totally undermine the actions seeking to achieve quality improvement and creating difficulties in using available information on performance as the basis for promoting change within the United Kingdom's NHS.

Service Quality Obstacles

Case Aims: To illustrate how managerial failings can impact the quality of service provision.

A key factor influencing the ability of employees to deliver adequate service quality is internal communication. Communication can either be formal (instruction manuals) or informal (from employee verbal interactions). Formal materials will detail standardized processes for addressing customers' needs. Informal interactions are important for filling in the gaps of knowledge between what employees want/need to know and what they are told during formal briefings or from manuals. Hence, Brunetto and Farr-Wharton (2008) undertook a study of a local government organization in Australia to gain further understanding of how communication flows can influence service quality in a public sector environment.

They concluded that quality of employee's level of dissatisfaction with communication processes with supervisors and management significantly affected their ability to deliver desired outputs. This is because employees perceived these communications were causing role ambiguity which, in turn, was damaging the quality of service provision to the general public. The view of employees concerning the cause of poor service quality was inadequate internal communications between managerial levels resulted in staff unable to undertake tasks, solve problems, and consequently effectively meet the needs of the client.

These findings caused the authors to agree with other authors who have claimed that the implementation of NPM reforms was less about a process to improve the effectiveness of service delivery and more about per capita cost-cutting in the provision of public goods. In their view, their study supported previously expressed concerns that the impact of recent reforms has reduced the effectiveness of Australia's local government organizations to provide employees with the tools, processes, and systems capable of meeting the service needs of customers.

Customer orientation

Accompanying the focus upon improving service quality, another dimension of NPM in relation to how lessons can be learned from the private sector is the issue of stronger customer orientation. Authors such as Cervera et al. (2001) have posited that adoption of customer orientation by public sector organizations would result in these entities exhibiting a more proactive response to their environments, destroy bureaucratic barriers, and provide new high quality services capable of satisfying social needs. In recent years, within the services marketing literature the emphasis has been on the benefits of 'relationship marketing'. This philosophy is based upon the perspective that given the intangible nature of services, the focus of the marketer is on the need to build closer relationships with customers as this then leads to stronger customer loyalty. In their assessment of how public sector bodies could enhance their operations, Da Silva and Batista (2007) have posited that relationship marketing should become a fundamental strategy that would drive all operational processes. In support of their perspective they quote the case of London Borough of Haringay investing in a sophisticated computer-based Customer Relationship Management system (CRM). This strategy has involved investment in an integrated, multi-channel, multi-agency system the aim of which is to allow employees to maintain a seamless, uninterrupted dialogue with customers. In support of their perspective on how customer orientation is an effective component of CRM the authors then state that

> The CRM solution links its contracted business partners to enhance the quality and efficiency of service delivery. The whole solution provides an instant snapshot of which residents are using each service, allowing the Council to measure which sections of society are under- or over-represented by the service. As a result, the council has improved efficiency efficacy of service delivery, enhanced customer-service staff skills, enhanced staff understanding of the Council's services, and increased the level of citizens, partners, and employees' satisfaction.
>
> (Da Silva and Batista 2007, p. 554)

It should be noted, however, that the authors identify the source of the data that led them to reach this conclusion was not the outcome of any research activities. Instead, it is based upon case materials published on the Web site of the company that sold Haringey their CRM system (Siebel 2003).

An outcome of the need for adopting a customer orientation is that some public sector agencies have diverted a significant proportion of their resources towards activities such as customer care programmes to persuade nurses to perceive patients as customers. The activities of Auckland City Council in New Zealand provide another illustration of the use of promotional campaigns to communicate an organization's commitment to serving the needs of the general public more effectively (Price and Brodie 2001). Unfortunately, such actions as well as placing even greater strain on already limited financial resources, do suggest that some public sector managers have not comprehended that marketing is based upon concepts that are not easily transferred to the public sector. A complication which can often frustrate this process is that unlike the private sector most PSOs face the problem of having to seek to fulfil the needs of highly diversified external and internal customer segments. As a consequence, creating quality standards and delivering services to meet such standards become an extremely difficult objective. Hence, there is rarely any benefit in management demanding total customer satisfaction. Instead, a more realistic philosophy is to seek to meet the needs of the more important, usually larger, customer groups whilst concurrently accepting that a significant minority of customers will remain dissatisfied with claims that the organization is exhibiting an adequate level of market orientation. Once a public sector organization has accepted that in the case of a highly diverse customer base not all customers can be satisfied, then this reality should receive emphasis during employee training on customer orientation. Furthermore, creation of understanding among all levels of staff within the PSO about the need to accept dissatisfaction among a small number of customers is a critical staff development objective. This then permits organization to avoid a small number of staff using examples of dissatisfaction among a small group of customers as the basis for criticizing the organization's overall achievement in relation to being customer-orientated (Schofield and Raynes 1992).

The fundamental role of marketing is the management of an exchange relationship between an organization and the organization's customers. Organizational performance is critically influenced by the ability to fulfil the needs of customers better than competition such that an exchange relationship is created in which the customer purchases the goods from their preferred supplier. Upon applying this concept to many public sector scenarios, the fundamental issue arises over 'Who is the customer?' This is because the recipient of the service, such as the patient in a UK hospital, is not the participant in the exchange relationship. Instead, this role is undertaken by the Government which funds the provision of service. As a consequence, in many public sector organizations, customer orientation requires an understanding that the public sector agency is engaged in the management of a triangular service provision scenario of the type illustrated in Figure 2.1. As most providers cannot expect Government departments to authorize funding sufficient to meet all of the demands made by service

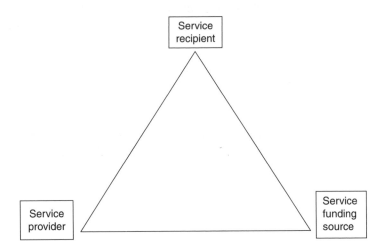

Figure 2.1   The service provision triangle

recipients, the provider will often be forced to ration service provision. The resultant outcome leads to a fundamental breach in marketing philosophy because the provider will be unable to satisfy customer needs.

In reviewing the implications of the inability to meet total customer needs caused Larson (1997) to point out that private sector organizations are able to use the principal of differential pricing to influence customer behaviour. For example, those who want faster or a broader range of services from their bank are offered the facility that by paying higher bank charges these customers can have access to their own personal banker. In the case of welfare services in a democracy, the fundamental driving principle is that of equality. As a result, although public sector agencies could offer multi-priced, multi-tiered levels of service based upon the willingness of people to pay, understandably this concept will usually be rejected by the majority of the general public. This situation leads Larson to conclude that as the philosophy of the welfare state is of public sector services that are made available on the basis of uniform equality of access, common service, and an equal cost basis, then any action intended to embed the private sector concept of customer orientation is likely to be unsuccessful.

This conclusion does not mean, however, that the public sector should reject all of the attributes associated with adopting a stronger customer orientation. A fundamental aspect of any form of effective service delivery is the use of information to gain a greater understanding of the needs of the multiple stakeholders. Kotler and Andreasen (1991), for example, have proposed there are four publics about whom the acquisition of information can assist the public sector service delivery process. These are the 'input publics' who supply resources, 'internal publics' who use the resources to produce goods and services, 'intermediary publics' who facilitate the distribution of the organization's services, and 'consuming publics' who are the users of the service. Each public has an exchange, but usually very different, relationship with the service provider.

Paarlberg's (2007) research on a US public sector agency also confirms the perspective that acquisition of additional understanding of customer needs can be beneficial in enhancing the quality of services delivered. He also notes that the public sector is usually a multi-customer scenario in which managers tend to favour emphasizing meeting the needs of the customer who is funding the purchase, whereas front-line staffs' sympathies will tend to be with those to whom the services are being provided. Under certain circumstances, Paarlberg (2007) suggests if this difference in perspective is not resolved, it will eventually create internal organizational dissent that can lead to a decline in service quality and a de-motivated workforce.

The Breaking Storm

3

The aims of this chapter are to cover the issues of:

(1) Governments' increasing dependence upon deficit spending

(2) The introduction of the euro and associated public sector spending rules

(3) The impact of population ageing on public sector funding

(4) The influence of globalization on developed nation economies

(5) The 2008 banking crisis and consequences for Government spending

Deficit spending

There are two primary mechanisms by which a country's public sector is funded, namely through taxation and Government borrowing. The benefit of taxation is that this immediately brings in revenues that have no associated liabilities. This is not the case with borrowing because in order to raise money Governments are required to issue bonds (or 'gilts') which pay interest to the lender. Hence, as well as being required at some time in the future to repay the face value on the bond, the Government also needs make interest payments. As a consequence, as public sector borrowing rises, so also does the scale of a country's public deficit.

During an economic downturn, tax receipts from both business and consumers tend to decline. Hence, if a Government wishes to sustain public sector spending, additional borrowing usually becomes necessary. Over the last 60 years, many Governments have become more interventionist and perceive that to reduce the social impact of economic downturns, increased public sector spending funded by additional borrowing will be necessary. Evidence exists that where such borrowing is directed towards infrastructure projects, such as building new roads and hospitals, direct benefit is offered through job creation and providing business with contracts that can compensate for a downturn in their sales to private sector customers.

During the period of industrial reconstruction following World War II, deficit spending was considered a highly effective tool through which to rebuild economies. Politicians seeking to justify their actions felt able to draw upon Keynesian economic theories to support the acceptability of deficit spending. What they seemed to ignore, however, was even Maynard Keynes considered deficit spending should be seen as a temporary measure. In his view, increased Government borrowing during a downturn was only justified if subsequently during the next upturn, tax inflows generate a surplus which would then be applied to reducing the scale of the public deficit. Where this does not occur even as an economy improves, tax inflows are unable to cover the scale of Government borrowing and a 'structural deficit' will merge. Should the financial markets perceive that a persistent, unmanageable deficit is developing, concerns will grow over the possibility that a nation's currency will have to be devalued. This, in turn, will lead to a Government being required to pay an interest-rate premium in order to attract new lending, thereby further raising the size of the structural deficit. A potential beneficial side effect of devaluation is this will make a country's products less expensive on world markets and in some cases the economic performance may improve due to an upsurge in export activity (Schettkat 2001).

By the 1980s, a series of economic shocks such as rising oil prices, the decline of competitiveness of Western businesses relative to the new Asian Tigers, and inflexible attitudes of the unions, especially in the public sector, led to both high inflation and rising unemployment in many developed economies. Some countries were affected more than others. The United Kingdom, for example, which was experiencing 'stagflation' due to the combined effect of rising prices and declining economic output became known as the 'Sick Man of Europe'. Politicians in some countries were so concerned about the potential for social unrest that they felt it was necessary to increase expenditure on programmes for the unemployed. Even they, however, recognized that unless inflation could be reduced, increased funding of public sector activity would be extremely difficult.

In terms of what was the most appropriate change in economic policy, a major complication was the contradictory views expressed by the world's economists. Some argued the only solution was a balanced budget achieved through higher taxation and reduced Government spending. Other economists vehemently opposed this solution on the grounds that such actions would severely damage the already much weakened developed nation economies (Eisner 1996). The view which began to prevail in the late 1980s was that inflation was the most dangerous factor impacting the economic survival of nations. This led to the emergence of consensus on the need for Western nations to de-regulate markets, reduce the influence of labour unions, and most importantly, adopt sound monetary policies. This view, especially in relation to sound monetary policies, was championed by influential institutions such as the Organization for Economic Cooperation and Development (OECD), the US Federal Reserve, and the European Central Bank (ECB). As a consequence, by the late 1990s, most Governments had accepted the need to insulate monetary policy from the actions of politicians by transferring the responsibility of managing the policy to their nations' Central Banks. These entities were assigned the aim by politicians of implementing actions designed to reduce inflation (Schettkat 2001). Central Bankers were also aware that in order to reduce inflation there existed a concurrent need for ways to be found for reducing public sector spending as a proportion of GDP.

One of the earliest critics of the seemingly uncontrolled continuing rise in post-war public sector spending was the American economist Henry Simons (Orcutt 2003). As early as 1980, he argued that in the United States, with legislators needing to ensure their re-election every few years, both the main political parties were using Government spending as a mechanism to ensure they retained the allegiance of the electorate. He pointed out that in the 1930s, public sector spending stood at 12 per cent of GDP, by 1976 it stood at 36 per cent of GDP, and assuming no change in the behaviour of politicians, it would reach 60 per cent of GDP by 2000. In addition to the huge inflationary pressures caused by increased Government spending, Simons held the view that the continuing rises in public sector expenditure reflected a policy of borrowing and ever-increasing taxation of those engaged in productive activities in order to fund the less productive sectors of society. This is because spending on non-means-tested entitlement programmes such as Social Security, Medicare, federal pensions, and farm aid had grown about 3.5 times faster than the rise in population over the last 30 years. In his view, legislation was required to cap level of public sector spending as a percentage of GDP and the Federal Reserve Bank should be given greater powers to influence the nation's monetary policies.

Despite warning from Central Bankers about the need to control public sector spending in the 1990s, most industrialized countries continued to run persistent deficits leading to rising debt-to-GDP ratios. In the United States, gross government debt as a percentage of GDP rose from 44 per cent in 1980 to 69 per cent in 1994. Over the same period, Government debt rose from 32 to 50 per cent in Germany, from 52 to 83 per cent in Japan, and from 58 to 129 per cent in Italy. To a large extent, this deterioration in fiscal balance sheets was due to politicians, in the face of declining productivity and increasing levels of structural unemployment, continuing to approve further expansion of expenditure on pensions and health care (Weiner 1995). With politicians apparently still favouring expenditure to support the socially disadvantaged in their societies, the issue facing Central Bankers was how their influence over monetary policy could contribute towards reversing the trend of public sector spending continuing to increase a percent of GDP.

As well as electoral acceptance of high public sector spending and the appealing morality of increasing social equality, politicians tended to express concern that reduced public sector spending would damage already somewhat fragile national economies. In response Central Bankers came to accept the concept that by using their control over money supply and interest rates, this could stimulate consumer demand leading to an aggregate improvement in economic growth to compensate for any decline caused by reduced public sector spending. Lower interest rates also had the advantage of lowering the cost of Government borrowing. Hence, not surprisingly politicians were also supportive of this concept. Unfortunately, although Central Bankers have been able to hold down interest rates well into the twenty-first century, their actions have not been accompanied by any attempts by politicians to introduce greater austerity into their nations' budgets.

Another factor influencing funding of Government deficits is the stability of a nation's currency. Where there are concerns over financial instability, this can cause a major increase in borrowing costs and lead to balance of payments problems. The importance of achieving financial stability within the European Union is the reason most member states decided to adopt a common currency the euro as a key step in achieving closer economic integration. In order for the euro to be a stable currency, member states need to exhibit highly responsible fiscal policies. It is for that reason that in theory countries would only be permitted to join the planned Economic and Monetary Union (EMU) if their annual public sector spending did not exceed 3 per cent of GDP and if their gross public debt did not exceed 60 per cent of GDP. Initially only Germany and Luxembourg met these criteria. This has meant that once a new country has been admitted to the EMU, they are expected to implement fiscal reform in order to ensure specified debt ceilings are achieved and maintained. One of the assigned roles of the European Central Bank (ECB) is to seek to counteract ill-advised fiscal expansion by national Governments in order that monetary stability and low inflation are to be maintained across all member states.

One of the problems facing the euro is that although monetary policy is based upon a single federal policy, countries still retain a degree of independent control over their economic, fiscal, and labour policies. Countries which join the euro are unable to use monetary policies such as adjusting interest rates to alter the value of their currency. As a consequence, there is a natural tendency in an economic downturn to increasingly rely upon higher public sector expenditure. This will typically lead to the creation of excessive fiscal deficits. It was for this reason that EU members who joined the euro agreed to the Stability and Growth Pact (SGP) the term of which are formally enshrined in the 1997 Amsterdam Treaty (Goodhart 2006). In signing the SGP, the following rules were agreed in relation to the role of the ECB and the behaviour of nation states, namely (Arestis et al. 2001):

(1) The ECB would remain independent and free from political pressures.
(2) No bailout of any nation's public deficit would be permitted.
(3) Monetary funding of Government deficits is prohibited.
(4) Member states will avoid exceeding deficit spending which exceeds 3 per cent of GDP.

It was recognized by the larger, more stable economies within the European Union that some nations, particularly Mediterranean countries and new entrants from Eastern Europe, already had very large public deficits. In an attempt to assist these latter countries develop more stable economies, structural and cohesion funds were agreed by which subsidies and other forms of financial assistance were made available. This redistribution of wealth also included the formation of the European Investment Bank which was assigned the role of assisting weaker nations in modernizing their economies.

The creation of the euro in 1999 occurred during a period of global financial instability following the banking crisis in Asia and the bursting of the dot.com bubble on Wall Street. Central Banks were concerned about ensuring financial stability and avoiding another recession and therefore decided to hold interest rates at their lowest levels seen since the 1950s. This decision stimulated consumer spending which sustained a period of economic growth. In those countries such as Greece and Italy further economic stimulus occurred as Governments approved increases in public sector spending. In theory, such actions were prohibited under the terms defined by their membership of the SGP. The stated intent of the SGP was where such behaviour occurred the EU would demand that Governments who breached rules on public sector spending would be required to pay non-interest bearing bank deposits to the ECB. Furthermore, these deposits would become non-refundable if the Government in question failed to adequately reduce public sector spending within the subsequent 2 years. In practice, it seems the EU Commissioners were always able to identify special circumstances which exempted countries from adopting more constrained public sector spending policies.

In other countries, such as the United Kingdom and the United States, where low interest rates were stimulating consumer-led economic growth as well, it also appears Central Banks had concluded that fiscal constraint was not a priority issue. As these countries headed towards the end of the first decade of the new millennium, it became apparent to the more foresighted economists and bankers that public sector deficits were approaching unmanageable proportions. Such views when expressed appear to have been ignored by the politicians. One can only presume this was because of their concerns that any attempt to restrain public sector spending might create an economic downturn and that reduced welfare spending would make it much more difficult for the political party in power to be elected into a further term in office.

Fiscal Reform

Case Aims: To illustrate the type of activities undertaken by a Government to create a more stable fiscal economic system.

In the 1980s and early 1990s, Mexico struggled with high fiscal deficits and debts resulting from two major economic crises in 1982 and 1995. Both crises had a profound impact on the Mexican economy and generated a contagion

(cont'd)

effect throughout the rest of Latin America. In 1982, Mexico became the first country in the region to default on its debt of $86 billion, triggering a spiral contagion effect throughout Latin America leading to a flight from these countries' currencies. In 1982, the Mexican budget deficit reached 16 per cent of GDP. In reaction to the crisis, the government introduced macro-economic adjustments including strong fiscal consolidation and price controls.

The 1995 crisis was triggered by the need to devalue the Mexican peso. In the wake of this action, GDP growth rate shrank by 6.2 per cent in 1995 and real wages fell by about 20 per cent. The Government was forced to introduce a number of reforms to deal with the crisis, including raising value-added tax from 10 per cent to 15 per cent. The Mexican economy made a rapid recovery and economic growth became positive during the first quarter of 1996. Since this crisis, Mexico has successfully followed prudent fiscal policies. The credibility of the autonomous Central Bank of Mexico has improved over time, and a sound monetary policy has helped to bring annual average inflation down from 35 per cent in 1995 to 5 per cent in 2008. The Government has reduced both the budget deficit and public debt over the past 10 years with the aim to achieve a balanced budget over the longer term.

In 2006/7, the downturn in the world economy began to severely impact the Government's attempts to sustain public sector reform. In part this was due to heavy dependency on oil revenue as the primary source of Mexico's public finances. The price of oil, like all commodities, is volatile. Mexican oil reserves and production levels are declining. Current oil reserves will only last another 10 years at present extraction rates. Investment is needed by the state-owned oil company in new technologies, increased capital for exploration of new fields, and introducing ways to improve productivity. The limited effectiveness of the tax collection system is reflected by tax revenues accounting for only 20.5 per cent of GDP, whilst elsewhere in OECD the average is 36 per cent. Business informality is high and this further reduces the level of taxes collected. Informality is when workers and firms do not have any interaction with the State and do not register with authorities, comply with regulations, pay taxes, or benefit from any labour or social protection.

In order to sustain economic reform the Government has introduced major new policies to address the underlying aspects of the country's structural challenges and to improve fiscal sustainability: These include the following:

- Creating a balanced budget rule.
- Establishing a formula for calculating oil-related revenues and institutionalizing the Oil Revenues Stabilisation Fund as well as the stabilization funds for infrastructure and for states' revenues.
- Establishing a clear timetable for the budget approval process in Congress, including a separate timetable for the budget process in an election year.

(cont'd)

- Stating that Congress cannot increase the overall budget balance proposed by the executive. Increases in expenditure have to be offset by decreases elsewhere.
- Assessing the budgetary impact for every new law proposed.
- Requiring the government to provide more economic and performance information to Congress.

New legislation was introduced which required public sector agencies to control personnel expenditure, implement more efficient execution of their spending activities, and greater autonomy was granted to ministries and agencies. These organizations are now required to develop performance indicators and to introduce austerity measures. There were legislative changes to public sector pension schemes to create a more sustainable pension system over the longer term. This reform relieves pressure on the Government's fiscal accounts by moving from a Pay-As-You-Go (PAYG) system to a system of individual savings accounts. The new system, which is fully funded, provides portable individual accounts for each worker and allows the transfer of employee pension rights between the public and the private sector.

Population ageing

When future historians would revisit the twenty-first century, one issue they would be attracted is the social and economic impact of population ageing (Johnson 2004). This trend reflects the fact that for some years in many industrialized nations, average age has been rising and older people are becoming the dominant group in most populations. There are two main causes for population ageing, namely increased longevity and declining birth rates. The longevity factor is mainly explained by improvements in health care provision. Since the World War II, most Governments have created some form of public sector health care system which offers free or subsidized services. Concurrently, major advances in medical technology have abolished many of the illnesses which in previous generations caused people to die at a much younger age (Yakita 2001).

Acquiring accurate figures about how population ageing impacts a nation's socio-demographics is complicated by the fact that much of the data collected by Governments uses the arbitrary classification that only people who are 65 or older are considered as being retired. Some people, however, are now retiring in their 50s or early 60s. Hence, the precise balance between older people in work and those who are retired is not usually available from Government statistics. Nevertheless, census data can still provide a reasonable indication of the proportion of retirees within a nation's population. United Nations' data show that in 2005, the 65+ age group in both the European Union and in the United Kingdom constitute over 16 per cent of the population. What is of even greater interest, however, is the United Nations' forecast that although the total population in Europe and in the United Kingdom will remain virtually unchanged between now and the year 2050, the number of 65+ individuals will increase by 65 per cent.

Governments confronted by such forecasts are concerned about what happens as the number of retired people increases and concurrently the number of people of working age decreases. This is because unless the shrinking number of people in work is prepared to accept major tax increases, public sector revenues will have to decline. Concurrently, as people are living longer, this will place even further pressure on Governments' abilities to fund state pensions and health care provision. Even before the 2008 banking crisis, observers of population ageing were predicting many Governments will soon be facing a potentially massive fiscal crisis (Jensen et al. 1995). On average the cost of public pensions and health care benefits consumes 12 per cent of GDP in developed nation economies. This figure is forecasted to rise to 24 per cent of GDP by 2040. Unless significant changes are made in the way Governments operate their welfare systems, funding this increase in GDP will require the working population to accept at least a 100 per cent increase in their personal tax burden. The potential scale of the impending crisis varies by country. In Europe and Japan, unless there are fundamental changes in Government policy, the crisis will deepen rapidly because low birth rates mean the size of the working population is declining. The United States will be less affected by population ageing because higher birth rates and a liberal immigration policy will result in a continuing expansion of the number of people in employment (Meeks et al. 1999).

In most countries, all citizens receive some form of state pension upon retirement. In most state pension schemes payments are usually on a flat rate basis, thereby resulting in all citizens receiving the same basic pension. This type of pension is funded on a Pay-As-You-Go (PAYG) basis which means people who are currently in work pay a social security tax that funds the pension payments of those in retirement. In most countries, payroll taxes from the current workforce are almost entirely consumed in covering payment of pensions for today's retirees. During the 1950s and 1960s, PAYG looked like a good idea. The labour force was growing and real wages were climbing by 2–5 per cent a year. Unfortunately, by the 1970s, in most developed economies declining labour force growth and economic slowdown had eliminated any advantages of PAYG which may have previously existed. In the United States, for example, social security pension payments and health care costs for the elderly seem likely to expand by 2.25 per cent and 4 per cent of GDP, respectively. As a result, by 2034, unless fundamental changes are not made to the Social Security System, it is estimated there will be no assets left in the Social Security Trust Fund. Similar outcomes are predicted across most developed economies because their schemes are also facing a massive funding deficit. The speed and scale of the arrival of the deficit scenario have been increased by population ageing. This is because as people live longer, the total payment they receive in retirement has significantly increased. It has been obvious to pension experts and politicians for over 20 years that reform was necessary. Should nothing be done, then public deficits could rise by some 5 per cent of GDP over the next 30 years and public debt could more than double (Bosworth and Burtless 1997).

Government pensions are now the main source of income for most retirees, providing over 40 per cent of total retirement income in the United States and up to 70 per cent in Germany. One obvious solution to the funding crisis is to cut pension payments. The problem is that because many old people have fairly modest incomes, in some cases causing the most vulnerable members of society living below the poverty line, most countries cannot reduce minimum pensions without increasing social distress among the elderly. Under these circumstances, an alternative option is to increase the retirement age. This is now being done in many Western nations (e.g. to 67 in the United States and United Kingdom). The other option available to Government is to raise the social security contribution of people in work, increase the contributions made by employers, and introduce higher levels of capital gains tax. In virtually every country there will be disagreement between the unions, business, and different political parties over which is the most acceptable solution (Durand 2003). The problem is that to date resolution of these differences has been extremely slow and unless more decisive action is implemented in the very near future, the funding crisis would become a massive drain on Government revenues. This then could only be resolved by withdrawing resources from other areas of public sector spending or lead to even larger, probably unmanageable, public sector deficits.

The Other Elephant in the Room

Case Aims: To illustrate the scale of a less well-publicized dimension of the pension funding problem which has been created by population ageing.

There exists two basic pension models: Direction Contribution (DC) and Direct Benefits (DB) plans. In DC plans, an employer usually provides a matching amount to an employee's contribution. All received funds are placed in an account that is invested and managed on the behalf of the employee. The employer is not responsible for the ending balance which is made available to the employee upon retirement. In contrast, DB plans represent a promise for the future. Employees participating in DB plans are guaranteed a specific pension. In the private sector plans in some countries, the employer is required to report the relationship between pension payment inflows and the total future pension liability (or 'pension benefit obligation'). In recent years due to some employers not ensuring the level of funding has been adequate and the increased volatility in the world's stock markets, major firms are now reporting very significant

(cont'd)

pension fund deficits. In many cases, this has resulted in these companies closing their DB scheme to new employees and adopting some form of DC-based individual employee investment plan.

Although there is reasonable data available on private sector pension deficits, less information is available on public sector schemes. This is becoming an increasingly important issue because virtually all public sector programmes are based upon DB plans and in many cases funding is reliant on a PAYG basis whereby the current workforce is funding the payments of retirees (Easterday and Eaton 2010). Historically public sector pay was lower than the private sector, but in the past employees felt compensation for lower earning was provided by being participants in a guaranteed, in many cases index-linked, payment system based upon years of service and final salary. Over the last 20 years, public sector unions in many countries have successfully negotiated salaries for their members similar to those in the private sector. What seems to have gone unnoticed is that there has been no revision in public sector pension schemes. This situation, when linked to longer life expectancy, now means that most public sector pension schemes are grossly underfunded and the scale of the funding deficit is growing at an exponential rate.

In recent years, politicians have exacerbated this situation by agreeing to upgrade pension benefits in lieu of wage increases for public employees (Mahoney 1992). This action reduces the level of funds needed to support pay rises and appeals to politicians because it provides a mechanism through which to defer payments to employees, thereby leaving a future government to find some way of resolving the even larger pension deficit which has been created by the action of today's politicians.

In the United States in 2006, the Federal Government's General Accounting Office concluded that in the case of State Government plans there was already a \$1 trillion deficit in terms of fund inflows versus pension payment liabilities. Furthermore, many of these plans are at significant risk of soon being unable to meet pension obligations for even their existing retirees. The scale of this deficit in the United States is evidenced by being equal to the emergency fund created by the European Central Bank in 2010 to manage the sovereign debt crisis in the euro zone. In 2007, the size of public sector employee obligations was estimated at being between 100 and 500 per cent larger than the annual operating budgets of most states in the United States (Ennis 2007). A similar position is also apparent in the United Kingdom where it is estimated that between 25 and 30 per cent of all local taxes are now needed to fund the pension payments being made to Local Government retirement employees.

The scale of the pension deficit situation has deteriorated further as a consequence of the recent banking crisis. In the United Kingdom, for example, some Local Governments had placed funds on deposit with the Icelandic banks

(cont'd)

which were then wiped out when these institutions failed. Other public sector pension managers were persuaded that better returns on their reserves could be achieved by purchasing CDOs from banks. These have subsequently become virtually worthless because they are constituted of significant levels of toxic debt.

Some politicians have been less enthusiastic about legislation requiring public sector pension funds to publish the same pension benefit obligation statements that are required of the private sector. Furthermore, in some countries, there is no legal requirement of Governments to include a figure for their public sector pension deficit in the country's national accounts. This is because a statement of pension liabilities is considered as future liability, thereby exempting these figures from inclusion in any statement of a nation's current public deficit. As a consequence, an accurate figure on the scale of the deficit problem which exists in relation to public sector pensions is almost impossible to obtain. In theory, however, based upon the deficit figure for the State Level funding gap in the United States and 25–30 per cent of current UK Local Government revenue being used to fund existing retirees, it would not seem improbable that inclusion of this liability in most developed nation public accounts would increase their national deficit by between 30 and 50 per cent. With organizations such as the IMF and the European Central Bank seeking greater clarification of the real scale of public sector deficits following the onset of sovereign debt crisis, more data may become available requiring a fundamental reconsideration of public sector pension programmes. Probable actions may include delaying the age at which benefit entitlement can commence, a freezing or reduction in pension payments to retired employees, a significant increase in the level of employee pension contributions, and replication of the private sector trend of adopting DC-based plans for new employees. Whichever of these actions are implemented they are unlikely to fully resolve the deficit problem and the other probable outcome is taxpayers may find themselves having to accept further reductions in the levels of public services or face tax increases specifically designed to reduce the public sector pension deficits.

Globalization

Even in the 1960s when the developed nations were enjoying an unprecedented increase in GDP, employment in smokestack industries such as coal, steel, and shipbuilding were already being lost to developing countries. By the 1980s, these job losses accelerated as manufacturers relocated their operations overseas to countries offering lower labour costs. Concurrently, manufacturers in Pacific Rim nations began to successfully enter world markets in sectors such as cars and consumer electronics. This latter trend led economists and sociologists to begin to consider how globalization which was resulting in declining GDP and rising unemployment in the developed nations might impact future public sector spending.

The debate between academics over the impact of globalization has centred upon the merits of some very divergent views. Some academics proposed that as GDP is a dominant factor in determining the level of public sector spending, as developed nation economies suffer in the face of globalization, the outcome would be a decline in public sector spending (Navarro et al. 2004). Others experts forecasted that globalization would cause greater volatility and uncertainty in international finance and trade. In response, Governments would be forced to implement expanded social policies to stabilize their economies through actions such as increased spending on programmes for the unemployed. This second perspective leads to the conclusion that globalization will lead to increased public sector expenditure in Western democracies. A third perspective is that on a global scale there will be convergence in public sector spending. This will occur because as developing nations enjoy higher GDP this will be reflected in increased spending by their Governments. Concurrently, falling GDP in developed economies caused by globalization will require a reduction in Government spending.

In seeking to determine which hypothesis is valid, econometricians have undertaken very sophisticated statistical analysis of economic and Government spending data. As far as providing a solid conclusion about which theory is correct, various studies have provided contradictory conclusions. In part this is due to the difference in data sets which have been analysed and the nature of the statistical techniques utilized. The other, probably more influential, factor is that there are a multitude of different variables influencing decision over the magnitude of public sector funding. As a consequence, being able to definitely isolate the specific influence of globalization has proved to be an extremely difficult empirical task.

Dreher et al. (2008) analysed data from 60 nations over the period 1971–2001. Their results provided no support for either the theory that increasing globalization would lead to a reduction in public sector spending or the alternative theory that the economic problems caused by globalization would result in an increase in Government spending in developed economies. These researchers did note, however, that the complex interactions which exist between variables influencing economic trends may result in a blurring of the influence of globalization to the point that no statistically significant results will be evident. Similarly Brady et al. (2005) who analysed data from 17 developed nation economies over the period from 1975 to 2001 also encountered severe difficulties in isolating the impact of globalization. They did suspect, however, that the data provided some indications that convergence between developed and developing nations may be occurring. As they noted, however, other intra-country economic or demographic pressures and the currently different Governments' preference on directing funds towards alleviating identified social problems are significantly more important, thereby complicating any analysis seeking to isolate the specific impact of global factors. Navarro et al. (2004), who studied economic data from leading OECD nations over the period 1980–2000 reached the conclusion that political orientation of the Government in power had the greatest influence on the scale of public sector spending. Their analysis, however, was unable to identify evidence of convergence. Their primary conclusion was that public sector spending in leading OECD nations over this period has continued to increase.

These empirical studies would tend to indicate that developed nation policy makers do not have to be overtly concerned about the adverse impact of globalization on public sector spending capability. It should be noted, however, that econometric studies face the problem that there is significant time lag between data becoming available, analysis being completed, and results being published in academic journals. As a consequence, even the most recently published findings have focused on the period leading up to the end of the twentieth century, whereas it is only more recently that the economies of China and India have begun to exhibit a level of exponential growth that is totally transforming the nature of international trade. Observers of this transformation consider the impact on the world economy will be even more significant than the emergence of the United States as the leading economy at the beginning of the previous century. Once this occurs, then any convergence in public sector spending between developed and developing nations may become more apparent.

In seeking to provide an assessment of implications of a shift in economic power from the Western democracies to countries in Asia, Swank and Steinmo (2002) have pointed out that major Western firms are removing capital from their developed nation operations and re-investing these funds into new ventures in Asia. For example, the US electronics company, Cisco Systems, has recently established their 'second headquarters' in India and Microsoft has established its second R&D centre in China. Furthermore, the profits generated from these new investments are being retained overseas to support further international expansion. As a consequence, globalization is altering the politics of taxation. This is because the fund inflow from corporate taxes in many Western nations is beginning to fall. Another dynamic is the increase over the last few years in the level of low-cost exports by Asian firms in sectors such as clothing and footwear. These are labour intensive sectors which in the past have played a critical role in sustaining employment in economically disadvantaged regions of Western economies (e.g. the clothing industry in North Carolina and the footwear industry in Italy). Despite actions by some Western Governments to protect domestic firms by limiting imports, there has been a huge increase in the volume of exports of low-cost consumer goods flowing in from developing nation markets from Asia. These imports are decimating domestic firms because they are unable to survive in the face of such intense price competition. This has two adverse impacts on Western economies, namely rising unemployment and a decline in the level of corporate taxes being generated by the few domestic firms which remain in operation in the affected sectors. The reaction of some policy makers to this situation is that this is not a major problem because the key source is the future economic growth and employment in developed economies in high-technology industries such as IT and telecommunications. These individuals hold the view that countries such as China were not a threat because they are only capable of producing low-technology, labour intensive goods. It would seem they have forgotten that in the 1970s the same observations were made about Japanese car manufacturers such as Honda and Toyota and manufacturers of consumer goods electronic such as LG in Korea. In fact, over the last 10 years, the Chinese Government has been investing heavily in the expansion of their industrial and technology base in order to move into areas such as computing and telecommunications. Furthermore, in an amazingly short period of time, Chinese firms in these sectors have already become significant players in world markets. For example, the Chinese company Huawei is now the second largest producer of telecommunications equipment in the world with annual sales of $21.8 billion. Other developing nations, such as Brazil and India, are also enjoying major success in expanding into the global market for high technology products. The scale of their growth is evidenced by the fact that in 2000, of the world's top 500 companies, only 26 companies achieving $0.7 million in total sales were from developing economy countries. In only 10 years by 2010, this figure has risen to 119 companies with annual sales of $5.3 billion (Wagstyl 2010).

To a certain degree developed nations have benefited from the explosive economic growth in China and India because they are exporting both products (e.g. machine tools from Germany) and services such as undertaking huge construction products to assist these countries modernize their infrastructure. However, the Governments in both these countries are committed to an economic policy of developing their own domestic expertise with the eventual aim of not needing to rely upon importing these products and services from developed nations. As this trend accelerates, Western nations can expect their level of exports to decline. Furthermore, total sales will be reduced as emerging nation companies achieve a greater share of global markets. Hence, over time, unless Western nations are able to find new ways of achieving and sustaining competitive advantage in their more advanced sectors of industry, the outcome will be the same as has occurred in sectors such as clothing and footwear, namely a very significant increase in the level of domestic unemployment across many other sectors of industry.

The views of some academics concerning this outcome are in stark contrast to previously published empirical researches that have concluded globalization is insignificant factor in relation to managing public sector spending. Tridimas (2001), for example, believes these new trends in the global economy will place a huge, possibly unmanageable, strain on Western democracies' public sector budgets. The probable outcome is that spending will have decline and ongoing provision of benefits for the socially disadvantaged will have to be massively reduced.

The banking crisis

The collapse of the US securities market in 1929 led to an extensive re-evaluation of the US banking system. The chairman of the Senate subcommittee examining these practices was Carter Glass, a vehement opponent of the affiliate system, under which banks conducted securities trading through affiliated, often wholly owned, institutions. His persistence in questioning this situation led to the enactment of the Banking (or Glass-Steagall) Act of 1933. This prohibited banks from being affiliated with any company engaged in the issue, flotation, underwriting, or public sale of stocks, bonds, debentures, or other securities.

In the late 1980s, the banking industry, especially in the United States and the United Kingdom, began to pressure politicians to remove the regulations which had been put to avoid a repetition of pre-war Great Depression banking collapses. The bankers' promised contribution to enhanced growth in GDP and related potential incremental tax flows seemed to be of sufficient appeal that by the mid-1990s a massive de-regulation of the banking industry had been approved. Politicians' confidence in avoiding another banking crisis was reliant upon their assumptions that their Central Banks and other regulatory agencies (e.g. the SEC in the United States and the FSA in the United Kingdom) had sufficient expertise to provide early warnings of potential problems or misbehaviour within the financial services industry (Kaufman and Wallinson 2001).

Concurrent with de-regulation, as part of their anti-inflation and economic stability policies, Central Bankers were keeping interest rates very low resulting in a sustained period of low inflation. Policy makers were pleased with apparent effectiveness of this new approach to monetary management. This was despite the fact that some economists (Wray 1993) and Central Bankers (Eisenbeis 1997) had expressed major concerns about the risks associated with de-regulation and excessive reliance upon a monetary policy which focused on retaining low interest rates. The rise in developed nations' GDP in the 1990s and early twenty-first century was achieved by an upswing in consumer spending based upon private citizens perceiving rapid increases in house prices and borrowing against this asset to either (a) speculate in the property market and/or (b) sustain their spending on enjoying a better lifestyle (Connelly 2008; Whalen 2008). What Governments did not seem to understand is that when the world is awash with money based upon uncontrolled lending to support a growing asset bubble, Central Bank monetary policy is unlikely to have a significant impact on any attempts to manage a country's economy (Nesvetailova 2005).

In the United States in the 1990s, bankers keen to expand consumer lending entered the sub-prime mortgage market offering low interest loans and reducing the level of assets that borrowers needed to have in order to secure a loan. This led people on limited incomes to believe they could finally afford to own their own houses, safe in the knowledge that the value of this asset would continue to rise. The banks' huge success in this market created a problem that their expanded balance sheet liabilities restricted further lending. Their solution was to bundle together the loans in a process known as 'securitization' and to sell these loan packages as *collateralized debt obligations* (or 'CDOs') to banks and other institutions such as public sector agencies and pension funds. As the scale of mis-selling of the sub-prime mortgages began to emerge and industry experts recognized that many CDOs were essentially toxic debt, the US banking industry went into crisis (Hoenig 2008). Some companies such as Bear Sterns and Lehman Brothers collapsed. Others such as Washington Savings & Loan were taken over by other larger banks. To avert a banking industry meltdown, the US Government approved a huge bail-out fund and implemented Quantitative Easing to sustain liquidity in the financial markets.

Meanwhile in the United Kingdom concern over toxic debt on their balance sheets caused European banks to severely reduce their inter-bank lending activities causing short-term interest rates to rise. Banks such as Northern Rock could not borrow the funds necessary to service outstanding loans and to avoid a run on these institutions and the UK Government was forced to take over major banks and assist other banks buy their smaller, even more financially distressed counterparts. Concurrently to sustain financial liquidity and to attempt to inject stability into the economy, the Bank of England initiated a programme of Quantitative Easing involving making available over £200 billion to the financial markets.

Within the European Union although major banks were carrying some toxic debts on their balance sheets due to their purchase of CDOs, these were not considered sufficiently large enough for the European Central Bank to initiate actions such as Quantitative Easing. In part this was also due to the fact that under the terms of the SGP this type of involvement in the European money markets was deemed non-permissible. Unfortunately, the European Union since the beginning of the new century had not been enforcing actions to ensure that all members of the euro zone attempt to bring their public spending under control. As the financial crisis in the banking system worsened and the world economy entered recession, it became apparent that countries such as Greece had been continuing to grow their economy funded in large part by increased borrowing on the short-term money markets. By mid-2010, it was clear that Greece was heading for financial meltdown and problems of a similar nature, but on lesser scale, were emerging in other Mediterranean countries such as Spain and Portugal. Initially it was hoped that similar to new Eastern European members who faced problems during the recession, the IMF would be able to make sufficient funds available to resolve Greece's sovereign debt crisis. Within a short time it became apparent that the scale of the sovereign debt problem was beyond the capacity of the IMF. Suddenly the conventional view that sovereign debt crises and the potential for default on gilts were only a problem in developing countries was altered overnight (Bauer et al. 2003).

Major European countries who are members of the euro such as Germany and France have been forced to support the ECB in the creation of a £1 trillion bail-out fund. In order for any EU member to qualify for these rescue funds their Governments are required to implement massive reduction in public sector spending and deficits through the immediate introduction of austerity measures such as raising taxes whilst concurrently cutting public sector pay and pensions up to 30 per cent. The response of the electorate in the more stable European economies has been to be fiercely critical of what they see as their taxes being used to save other, more profligate spenders elsewhere in the European Union.

In the United Kingdom, actions to rescue the banks and stabilize the money markets led to the creation of a public sector deficit estimated at £163 billion. This figure represents 12 per cent of annual GDP and is the largest deficit of any EU member state. By remaining outside the euro zone, the United Kingdom has been able to avoid significant contribution to the ECB bail-out fund. However, the Conservative–Liberal coalition which came to power in May 2010 has been forced to initiate immediate actions to reduce the deficit through a mixture of public sector spending cuts and raising the levels of both personal and corporate taxation. Some developed nations such as Australia, Canada, and New Zealand have to a large degree been unaffected by the recession or inappropriate banking practices. The outlook for many developed nation economies, however, is for an extended period of austerity involving major reductions in public sector spending accompanied by a massive restructuring of the nature and quantity of public services being delivered. Under these circumstances, senior managers in public sector organizations will face the 'mission impossible' task of responding to pressure from politicians to sustain services delivery but with much reduced resources.

The Bank Wars

Case Aims: To illustrate that there are rarely any real financial benefits to be achieved by companies triggering brand wars in mature markets.

In most cases, the usual outcome of brands entering into head-to-head confrontations in a mature market is there is rarely any fundamental increase in a company's total number of customers, but the cost of the war will be reflected in all parties facing a reduction in operating profits (Thompson 1999). The deregulation of the UK financial services sector in the 1980s was eventually to lead exactly this depressing outcome. Deregulation caused the UK banks to become much more interested in using mass marketing techniques to attract additional business. By the 1990s, some of the United Kingdom's leading High Street banks were engaged in fierce battles to steal each other's retail customers. In the case of NatWest, having triggered a promotional spending spiral by entering into an unsuccessful battle for market leadership with Barclays, the bank's weakened financial position was a contributor to the bank eventually being taken over by the Royal Bank of Scotland (RBS) in 1999.

Instead of learning from the NatWest mistake, another brand war broke out between financial institutions seeking to achieve market leadership in the UK consumer mortgage market. The existing traditional UK consumer mortgage model was based upon lending depositors' money to borrowers who wanted to

(cont'd)

buy their own home. Essentially market leadership was based upon being able to attract and encourage more consumers to open savings accounts which, in turn, permitted the institution to fund more mortgages than the competition. Then Mr Applegate, the CEO at Northern Rock, had the apparently brilliant idea of borrowing money in the short-term money markets where prevailing interest rates were much lower than rates being paid to savers. These cheaper funds could then be used to offer mortgages at a lower interest rate than other mortgage lenders in the market. The outcome was Northern Rock embarked on a battle for market share which saw Mr Applegate being lionized in the financial press for bringing more aggressive, modern thinking into the conservative world of UK banking (Urry 2003). All was going according to plan until 2007. Then the sub-prime mortgage disaster in the United States caused banks to become increasingly wary about lending money to each other. Money became scarce and short-term interest rates rose dramatically. This left Northern Rock in the position of being unable to pay off loans that were coming due or to raise additional loans to service the institution's rising cost of the money market debts which had already been incurred. As word spread about the problem, there was a run on Northern Rock as worried UK consumers rushed to remove their savings. The queues that formed outside Northern Rock, the country's fifth-biggest mortgage lender, represented the first bank run in Britain since 1866 (Anon 2007b). The chancellor's, Alistair Darling's, attempts to reassure savers seemed to only lengthen the queues of people outside Northern Rock branches demanding to get their money out. The run did not stop until Mr. Darling gave a taxpayer-backed guarantee that all the existing deposits at Northern Rock were safe. Nevertheless, as the scale of the problem within Northern Rock became known to the UK Treasury and the financial regulators, in the end the only way the UK Government was able to resolve the situation was to nationalize the bank (Ritson 2007).

The lesson that both senior managers and marketers should learn from such events is that the best response to a brand war is usually to stand back, wait until the dust has settled, and then move on to exploit the opportunities created by those firms whose financial position has been weakened. Regretfully it is often the case that the CEOs of one or more of the largest companies perceive a brand war as a personal affront to their reputation and hence seek to become embroiled in the battle. Such was the case with HBOS which was created when RBS acquired Halifax, one of the United Kingdom's largest mortgage lenders. The HBOS CEO, Mr Andy Hornby, had established a reputation for being extremely aggressive in his response to any threat from competitors. Hence, when it was understood that Northern Rock was achieving market share growth by borrowing short-term funds via the money markets, Mr Hornby's reaction was to duplicate the model. As a consequence, this decision sparked off a bank war between most of the mortgage lenders in the

(cont'd)

UK banking system. In mid-September 2008, after a huge collapse in the value of HBOS shares, the only viable solution was for the UK Government to assist the bank to consider a takeover offer from the more conservatively managed Lloyds-TSB. Explaining the demise of HBOS, Mr Hornby was quoted as stating 'we found ourselves impacted by the wholesale market shutting down. We were particularly dependent upon wholesale funding' (Anon. 2008). This was not a particularly surprising statement given that HSBOS in their fight to retain market domination had by September 2008 created a lending gap of almost £200 billion between the bank's mortgage assets and liabilities.

Stakeholders, Values, and Ethics

4

The aims of this chapter are to cover the issues of:

(1) The concept of organizational responsibility in relation to stakeholders
(2) The stakeholder concept in relation to public sector organizations
(3) The influence of embedded values on organizational behaviour
(4) The influence of culture on organizational behaviour
(5) New Public Governance Management (NPG) and networks
(6) The role of ethics in guiding management and employee behaviour

Stakeholders

In terms of developing a strategic plan for managing a resource-constrained world, managers require clear guidance on what are their organization's fundamental objectives in relation to future performance. On ongoing debate in the private sector, especially prevalent following major financial scandals such as Enron or the collapse of the United Kingdom's RBS, is whether the purpose of a strategic plan is merely to achieve the goal of maximizing shareholder value or should fulfil a wider requirement to exhibit a sense of social and moral obligations aimed at meeting the needs of other stakeholders (e.g. customers, suppliers, and the communities in which their operations are based).

Supporters of the stakeholder perspective in the private sector usually base their argument on the benefits to the wider community from corporations exhibiting social responsibility. Those who oppose such views and point out that the primary responsibility must be towards shareholders often base their argument on the fact that in many countries, there exists a fiduciary responsibility towards protecting shareholders. In the United States, for example, a clear articulation of the primacy of the shareholder value maximization was the ruling by the Michigan State Supreme Court in Dodge vs. Ford Motor Company, 1919. Henry Ford wanted to invest Ford Motor Company's considerable retained earnings in the company rather than distribute it to shareholders. The Dodge brothers, minority shareholders in Ford Motor Company, brought suit against Ford, alleging that his intention to benefit employees and consumers was at the expense of shareholders. In their ruling, the Michigan court agreed with the Dodge brothers and stated that the business corporation is organized and carried on primarily for the profit of stockholders. The court ruled that the powers of the directors must be employed for this end (Sundaram and Inkpen 2004).

Those who believe in serving the needs of stakeholders will often claim that if one permits managers to pursue the aim of maximizing short-term profitability, thereby enhancing quoted share prices, this can lead to extremely adverse outcomes such as the Union Carbide Bhopal Plant Disaster of 1984 or women prescribed the tranquillizer Thalidomide giving birth to children being with major birth defects. There clearly is some validity in this perspective (Schrenk 2006). In attempting to resolve this dilemma, Madden (2005) has presented an alternative position which proposes that firms should only seek to maximize shareholder value, but that this aim should be specified as long-term objective. In his view if management has embedded a culture based upon continuing to generate a much higher return on capital relative to the cost of capital over the long-term, then this goal will remove the temptation to implement actions that immediately increase short-term profitability. This is because in virtually every case short-term profit maximizing activities will usually distort and damage longer-term performance. Thus, for example, US banks which became involved in the sub-prime mortgage market did enjoy a very major increase in short-term profitability. However, once the non-viability of these loans became apparent, these same banks either collapsed or were forced to drastically downgrade the values of assets on their balance sheets.

Although originated in relation to strategic management theory in the private sector, the concept of seeking to satisfy the needs of multiple stakeholders was recognized as an issue also of relevance to the public following the introduction of NPM. McAdam et al. (2005) have noted, however, that differences which exist in between multiple stakeholder scenarios in public versus private sector organizations do present fundamental operational problems that must be addressed in attempting to adapt the concept for use in the public sector. In their view, simply translating the language of the private sector stakeholder model with minor modifications upon introduction within the public is unlikely to be sufficient. This is because the basic model is unlikely to accurately or appropriately represent the interests and needs of the stakeholders in public sector environments.

The purpose of a stakeholder model in any organization is to determine how performance will impact and fulfil the needs of each stakeholder group. In the context of the resource-constrained world now facing public sector organizations, the purpose of stakeholder analysis is to determine how changes in ongoing service provision will impact specific client groups. Such changes may occur following fundamental re-engineering of internal processes, structures, and management systems that would emerge once the imposition of major budget reductions takes place (Martin, 2000). In the context of utilizing stakeholder analysis the process assists in determining appropriate plans to ensure the delivery of value to all those impacted by the activities of the organization. Wisniewski and Stewart (2004) stress the need to fully consider the diversity when adopting a stakeholder approach to define future performance in PSOs. They suggest there is a requirement for differing 'stakeholder windows' to be considered when assessing the relevance of public sector performance measurements. Various stakeholders will exhibit differing and possibly conflicting performance outcomes. Hence, in their view a 'one size fits all' approach to optimizing stakeholder values in the public sector is unlikely to be successful. The implication of this conclusion is that a key antecedent to the successful development of future plans in a public sector organization will be the development of accurate answers to the following questions:

(1) Who are our stakeholders?
(2) How can stakeholders be categorized to identify areas of common need?
(3) What are the needs of each of the identified stakeholder groups?
(4) How can synergies and dichotomies of need across groups of stakeholders be most effectively addressed and resolved?

In view of the fact that different and potentially conflicting performance requirements among stakeholders will be identified in such an analysis, the public sector strategist will need to utilize a system which provides a framework for assessing the suitability of alternative plans. To achieve this aim, Moullin (2002) developed a public sector version of the balanced scorecard approach to strategic management. His system is constituted of ensuring the validity of the following organizational components:

(1) Strategy is concerned with key performance outcomes that justify the existence of the delivered services.
(2) Service is about how the organization's outputs meet the needs of both users and other key stakeholders.
(3) Operational excellence is concerned with effectiveness of process, structures, and of staff.
(4) Financial performance focuses how the organization achieves optimal management of allocated funds and the cost-effective utilization of assigned budgets.
(5) Innovation and learning are concerned with exploiting innovation and entrepreneurial behaviour to create added value for service users and other key stakeholders.

Process implementation

The concept of adopting a stakeholder approach to strategic planning in the private sector has gained in acceptance over recent years and tends to be strongly recommended in most leading academic texts. Most writers, however, do add the caution that the stakeholder approach is much more difficult to successfully implement than the more traditional model of optimizing long-term shareholder value. In commenting upon these difficulties, Freeman and Liedtka (1997) proposed there are four normative principles that are critical to the success of the organization and the organization's stakeholders. These are as follows:

(1) *Stakeholder co-operation* through which value is created that permits stakeholders to jointly satisfy their wants/needs.

(2) *Complexity resolution* whereby the complex needs of individuals belonging to various stakeholder groups are identified and different groups seek to jointly determine how differences can be resolved.

(3) *Continuous creation* whereby stakeholder co-operation emphasizes innovation as the basis for indentifying common values that can provide new sources of benefit to stakeholders.

(4) *Internal competition* which arises because stakeholder differences and the focus within the organization are to effectively manage these tensions which exist because of the two behaviour traits of co-operation and competition amongst internal stakeholder groups.

The added complexities which emerge upon the introduction of stakeholder models in the public sector are evident when attempting to implement the aspect of NPM philosophy that advocates the private sector should compete for work currently undertaken by Government agencies. In commenting on this situation, Rucker (2003) points out that implementation requires convergence in compatible needs between the culture of private sector bidders, culture within the impacted Government agency, the values of public sector employees, the values of the employees among private sector bidders, the general public to whom services are to be delivered, and the third party values of politicians supporting change.

A significant difference in relation to organizational culture is the orientation towards optimizing shareholder value in private sector organizations versus the emphasis of the organization fulfilling the role as servants to the general public in the public sector. Where private sector bids are used to provide outsourced services, this action can often further heighten the level of dissent between stakeholders. Public sector unions can be expected to adopt an adversarial attitude should they perceive there is inadequate concern over equity and fairness in outsourcing jobs to the private sector. The general public may perceive that as taxpayers they are funding the provision of services yet have no ability to ensure that there is no decline in the availability of services following the implementation of outsourcing. In the face of such problems, it may be the case that any attempt to achieve convergence in stakeholder values becomes an impossible aim. This is because policy makers have adopted the overriding principle that the fundamental aim is to achieve a reduction in the costs of service delivery. Should this result in a divergence of opinion between different stakeholder groups, then the policy makers may conclude this is an acceptable casualty in the war to reduce public sector spending.

Barriers to Stakeholder Implementation

Case Aims: To illustrate some of the problems associated with implementing a stakeholder approach in the public sector.

Stakeholder interactions are usually much more complex inside public sector organizations. As a consequence, the case materials on utilization of stakeholder models in the public sector usually conclude that in some situations, despite articulated good intentions, implementation can be fundamentally flawed. Research on stakeholder behaviour in a major UK hospital provides an example of the tensions and obstacles which can arise in using a stakeholder approach (Carruthers et al. 2007).

The researchers collected data from a representative sample of stakeholders. These included the director of cardiac services, heart specialists (clinicians), business managers, technical staff, nursing staff, and health care purchasers from the local health care authorities. The conclusions reached concerning relationship dynamics found the purchasers saw themselves as being in a position of power because they could determine to which hospitals they will award contracts. These purchasers expressed concern about investing considerable funds only to observe limited returns in relation to treatment outcomes, volume of work, and patient waiting lists. Both purchasers and providers identified the lack of a shared culture inside the hospital which was reflected by a behaviour trait of many individuals essentially doing what they pleased. This was most apparent among clinicians whose self-interest seemed to be a major barrier to delivering patient-centred care. The view of hospital managers was that the new realities of NPM which require greater attention to meeting performance indicators are not incompatible with the delivery of high quality health care. There was little attempt to foster co-operation between administrators and medical staff. This failure of stakeholders to successfully integrate their different corporate attitudes created an environment that was unable to effectively facilitate the co-operation needed to optimize the value of output in a world of increasingly scarce resources.

The opinion of hospital staff was that identifying compatible objectives was rendered impossible because resource priorities often have to be revised due to the activities of politicians creating artificial, often irrelevant, targets

(cont'd)

which are then publicized using phrases such as 'a new patients charter'. The problem this type of behaviour creates is then amplified once latest issue which has come to the attention of the politicians ceases to be of interest and is then replaced with a decision by politicians to invoke action in relation to a completely new series of performance indicators. Even the purchasers recognize the problems that are created by their requirement of the hospital to deliver increasingly large quantities of information that they need to assess performance against an ever-rising number of performance indicators. Possibly even more worrying is that many respondents expressed the concern that in the move to a stakeholder-orientated management model, meeting the needs of one key stakeholder group, the patients, seems to be increasingly ignored.

In discussing the results of their study, Carruthers et al. (2007) concluded that the problem with introducing stakeholder models into the public sector is there is a marked difference between a 'propensity to co-operate' mindset and the reality of whether a 'capacity to co-operate' actually exists. This conclusion is based upon their observations that although the various stakeholder groups perceive the benefits of greater co-operation, in the face of threats over personal freedom, resources being diverted to other groups, or performance indicators being ignored in order to sustain the quality of patient care, actually being able to co-operate with others becomes an impossible objective. The implications of these findings are that although the stakeholder model is intuitively appealing, in a world of increasing demand for public sector services, but a declining availability of resources, the approach is critically dependent upon the skills of an organization's senior managers to achieve convergence of purpose among internal stakeholder groups. If this cannot occur, then the probable greatest casualty will be the general public who will encounter a decline in either the volume or quality of delivered services.

Embedded values

Private sector service firms exhibit a number of characteristics which differentiate them from tangible goods businesses. These include product intangibility, perishability, the interchangeability of suppliers, and heterogeneous customer demand. Additionally, because of the high labour content associated with the delivery of many services, organizations can face significant difficulties in ensuring consistency of service quality. In recognition of these problems, two key attributes of successful service firms are (a) a viable strategic model which recognizes the difficult nature of the market conditions facing these organizations and (b) the critical need to embed the same values throughout the entire workforce.

In reviewing the need to embed common values across the entire business operation, Campbell (2000) proposed that this objective requires an organization's leadership to have the ability to ensure the following outcomes:

(1) The goals of the organization must be communicated and embodied in the culture of the organization.

(2) Overseeing the communication processes necessary in order to stated value is permeated through all levels of organizational hierarchy.

(3) Exhibiting a behaviour trait in relation to decisions and actions that demonstrate the individual's unwavering commitment to the organization's stated values.

(4) Making any changes in organization's structure and processes that is necessary to support the effective utilization of defined values. This ensures no forms of bureaucracy remain which might be resistant to accepting these values.

(5) Ensuring that managers at all levels demonstrate a commitment to these values through their behaviour and by the way they reinforce the behaviour of others. This is necessary because any manager who shifts positions and exhibits contradictory values will undermine the trust and confidence of their staff.

(6) They must ensure that organization's values assist people within the organization to be motivated to have commitment towards producing outstanding results.

Southwest Airlines

Case Aims: The role of leadership to ensure the delivery of high quality services.

An example of an individual whose strong leadership ensured the long-term success of a company in the intensely competitive airline industry is the founder of Southwest Airlines, Herb Kelleher (Reich 1994). His strategic model was based upon recognizing there was growing demand in the United States for lower airfares. He perceived significant weaknesses in the strategic 'hub and spoke' model used by the major airlines and inflexibility in the operational processes being utilized in the industry. His alternative strategic model was to fly direct routes and by introducing more flexible working patterns, generate much higher productivity from the company's aircraft fleet. On a typical day, Southwest Airline planes are in the air 11 hours, versus an industry average of 8, and the company achieves an average of 10.5 flights per gate each day compared with an industry average of 4.5. The company also has much leaner, six-person ground crews who can turn around a plane for the next flight in just 15 minutes, compared to an average of 1 hour required for the most major airlines.

(cont'd)

To achieve these outstanding results, Herb Kelleher has ensured that all employees share the same values, namely by working together and helping each other, and the company delivers outstanding customer satisfaction and thereby outcompetes other airlines. He has also created an environment where the message is 'work can be fun' with staff doing zany things to keep their passengers smiling throughout their trip. He has also instilled a strong belief in the importance of sharing information and ensuring managers at all levels are deeply involved in providing encouragement for the efforts of their staff. Another important value is loyalty to employees which is reflected by a policy of investing in training to upgrade existing skills and ensure wherever possible that filling of higher-level jobs is achieved through internal promotion.

Fedex

Case Aims: To illustrate the importance of shared values in a service environment.

An example of a service business which has been highly successful due to lucra- tively embedding common value throughout the workforce is Federal Express (or 'Fedex'). This is a company whose achievements are somewhat amaz- ing because the primary competitor has been Government-owned, and often heavily subsidized, national postal services. The company's founder Frederick Smith had the vision of combining existing technologies with developing new approaches to logistics handling of trucks and aircraft to create a delivery ser- vice superior to that of the US postal service (Gordon 1992). Smith recognized the critical importance of embedding common values throughout the entire Fedex workforce. At the core of the Fedex operation is his philosophy of People, Service, Profit (P-S-P). The People component reflects the embedded value that employees are the company's most important asset. Their commitment permits the delivery of service levels superior to any other organization. Superior quality then naturally leads to the generation of profits. The P-S-P philosophy is pre- sented to employees as an unbroken circle where there are no clearly definable points of entry or exit. The People link is supported by Profit, which is supported by Service, which is supported by People. Each link upholds the other and is, in turn, supported by them.

The company is also a strong supporter of the use of performance indicators to identify areas where performance can be enhanced. Unlike the public sector where policy makers and politicians seem to believe adding more performance indicators on top of existing standards would improve performance, the Fedex system is extremely simple. It is based upon the measurement of only three

(cont'd)

'critical satisfaction' factors, namely timeliness, loss or damage, and error. Together these are used to assess performance and where problems are identified, action can be implemented to ensure even higher customer satisfaction levels in the future.

The simplicity of the performance measurement system, when linked to the computerized collection of process activity data in real time, permits teams to self-assess their productivity at the end of every shift. In those cases where a service problem is identified, Quality Action Teams (QATs) are formed to seek a solution. These teams will be constituted of employees who have the skills to identify and resolve the identified problem. In some cases, the QAT will contain representatives from customer companies when this added knowledge is deemed a more effective approach to ensuring quality improvements can be implemented. The QATs receive no additional compensation for their achievements because employees accept the corporate value that quality is considered fundamental to fulfilling the organization's strategic objectives. Hence, the only recognition of success is the members of the most successful QAT outcomes are invited to make national level presentations to senior management to describe the outcomes of their actions. The best presentation is then given the chance to travel to the Fedex Head Office in Memphis to repeat their presentation to the Fedex Board of Directors.

The reality facing developed nations is that expansion of public sector resources by increased taxation is increasingly an impossible task because eventually neither their citizens nor corporate taxpayers will remain sufficiently motivated to make greater contributions to enhancing GNP. Another reality is public sector organizations can no longer expect year-on-year budget increases to be able to offer employees an annual wage increase. Under these circumstances, public sector organizations will be required to deliver greater value in the provision of services whilst making the best and the most productive use of increasingly scarce resources. Management and employees will be required to interpret stakeholder demands and expectations in order to ensure that the most important and appropriate public services continue to be delivered. This can only be achieved through an ongoing dialogue between stakeholders and public sector organizations, with stakeholder discussions occurring at all levels within these organizations.

In reviewing the values determining the behaviour of public sector employees in the United States, Henderson (2004) concluded that the dominant value for the last 120 years can be labelled as 'merit'. In his view, merit is the basis which determines exhibited values, attitudes, and beliefs of civil servants. Merit avoids politicians using patronage to create public sector agencies which respond to politicians' demands in ways potentially detrimental to the needs of the general public for whom these agencies were created. Generally speaking, it has been found that as a group public sector employees in the United States are somewhat more liberal, tolerant, and better educated than the population at large. They are motivated by economic incentives, job security, being appreciated for their efforts, and being involved in undertaking tasks which they believe are extremely worthwhile.

In terms of summarizing the core values to be found among public sector employees in the United States, Henderson suggests these include:

(1) Neutrality and objectivity in the sense that public servants exhibit unbiased opinions in relation to the views of different political parties and as a result they are able to avoid acting in a partisan fashion when it comes to advising the Government on public sector policies or undertaking the tasks associated with implementing public policy. Neutrality also permits public sector employees to serve the general public objectively, in accordance with laws and rules and being impartial when providing services to any particular creed, gender, race, ethnicity, age, or other such variables.

(2) Professionalism and expertise in the sense that public sector employees are competent to do their work and their performance is measured in relation to specified professional standards. In many cases, independent professional organizations exist which specify and maintain required standards (e.g. doctors, lawyers, and engineers are respectively covered by the standards of the American Medical Association, American Bar Association, and The American Society for Public Administration).

(3) Transparency and accountability in the sense that public sector employees are expected to avoid both impropriety and the appearance of impropriety by being open to scrutiny, responsive to the public, and accountable for their actions.

(4) Belief in equity, the rule of law, constitutional norms, private property, and a workable legal order.

Common Values in Public Services

Case Aims: To illustrate that acceptance of common values can assist public sector employees respond to the need to deliver services.

Some years before the scale of the sovereign debt facing the European Union was recognized, the welfare state in Scandinavian countries was already beginning to face problems. In Denmark, for example, the welfare state (i) represents approximately 50 per cent of the national economy, (ii) requires one of the highest levels of taxation in the OECD countries, (iii) consists of approximately 30,000 public institutions, (iv) employs approximately 1 million persons

(cont'd)

(or 20 per cent of the entire population), and (v) to a large degree has established a monopoly on providing services to the country's citizens. As a consequence, the political system and public institutions in Denmark operate in a way which is near to Weber's ideal type of bureaucratic rational organization that has been combined with Frederick Taylor's principles of scientific management to achieve organizational efficiency.

A critical factor in public sector organizations continuing to deliver adequate services during a period of sever austerity is the need to ensure appropriate values are embedded across the entire workforce. In order to determine how this can be achieved Pedersen and Rendtorff (2004) undertook an in-depth study of events within the Aalborg Municipality in Denmark. To communicate the need to adopt common and appropriate values, the senior management team developed the slogan 'Down with the old internal kingdoms, focus on stakeholders and transparent decision-making processes.'

To embed the philosophy underlying the slogan, a project was initiated called 'Core Values in the Administration of the Mayor'. The aim of the project was to involve all the staff in defining the future common values of the organization. From a list of over 40 identified values, the following 6 core values were selected as representing the organizations core values:

(1) We are committed and we take responsibility for what we do.

(2) We are open-minded and we are honest.

(3) We treat other persons with respect and we trust other persons.

(4) We are well-skilled and we want to have the necessary competencies to do a good job.

(5) We are willing to co-operate with all relevant partners.

(6) We are proud of being in the administration of the Mayor.

In order that staff could integrate these values in their daily work, a series of training events in areas such as behaviour, decision-making, and communication were undertaken. The aim was to assist staff to take ownership of the values which they had defined in order that these could be embedded across the entire organization. In relation to provision of services, senior managers in the organization had to interpret the decisions of the politicians in order to understand how these should be reflected in the production and delivery of services. This was achieved through dialogue with politicians and other stakeholders such as senior civil servants who are responsible for making funds available. The aim of these dialogues was to gain an understanding of what are the demands and expectations of stakeholders. It was apparent that the newly embedded core values were of critical assistance in this process. They were also of assistance

(cont'd)

to senior managers during dialogue with their staff to determine how the demands of external stakeholders could be translated into deliverable actions understood by the entire workforce. Pedersen and Rendtorff concluded that a value-based approach to management was important in terms of supporting decision-making about how and what services to deliver. This is because values can act as a facilitator by (a) generating focus on important issues in both the dialogues and their interpretations and (b) being used to make sense at different levels in the organizations of what is required by external stakeholders.

Acceptance of common values is also extremely important in providing the justification for defining rules and procedures upon which service production and delivery can be decided. Values when linked with defined rules assist staff communicate, explain, and defend the reasons for their decisions made interacting with others inside the organization and, most importantly, with the general public. Based upon their observation of process, Pedersen and Rendtorff determined that value-based management gave staff greater flexibility when seeking to resolve service provision problems. The embedded values are also supportive because top-down directive leadership can be replaced by a bottom-up approach to decision-making.

The researchers also found evidence that common values can assist managers overcome tensions that can arise in seeking to deliver adequate services in the face of constrained resources. Confrontation and compromise appear to have been reduced because middle managers assisted by the new embedded values seem to act with greater honesty and integrity when working with their staff. Additionally, middle managers utilize the organization's values as the basis for justifying their decisions about how best to deliver high quality services to the general public.

Culture

Bozeman (1987) argued that Government organizations tend to represent their society's values to a greater extent than do private businesses. This is because members of society view their Governmental organizations as more reflective of their own values than they expect of any commercial business. The general public, who perceive themselves as part-owners of their Government organizations, often feel that these entities should reflect society's values. With the aim of assessing the validity of this perspective, Khalid and Pearce (1993) undertook a comparative analysis of the behaviour of public sector managers in Saudi Arabia and the United States in relation to how managerial activities are reflective of societal values. Saudi managers reported that their organizations were less rule-bound, used more non-merit criteria in personnel decisions, and were characterized by greater nepotism than their US counterparts. Behaviour patterns in Saudi organizations held constant even when managers worked with, or were supervised by foreigners. These results caused the authors to conclude that behaviour of managers in Saudi Government organizations closely reflected the ideals and values exhibited within general society.

In relation to the issue of how national culture influences employee values in public sector organizations, Asia presents a very different environment than organizations more frequently studied such as those in United States and Europe. In a Confucian-oriented society, such as Korean, people think of themselves as part of a hierarchically organized world with commitment to family being an ordained responsibility. Order and harmony, rather than competition and adversarial relations are considered supreme values, to be upheld by the conduct of employees in public sector organizations. As a consequence, Cho and Lee (2001) posited that Korean public managers can be expected to perceive their job as offering higher levels of prestige, centralization, and general job satisfaction than their private sector counterparts.

To test their hypothesis, these researchers undertook a comparative evaluation of the values of public sector managers and their counterparts in the private sector. Compared to private sector managers, Korean public managers score higher on value commitment and commitment to stay with their organization even in the face of problems or increasing workload. Korean public managers also score highly on their acceptance of the need for perceived centralization. Perceived prestige score is significantly higher in the public sector, indicating that Government sector managers clearly perceive that they get more prestige and recognition from society than do bank managers. This can be contrasted with the situation found in United States, where private sector managers perceive much higher job prestige and recognition from their society than do their counterparts in the public sector. Korean managers in both sectors show a moderate level of value commitment, although private managers score higher on the value commitment to their employers than do public sector managers.

Organizational culture reflects the widely shared and strongly held values of the workforce which in turn influence behaviour in the execution of assigned tasks. Employee values represent preferences for alternative outcomes as well as means of achieving those outcomes. One approach to visualizing alternative forms of organizational values is to assume there are two variables that are dominant influencers, namely Orientation and Control. As summarized in Figure 4.1, these two dimensions result in four different value philosophies that might be exhibited by an organization.

Parker and Bradley (2000) posited that any changes in the advent of NPM strategies in Queenlands, Australia, public sector agencies will be reflected in the nature of ongoing organizational behaviour. They note that the Queensland public sector has undergone a process of change in which departments have been encouraged to depart from a traditional bureaucratic model with its emphasis on rules, procedures, and stability and to adopt a NPM philosophy. The

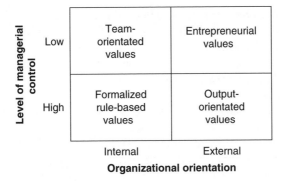

Figure 4.1   Alternative organizational values

new philosophy has sought to achieve a greater orientation towards change, flexibility, entrepreneurialism, outcomes, efficiency, and productivity. It also includes encouragement of a more participatory, team-orientated, and flexible approach to task implementation as the basis for engendering a stronger sense of organizational commitment among employees.

To assess whether the introduction of the NPM model has achieved the value shift being sought by politicians and senior Government officials, they undertook a study of six different Queensland public agencies. They utilized a research model designed to permit these agencies to be mapped in relation to the values philosophies similar to those shown in Figure 4.2. Their research hypothesis was that the introduction of the NPM model would mean a formalized, rule-based values philosophy would no longer be very evident in these six agencies. The data acquired, however, did not support this hypothesis. In all of the agencies there remained a hierarchical culture based upon enforcement of rules, conformity,

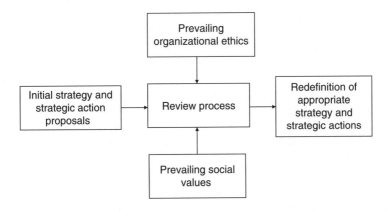

Figure 4.2   The ethical review process

and attention to technical matters. Their conclusion was that despite external pressure to implement change, the values model found within the Queensland public sector organizations clearly reflected the retention of the traditional model of bureaucracy and the operation of public administration model that rely on formal rules and procedures to ensure tight control over employee behaviour.

Parker and Bradley concluded that their findings are suggestive of the inability of public sector managers to effectively manage a culture change. This is possibly due to the fact that existing organizational culture is deeply ingrained in the underlying norms of an organization and cannot be altered by merely relying upon edicts issued by senior managers. They also suggest that despite what may be a prevailing political ideology, many private sector management practices cannot be introduced in the public sector. This is because public sector employees believe that the very different nature of public sector services means these cannot be delivered in the same manner as the production of goods or delivery of services in the private sector. Consequently, the prescriptions of organizational values which are drawn from the experience of successful private sector companies may be unsuitable for application within public sector organizations.

New public governance

Until the 1980s, the prevailing theories of business were based upon the assumption that organizations perceive themselves as engaged in competitive, often adversarial activities in relation to other firms and during any interactions between buyers and sellers. Research initiated by the Nordic business schools produced evidence which contradicted this prevailing wisdom. These researchers found examples where firms succeeded as the result of a willingness to collaborate with each other. They also concluded that collaboration often involved a large number of firms creating networks to jointly improve performance in situations such as seeking to enter new overseas markets. Further impetus to network theory was added by recognition that small firms often engage in formal and informal networking in order to gain access to information and resources which are not available inside their own organizations (Curren et al. 1993).

There is a tendency in academia when a new paradigm is identified for some researchers to claim a new managerial form is superior to any others and should be adopted by all organizations. Such was the case with networks. Some early studies tended to present these entities as the most effective solution to managing in post-industrial societies. This view was so prevalent in the 1990s that some Governments were persuaded to divert a significant proportion of their economic support programmes for small business into schemes to persuade firms to create networks (Chaston 1996). As is often the case with new academic theories, as more understanding was acquired, the claims of the superiority of network structures proved to be less valid than originally thought. Researchers such as Lorenzoni and Baden-Fuller (1995) concluded that networks were not always the best solution and that even where these new entities have been formed, there are a number of critical factors such as power differentials among members and level of achieved trust that will determine whether the network structure can be successful.

The concepts of collaboration and networks subsequently entered the realms of public sector management theory. Similar to the evolution of theory in the private sector, some academics decided that networks offer a superior managerial paradigm for PSOs. Crosby and Bryson (2005) perceive networks as having the capability to assist diverse stakeholders to make sense of a common problem, commit to collaborating with each other, develop new public sector policies, and work together in developing superior outcomes. In the 1990s, emerging evidence of the failings of NPMs was explained as being caused by Governments implementing a system based upon top-down, hierarchical approach which directed PSOs to implement highly prescriptive actions without being permitted to modify process to fit differences in local circumstances. Kooiman (1999) posited that networks permitted greater understanding of public sector relationships and issues which could lead to the implementation of more effective solutions.

Discourse between academics about the benefits of the network approach in the public sector identified the concept as providing new ways of governing. These interactions led to the conclusion that the world was entering a new stage in the evolution of public administration which eventually was labelled as New Public Governance (NPG). Politicians were enthusiast acceptors of network theory and began to avidly promote 'partnerships' and greater interagency co-operation between Government departments, PSOs, private sector companies, and third sector organizations (DWP 2004). Unfortunately, many supporters of the concept of NPG failed to learn from the lessons existing within the private sector that the formation and successful operation of networks are a complex, and often highly problematic, process. Few in Government appeared to heed warnings that collaboration in the public sector is unlikely to achieve a beneficial outcome unless there is a genuine need and real agreement by all involved parties that the most effective solution will emerge through cross-organizational collaboration (Mattessich et al. 2001). This is because, as been known in the private sector for over a decade, there are a number of key determinants of performance that need consideration when seeking to utilize networks as a platform to solve problems. Given the following critical factors listed below, it seems unlikely that NPG will face severe problems as a practical paradigm for politicians or PSOs struggling to manage major cuts in public expenditure:

(1) Participants must agree over a common purpose, strategy, and outcome to be achieved by the network.

(2) Participants should exhibit high levels of integrity, thereby creating a high level of trust between all network members.

(3) Participants must share common goals in relation to the delivery of services.

(4) Participants should perceive the success of the network as being more important than achieving the performance goals that have been specified for their own organizations.

(5) Participants should perceive that retaining resources for use within their own organization is less beneficial than allocating these same resources for use by the network.

(6) There must be genuine recognition of the value that each participant brings to the network and that no individuals or organizations make false or misleading claims about their role in delivering the outcomes achieved by the network.

(7) Participants must share the same cultural values which are based upon believing there are significant advantages from exhibiting a participative orientation towards problem solving and task execution.

Ethics

Over the next decade, public sector senior managers will face the mission impossible task of sustaining delivery of the same or even an increased level of services but with significantly fewer resources. It will prove extremely difficult to retain staff loyalty and commitment when employees are facing increasing complaints from the general public over the scale or quality of service provision. Staff will be expected to continue to exhibit a high level of professionalism despite having fewer resources with which to fulfil their assigned job roles.

Ethics involve moral formulae concerned with right and wrong, thereby providing the basis for guiding appropriate socially accepted conduct. An ethic can be considered to be constituted of two elements, namely the act itself and the human conviction underlying the act (Jayaraman et al. 1993). An act contains the four attributes of intent, motive, consequences, and justification. Hence, in assessing the nature of any act, it is necessary to determine which, if any, of these attributes is rendered unacceptable or immoral. In terms of decision-making within a PSO it is necessary to select acts which optimize service delivery responsibilities whilst remaining within the legal and ethical boundaries of society in relation to prevailing environment conditions. For the leaders of these organizations, as the availability of allocated resources decline in the face of Government cuts, these individuals will need to constantly assess whether changes in plans and the implementation of strategy will continue to be considered as ethically acceptable by the general public. Achieving this objective will require a review of the elements summarized in Figure 4.2.

In some cases, the impact of changing ethics and social values may require a fundamental re-appraisal of a PSOs' future plans. The PSOs that are more likely to succeed during the re-definition of service delivery processes are those which have created an entrepreneurial culture at the core of their operations. An entrepreneurial orientation usually permits more flexible, 'out-of-the-box' thinking. This is usually a fundamental requirement when seeking to respond to significant change in long-standing industrial, market, or societal conventions.

The dilemma which can emerge is the organization is unable to identify new actions that can be accommodated within prevailing ethical or societal values. This is because the leadership may decide that unethical acts are justifiable in order to ensure the survival of the organization. For example, an organization whose future is critically dependent upon a merger with another organization may face the dilemma that many of the current employees may be made redundant. Under these circumstances, the leaders of the organization must decide whether job security is more important than delivery of the best possible level of services. Such dilemmas are not easy to resolve. Any individual who considers himself/herself as an ethical person may find his or her personal values severely tested when facing a decision that could reduce the scale of his or her operations or cause a significant number of his or her employees to be made redundant. Some leaders can be expected to be supportive of a paraphrased view expressed by the famous University of Chicago economist, Milton Friedman (1970, p. 25) who argued that:

> ...there is one and only one social responsibility of any organisation – to use its resources and engage in activities designed to ensure survival so long as it stays within the rules of the game, which is to say, engages in activities without involvement in deception or fraud.

In assessing the validity of Friedman's perspective, Gallagher (2005) felt that merely relying upon the position that the organization has remained within the confines of existing legislation may not be an astute claim by the leadership. This is because managers must recognize that where their actions do not align with society's broader view of ethical behaviour, this may place the future of the organization at risk. Relying upon the legal system to ensure the staff observe an organization's confidentiality rules is an increasingly impractical concept. The age of e-mails, 'hacks', and the willingness of employees to reveal organizational misbehaviour means unfavourable information will often become known to the general public. Furthermore, in many developed nations, special interest groups external to the organization can often invoke a civil legal action to force an organization to release this information into the public domain. Hence, acting ethically in relation to both laws and broader societal values is an invaluable insurance against actions that might sometime in the future damage the organization's reputation or undermine an ability to remain in existence.

Based upon evidence from the private sector concerning organizations facing extremely difficult external environments or resource limitations, sustaining employee commitment is often critically dependent upon how the staff are perceiving their senior managers and influential external stakeholders are exhibiting high levels of ethical behaviour. Unless this trait is overtly apparent, staff may adopt the view that acting unethically is totally acceptable when seeking to achieve their own personal goals or fulfilling the tasks or responsibilities which they have been assigned. In an ethical organization individuals lead by example, exhibiting behaviour which is morally good and correct, as opposed to what is merely legally or procedurally right (Mendonca 2001). To achieve this outcome, leaders need to be guided by altruism. This will be reflected by being concerned about others even when this may involve considerable personal sacrifice or inconvenience. Ethical leaders in public sector organizations must perceive that their organization's ongoing existence will be of benefit to society. An assessment of ethical behaviour will need to encompass responsibilities including the delivery of services most appropriate to a nation's need, providing employment, fulfilling responsibilities in relation to the use of resources, protecting the environment, and optimizing the use of scarce financial assets in order to positively contribute to improving the quality of life for the nation's population. Effective leaders need to be able to evaluate the *status quo*, formulate, and articulate a vision that may involve personal sacrifice but which builds trust among their followers. This philosophy can be contrasted with most unethical people. They exhibit egotistical behaviour, only think about themselves with no concerns for others (Conger and Kanungo, 1998).

A Spreading Contagion

Case Aims: To illustrate the hazards of permitting individuals to exhibit a behaviour trait based upon the motivation for maximizing immediate personal wealth.

In the period leading up to the recent banking crisis, a number of examples began to emerge about executives failing to exhibit integrity. The CEO of United States' largest insurance broker, Marsh and McLennan, resigned after it was alleged the company engaged in bid rigging and secretly restricted clients' choice of carriers to the paying higher commissions. International Group (AIG), one of the largest insurance companies in the world, was compelled to admit that their approach to accounting may have been misleading to investors. The company apparently used a variety of complex financial instruments and partially owned offshore re-insurance companies to smooth earnings and increase financial reserves. Following a federal review of accounting practices at Fannie Mae, the Governmental-back public sector organization responsible for underwriting homeowner mortgages, irregularities emerged that required a $9 billion balance sheet adjustment. Another area of current concern is the ethical behaviour of senior management in relation to their high levels of personal compensation. In the private sector, only a year after the banking crisis the major players have again started paying huge bonuses to their senior executives. This is despite that in some cases these institutions had only remained in business due to huge bailouts by their respective Governments (Sayles 2006).

(cont'd)

It seems the concept of working for the good of shareholders, customer, and employees as an unbreakable rule in the private sector has long since disappeared. Instead, improving one's status and achieving high remuneration seem to have become the primary goal of many senior managers. The problem is that this short-term, self-interest orientation usually results in severely damaging the long-term performance of the organization. This is because the monies expended on current salaries and fringe benefits are then unavailable for investment in the innovation that can provide the basis for sustaining long-term corporate performance.

The problem which is increasingly confronting managers in the public sector is the contagion of self-interest and unethical behaviour now seems to be infecting some public sector employees and their political masters. Following the introduction of concepts such as 'Performance-Related Pay'(PRP) into the public sector, civil servants are being rewarded for fulfilling cost reduction targets even in cases where such actions have seriously damaged their role as protectors of their citizens and of the public good. In the most extreme examples it does appear that possibly bonuses have been paid to civil servants who reduced expenditure on vital military equipment, thereby putting members of the armed forces at risk when operating in battle zones such as Iraq and Afghanistan.

In Europe, politicians in certain countries such as those in the Mediterranean region had previously promised to exhibit more responsible fiscal behaviour in order to become members of the euro zone. Yet, as has been evidenced by the 2010 sovereign debt crisis in countries such as Greece, it is apparent that these politicians had no intention of actually exhibiting greater fiscal responsibility. Furthermore, one suspects some of their actions were only made possible through supportive actions by their country's senior civil servants providing guidance over how to hide data on actual fiscal spending and using the accounting laws to justify what were probably highly questionable financial transactions.

Even in the more fiscally responsible nations politicians seem to be placing self-interest ahead of setting a good example for the rest of the society. In the United Kingdom, for example, during 2009, it emerged that some politicians were abusing the Parliamentary expense system by making somewhat dubious claims such as cleaning the moat at their country house, repeatedly flipping their home address to avoid capital gains taxes, and purchasing DVDs for home entertainment purposes.

In the private sector, some leading companies have accepted that immediate action must be taken when it emerges that corporate misbehaviour has occurred within their management team. Additionally, there is greater emphasis on recruiting senior managers who have a track record in which integrity and commitment have been primary reasons for their successful careers. There is also support for the idea that a new approach to senior executive compensation

(cont'd)

is required in order to eradicate short-term decision-making aimed at maximizing personal income. Unfortunately, a similar debate has yet to occur in relation to the behaviour of politicians and senior public sector managers. However, unless ways to be found to upgrade ethical standards in Government and within PSOs, it is probable that some nations will continue to struggle to implement actions that can reverse the declining standard of living which many electorates are facing for the foreseeable future.

Strategic Planning 5

The aims of this chapter are to cover the issues of:

(1) Theories concerning the applicability of strategic planning to enhance organizational performance

(2) The variations in academic opinion which exist over the nature and purpose of strategic planning

(3) The relevance of strategic planning in public sector organizatons

(4) The concept of entrepreneurship and the use of innovation to challenge existing conventions

(5) The concept of entrepreneurial strategic planning

(6) Enhancing the performance of public sector organizations by adopting an entrepreneurial orientation

Emergence of theory

As the wealthiest and most successful economic power of the twentieth century it is to be expected that the majority of prevailing management theories have originated from business schools in the United States. These theories have emerged from both research and examination of effective management practices in United States' largest corporations. In the 1920s and 1930s, as the operations with these corporations, especially among manufacturers exploiting mass production and economies of scale to produce lower-cost standard goods, became ever more complex, senior managers sought new ways of reviewing current performance and developing plans to guide the direction of future activities. One of the leading proponents of introducing a more structured, formalized strategic approach to business planning was Alfred Sloan, the CEO of General Motors (or GM). During his years in office, Sloan guided the company to attack and ultimately overtake the Ford Motor Company to become the world's leading car manufacturer. A factor in this success was GM's recognition that consumers wanted greater choice and variety when purchasing an automobile. To fulfil this need, GM developed a much broader product line than Ford, as well as marketing products under a variety of different brands names such as Chevrolet and Pontiac. In contrast, Henry Ford's orientation towards producing ever more affordable cars was reflected in the manufacture of a much more restricted product range. This philosophy is aptly summarized by Henry's famous statement that 'customers can have any colour they want, as long as it is black'.

Although there has been an evolution of academic thinking over the last 40 years concerning the nature of the strategic planning models that have been used to achieve business success, many of the currently accepted, fundamental principles were in place by the 1960s. Learned et al. (1965), for example, in proposing a process to identify a successful strategy suggested that all organizations needed to develop a set of goals and policies that provide the basis for defining the nature of future operations. These authors also felt that to achieve this aim, organizations should determine their relevant internal strengths and weaknesses in order to specify which distinctive internal competences can best ensure the organizations' strategies are appropriately aligned with the opportunities and threats which exist in organizations' external environments.

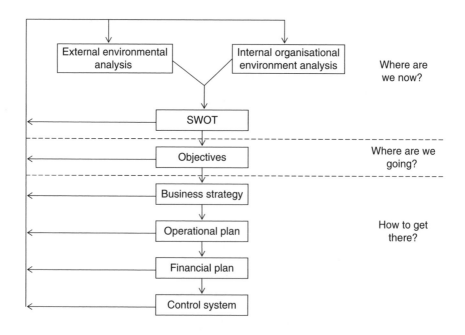

Figure 5.1   Standard linear sequential strategic planning model

Accompanying this activity should be actions within the organizations that ensure functional departments are acting in an integrated fashion to support the selected approach to optimizing performance in the face of identified future environmental conditions. This approach, which is summarized in Figure 5.1, involves asking the three questions of (i) 'Where are we now?', (ii) 'Where are we going?' and (iii) 'How to get there?'

The Canadian academic Professor Henry Mintzberg, a prolific writer of articles about strategic management, observed that 'the term strategy has been defined in a variety of ways, but almost always with a common theme, that of a deliberate, conscious set of guidelines that determines decisions into the future' (Mintzberg 1979, p. 68). One issue of difference which exists between academics is the breadth of organizational issues that should be contained within a definition of 'strategy'. For example, Hambrick and Fredrickson (2001, p. 148) argue that the company's mission and objectives should stand apart from strategy, because their role is to guide strategy. As a consequence, these authors propose the definition that 'strategy is the central, integrated, externally orientated concept of how we will achieve our objectives'. This viewpoint can be contrasted with the somewhat broader definition provided by Hall and Sais (1963, p. 150) who propose that 'strategy is a statement of the vital missions of the organisation, the goals which must be attained and the principal ways in which resources available are used'.

The strategic planning debate

In crafting new theories academics tend to be very careful to state the external environmental conditions and operational assumptions that apply in relation to the conclusions that can be drawn about a specific scenario. Unfortunately, politicians and their advisors often only utilize those aspects of any theory that support their proposed policies, whilst ignoring the various caveats and application assumptions that were stated by the theory's originator (Greenspan 2009). One would imagine, for example, that the UK economist Maynard Keynes would be less than happy to be quoted as the justifier for the current deficit spending schemes of Central Banks in the United States and Europe to buy bad debts and to rescue commercial banks. It is also doubtful that Milton Friedman would be too pleased to hear that it was a *laissez-faire*, free market theory which created the conditions fundamental to the cause of the 2007 sub-prime crisis. Similarly, Harry Markowitz, also of the University of Chicago, would be aghast to find that having developed the basic principles of risk management modelling, he is now to be held responsible for the banks using his ideas to create sophisticated approaches to debt collateralization that led to a meltdown in the world's financial markets.

Within the world of academia there is also a tendency for some individuals to embrace the latest successful management idea without apparently understanding the relevance concerning how a specific theory was originally framed.

Such persons present theoretical models to their students without explaining the caveats underlying espoused ideas or failing to recognize that a certain text was written within a specific contextual framework. In relation to strategic planning, one such example is provided by the theories proposed by the Harvard Professor Michael Porter (1985) whose views on competitive advantage must be one of the most frequently quoted strategic management model in business schools across the world. It is not unusual for some academics to fail to communicate to their audiences the context in which the original text was written: namely that Porter was seeking to evolve a framework to demonstrate how in the 1980s US Corporations were losing market leadership to newly emerging sources of competition from Pacific Rim countries. Even more worrying is the tendency of these same academics to present Porterian principles as fixed, inviolate rules. This occurrence is despite Porter's (1991, p. 102) own observations that:

> There is no one way of positioning in an industry, but many positions involving different choices of the type of advantage sought.... Several positions can be attractive in absolute terms and a variety of positions may be the most attractive...

Over the years, there have been significant differences in opinion amongst academics about the nature, purpose, and process of strategic planning. A key factor influencing this debate is some researchers, in seeking to validate the effectiveness and applicability of the linear, sequential strategic planning model shown in Figure 5.1, have found real-world management practices are often at variance with espoused processes. As a consequence, some of these researchers have proposed what they believe are alternative, more appropriate process models that organizations might utilize in the crafting of future strategies.

One the most vocal critics of the linear sequential process model is Professor Henry Mintzberg. In reviewing the different typologies concerning strategic planning within the academic literature, he described the linear sequential planning process as belonging to the 'Design School' approach to management (Mintzberg 1990). Two other typologies which he feels share the same philosophy of using detailed analysis leading to the prescriptive definition of an optimal strategic solution are the 'Planning School' and the 'Positioning School'.

Minztberg's believes that validation of management theories should involve an assessment of the degree to which a concept provides organizations with effective decision tools. He concluded that in many organizations, strategy actually evolves gradually over time as managers make sense of what influences performance and thereby acquire a deeper understanding of the factors influencing success. Mintzberg's (1999) typology for this type of strategic behaviour is the 'Learning School'. He considers the typology shares a number of common traits with other views on strategic process management such as the 'Power School', the 'Cultural School', and the 'Environmental School'. In comparing these similar approaches with the Design School philosophy, he feels the former support the perspective that strategies emerge through experience and cannot be defined on an *a priori* basis through the analysis of historical organizational activity.

Mintzberg's fundamental concern with the Design School is the specification of a deliberate, detailed strategy cannot be achieved with any real degree of absolute confidence in today's increasingly uncertain world. The reaction by other academics has been to question the validity of Mintzberg's viewpoint. Ansoff (1991) posited that a drawback of the Learning School and other related typologies is their approach is essentially descriptive. This means the manager is not offered any guidance about how to acquire any quantitative understanding of external environment facing the organization. He also rejects Mintzberg's view that Design School models are static. In Ansoff's opinion, strategic modelling has evolved over time and is able to accommodate the influence on organizational performance of increasingly uncertain futures.

The debate over the validity of prescriptive versus descriptive management models can be extremely confusing for both students and management practitioners seeking guidance upon the most effective process model through which to develop a strategic plan. Ultimately, the choice rests with the individual. The majority of students and management practitioners from Western countries do tend to be rational, logical thinkers who prefer to reach a conclusion based upon quantitative analysis of the variables impacting organizational performance. As a consequence, these individuals, despite articulated criticisms of process weakness, still tend to favour systems which are reflective of the Design School approach to strategy formulation. In seeking to provide added justification for this approach to strategic management, Liedtka (2000, p. 29) suggested that:

> Design offers a different approach and would suggest processes that are more widely participative, more dialogue-based, issue driven, conflict-using rather than conflict-avoiding, all aimed at invention and learning, rather than control.... Finally and perhaps most importantly, we should recognize that good designs succeed by persuading, and great designs by inspiring.

Public sector strategic planning

A key area of emphasis under the banner of NPM was the need for public sector organizations to adopt a more proactive orientation towards the influence of the external environment on the operations and the optimal exploitation of available internal resources. This was deemed necessary in order to achieve an economic, effective, and efficient delivery of services. The perspective led to the concept of strategic planning being introduced into the public sector to assist management develop more appropriate plans for managing an increasingly complex world whilst learning to cope with a capped, or sometimes declining, resource base. In terms of defining the purpose of using strategic planning in the public sector,

Bryson (1995, p. 11) has proposed the activity is ' a disciplined effort to produce fundamental decisions and actions that shape the organisation, what it is, what it does and why it does it'.

Early attempts at introducing strategic planning into the public sector from the private sector frequently met with failure. This was because consultants hire to advise public sector agencies and the training they provided to public sector managers frequently failed to define the nature of the differences which exist between the two sectors. As a consequence, insufficient attention was given to how private sector process models needed to be revised to reflect the operational realities confronting the public sector manager. One of the most fundamental difference between the two sectors is the nature of the customer and degree of freedom which exist in the availability and allocation of resources utilized to deliver services that are available to an organization (Ring and Perry 1985).

In a private sector organization, strategic planning is a fundamentally simple process in that the organization having determined the nature of customer need can then determine how best to meet these needs with the aim of optimizing the use of available resources in a way which ensures achievement of delivering long-term value to the shareholders. This can be contrasted with the public sector where, as summarized in Figure 5.2, the public sector provider has to attempt to satisfy the needs of two customer groups: namely (i) the 'contracting customer', usually a legislative entity who decides the nature of the services to be delivered and the level of resources available and (ii) the 'served customer' to whom the organization delivers services. In relation to meeting the needs of the served customer, this process is significantly more complex than in the private sector. This is because although the served customer may have clearly understood the needs, the ability of the provider to satisfy the served customer is controlled by factors such as the 'service role' defined by the legislators and the performance indicators which the contracting customer decides should be met in order for the provider to receive the resources which have been promised by the legislators.

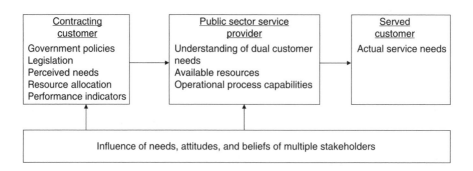

Figure 5.2   The public sector dual customer model

In their analysis of the strategic planning models, Ring and Perry posited that the five following contextual issues can be expected to complicate the process model in public sector organizations:

(1) The specific nature of the policies and desired service outcomes are often ill-defined by the contractual customer who creates problems for the managers in the provider organization seeking to interpret specific definitions of their service provision role.

(2) A public sector provider plan will be exposed to a much closer examination and scrutiny by legislators, policy makers, the media, and the general public.

(3) There are a much greater number of stakeholder interests and influences which need consideration in the creation of an effective plan.

(4) The actions of the legislators or policy makers can often lead to the creation of artificial time constraints either by not being prepared to define resource availability beyond a single financial year or because there has been a decision to introduce new legislation which the provider is required to instantly incorporate into existing service provision activities.

(5) Coalitions and alliances that the service provider may have formed to enhance or expand service delivery often prove to be unreliable due to the instability or unpredictable behaviour of the partner organization(s).

In analysing the nature of strategy, Mintzberg (1979) has proposed that there are three outcomes from the strategic planning process. These are (i) the 'deliberate strategy' (i.e. the intended strategy of the organization), (ii) the 'unrealized strategy' (i.e. the intended strategy that was never implemented), and (iii) the 'emergent strategy' (i.e. the realized strategy that was unintended). Ring and Perry have concluded that given the complexities associated with fulfilling the needs of the contractor customer, artificial time constraints, and the instability of collaborative relationships, public sector providers can be characterized as being low on successful implementation of a deliberate strategy. Instead these organizations' actual strategies can be expected to be of an unrealized and emergent nature. The implications of this conclusion is that to be successful in a public sector organization, managers need to be very flexible, willing to accept sudden changes in time schedules by legislators, and able to rapidly develop an alternative strategy in the face of sudden changes in the agency's external environment or access to available resources. To fulfil these managerial requirements probably demands a higher level of adaptability than is demanded of the average private sector manager. This is because the public sector manager will often face scenarios where there is the need to be creative in the development of new solutions following an unexpected, but ill-defined, change in policy by the contractor customer. Furthermore, in order to meet tight timescales that may be associated with new legislation, the manager may be forced to risk implementing new strategies before it has been feasible to gain the approval or acceptance by all the key stakeholders who may be impacted by the latest change in Government

policy. In a world where many developed nations in response to growing problems over the size of the public sector deficits, Governments are being forced to
instigate major policies based upon significant reductions in financial resources,
the need for public sector managers to exhibit flexibility and adaptability can be
expected to dramatically increase for the foreseeable future.

Reviewing documented evidence concerning early experiences of strategic
planning in the public sector led Bunning (1992) to posit that some managers
have concluded that planning ahead is impossible, dangerous, or a waste of time.
Factors influencing this perception include:

(1) Strategic planning requires involvement of outside groups such as customers during the environmental scanning process which can cause these
stakeholders to develop heightened expectations which subsequently cannot
be fulfilled.

(2) With funding often based upon a 1-year basis, there is little point in adopting
a longer-term perspective.

(3) Formal, long-term plans can lock the organization into actions which are
difficult to revise should future circumstances undergo change.

(4) The existing Governments may not be re-elected and plans to respond to
their manifesto may become redundant.

(5) Planning can create resource allocation dilemmas which lead to unrest
within the organization among those groups whose resources are adversely
impacted by a new plan.

(6) Once publicized, the plan can arouse criticism and dissent among those most
adversely affected by defined priorities and activities.

Whilst working with public sector managers in the introduction of strategic planning into their public sector organization, Bunning encountered adverse perceptions concerning the benefits of undertaking the activity. Common behaviour
traits include perceptions that strategic planning is a ritual to be performed essentially to meet the expectation or demands of others, particularly Governments
or funding agencies. A common perception is the focus in the planning process
is not so much on what is to be ultimately achieved but rather on the production of a plan on paper, so allowing the organization to be eligible to acquire
the desired resource inputs. Managers engaged in the planning process tend to
exhibit conformity and/or cynicism. There is also a significant decline in attention and energy once the plan is created and the resource decisions are made.
Another problem is during the decision-making process, the focus and attention often centre upon the technical feasibility of various alternatives proposals,
rather than to perceive planning as an interactive process requiring consideration of political, social, and technical viability issues. The resultant outcome is
the setting of rational, impersonal goal which causes staff problems over prac-
ticality when implementing actions specified in the plan. A third problem is

the tendency to adopt a consensus approach to decision-making, where the aim is to identify a strategy which is not objectionable to any of the major internal organizational stakeholders. As a consequence, the needs of the clients and the general public tend to be subordinated to satisfying the needs and concerns of key internal stakeholders. In Bunning's view, this latter behaviour trait means that the underlying dynamic during the strategic planning process is that of internal political bargaining with acceptance that irreconcilable differences exist between internal and external stakeholders.

Bunning expressed the view that strategic planning in many Government agencies has not led to any significant changes or improvement in performance. In his opinion Government agencies are typically more reactive than proactive. Innovation and change are to be avoided because established policies and organizational culture will create insurmountable obstacles to the adoption of any really radical new ideas. In most cases, this situation means that a prerequisite for successful change and development is the appointment of new senior managers who are open to accepting the concept of identifying and implementing new ways of working inside the organization. Accompanying the appointment of new senior staff, there may also be the need to overcome entrenched opposition which can only be achieved by implementing a fundamental restructuring of the organization.

The conclusion that can be drawn from Bunning's observations is that the probability of strategic planning leading to change in a public sector organization can be enhanced by actions which include:

(1) Making strategic planning the responsibility of senior line managers rather than staff experts, with the chief executive officer acting as the leading advocate within the planning process.

(2) Communicating the rationale and need for strategic planning and more effectively preparing managers by ensuring they have developed appropriate knowledge, skills, and attitudes.

(3) Moving beyond vague goals that are acceptable to everybody towards definition of clearly articulated specific strategic actions and performance objectives.

(4) Avoiding the creation of lengthy strategic plans containing highly detailed specification of operational activities because this can lead to the key strategic issues becoming obscured.

(5) Ensuring that in the development of detailed operational plans these are led by teams which include individuals from the lower levels of the organization.

(6) Ensuring all the plans are linked to assigned budgets in order that financial resources are effectively allocated to key areas of intended activity.

(7) Ensuring that the plan achieves a clear match between the proposed strategies and organizational culture.

(8) Ensuring that where new behaviours are required by staff in the implementation of the new strategic plan, these are clearly specified and acknowledged in the plan.

(9) Ensuring an effective control system has been created for monitoring actual versus planned performance objectives and that this system, when variance emerges, has the capability to diagnose the cause of identified differences between actual versus planned outcomes.

Plant (2009) feels that in the case of public sector organizations the link between the strategic plan and the organization's budget only tends to emerge when strategic priorities have been identified and budgeted funds are received. As a result, organizations can find themselves facing the situation of having many more strategic service provision responsibilities than the funds available to support all these activities. When this situation occurs and funding for specific strategic priorities has not been forthcoming, there is a sense in the organization that the plan, therefore, will not result in achievement of key performance goals. In his view, public sector organizations, especially in a world of decreasing financial resources, should not base strategic decisions purely on the amount of funding available at any specific point in time. Instead, there is a requirement to fundamentally assess the long-term strategic role required to effectively fulfil the service needs of the organization's external stakeholders.

Plant suggests that to achieve this aim, the strategic planning process should focus not on funding, but upon identifying gaps between strategic goals and actual performance. The objective of the plan is to determine how and to what degree identified gaps can be closed. Having defined performance goals at the beginning of the year, actual achievements can be regularly assessed throughout the year and again at the beginning of the next annual planning cycle. This author proposes that by linking the performance management system to a strategic plan this permits:

(1) Objectives being defined against which progress can be measured

(2) Tracking input resources, assessing outcomes, and determining efficiencies

(3) Service delivery evaluation which is the primary outcome responsibility of the organization

The complex, uncertain, and rapidly changing public sector environment demands flexibility, adaptability, and the capacity to anticipate and immediately address emerging issues. Public sector organizations are increasingly dependent upon their frontline staff to deal with challenges of sustaining the delivery of high quality services even when faced with increasingly scarce resources. This requires that these staff have the capacity and ability to act independently in the delivery of the service goals specified in the strategic plan. Key capacity and ability skills which they require include the authority to make decisions, the necessary expertise to exercise this authority, an understanding of the impact of their decisions on the organization, and a willingness to share in the consequences of their decisions. This outcome is not possible if senior management undertake the strategic planning process and development of performance management criteria without involving lower level staff.

Plant suggests that involvement of lower level staff will actually strengthen the strategic planning process and lead to the identification of more appropriate performance measures. This is because these individuals bring real-time knowledge of the service delivery process and provide useful feedback on the outcomes of implementing the organization's strategic plan. He also posits that there is a need for different types of performance measures which require the strategic performance variables to be closely linked with systems for assessing operational and performance evaluation variables. The purpose of strategic measures is to provide an overall perspective on the ability of the public sector organization to attain the strategic goals associated with the provision of a portfolio of services. Operational measures provide an assessment of the efficiency and effectiveness of actual service delivery. Evaluation measures provide data on outcomes or results of services provided in relation to achieving satisfaction among the clients being served.

In the development of an effective measurement system, Plant stresses that establishing performance measures does not provide the basis for ensuring strategic success. In his view, public sector organizations have a tendency to develop too many measures; staff rarely understand why information is being collected or how performance measures assist the organization to optimize the service delivery process. In these situations, the performance measures can become an unnecessary administrative burden with resource and time being allocated to the collection of data which have little value in terms of managing the effective implementation of the organization's strategic plan.

In assessing other problems that can occur in the strategic planning process in the public sector, Popovich (1998) proposed that these can include:

(1) A failure by senior management to accept the need for performance measurements that can provide feedback on the efficiency and effectiveness of service delivery when assessing future service provision strategies in relation to available resources.

(2) Senior management seeking to avoid exposing internal problems to external stakeholders and hence wishing to severely restricting the release of performance measurement information to the general public.

(3) Senior managers using performance measures to retroactively punish failures uncovered by measurements indicating adverse performance instead of creating a culture that rewards identification of mistakes and actions to improve future service delivery.

(4) Senior managers failing to exhibit the leadership skills required to ensure that service strategies are effectively implemented and that one of the organization's top priorities is to use performance measures to enhance future performance.

Progress Report

Case Aims: To illustrate the degree to which a strategic planning philosophy has been adopted by local Government operations in the United States.

In the face of rising inflation and declining tax revenues, municipal authorities in the United States first began to introduce a strategic approach into the planning process in the mid-1980s. To determine the degree to which the subsequent two decades have influenced the ongoing utilization of this planning philosophy, Poister and Streib (2005) undertook a large-scale survey of CEOs in municipalities across United States. They found that 56 per cent of respondents still had yet to move towards utilizing strategic planning. Of the 44 per cent who are utilizing this approach, the majority are restricting involvement in the process to senior managers and elected officials. Less than half of these organizations are involving their lower level staff in the activity. In terms of the overall purpose of the planning process, 92 per cent utilized the activity to define performance goals, 82 per cent to assist in developing a vision for the future, and 78 per cent for the identification of appropriate action plans. Slightly fewer organizations (72 per cent) utilized the activity to identify external shareholders' needs and concerns. Only 60 per cent of respondents used the activity to assess internal capability, 52 per cent to identify strengths, weaknesses, opportunities, and threats and even fewer (36 per cent) to take this opportunity to assess the feasibility of proposed future strategic actions.

In relation to nature of the outcomes achieved, the researchers concluded that although 44 per cent had reported use of a strategic planning philosophy, only 37 per cent had a fully documented strategic plan, only 33 per cent linked the plan to budget priorities, and only 22 per cent had defined performance measures to be utilized to track actual performance versus targets that had been defined by their strategic plan. In those organizations where the budget is linked to the strategic plan, 84 per cent reported that there is clear focus on using any new funds and capital expenditure activities to enhance achievement of specified strategic aims. However, only 48 per cent reported that the budget is linked to a performance assessment system designed to ensure the allocation of internal resources is closely linked to achieving service delivery outcomes specified in the strategic plan.

Of those municipalities which had a strategic plan, 95 per cent indicated that assessment of performance by senior managers is linked to the plan, but only 64 per cent utilized the same approach when undertaking annual assessments of the achievements of department heads within their organizations. Similarly, only 50 per cent of these respondents indicated that performance measures are in place which permit a detailed assessment of actual organizational achievements in areas such as service delivery in relation to targets specified in their strategic plan.

(cont'd)

In terms of satisfaction over the use of strategic plans to assist effective management of their organization, of those municipalities which had a plan, over 80 per cent were very satisfied/satisfied that the existence of a plan has enhanced their ability to define outputs associated with their role as providing appropriate services to the general public. As far as actually achieving specified goals, only 30 per cent reported that between 60 and 80 per cent of aims had been achieved and even less (10per cent) than between 80 and 100 per cent of their service delivery aims had been delivered. The two most important identified benefits of strategic planning were delivery of higher quality services (89 per cent) and clarification of the organization's future goals and vision (85 per cent). Other identified benefits included improved decision-making (83 per cent), more efficient management of operations (81 per cent), enhanced communications with external stakeholders (79 per cent), and providing clearer direction to employees over assigned tasks and responsibilities (61 per cent).

Poister and Streib's overall conclusion was that even after 20 years, there still remained a significant need for many more municipalities to adopt a strategic planning approach. Those municipalities with a strategic plan have been successful in linking strategic aims to the determination of annual budgets and specifying overall performance output targets for the delivery of services. The researchers were surprised, however, that only a minority of these organizations were linking their strategic plan with a performance measurement system that would assist in identifying the nature of gaps which might exist between planned and actual service delivery outcomes. The positive outcome reported by the study is that those municipalities which have adopted a strategic planning philosophy believe the benefits achieved greatly outweigh the costs associated with the creation and operation of this approach to determining future performance aims. Nevertheless, given that only 44 per cent respondents reported the utilization of a strategic plan to manage in a world of declining resources, the authors did feel that there remains an urgent need for more public sector bodies to adopt a philosophy of using strategic planning to define and guide their future operations.

Entrepreneurship

It is critical to recognize that current strategic management theories were evolved and validated through research during the second half of the twentieth century during which for much of the time business environments were relatively benign. Probable forces for change were easily identifiable and adequate time usually existed to implement appropriate strategy revisions. As a consequence, the outcome of planning models such as that shown in Figure 5.1 is future organizational aims could be based upon a simple extrapolation of past performance.

Organizational leaders in both the private and public sector, university graduates unable to find a job, or experienced managers who have lost their jobs as a result of the latest recession, all have cause to wonder whether a philosophy based upon extrapolation of past results to forecast future outcomes can continue to provide an effective planning model to ensure the future survival of organizations.

It is worth remembering, however, that the problems currently facing the world in the first decade of the twenty-first century are not new. During the Great Depression of the 1930s, banks went bust and unemployment rose to almost 25 per cent of the total workforce in many nations. These events prompted a number of academics to re-examine the validity of capitalism as a viable economic principle. One group, the 'Austrian School of Economics' was profoundly concerned by the future of capitalism in the face of widespread acceptance of pro-socialist models such as communism in Russia and the emergence of extreme right-wing, authoritarian regimes in Western Europe. The Austrian economist were a small island of believers in a philosophy of free markets surrounded by some very hostile adversaries such as Hitler and Stalin who claimed they offered the nations much superior economic systems. One of the most influential theorists within the Austrian School was Joseph Schumpeter (1950, 1942). He held the view that capitalism can be expected to go through periods of 'creative destruction' caused by organizations becoming too fixed in their ways and unable to implement the changes required to sustain their ongoing survival.

Schumpeter posited that the trigger for creative destruction and economic change is innovation. This causes existing, non-effective institutional frameworks to be replaced by a solution offering superiority over existing propositions. He identified that the source of change is the entrepreneur. The activities of the entrepreneur result in the emergence of a new, significant innovation which Schumpeter described as a 'meta-events'. Two examples of a meta-event are the invention of the internal combustion engine and the Internet. The term 'meta-event' was used by Schumpeter to communicate that the scale of a new innovation has the potential to dramatically reduce the viability of existing industrial policies and practices. The outcome is that the new innovation can be expected to severely reduce the long-term profitability of organizations who fail to introduce fundamental change into their current operational processes and activities.

With the Austrian economist Joseph Schumpeter as a regular guest at his parents' dining table in Vienna, it is perhaps not surprising that the US management theorist Peter Drucker acquired a fascination with the strategic implications of entrepreneurship. Drucker shared Schumpeter's view of entrepreneurship being a 'meta-economic event' which causes a major market change. He described this type of innovation as being 'firstest with the mostest' (Drucker 1985a). His examples of this type of entrepreneurship included DuPont's development of nylon and more recently, Steve Jobs creation of the Apple computer.

Drucker (1985a, b) did not, however, restrict his view of entrepreneurship to being confined to meta-economic events. In his opinion, other forms of innovation should also be considered as entrepreneurial. He posited that the original innovator may make mistakes, thereby permitting market entry by another firm. He described this type of innovation as 'creative imitation' and proposed that it can only occur after another organization has demonstrated the existence of a new market opportunity.

Another form of innovative behaviour was labelled by Drucker as 'entrepreneurial judo'. Similar to creative imitation, other firms have already either demonstrated the existence of a market or have developed the new technology capable of supporting the creation of new products.

Entrepreneurship and Future Performance

Case Aims: To demonstrate that in today's volatile world successful private sector organizations recognize the importance of adopting an entrepreneurial philosophy to sustain performance.

Management theories have little relevance unless they can be demonstrated to offer practical applications in the effective operation of organizations. To capture the views of major firms during the 2008 global downturn, IBM (2008) surveyed over 1000 CEOs of major businesses across the world. These individuals expressed the view that in the face of the worst recession since the 1930s, long-term survival and growth is critically dependent upon sustaining spending on innovation and embedding an entrepreneurial culture across their entire organization. Many CEOs perceived themselves in the role of the venture capitalist responsible for managing a portfolio of different business operations. Their primary responsibility is for picking winners, ensuring internal support for existing and potentially very successful future business activities, and weeding out those areas within their firm's portfolio which could be drain on future profitability.

Similar to an earlier IBM survey in 2002, the CEOs considered the market and new technology are key influencers of future performance. In the previous study, however, CEOs made no comments about the need to monitor macro-environmental trends. By 2008, no doubt in response to the unexpectedly severely damaging impact of the global recession, respondents now consider that understanding and responding to macro-environmental forces have become an issue as crucial as avoiding business losses due to competitors making a pre-emptive move to introduce new technology.

The vast majority of CEOs believe there is a need for their organizations to utilize a business model which focuses upon delivering greater value to customers and other supply chain members. For 39 per cent of respondents delivering value will require innovative actions aimed at building closer collaboration with customers and supply chain members. In many cases, this will require fundamental revisions in the business activities undertaken inside their own organizations. For 23 per cent of respondents, innovation will be about developing new ways of managing markets to deliver increased value by

---

(cont'd)

actions such as upgrading quality or reducing prices. Only 18 per cent of respondents perceive their organizations will be engaged in the highly entrepreneurial activity of either redefining their existing business operations or creating an entirely new business models within their industry. A unifying attribute across this latter group of organizations is they are amongst the highest performers in terms of profitability and ROI within their respective industrial sectors. These 'outperformers' hold a common view that entrepreneurial innovation permits the generation of higher profits permitted which in turn permits their organizations to remain ahead of competition by being able to make further investments in new forms of innovation.

Defining entrepreneurship

Given the importance that the CEOs of major corporations now place on 'entrepreneurship', it is somewhat disconcerting to find this topic is another area of management theory which is apparently sometimes misunderstood by academics. In recent years, for example, there has been a tendency for the term to be used interchangeably with small business management. In reality most small firms are in no way entrepreneurial. This is because their operations merely duplicate the activities of numerous other businesses operating in the same market sector. A more informed view of entrepreneurship is that proposed by those academics who have sought to understand the process through research. They have universally concluded that there is no relationship between the size of a firm and an ability to be entrepreneurial. Hisrich and Peters (1992, p. 11), for example, described entrepreneurship as the process of 'creating something different by devoting the necessary time and effort, assuming the accompanying financial, psychological, and social risks and receiving the resulting rewards of monetary and personal satisfaction'. Miller (1983) suggests that the entrepreneurial orientation of a firm is demonstrated by the extent to which top managers take risks, favour change, and exploit innovation to achieve a competitive advantage. Hills and LaForge (1992) concluded that being a successful entrepreneur requires the presence of certain attributes: namely an ability to exploit innovation and to develop a unique operation that supports business growth. Georgelli et al. (2000) proposed the skills of entrepreneurship are a capacity for changing business processes and the launching of new products or services. Covin and Slevin (1988, p. 219) defined 'entrepreneurial orientation' in terms of the extent to which 'managers are inclined to take business-related risks, favour change and innovation, and compete aggressively with other firms'. They developed a measure of entrepreneurial orientation based upon previous theorizing by Khandwalla (1977) and Miller and Friesen (1982).

Du Gray (2004) posits that entrepreneurship no longer just refers to the creation of an independent business venture or the characteristics of model entrepreneurs or successful independent business people. Instead, it now refers to the ways in which economic, political, social, and personal vitality is best achieved by organizations of all types including non-profits and governmental agencies. Morris and Jones (1999, p. 74) have proposed the following working definition for public entrepreneurship being 'the process of creating value for citizens by bringing together unique combinations of public and/or private resources to exploit social opportunities'. In terms of why entrepreneurship occurs in the public sector factors of influence appear to include uncertain environments, devolution of power, or re-allocation of resource ownership.

Kearney et al. (2009) believe entrepreneurship in the public sector, unlike the private sector, does not rely upon particular attributes of a specific individual but on a group desire for organizational change. This is because opportunities for innovation in the public sector arise from circumstances peculiar to the public sector and that innovation is much less focused on commercial considerations. Instead, the aim is to sustain or enhance service provision in the face of resource constraints. Based upon the existing literature on entrepreneurship in public sector organization, these authors propose that a set of internal environmental dimensions exists which stimulate or constrain public sector innovation. These variables include structure, decision-making, control, reward/motivation, and culture.

Morris and Jones (1999) assert that innovativeness in the public sector will tend to be more concerned with novel process improvements, new services, and new organizational forms. The issue of risk is a central component to the study of entrepreneurial behaviour. Hence, it can be assumed that innovative public managers must be prepared to take risks and appreciate they can expect to face bureaucratic and political obstacles from other, more conservatively orientated managers. Proactiveness refers to a posture of anticipating and acting on future wants and needs linked to the associated activities of being concerned with implementation and undertaking the appropriate course of action in order to bring an entrepreneurial concept to fruition. This involves a high level of commitment, perseverance, flexibility, and adaptability, plus a willingness to take responsibility for possible failure. Morris and Jones consider public sector proactiveness involves an emphasis on anticipating and preventing public sector problems before they occur. Effective actions will include creative interpretation of rules and leverage of scarce resources. In relation to the stimulus leading to the emergence of entrepreneurial activity in the public sector, a number of factors are perceived as key influencers. A very common factor is the emergence of new political policies created by legislators responding to their perception for the need to implement actions in relation to the ongoing provision of services. A related issue is where political change is accompanied by a significant reduction or re-allocation of public sector budgets.

Planning and entrepreneurship

The perspective about the key role played by structured, highly formalized business plans in the successful operation of any type of business is reflected by the importance given to the topic in most university programmes on entrepreneurship. For example, one group of US academics, in writing about the effective delivery of entrepreneurship programmes proposed that 'entrepreneurship should be defined as a profit-orientated activity which applies principles of strategic management and planning in the development of a business and the promotion of its growth' (quoted in Chaston 2009, p. 31). Given widespread acceptance of this view within the academic community, it is perhaps not surprising to also find that many texts on entrepreneurship stress the importance of developing a detailed plan to identify opportunities and to define how various elements of the organization will contribute to achieving the firm's specified performance goals.

Published evidence does appear to support the view that under certain conditions, entrepreneurial organizations can gain benefit from creating a strategic business plan to guide their operations (Ibrahim et al. 2004). One of these conditions in the private sector is that of market stability. This is because when an industrial sector enters maturity, a dominant technology prevails, market growth is minimal, then even small firms can benefit from using detailed business plans to guide future operations (Robinson and Pearce 1984). Another appropriate condition is when a detailed plan might be prepared for a large firm which has a diverse range of business units, all actively pursuing innovation. In such situations, senior management will benefit from being provided with detailed evaluations of the various projects in progress to determine which have the greatest prospects for success. This type of planning review will assist decisions such as the allocation of scarce resources across the organization and reaching decisions about the financial implications associated with significant expenditure on a diverse range of new capital assets (Berry 1998).

McCarthy and Leavy (1998) and McCarthy (2003) posit that when reaching conclusions about the relevance of developing business plans, one should take into account the leadership style of the individuals concerned. Their studies reveal that the *charismatic entrepreneurs* tend to be driven by the strength of their own convictions, they exude massive self-confidence in their ideas, and are passionately certain their venture will succeed. Such individuals rarely perceive the need to develop a detailed business plan and cannot understand why potential investors, without being provided with a plan, will question the probability of commercial success. In contrast, the *pragmatic entrepreneurs* tend to adopt a more conservative attitude when assessing opportunities and are not prepared to commit their own or others' resources unless there is clear evidence that success is reasonably certain. This latter type of entrepreneurs tend to believe business planning can be an effective process through which to identify appropriate future actions.

Despite the extensive support which planning as a key business process has received in the academic literature, a question still exists about the degree to which the development of a business plan can have a positive influence over the performance of entrepreneurial firms (Shrader et al. 1989). Some researchers, when attempting to validate the relationship between planning and performance, have not been able to reach any definite conclusions. This outcome is supported by observations of the actual behaviour of entrepreneurs. These reveal that many successful smaller, entrepreneurial firms do not appear to bother with developing a formal, annual business plan (Carson 1985). Researchers such as Allison et al. (2000) and Kets de Vries (1977) have also concluded that few entrepreneurs engage in formalized, long-term planning or follow highly structured, logical models of business process. Instead, there is a tendency to act on the basis of instinct, intuition, and impulse.

Mintzberg's observations of entrepreneurs also caused him to become a strong supporter of the perspective that successful entrepreneurs may often avoid utilization of detailed business plans during the development of future strategy. Possibly Mintzberg's most well-known example of this orientation was provided in his longitudinal case study of Sam Steinberg, the founder of highly successful Canadian retail group Steinberg's (Mintzberg and Waters 1982). At its peak this was a multi-billion dollar business empire containing a portfolio of 191 supermarkets, 32 department stores, 33 catalogue stores, 119 restaurants, 15 pharmacies, 25 shopping centres, a flour mill, a sugar refinery, and a food manufacturing operation. During the company's rapid expansion in the 1950s, Sam was famously known for standard response of 'who knows' when answering questions from the financial community and the business press about his future plans for his business.

Drucker (1994) was another very influential academic who has been supportive of Mintzberg's ideas concerning the Learning School approach to strategic planning. He is somewhat sceptical of the subject of the practical benefits of highly structured, formalized, linear planning. Having observed the process in numerous corporations, Drucker concluded that long range planning in many firms is merely concerned with organizational policies and the analysis of information. In his view, planning should involve acquiring new knowledge that can assist in developing a better understanding of potential future external environmental conditions to determine the most appropriate future opportunity for the organization. In presenting his 'theory of business', Drucker (1994) proposed that an effective planning model should be constituted of the three phase process of (1) accumulating assumptions about future environments, (2) specifying mission, and (3) determining which internal competences are required to achieve future performance aims.

In view of the contradictory evidence concerning the benefits of formalized planning in entrepreneurial firms when combined with the potential problems caused by poor research methodology or data analysis, it is impossible to reach a solid and certain conclusion on this issue. Possibly the safer option is to accept a contingency approach, namely for certain firms in certain industries managed by

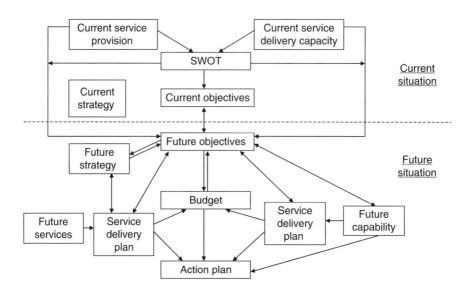

Figure 5.3   Components in an entrepreneurial approach to public sector strategic planning

certain individuals facing certain circumstances, the use of a formalized, structured strategic plan will contribute towards improving business performance. It also appears reasonable to conclude individuals engaged in managing an entrepreneurially orientated organization in a complex and changing environment may find that the strategic planning process is not an advantageous method through which to reach key business decisions.

In those cases where the public sector organization has adopted an entrepreneurial orientation but prefers to sustain a philosophy of developing a strategic plan to guide future activities, the issue arises of what would provide the most appropriate planning model. Anderson and Atkins (2001) have concluded that the classic linear sequential model has limited appeal to entrepreneurs. This is because they perceive that there is great complexity and interaction between the variables which need simultaneous consideration when determining future actions. As a consequence, entrepreneurs who utilize some form of structured planning process tend to adopt what Chaston (2009) refers to as a 'spider's web' approach. It seems reasonable to propose that this type of model, summarized in Figure 5.3, is suitable for use by an entrepreneurial public sector organization.

Leadership

The aims of this chapter are to cover the issues of:

(1) The attributes required of effective leaders

(2) Specific problems facing leaders in public sector organizations

(3) The new pressures placed on leaders by the advent of NPM

(4) The importance of transformational leadership in the effective management of change

(5) The role of entrepreneurial leadership in the provision of services and revising internal operational processes

Leadership theory

An area where there is a diversity of academic theories is the subject of organizational leadership. Despite such variation, most theories accept that the success or failure of organizations, political parties, and even nations is often dependent upon the behaviour of the individual who is currently fulfilling the leadership role. This role is critical because this individual has the primary responsibility for defining the purpose and vision of the entity which he or she is leading.

A critical aspect of effective leadership is the relationship which exists between the leader and those who require to be led. This is because leaders rarely have the sufficient power over people to ensure everybody does exactly what they have been told. Effective leadership usually involves working with people to gain their support and collaboration. Hence, leaders have to take into account the needs and interests of the people for whom they are responsible. Leader/employee alignment can only be successful if an appropriate culture has been established within an organization. If the leader desires innovation and creativity, then the culture must be supportive of employee behaviours such as challenging proposals, questioning the validity of ideas, and being permitted to express dissenting opinions. Many leaders, especially those of the 'command and control' variety, will not countenance dissent. They tend to believe they are always right and that they know what is best in terms of what needs to be done. Leaders of highly creative organizations accept that no one person can always be right. Their role as leader is to stimulate creativity by being willing to accept new ideas and being open to having their views challenged by others (Chaston 2009).

Effective leaders must provide themselves with access to the time and space needed to be able to think deeply about priorities and future plans. This will typically involve regularly standing back from day-to-day affairs in order to be able to spend time thinking. Concurrently, however, the leader must show sufficient mastery of day-to-day events so that the individual retains credibility in the eyes of their staff. To achieve these joint goals, a leader must be both a visionary and at the same time have their feet planted firmly on the ground, or in other words be 'both a dreamer and a doer'. As a doer the leader must know the tasks in which to become involved and those tasks that should be left to others. Excessive attention to detail can result in the leader becoming so embedded in organizational minutiae that important activities such as strategic decision-making remain uncompleted because there is no thinking time left available within the day.

Stephen Covey, in summarizing his views about the role of leaders, distilled his views and experiences into a model which he entitled *The 7 Habits of Highly Effective People* (Covey and Gulledge 1992; Carlone 2001). The habits he proposes are:

(1) Leaders should initiate and then continue to pay constant attention to mission, vision, values, and principles

(2) Leaders should initiate early involvement of others in defining and implementing action

(3) Leaders should encourage and promote widespread feedback and comment within the organization

(4) Leaders should ensure they make timely communications about what is going on within the organization to the entire workforce

(5) Leaders should not try to rush events and must allocate sufficient time for processes to work

(6) Leaders should exhibit commitment and follow-through (i.e. 'walk the talk')

(7) Leaders should encourage sub-units such as individual departments to develop their own mission statements, but these must be compatible with the overall organizational mission

A significant problem for all leaders in a rapidly changing and increasingly volatile world is organizational structures often need to be revised. To date, no single generic re-structuring model has evolved that can be applied as a solution to all the problems which may be encountered (Nohria and Berkley 1994). In their analysis of today's organizations, these researchers observe that the world is no longer constituted of organizations being stable, unitary entities built upon rules, and procedures and norms led by leaders who are able to be rational, universalistic thinkers. Organizations are now more unstable, founded upon uncertainty, and facing the need to respond very rapidly to changing external environmental circumstances. This has forced leaders to reconsider issues such as appropriate organizational strategies and structures. Strategy is no longer a matter of determining external environmental conditions and then using an appropriate positioning to match the organization's output portfolio to effectively meet customer needs. Effective strategies now depend upon an intent that leverages the organization's unique, distinctive internal competencies to minimize any gap which exists between customer expectations and the organizations capability of meeting these needs. Structures often have to evolve from the classic hierarchical model led from the top into new entities which are flatter, more flexible and within them lower-level staff are empowered to reach and then implement their own decisions. Accompanying this structural change is a requirement to move away from narrow assessment of performance based on the quantity of services delivered. Instead, organizations must assist all staff fully understand the factors influencing success by expanding performance measurement to include internal assessment measurements which encompass wider issues such as quality, product performance, logistics, customer satisfaction, and employee competence.

On the basis of a number of extensive long-term studies across some organizations, Nohria and Berkley have concluded organizations that outperform their sector peers have leaders who ensure their organization excel in the following four primary practices:

(1) Strategy – devising and maintaining clearly stated, focused statements of purpose
(2) Execution – developing and maintaining flawless operational execution
(3) Culture – developing and maintaining a performance-orientated culture
(4) Structure – building and maintaining a fast, flexible, and flat organization

Public sector leadership

The introduction of NPM was accompanied by a number of changes in what politicians have required in relation to the ongoing operational practices of public sector agencies. There was an emphasis on continually seeking new ways of improving the quality of service delivery. To achieve this goal, Governments have promoted the use of techniques originally developed in the private sector such as business process re-engineering, process mapping, lean thinking, and benchmarking. Output demands on public sector agencies have been tightened and new procedures for ensuring performance-based contract compliance have been introduced. This has been accompanied by public sector organizations being required to assess performance against an ever-increasing proliferation of key performance indicators and closer oversight by external auditors.

In some countries such as the United Kingdom, public sector organizations have been instructed to move towards engagement in lateral partnerships (e.g. crime and disorder partnerships involving the local authority, the police service, and the health service), vertical partnerships, and vertical multi-level governance (e.g. between local, regional, and national agencies). Public sector agencies are also expected to become active members in networks constituted of different public agencies and in some cases also involve private and voluntary sector organizations in the delivery of services.

Pedersen and Hartley (2008) have concluded that these fundamental changes have meant that leaders in the public sector, by being required to deliver clearly defined performance targets often with inadequate resources, are increasingly being placed into 'no-win' situations. This is because whatever they do will cause adverse reaction and comment from one or more stakeholder groups. Furthermore, many of these leaders are now expected to achieve ever-improving and sustainable performance even though their annual budget has been reduced. Even where there are increases in government spending, as has happened for the past few years in the UK National Health Service (NHS), publicity about budget increases can lead to rising undeliverable expectations among the general public about the delivery of more, higher quality or faster services.

Public sector leaders are being forced to find ways of managing the inherent policy tensions emerging from inside their own organizations. These are arising as staff attempt to fulfil their assigned tasks in an increasingly uncertain world in which politicians frequently introduce new, additional, often ambiguous, performance indicators. An added burden facing these by leaders can be the need to respond to criticisms by politicians as these individuals seek ways to divert criticism away from their policies by suggesting the real problems exist within the public sector agencies responsible for delivering services.

An even greater problem for public sector leaders is their strategic decisions can no longer be defined solely by their own professional perspective of what is best for the optimal delivery of services and meeting the concerns of the general public. Professional standards are now often supplemented by demands from politicians and senior civil servants for greater efficiency, productivity, user satisfaction, responsiveness, and adherence to external defined standards of conduct. This requires that to be effective the public sector leader must be able to decode, challenge, and develop varied sets of values, goals, and knowledge systems in response to the demands created by the introduction of new management philosophies such as NPM and managing through partnerships. The leader in a PSO will often face divergent rationales from different stakeholders and is sometimes forced to select not the most appropriate strategy, but the one which is most likely to minimize stakeholder dissent. The leaders are also usually required to be accountable for their decisions but in many cases have been assigned an inadequate degree of independent authority. Instead, they are frequently required to postpone decisions until the issue has been referred to some higher level within the public sector bureaucracy. This means that management processes are no longer built upon a specific hierarchy which clearly defines the level of responsibility which has been assigned to a leader. Instead, leaders find that in order to implement key, often time-constrained decisions, they have to navigate their way through an ill-defined network-like structure to identify who exactly holds ultimate responsibility for approving their proposals. This situation creates uncertainty for the leader because the individual is unsure of what are the current rules by which politicians and senior civil servants expected the individual to abide in reaching what is considered by stakeholders as being the most appropriate decision.

Political Skills

Case Aims: To illustrate that to be successful public sector leaders need a high level of political skills.

As politicians become more involved in defining the strategic direction of public sector agencies, their leaders can expect to be faced with having to work with individuals whose primary interest is ensuring the effective delivery of a political manifesto. The other problem which can arise is frequent changes in the politicians who are assigned responsibility for a specific Government department. When a new political head is appointed, especially if they have a political view different from the previous incumbent, there is tendency to ignore decisions made by their predecessors and instead impose their own views on what should happen next. The risk for the leader of the public sector agency is they may focus on decisions related to technical or professional standards and ignore the need to exhibit the political skills needed to persuade their superiors of the reason why implementing their existing strategy is the best solution.

To demonstrate the importance of public sector leaders exhibiting a high level of political skills, Peled (2000) presented a case study comparing the outcome of two projects in Israel to computerize public sector operations. One project was led by an outstanding Government scientist and the other by a highly experienced bureaucrat. The scientist was determined to build a state-of-the-art system. Unfortunately, he had neither the patience nor the willingness to fight opponents or endure the painfully slow decision-making processes in the ministry where he was working. In his view, the key issue was to ensure the new computer system used the most effective and technologically advanced hardware and software. He was suspicious that some of his colleagues in the ministry were not adequately qualified so he recruited individuals from academia and the private sector whom he trusted to work on the project. He wrote the project requirements in complete isolation without attempting to seek advice or guidance from other managers within the ministry. Resistance to his behaviour emerged from both inside and outside the ministry. His ministry is responsible

(cont'd)

for supervising two semi-autonomous institutions that execute computer projects. These organizations were already working on similar projects but the scientist refused to co-operate with the other institutions on the grounds that their approach was too expensive, progressing too slowly, and did not meet his standards. He defended his lack of co-operation, saying that his project was a huge technological leap forward rather than the regular 'meat-and-potato' projects that these other institutions were accustomed to executing. Eventually, having become frustrated by what he perceived as obstacles continually being placed in his way by bureaucrats, he resigned.

The reality is this individual worked alone and refused to listen to advice. He had his own independent mind, his own partners, and his own technologies. He did not wish to be integrated into the activities of the ministry. His aim was to be seen as being involved in the forefront of technology and tried to control the decision-making system instead of co-operating with it. This was unacceptable to the ministry and the day he left, his project was terminated.

In contrast, the experienced bureaucrat, although he found senior civil servants seemed to block his every move, sometimes formally and sometimes through backstabbing, realized that project success required the formation of an alliance of supporters. Observing attitudes within the ministry, he searched for potential allies outside the organization. Aware of the fact that hostility, fear, and mistrust of relationships existed within the ministry he decided to drop the strategy of implementing a large-scale, highly centralized project. Instead, he decided to adopt a new decentralized strategy by working with the ministry's nine external, geographically dispersed service centres. His decision was based upon the realization that instead of attempting to create a single, unified system, the first phase should involve working in partnership with each service centre implementing pilot projects. Once all service centres were using the same system, he could later merge these systems into a larger, centralized operation. In his view, his success was due to avoiding being perceived as managing a highly complex technical project. Instead, he presented himself in the eyes of the ministry decision-makers as an effective administrator who was able to co-ordinate his team's abilities to generate ideas, evolve effective work plans, identify appropriate strategies, and define effective operational policies. He also was a great believer in by-passing problems inside the ministry rather than tackling them head-on. His project was successful and the view of others was the secret to the success was highly developed political skills which he exhibited as the programme leader.

Leadership effectiveness

From a review of the literature, Turner (2007) concluded that successful leaders in public sector organizations need to exhibit the following traits:

(1) *Self-Knowledge* which involves understanding of one's own values and motivations, including an understanding of one's personal vision, beliefs, and aspirations plus an ability to critically assess one's strengths and weaknesses as a leader. Self-knowledge also enables the individual to assess how his or her leadership skills impact their organization and assists him or her to identify any personal skills gaps.

(2) *Personal Accountability* which involves being prepared to be held accountable for failings in organizational performance. An effective leader will exhibit a strong personal commitment to guide the organization's staff as they seek to overcome the challenges that may confront the organization. To be effective, the leaders must be willing to act courageously and being prepared to risk personal embarrassment or even to suffer loss of their job when reaching decisions which may be deemed to be in conflict with the views of key stakeholders.

(3) *Strategic Thinker* which involves being able to guide the organization in identifying customer needs and understanding how the organization adds value through the provision of appropriate services. Fulfilment of this responsibility involves ensuring the organization has the ability to scan internal and external environments, acquiring necessary resources to capitalize on strengths and opportunities, and concurrently overcoming weaknesses and threats. Strategic thinkers also must have the capability to make difficult decisions and be prepared to take risks after weighing up the potential costs and benefits.

(4) *Engaging with Others* reflecting the key role of the leader is to direct the activities of others and support a team-orientated approach towards fulfilling assigned organizational responsibilities. Successful leaders have the ability to call upon resources and support from a broad network of allies both inside and outside the organization.

(5) *Harnessing Knowledge* because success in achieving an organization's mission is reliant upon the ability to capitalize on the expertise, insights, and creativity which exist among employees, clients, suppliers, elected officials, and top managers. Leaders must ensure that within the organization an environment exists in which ideas and expertise can be identified and effectively exploited.

(6) *Organizationally Specific Skills* which require the leader to have the interpersonal and technical skills to ensure alignment with the organization's mission, culture, resources, and strategic needs.

One perspective on the effectiveness of a leader is the individual is only as effective as their ability to gain the support and co-operation of the organization's workforce. Many of the changes associated with NPM initiatives have focused on the reform of bureaucracies. Typically these reforms involve changes within the basic bureaucratic model rather than any attempt by leaders to introduce a fundamental shift towards creating radically new organizational forms Hence, in most cases, the end result is not a de-bureaucratized organization, but instead merely a 'cleaned-up bureaucracy'. In commenting upon this trend, Hales (2002, p. 52) suggests that many bureaucratic reforms retain '. . . the defining features of bureaucracy – hierarchical control, centrally imposed rules, and individual managerial responsibility and accountability'.

Hales (2000) notes that this move towards what he labels as 'bureaucracy-lite' organizations somewhat contradicts academic writings in the 1990s that predicted the appearance of new forms of managerial work, linked to the necessary development of 'post-modern,' 'networked', or 'post-bureaucratic' organizations. Two key characteristics are often emphasized in writing concerning how to enhance the effectiveness of public sector organizations. The first is that within these organizations the responsibility for leadership functions will shift from managers to 'empowered' employees, either acting as individuals or as members of self-managed teams. The second new characteristic was that the external boundaries of these organizations would be less distinct. This would be accompanied by an 'unbundling' and outsourcing of service delivery activities to outside agencies. Consequently, the distinct, traditional role of the leader was forecasted to disappear. Their replacement would be a professional 'knowledge worker' charged with a generalist, entrepreneurial, leadership role. This leader would focus upon stimulating inspiration, co-operation, networking, and proactive instigation of change in place of the traditional command, control, and administration approach to leadership.

Subsequent observations of actual organizational change within public sector organizations have raised doubts about the validity of these claims concerning the new forms of leadership. As a result of his own research, Hales concluded that even in leadership roles in organizations which have been granted greater operating autonomy there still continues to be a preference for the leader to exhibit a conventional direction and control orientation rather than acting as entrepreneurs or 'orchestrators' of teams. In his opinion, one key reason for this outcome is actions to create more effective organizational structures still demand strong control from the centre. Instead of the emergence of post-bureaucratic, network entities, public sector organizations have been found to retain the principle of hierarchical control even though some entities have created flatter strategic unit structures in which middle managers are free to operate as autonomous decision-makers. Once leaders and managers realize that claims and promises to create more flexible, adaptive organizations are basically 'political spin', not reality, then their tendency is to revert back to the traditional behaviour pattern of concentrating on undertaking routine, day-to-day tasks and retaining close control over the activities of subordinates.

Employee De-Motivation

Case Aims: To illustrate how a leadership style biased towards centralization and control can adversely impact employee attitudes.

(cont'd)

A leader is only as effective as their ability to gain the support and co-operation of the organization's workforce. Jones and Kriflik (2006) suggested that the most appropriate way of assessing public sector leadership effectiveness in a 'cleaned-up bureaucracy' is to research the perceptions and experiences of subordinates in those organizations which have undergone change. This perspective reflects these authors' opinion that in many cases subordinates in 'cleaned-up' public sectors bureaucracies feel they are more powerless than prior to the restructuring when the staff worked in an environment constituted of hierarchical command, extensive formalization, technical narrowness, and standardized procedures.

To gain further understanding of such situations Jones and Kriflick undertook a study of subordinate attitudes and behaviour in major Australian public sector agency following the introduction of NPM. When this organization, which is presented as an anonymous case by the researchers, was first established it operated as a decentralized entity consisting of five regional operations, each led by regional director. Each region had a high degree of autonomy and was able to exhibit a high degree of flexible decision-making. With the advent of NPM in Australia in the mid-1990s emphasis on decentralization and autonomy began to change. Due to external pressure from politicians for a revised strategy of refocusing the core business to optimize effectiveness and efficiency, this led to demands for greater centralized accountability and control within the case study organization. A new CEO was appointed, regional autonomy was progressively dismantled, and major functions were standardized. Senior managers were placed on short-term performance-based contracts and a series of goals, objectives, and targets were cascaded downwards throughout the whole organization.

Based upon interviews of staff within the organization, the researchers concluded the staff's primary concern was a desire to perform at their full potential. The view held by staff is an effective leader is somebody who is able to interact with them in order to liberate, unleash, and facilitate their movement towards achievement of their full potential. Staff expressed the view that the new leader's emphasis on centralization removed the flexibility and discretion of subordinates to reach decisions most appropriate for local circumstances. They now found themselves constrained by standardized policies with rules and monitoring systems being introduced by the organization's new leader who claimed these were 'best practice' procedures. In their view, the new culture was one of 'fitting in, following orders, meeting targets and making your boss look good'.

Staff did not question the overall need for the organization to achieve greater competitiveness, efficiency, and productivity. What troubled them was the 'personal price' they were having to pay to achieve a strategic vision that had been devised by what they perceived as a new, remote, faceless leadership. The subordinates began to require that their more immediate superiors protect

> **(cont'd)**
>
> them from the more extreme measures devised by the organization's senior leadership. In terms of assessing the effectiveness of their immediate leaders within the organizational hierarchy, those who received high ratings from staff were those who understood the needs of subordinates, exhibited a high level of concern for their welfare, and were willing to accept the responsibility of shielding staff from the more disruptive aspects of the organization's new operational philosophy.

Leading change

In most cases, in order to be effective in today's organizations, a leader usually needs to motivate and inspire the workforce by exhibiting an orientation towards promoting participative decision-making across the organization (Kim 2002). Nevertheless, there will be occasions when it is necessary for a leader to act autocratically, impose decisions, and mandate the actions required of all staff. This scenario will arise in those cases where the public sector organization is facing a massive financial crisis and immediate action is demanded in order to avoid a major reduction in the provision of services or in some situations to avert closure of the operation. In the United Kingdom, for example, in recent years due to the implementation of inappropriate strategies or a failure to create effective managerial controls to monitor actual performance, a small number of universities are now in a perilous financial state with operating costs exceeding revenue. With the announcement of future cutbacks in 2010 as the UK Government struggles to manage the country's public sector deficit, more institutions can be expected to face financial viability problems. Furthermore, the central funding body, the Higher Education Funding Council for England (HEFCE), has demanded that certain institutions refund grants because HEFCE has determined these funds have been inappropriately utilized. Hence, over the next few years, it can be expected that new vice chancellors will be appointed to some universities who will find it necessary to act autocratically and mandate immediate actions such as making staff redundant in order to 'balance their institutions books'. Such individuals will be unpopular with their staff who will no doubt express vocal criticisms about the leadership capabilities of their new vice chancellor.

With Western corporations facing the need to implement fundamental strategic changes in the face of increasing competition from Pacific Rim countries, Burns (1978) raised the issue of whether there was a need to change the nature of leadership in organizations based in Western nations. Burns rejected the idea that leadership involves the imposition of decisions on the workforce without seeking their views on how to attain future organizational goals. In his view, the effective management of change can only come from individuals who understand leadership is a mutual interaction and creation of collaborative relationship that ultimately leads to a fundamental improvement in ongoing operations. Burns entitled this latter approach as 'transformational leadership'. This is exhibited by individuals in recognition of the need to assess their own actions in relation to the higher level needs and values of their workforce.

Another supporter of the benefits of transformational leadership, Bass (1988) has a somewhat different perspective about the nature of this leadership style. Bass argues that transformational leaders seek to arouse or alter the needs of followers, not to discover them. This is achieved by raising the level of awareness and acceptance of designated goals across the workforce and persuading staff to transcend their own self-interests for the sake of the larger group and/or organization. As such, Bass narrows the moral foundation associated with transformational leadership concept. Nevertheless, he does conclude that usually it is the leader's long-term interest to act with integrity and exhibit a level of moral principles.

With the management of change becoming a fundamental aspect of NPM philosophies, the issue has arisen over the validity of introducing transformational management into the public sector. In relation to this issue, Burns posits there are three types of leadership values: ethical, modal, and end. Ethical values are character tests such as sobriety, chastity, abstention, kindness, altruism, and other rules of personal conduct expected of the leader by society. Modal values attributes such as integrity, honesty, and accountability. These are the values which are usually shared by all effective leaders and not just confined to those exhibiting a transformational style. End values cover issues such as liberty, equality, justice, and community. In Burn's opinion, these latter values are the core attributes of transformational leadership whereby the individual seeks fundamental changes in society, enhancement of individual liberty, and the expansion of justice and of equality of opportunity. Not surprisingly authors such as Denhardt and Campbell (2006) perceive that these values are a strong justification for public sector organizations engaged in change will only succeed following the appointment of transformational leaders.

Denhardt and Campbell posit that the need for transformational leadership in the public sector is further strengthened by the fact that decisions made by leaders in these organizations affect both their own workforce and also in many cases, the general public. In their view by expanding consideration of how leaders' decisions impact society as a whole, the concept of transformational leaders is linked to the concept of democracy and community involvement transformation. Burns argues this perspective is central to the concept of public sector leaders being assigned the objective of seeking to achieve fundamental changes in society, enhancing civil liberties, and achieving equality of opportunity for all. Denhardt and Campbell believe the appointment of public sector transformational leaders will have a critical influence on how these organizations act with integrity and effectiveness in the face of ever-increasing resource constrain, thereby achieving the goals of sustaining employee motivation and concurrently being perceived as acting in the best interests of a nation's citizens.

Entrepreneurial leadership

In every age of humanity, leaders have faced the need to respond to fundamental change. Currently leaders are faced not only with an ever more rapidly
changing world, but because of the impact of new technologies, also an ever-
increasing number of alternative options (Nanus 1992). Nanus is critical of
conventional theories of management. In his opinion, they place excessive
emphasis on the relationship between the leader and followers as exemplified
by theories associated with factors such as trust, empowerment, reward, participation, collaboration, and culture. In his opinion, the twenty-first century
world demands that leaders pay as much or even greater attention to changing
external environments. This external orientation should not just be concerned
with issues such as customers, suppliers, and competition. It must be widened
to encompass broader social, political, international, and institutional environments. Nanus proposed that the following three sources can be utilized to assist
leaders develop images of the future:

(1) *Signposts* – these are the multitude of information sources concerned
    with long-term trends such as demographics, economics, and resource
    sustainability. The other important signposting is that concerned with
    the plethora of data describing improving, new, and newly emergent
    technologies because these will often be the catalyst for fundamental change.

(2) *Values* – these will influence the attitudes and behaviours of both customers
    and employees in the future. Changing values such as increasing concerns
    about the future of Planet Earth can be expected to impact future oppor-
    tunities. Value shifts among employees can influence both the ability of the
    organization to sustain a future mission and also may demand revisions in
    relation to the nature of the work environment.

(3) *Frameworks* – these are selecting and refining the mental models which lead-
    ers find most useful in framing and reviewing the implications of responding
    to a changing world. Preferred frameworks will be influenced by the educa-
    tion and experience of individual leaders. Some will feel more comfortable
    with structured systems based upon sound quantitative and qualitative evi-
    dence from respected sources. Others, typically the more entrepreneurially
    orientated leaders, will prefer to rely upon unstructured environmental scan-
    ning accompanied by the use of intuition to select those futures which seem
    the most relevant to their specific organization.

Some academics and management practitioners are beginning to express doubts
about whether many leaders are capable of proposing a new vision that can
ensure the long-term survival of their organizations in the face of such a rapidly
changing world where technological advance is continually forcing a rethink of
prevailing economic and industrial forecasts. Certainly private sector examples
such as IBM failing to appreciate the impact of the PC on the computer industry,
the music industry not appreciating the implications of peer-to-peer data sharing
via the Internet, and Hollywood not comprehending how the DVD would alter

the dynamics of the film industry all provide adequate justification for such views. Should this perspective about the inabilities of many leaders be a valid perspective, the issue then arises of whether there is a need for a new type of leader. Fernald et al. (2005) in reviewing this topic have concluded that the replacement model for guiding the future identification, development, and selection of leaders should be that which they refer to as the 'entrepreneurial leadership' model.

Essentially these writers are proposing that on the basis of a review of the leadership and entrepreneurship literature, there are certain attributes which are shared by individuals who are seen as being successful in the leadership role. Table 6.1 summarizes both these shared and unshared key attributes:

Table 6.1   Successful entrepreneurs and leaders

Shared Attributes	
Entrepreneurs	**Leaders**
Visionary	Visionary
Achievement orientated	Achievement orientated
Creative	Creative
Flexible	Flexible
Persistent	Persistent
Risk-takers	Risk-takers
Patient	Patient
Able to motivate	Able to motivate
Unshared Attributes	
Autonomous	Able to listen
Tolerant of ambiguity	Able to communicate
Passionate	Able to work with others
	Charismatic
	Committed to mission
	Honest
	Strategic thinker
	Trustworthy

In considering the role of the entrepreneur as leader, it is necessary to recognize there are two dimensions influencing fulfilment of this function: namely the degree to which the individual is capable of (a) challenging existing conventions in the creation of his or her vision and (b) inspiring others within the organization to accept and believe in his or her vision for the organization (Eccles and Nohria 1992). The interaction between these two dimensions generates the alternative leadership scenarios illustrated in Figure 6.1.

The Caretaker Leader is an individual who perceives the future purpose of the organization is to continue to implement existing practices and processes. The individual is satisfied with the capabilities of the workforce to fulfil their assigned roles in delivering the organization's strategy. Hence, the individual does not become engaged in activities aimed at inspiring staff to direct their energies towards delivering the organization's future vision. This can be contrasted with

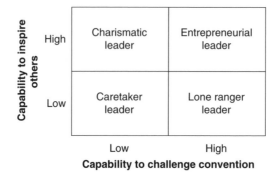

Figure 6.1   Alternative leadership capabilities

the charismatic leader. Although this individual may not always believe there is any need for the organization to fundamentally alter existing strategies or processes, the individual does have the ability to inspire others to share the same vision for the future.

Entrepreneurs are individuals who perceive that achieving future aims will require the challenging of existing conventions. The Lone Ranger leader is a highly effective entrepreneur in terms of identifying new, innovative opportunities. These individuals, however, lack the skills, or do not perceive the need to expend efforts ensuring others share their vision for innovation and change. Such individuals are most often the founders of a new, small business who have a preference for adopting an autocratic approach to management. This is because they believe their personal enthusiasm is all that is needed to ensure successful delivery of their vision for the organization (Chaston 2009). As organizations grow in size and complexity, merely relying upon the enthusiasm of the founder is an inappropriate managerial philosophy. Success is vitally influenced by the contributions being made across the entire workforce. Under these circumstances, it is critical that the entrepreneur has the capability to inspire and motivate others in order for the organization to deliver the vision that the leader has for the organization.

The important aspect of this view of entrepreneurial leadership is that it goes beyond the traditional emphasis about the charisma or personality traits of the leader. Instead, the emphasis is about in order to be effective, leadership capabilities must be closely linked to ensuring the overall capability of the organization in relation to key issues such as strategy, systems, and structure. A strong proponent of this orientation is the University of Michigan academic, David Ulrich. He refers to this aspect of the management process as 'results-based' leadership and he champions the idea that leaders should focus on promoting the following six organizational capabilities (Finnie and Early 2002):

(1) The ability to build the next generation of leadership

(2) An ability to establish a strong culture and firm identity in the minds of both employees and customers

(3) An ability to collaborate with teams and work across organizational unit boundaries

(4) An ability to generate and generalize ideas that have impact on future performance

(5) An ability to be disciplined and deliver what is promised

(6) A capacity to change and adapt quickly

Moon (1999) has proposed the existence of three different dimensions for managerial entrepreneurship: namely product-based entrepreneurship, process-based entrepreneurship, and behaviour-based entrepreneurship. Product-based managerial entrepreneurship emphasizes the quality of the final outcome (product or service) that an organization produces. Process-based managerial entrepreneurship refers to the improvements in administrative procedures, intra-organizational communications, and intra-organizational interactions. The literature strongly suggests the leaders of process innovation need to create a culture of flexible decision-making processes, open communication processes, and simplification of the work processes as a very common aspect of process change is the reduction in the level of 'red tape' inside organizations. In the public sector it is very usual for leaders seeking to stimulate innovation by promoting a commitment among staff to reduce bureaucracy as a mechanism for enhancing internal effectiveness and efficiency. Behaviour-based managerial entrepreneurship, which refers to the propensity for risk-taking, involves leaders promoting actions to deliver organizational change and to increase the level of innovative decision-making within the workforce.

In reviewing the effectiveness of innovation strategies, Moon posits there are a number of potential obstacles facing the entrepreneurial leader, the most important of which, hierarchy and formalization, are extremely prevalent in public sector organizations. A hierarchical system creates managerial difficulties in relation to the effectiveness of controls, co-ordination, and communications within organizations. Minimization of hierarchy is regarded as a required structural attribute of entrepreneurship. As the number of levels of hierarchy increases, this can result in reduced organizational sensitivity to issues such as meeting the needs of customers or sustaining an adequate level of service quality (Covin and Slevin, 1991). Moon also suggests that hierarchical structures tend to contain a higher level of red tape. This is because the customers and the employees often need to engage in various levels of administrative procedures before a final decision can be made.

Formalization is the degree to which organizational activities are manifested in written documents regarding procedures, job descriptions, regulations, and policy manuals (Hall, 1996). The existence of huge amounts of paperwork and written rules tends to cause administrative delay and poor communication both inside and outside an organization. A high level of formalization in relationships between managers and employees may also contribute to adding to the volume of red tape within an organization. Leaders who support formalization can expect to find that this management style will reduce the propensity for risk-taking because staff are likely to perceive that their ability to make innovative decisions is constrained by extensive rules and regulations.

Staff are usually able to fulfil their assigned tasks if the leadership has artic-ulated a clear mission and vision for the organization. These definitions assist staff understand their role in satisfying customers and implementing strategies that contribute to the organization achieving the goals that have been set by the leadership. Effective mission statements also indicate to staff the risk-taking propensity of their leadership and the degree to which the leadership is pre-pared to delegate risk-taking activity to members of the organization's workforce (Hills and LaForge, 1992). Closely linked to the issues of vision and mission are the levels of ethics and personal integrity which leaders expect employees to exhibit. Ethics define the moral values, beliefs, and rules that influence the way staff interact with each other and with the organization's external environment. Where leaders perceive staff exhibit a strong commitment to a high level of eth-ical behaviour, this increases their willingness to support actions to reduce the level of red tape within the organization. Moon proposed that entrepreneurial leaders need to exhibit trust in the actions and decision-making of staff. High levels of exhibited trust can contribute to a more co-operative, team-orientated work environment. Additionally, trust can promote a more efficient allocation of resources by lowering the time and costs associated with deciding how available resources can be mobilized in a way which would optimize the provision of high quality service outputs.

To gain further understanding of the factors influencing entrepreneurial behaviour in public sector organizations, Moon undertook a survey of gov-ernment agencies in New York State. In relation to process-based managerial entrepreneurship, he found the level of perceived red tape is the most important influencing variable affecting entrepreneurial behaviour. Two other variables, hierarchy and formalization, were also important, but had less impact than the perceived scale of red tape within these organizations. Analysis of risk-taking propensity of leaders suggests these individuals are perceived to take greater risks when the organization is more highly centralized. In contrast, lower level staff are more risk-averse when their organization exhibits a high level of centralized control. Risk-taking tends to decline as the level of hierarchy increases. This can be contrasted with trust and mission clarity which were found to be positively associated with the perceived risk-taking propensity of both leaders and staff.

Another key attribute of successful entrepreneurs is these individuals are realists who recognize the importance of avoiding situations where insurmount-able obstacles are evident. Given the high level of hierarchical control and the rules-based autocratic orientation frequently encountered in public sec-tor organizations, it can be expected that few entrepreneurs are likely to be attracted to the idea of seeking a career within this sector. As a consequence, it seems reasonable to conclude that many public sector providers will con-tinue to remain bureaucratic, hierarchical organizations led by individuals who (a) favour top-down non-participative management and (b) a strong orienta-tion towards fulfilling the requirements of being seen to 'tick the boxes' for whatever performance assessment scheme has been imposed by their funding bodies. Under these circumstances, strategic planning, where utilized, can be expected to be based on a Design School approach with the primary aim of producing a document to satisfy the demands of key stakeholders. These documents are unlikely to contain content which can actually assist employees in terms of identifying and guiding the changes needed to sustain service provision in the face of an expected ongoing reductions in financial resources.

Daring to Lead

Case Aims: To illustrate the obstacles confronting leaders in the public sector and the benefits of exhibiting an entrepreneurial leadership style.

An example of a research study which sought to understand the relevance of entrepreneurship within the public sector was that undertaken by Exton (2008). The research examined a programme entitled Improving Working Lives (IWL) within the UK NHS system. The aim of the initiative is for NHS bodies to become a 'world class model employers'. Utilizing a longitudinal case study approach, the researcher observed the implementation of the initiative in different NHS units and the degree to which project leaders were permitted to exhibit an entrepreneurial leadership style.

In Case A the project leader overcame obstacles of poor top-down communication, hierarchical management styles, and non-engagement of staff by activities such as innovative posters, saturating areas with flyers, and introducing inter-departmental seminars. The individual initiated the dissemination of policy information that the organization had a duty to provide and ensure communication channels were sufficiently open to encourage a free flow of information. Informing staff about the HRM policies in relation to flexible working, she identified that despite the appropriate policies now being in place, 'the staff did not know about them' or their entitlement to use them. The solution to overcoming the traditional need to depend on senior management support and limited access to resources was to locate new resources plus persuading people to champion innovation and improvement across the organization. The individual also elected only to work with people who were also willing to find ways of by-passing the obstructive behaviour of certain managers at various levels within the organization.

The project leader in Case B felt obligated to respect the views of the senior manager who had appointed the individual. This senior manager stressed the need to tow the corporate line, be compliant in leading agreed changes, and to ensure that the project outcome met the criteria for permitting the correct 'ticking of every box'. This project leader also relied upon using the existing management hierarchical structures to communicate with staff. This led to a failure to engage staff within the organization and hence the individual was

(cont'd)

unable to utilize the potential of staff to be contributive, active partners in the initiative being undertaken.

From the outset in Case C, the project leader had received a clear organizational commitment by the Board, senior management, staff, and the trade unions to work in partnership. This supportive culture permitted the leader to embed the required changes throughout the entire organization. The individual benefitted from being an enthusiastic and a skilled negotiator capable of communicating effectively with staff at all levels and retaining the support of the Board at all stages of the initiative. She developed innovative ways of overcoming the challenges of engaging staff and overcoming objections raised by managers across a highly geographical dispersed organization.

On the basis of her analysis of the case materials, Exton's (2008, p. 220) overall conclusions were that:

> ... there is a clear distinction made between entrepreneurs and champions working within the NHS.... Champions can be appointed to lead agreed changes within a given set of parameters, involved in both the design and implementation phases to monitor and administrate. However mere compliance with regulatory measures ('ticking boxes') is often achieved by diverting resources to achieve a specific measurable outcome in ways which do not necessarily lead to sustained change or improvement. Entrepreneurs faced with inconsistent objectives and ambiguous goals... reject compliance and challenge the status quo. They use the need to achieve performance targets as a lever that enables them to design and lead fundamental changes in organisational practice and behaviour. Entrepreneurs forge creative and unpredictable solutions, often in the spaces between formal organisational structures and protocols; performance targets are achieved as a by-product of new ways of working.... Part of the skill of the entrepreneur is to pass ownership of the change process and the new ways of working to the organisation as a whole, to embed it in day-to-day practice.

Strategic Planning Tools

7

The aims of this chapter are to cover the issues of:

(1) The various analytical tools available to the strategic planner

(2) Examining the application of the Product Life Cycle (PLC) and Boston Consulting Group (BCG) models in evaluating public sector service portfolios

(3) Analysing the nature of the external market confronting a public sector organization

(4) Determining the internal capabilities of the public sector organization

(5) The utilization of an external opportunity/internal capability planning matrix

(6) Summarizing scenarios by the utilization of a SWOT analysis

(7) Managing forecast uncertainty using scenario planning

Strategic analysis

The majority of management texts adopt the conventional approach of treating strategic planning as a rational–analytical process involving the detailed examination of available data using a number of different planning tools as the basis for reaching conclusions and determining appropriate actions. Use of these strategic decision tools typically involves a logical sequential approach of the type summarized in Figure 7.1. Within this process the application of appropriate tools permit the assessment of external scenarios and the internal capabilities of the organization. The results of these analyses provide the basis for decisions to be made about whether to expand current operations or to diversify into new areas of business (Ansoff 1965).

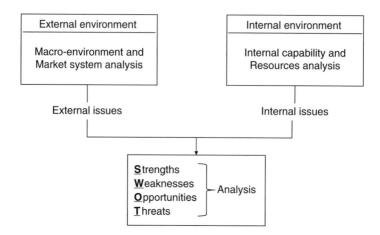

Figure 7.1   The 'Where Are We Now?' Rational–analytical process model approach

Most of the standard strategic planning tools have their supporters and detractors. Mintzberg (1994a) posits that most models and tools are based upon a rational–analytical approach. In his view these are inapplicable in modern environments. This is because these are too volatile, data are incomplete, or alternatively, there is need to reach a rapid decision which vitiates the possibility of undertaking a detailed in-depth review of the facts. This perspective is clearly supported by observations of managers operating in volatile external environments where the urgency of required actions necessitates key decisions being based upon an intuitive approach to decision-making (Khatri and Ng 2000).

Criticisms of the rational–analytical approach do not, however, provide adequate justification for concluding that managers should never consider utilizing available tools. This is because logical sequential analysis can provide frameworks that are invaluable for assisting organizations gain a fuller understanding of prevailing situations and future trends. The knowledge generated can often also provide the basis for assisting managers acquire a more enlightened understanding of the alternative strategic options available to the organization. Nevertheless, public sector managers when using such tools do need to ensure an important caveat is met: namely the analysis is only of benefit when the outcome is more informed decisions are reached in relation to achieving the long-term strategic goal of maximizing stakeholder value.

Managing time

Observing the success of brands such as Kellogg's Cornflakes or Heinz Ketchup one might be forgiven for assuming that in the private sector strategy of becoming brand leader and then defending the brand against competitive threats through promotional activity is an excellent strategy through which to maximize

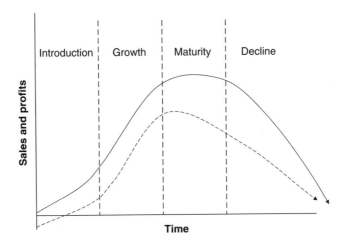

Figure 7.2   The product life cycle curve

long-term shareholder value. In most markets, however, products rarely survive unchallenged for very extensive periods of time. This is because changing customer needs or the advent of new technology rendering current products obsolete is an ever-present threat. A very useful analytical tool for identifying such trends is the Product Life Cycle (or PLC). As summarized in Figure 7.2, the PLC describes how sales revenue over time will pass through the four phases of Introduction, Growth, Maturity, and Decline.

Academics such as Hofer (1975) have proposed that the PLC concept is a very effective tool for assessing market conditions and changing profitability as the basis for determining whether there is a need to revise strategy as an organization's various products enter a new phase on their respective sales curves. The Introduction phase on the PLC is concerned with the launch of completely new product with the emphasis being on marketing activities to persuade customers to try the new goods. As sales tend to be low relative to operating expenses, during the early part of the Introduction phase, the product will generate a financial loss. The Growth phase is where new customers are entering the market and existing customers are becoming repeat users. The strategic focus will be on increased marketing activity coupled with investments in fixed assets to support capacity expansion. During this phase with sales rising faster than expenses, profits will rise. Eventually all of the potential customers will have been attracted into the market and hence sales will plateau as the product moves into the Maturity phase. With the only source of Growth coming from stealing sales from competition, marketing expenses will usually rise and average prices will tend to fall. The outcome is that as the product progresses through the Maturity phase, profits will downturn. Eventually customers will decide that another, usually newer or different product, is of more interest and the existing product will enter the Decline phase. Companies will use lower price to sustain sales and hence during the last phase of the PLC profits will usually fall dramatically.

There has been some criticism of using the PLC concept on the grounds that in the real world, sales curves rarely follow the precise pattern of the type shown in Figure 7.2. In an attempt to determine the validity of these criticisms, Anderson and Zeithmal (1984) undertook a detailed statistical analysis of the Profit in Marketing Strategy (PIMS) database which contained detailed financial records for over 1200 US manufacturing firms over the period 1970–1980. They concluded that certain variables behaved as the PLC theory predicts. For example, as products progress through the PLC, product changes become less frequent. The scale of technological change declines as the product moves from Growth into Maturity, whilst concurrently the breadth of product lines tends to increase. The longer the product remains in Maturity, the more intense the level of competition. Hence, companies find increasing difficulty in offering a product which is perceived as being different from competitors' offerings and both prices and profitability will usually fall significantly. In relation to R&D expenditure this tends to decline once the product leaves the Introduction phase but operational process R&D tends to increase for most of the Growth phase. Expenditure on any form of R&D falls during Maturity and is further reduced in the Decline phase. Towards the end of the Growth phase investment in capacity expansion is lowered and upon entering Maturity, the primary emphasis is a shift towards maximizing operational efficiencies.

Similar conclusions concerning the strategy management of different phases of the PLC were also evident in research undertaken by Thietart and Vivas (1984) involving a cross-sectional study of over 1000 firms within the PIMS database. The study involved selecting firms in the Growth, Maturity, and Decline phase on the PLC curve in various consumer and B2B sectors of industry. Performance in relation to (a) market share and (b) revenue was assessed in relation to a series of strategic behaviour variables such as product differentiation, pricing, marketing mix, R&D, and capital expenditure. The results of their study caused Thietart and Vivas (1984, p. 1405) to conclude that:

> ...the PLC approach can be used prescriptively for allocating effort and resources among different activities of the firm. It can also be useful for choosing and implementing strategic actions dealing with the financial, marketing, production and R&D aspects of the firm as the product moves from one stage to another.

The nature of service provision in the public sector also varies over time as suggested in the Service Life Cycle Curve shown in Figure 7.3. This diagram proposes that similar to the PLC concept in the private sector, the demand for a public sector service can be expected to vary over time and can be divided into four phases. Instead of mapping costs on a public sector PLC curve, the other dimension in the model is the supply of services over time. During the Introduction phase demand is known to exist but the public sector has yet to implement

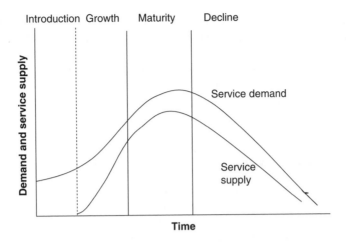

Figure 7.3   A public sector service life cycle curve

action to introduce the required service. Once the service is launched, then during the Growth phase both demand and supply will increase. Eventually the majority of customers seeking the service will have made contact with a service provider and in the Maturity phase demand and supply will tend to plateau. Eventually demand is likely to begin to fall due to circumstances such as an alternative service(s) becoming available (e.g. demand for Government postal services in the face of increased use of e-mails, mobile telephones, etc.) or fewer customers no longer perceive and/or require that they need the service (e.g. the provision of public transport in rural areas following population migration to urban areas). The other important attribute of the Service Curve is the gap between demand and supply. This reflects the fact that in most cases public sector providers have rarely been granted sufficient resources by Government that permits the provision of services to equal total customer demand.

Many public sector organizations deliver a range of different services. Hence, planners within these operations can use the Service Curve to assess the phase of each service and by knowing the link between supply and demand, determine the probable resource demand each service will place upon the organization over time. During the Introduction phase the service provider will rarely be able to determine the nature of, as yet, totally unsatisfied demand. Once the level of demand becomes better understood and it is apparent that the Government is prepared to make the new service more widely available, the strategist can begin to determine the resource implications associated with this service proposition being launched. Demand will begin to rise as an increasing number of potential customers begin to be aware of service availability. By tracking demand for a service, the strategist can assess when this has moved into the Maturity Phase. At this point no significant further increase in demand means that additional resources will not needed to be added to the organization's asset base. Eventually it is probable that service demand will decrease. This is due to factors such as the Government deciding a specific programme should be withdrawn, the number of customers declining for reasons such as economic or socio-demographic change, or the current service being replaced by what is considered to be a more effective or efficient service solution.

Managing portfolios

A private sector strategic tool that links profitability and cash flow in different phases of the PLC is the Boston Consulting Group (BCG) Matrix. In addition to the position of a product on the PLC, the other dimension used in the Matrix acknowledges the fact that products enjoying a high market share tend to achieve a higher Return on Investment (ROI) than poorer performing products (Buzzell et al. 1975). The combined effect of these two variables results in a matrix as shown in Figure 7.4 which proposes there are four different product types, each of which offers alternative strategic options.

Once a product has entered the Maturity phase on the PLC, it is very unusual for a brand leader to lose market share to competition and sustaining market position usually requires a low level of expenditure as a percentage of sales. Thus, the Cash Cow is so named because of the very positive cash flow and high profits generated. Once a market has moved into Maturity, the chances of a less successful product ever achieving sales growth by stealing market share from larger brands are minimal. Hence, the descriptive label of Dog. The sooner a product achieves market leadership, the greater the probability that this leadership position is retained. Hence, a product with a high share during the high market growth phase is known as Rising Star because it represents the next generation

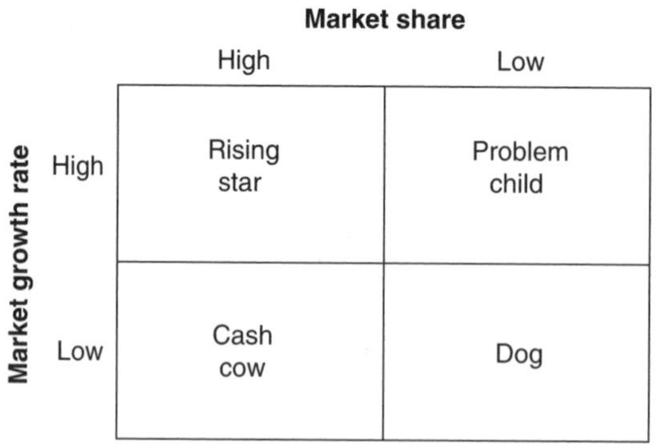

Figure 7.4   The Boston Consulting Group matrix

of Cash Cow. A product which has a low brand share during the early phase of the PLC is very rarely able to steal sales from the brand leader. This product is known as a Problem Child because the most likely outcome is the item will evolve into the next generation of Dog.

The conceptual idea underlying the BCG Matrix is that the firm should examine the state of current product portfolio. In those cases where Rising Stars and Cash Cows are identified, these products should receive priority in terms of future strategic plans to maximize shareholder value. Conversely, Problem Children and Dogs should usually be considered as products which will make little future contribution to either cash flow or profitability. Hence, it is suggested that these products should probably be de-emphasized in terms of being allocated any significant level of resources in any future plans.

The BCG Matrix has been widely accepted by planners as an effective simple tool through which the strategic priorities should be determined. As with any tool, however, caution should be exhibited in blind acceptance of the prescriptive rules associated with utilizing the model. Hence, some academics have expressed concern that rigid adherence to espoused theory can mislead managers into reaching strategic decisions without taking a broader view of other variables which influence organizational performance. Wensley (1982, p. 153), for example, expressed the view that 'the BCG matrix fails to reflect the full impact of competitive expectations and risk...the approach should not dominate any analysis of the specific nature and critical ambiguities in any strategic option'.

Despite these criticisms, the tool can be used by the public sector strategist to assess the future emphasis which should be given to the various services which constitute an organization's portfolio of service outputs. Thus, for example, a college might assess which courses should provide the focus of future core activities. Courses with a low market share are probably those which are more effectively delivered by another educational provider. In contrast, high share courses are those at which the college excels. Hence, the college planners might wish to consider phasing out the low share courses, the Problem Children and Dogs within the portfolio, and to allocate the resources released into further expanding the Cash Cow and Rising Star programmes.

Montari and Bracker (1986) have identified an interesting variation on the BCG Matrix for application to public sector scenarios. These authors have suggested that the two key dimensions are the ability of (a) a service to attract funding and (b) the public sector agency's effectiveness as a provider. By replacing these authors' 'ability to attract funds' dimension with a new dimension labelled 'growth rate in Government funding', one can create a matrix of the type illustrated in Figure 7.5. Similar to the scenario proposed for the college example, users of the matrix in Figure 7.5 should focus on phasing out the Problem Children and Dogs which they are poorly equipped to deliver. Resources which are released can then be re-allocated to the organization's Rising Stars and Cash Cows.

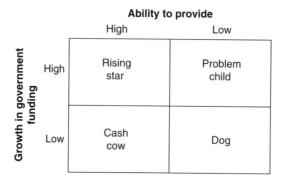

Figure 7.5   An alternative Boston Consulting Group matrix

Market analysis

Ultimately what determines revenue in the private sector is the nature of the market(s) in which an organization operates. The scale of success is influenced by factors such as the number of customers, the average expenditure/customer, and the nature of competition. However, organizations do not operate in isolation within a market. They are part of a complex system in which a number of different variables will have significant influence over customer demand. One variable which has received major attention in the strategic planning literature is the influence of competition. The Harvard Professor Michael Porter (1980) concluded that in assessing competitors there is a tendency among firms to place too much emphasis on responding to other companies operating at the same level with the market system. An example of this philosophy surfaced when the world's major airlines who were so busy engaging in a brand war between each other ignored the real market threat, namely the emergence of the low price budget carriers. To assist organizations undertake a detailed assessment of competition during the strategic planning process, Porter developed his Contending Forces model. In this model he proposed sources of competition are (i) other firms within the same market level, (ii) firms located upstream in the market system, (iii) firms downstream in the market system, (iv) new entrants, and (v) substitute goods.

There can be a tendency for public sector planners to give only minimal attention to the issue of competition because they perceive this as a factor which is much less critical than organizations in the private sector. Such a viewpoint is somewhat dangerous because a key reality in the public sector is that all organizations are competing with other public sector operations to maximize their share of increasingly scarce Government-funded resources. By undertaking an analysis of the type suggested in Figure 7.6, the public sector strategist is more likely to determine which other agencies represent the most important threats in terms of being able to acquire a larger share of available funds in the future. Figure 7.7 illustrates an example of how a regional agency providing business start-up

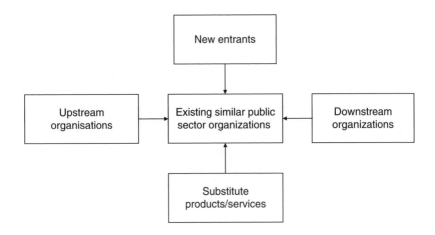

Figure 7.6   Sources of potential competition for available scarce resources

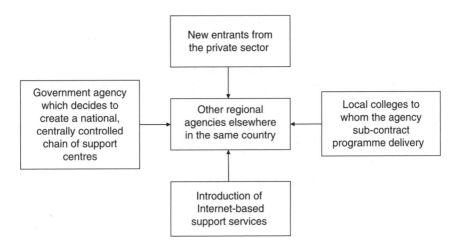

Figure 7.7   Example of a public sector contending forces analysis

support for the unemployed might utilize the model to identify potential competitive threats. Once these threats have been prioritized, the management of the agency is in a more informed situation in terms of implementing actions appropriate for ensuring major competitors are unsuccessful in their activities to be granted a larger share of available Government budgets.

Macro-environmental analysis

Another set of factors influencing service provision in both the private and public sectors is macro-environmental variables such as economics or technology which have a generic influence on the total demand for services. As macro-environment factors have a more diffuse impact on customer behaviour, it is more difficult to accurately forecast how a change in this type of variable will be reflected in future trends in the demand for services. The conventional tool utilized in an analysis of macro-environmental factors is a PEST analysis where the acronym summarizes the four variables of Politics, Economics, Sociological, and Technology. The actual number of potential influencing variables within the macro-environment is greater than the four covered by the PEST acronym. As a result, various writers have proposed longer acronyms depending upon which other key variables they consider critical influencers of the market system are analysed. One of the most frequently utilized extensions of the concept is PESTLE in which Legal and Environmental is added to the four original PEST variables.

Internal capability

As understanding of the strategic planning process has evolved over time, there has been growing recognition in the private sector that because most organizations have a detailed understanding of market opportunity, success will often depend upon a firm acquiring an internal capability (or competence) that provides the basis for outperforming competition (Day and Wensley 1988). An example of this scenario is provided by the US consumer goods giant Procter & Gamble. This company's superior competence in product development and mass marketing has permitted the firm to enter a diverse range of new markets such as disposable diapers (Pampers) and snack products (Pringles).

The concept of focusing upon the importance of developing superior internal capabilities has become known as the resource-based view (RBV) of the firm. In terms of resources which provide the basis for evolving a competitive advantage, these can be of a tangible or an intangible nature. Given the evidence which exists that supports this strategic philosophy, this suggests there is a requirement during the planning process for public sector organizations to also undertake an assessment of internal capability as part of their strategic analysis.

The primary activity of any organization is to acquire inputs, add value by internal activities concerned with transforming inputs into outputs, and make these outputs available to customers at a price higher than the costs of production. By capturing the essence of this process, one of the most widely applied tool for undertaking internal analysis is the Value Chain model proposed by Michael Porter. He described the value chain as 'a collection of activities that are performed by the organisation to design, produce, market, deliver, and support a product or service' (Porter 1980, p. 35).

As summarized in Figure 7.8 an organization is engaged in five different core activities in the acquisition of inputs, input transformation, distribution, environment management (or 'marketing'), and provision of services. Underpinning these core activities are individuals, groups, or entire departments fulfilling the support roles needed to optimize the value transformation process. Any internal analysis using this model seeks to determine which core and support activities are undertaken effectively, which could be enhanced, and which, by being superior

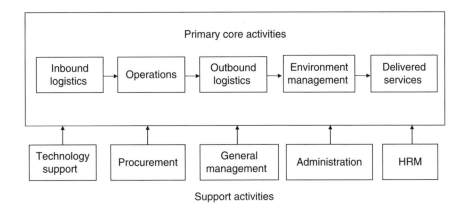

Figure 7.8   A generic value chain model

to activities undertaken within other public or private sector service providers, can provide superiority in some aspect of value generation activities (Valentin 2001).

Another analysis tool which can have application in the public sector is the Service-Profit Chain model shown in Figure 7.9. This was developed by Heskett et al. (1997) to assist private sector organizations. Subsequently, Steinke (2008) has validated that the model's components and operational philosophy are transferable to non-profit scenarios. This is because the same aim exists in either sector: namely by placing greater emphasis on service quality management this can possibly facilitate an improved work environment and higher customer satisfaction. Another possible outcome of such an analysis is that by focusing

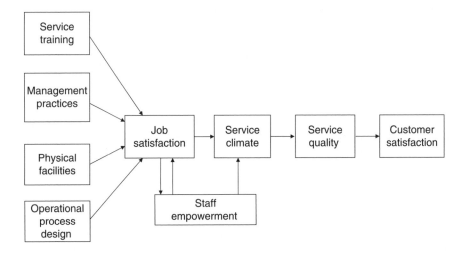

Figure 7.9   A public sector service-chain model

upon key internal components of process delivery the strategist may identify organizational activities that could provide the added advantage of reducing operational costs associated with the service delivery process.

Organizations that wish to be successful in financial terms should not focus on profits. Instead, the focus should be on understanding the enablers of profit. These are the organizational inputs: namely the employees and the resources that are required to for assigned tasks to be completed successfully. In terms of utilizing the model, Heskett et al. propose that the organization should analyse the interactions between the variables which constitute service provision. By identifying areas of strength and weakness, actions can be implemented to upgrade the performance of one or more components. This will achieve the outcome of delivering greater customer satisfaction. The model is designed to reflect the fact that there is a discernable manageable sequence of variables that form a chain reaction to produce the end result.

To determine the validity of the model in the public sector, Steinke undertook a study of Canadian hospitals. The data acquired caused her to conclude that the structural elements within the model such as service training and managerial practices do have an impact on the level of job satisfaction among medical staff. This in turn causes staff to feel they have greater control over fulfilling their assigned tasks whilst concurrently fostering greater excellence in the hospital's service climate. As a consequence, service quality is enhanced along with clients' perceptions of higher levels of service quality.

Given that many employees in the public sector perceive that profit is a concept only of relevance to the private sector, it is probably advisable as proposed in Figure 7.9 to refer to the model as a Service-Quality Chain. More importantly, the omission of the word 'profit' does mean the model can provide an effective vehicle for the strategist seeking to gain insights from staff in public sector organization concerning actions that might improve service quality or contribute towards stabilizing or reducing operation costs.

One potential drawback of the Value Chain model is the focus on internal activities may result in a rather narrow, short-term assessment of competence. To overcome this problem, Kaplan and Norton (1992a, b) proposed the need to adopt a broader, much longer-term measurement of capability by assessing internal capability in relation to the four difference perspectives of financial, business processes, customer views, and growth through learning. Their analysis provides the basis for defining each perspective, objective, and performance measure. These definitions can provide the foundations upon which the organization's overall future aims can be established and appropriate strategies defined.

Another approach to emphasizing the long-term competitive advantage associated with internal capability is to recognize the firm is a member of a sectoral system which contains other organizations able to offer complementary capabilities. In recent years, this recognition has led to the evolution of the supply chain concept. Extending the Value Chain model to include other organizations upstream or downstream within a sector is an effective planning tool which permits firms to rethink their long-term goals and implement strategies such as forming collaborative relationships which enhance the overall capabilities and competitive advantage of participants in this form of operational relationship. Such an approach can also result in significant cost savings and efficiency gains which enable an organization to redeploy resources to strengthen and grow core capabilities to support entrepreneurial activities such as new product development or market diversification (Evans and Smith 2004).

The integration of supply chains does require a shift in organizational attitudes from the more traditional adversarial relationships which can exist between suppliers and customers towards a more collaborative relationship. Evidence from industries which have achieved a shift in attitudes (e.g. car manufacturers and component suppliers; retailers and branded goods manufacturers) demonstrates that integration can assist in reducing costs, enhancing quality, and shortening order-delivery cycles. In commenting on why supply chain integration contributes towards significantly enhancing organizational performance, Myers and Cheung (2008) believe the most critical issue is the increased knowledge sharing which occurs between supply chain members. In addition to data interchange there are other types of knowledge exchange which they believe can be even more important such as operational know-how, managerial skills, and exploitation of new technology.

Myers and Cheung posit there are three types of knowledge sharing within supply chains, namely:

(1) *Information sharing* which takes place when organizations exchange important data about customer needs, demand levels, logistics, and supply availability.

(2) *Joint sense-making* that occurs when supply chain partners work together to solve operational problems, analyse and discuss strategic issues, and facilitate communication about the relationship. Since individual partners often interpret the same information differently, inter-organizational teams can help create a common understanding.

(3) *Knowledge integration* which occurs when supply chain partners develop relationship-specific memories, providing everyone with a common understanding of routines and procedures governing the relationship. This often results in collective problem solving that benefits both the organizations and the supply chain as a whole.

In commenting upon the tools available for undertaking an assessment of internal capability, Peters (1984) expressed concern that excessive emphasis on capabilities such as expertise in the production of services or logistics may result in the analyst ignoring key competences in the 'soft aspects' of the organization such as employee commitment or visionary leadership. To overcome this problem, he proposed that an internal analysis should also examine variables such as people, systems, and organizational structure. Afuah (2009) in seeking to evolve a tool which encompasses an assessment of both hard and soft variables, whilst concurrently including coverage of external environmental issues, has proposed

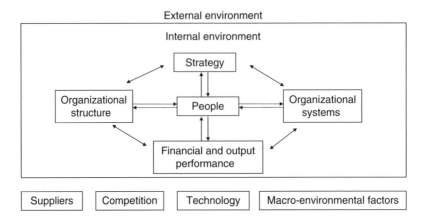

Figure 7.10   A generic S3PE framework

his S3PE Framework. As summarized in Figure 7.10, his model includes coverage inside the organization of soft issues such as people and hard data on matters such as financial and market performance. To re-enforce the key concept that there are inextricable links between external and internal environments, within the S3PE model the organizational core is presented as being surrounded by key external influencers.

Combined assessment

A criticism of tools such as the PLC and BCG matrix is these only provide an analysis of external situations. Similarly, a Value Chain analysis for a single organization focuses upon internal organizational issues. Ultimately the development of strategy requires an assessment of the interaction between the external environment and organizational capability. A tool which was developed to overcome this criticism is the GE-McKinsey matrix. The private sector strategist can utilize the technique to simultaneously examine both the degree of market attractiveness and the level of capability within an organization to exploit a specific market sector. Usually, the tool bases an assessment of internal capability in terms of being low, average, or high and in the case of markets, these being of low, average, and highly attractiveness. The analysis results in a 3×3 matrix in which the combined scores for capability and market attractiveness provide guidance over the most appropriate future strategies.

An identified weakness of the original concept is the nature of the analysis tends to cause managers to focus on existing markets and to identify near-term strategic actions. One way of avoiding this problem is to adopt a slightly different definition of the matrix parameters by re-directing the analysis to examine new entrepreneurial strategic opportunities. In the case of public sector organizations, this approach can be achieved by assessing the attractiveness of future

Future Service Provision Opportunities

		Low	Average	High
		1	**2**	**3**
	Low	Not A Strategic Opportunity – Avoid Involvement	Potential Strategic Issue – Monitor Developing Situation Very Closely	Major Strategic Risk – Assess Future Organizational Viability
		4	**5**	**6**
Internal Entrepreneurial Capability	Average	Not A Strategic Opportunity – Merely Continue To Monitor Situation	Average Strategic Opportunity – Sustain Ongoing Innovation Activities	Major Strategic Opportunity – Increase Investment To Upgrade Entrepreneurial Capability
		7	**8**	**9**
	High	Not A Strategic Opportunity – Transfer Entrepreneurial Capability To Other Activities	Potential Strategic Opportunity – Examine Exploiting Entrepreneurial Capability To Other Activities	Major Strategic Opportunity – Sustain Actions To Sustain Leadership Capability

Figure 7.11   Entrepreneurial assessment matrix

service provision activities in relation to the internal entrepreneurial capabilities of the organization. The outcome is a matrix of the type illustrated in Figure 7.11.

SWOT analysis

The SWOT analysis (strengths, weaknesses, opportunities, and threats) is an extensively used strategic planning tool. The purpose of the technique is to identify and describe an organization's internal strengths and weaknesses in relation to current and future operations. This is accompanied by an assessment of external factors which could have positive or negative impact on future performance (Mayer and Vambery 2008).

One potential risks with the conventional SWOT analysis identified by Lippitt (2003) is the technique can lead managers to create a somewhat static model which ignores the rapidly changing nature of external environments. She identified six attributes for a SWOT to be of real benefit to an organization. These attributes are the SWOT should be objective, dynamic, reflect all available information, identify possible alternative scenarios, and comprehend the consequences for the organization as events shift both inside and outside the organization. In her view the presence of these attributes enhances flexibility, commitment, focus, and the potential for the development of a more successful strategy.

In their review of the strategic implications associated with the key issues identified in a SWOT analysis, Sherman et al. (2007) have proposed that there are four basic outcomes. Each of these outcomes provides the basis for following generalized guidance about the possible future direction for an organization:

1. Where strengths outweigh weaknesses and opportunities outweigh threat this outcome is supportive of a growth strategy.

2. Where strengths outweigh weaknesses but threats outweigh opportunities this outcome is supportive of a maintenance strategy.

3. Where weaknesses outweigh strengths and opportunities outweigh threats this outcome is supportive of a harvesting strategy.

4. Where weaknesses outweigh strengths and threats outweigh opportunities this outcome is supportive of a retrenchment strategy.

Although widely used in strategic planning, there has been some criticism of the SWOT tool on the grounds that it (a) is a static definition of current circumstances and (b) fails to demonstrate the relationships which exist between internal and external factors. To overcome these criticisms, Weihrich (1982) evolved the Threat, Opportunity, Weakness, Strength (TOWS) analysis tool. In commenting on this latter technique, Ruocco and Proctor (1994) posit that the TOWS method enhances creative, more long-term thinking by managers, thereby offering a tool which overcomes Mintzberg's criticism of the Design School approach to strategic planning for being insufficiently innovative.

As illustrated in Figure 7.12, the output from a SWOT provides the dimensions for the TOWS matrix. By combining strengths with opportunity it is

Factors of Influence	Identified Organizational Strengths	Identified Organizational Weaknesses
Identified External Opportunities	Strengths & Opportunities Maxi-maxi Strategies	Weakness & Opportunities Mini-maxi Strategies
Identified External Threats	Strengths & Threats Maxi-mini Strategies	Weaknesses & Threats Mini-mini Strategies

Figure 7.12   A TOWS matrix

proposed that a maxi-maxi strategy can be defined as which has a high probability of success. A maxi-mini strategy is one which is designed to exploit organizational strengths to overcome identified threats. The mini-maxi strategy is designed to minimize weaknesses by exploiting identified opportunities. The combination of threats and weaknesses represents the most vulnerable position for the organization and hence is known as a mini-mini strategy.

SWOT in Action

Case Aims: To illustrate the application of the SWOT tool in a public sector situation.

An example of the utilization of a SWOT analysis as a key interim step in the formulation of a future strategy is provided by Vijayaraghavan's (1995) analysis of the situation facing India's State Transport Undertakings (STUs) which are Government-owned operations providing bus services across the country. The STUs are primarily assigned the social support role of providing public transport in rural areas. In urban areas where population density and per capita income is higher, bus services are provided by highly profitable private companies. The need for the analysis of the STU operations was that by mainly being restricted to delivering services in rural areas, this has led to an increasing funding deficit because many STUs are operating at a loss.

From his analysis, Vijayaraghavan presented the following conclusions in relation to SWOT analysis.

Strengths

(1) Major coverage of service provision across the entire country

(2) Well-established extensive infrastructure

(3) Well-qualified workforce

(4) Well-defined rules and procedures for defining employee tasks and activities

(5) Well-defined organizational structure and planning capability

(6) High-level of public goodwill for services provided

(7) Highly liquid cash flow situation

(8) Major provider of employment opportunities

(9) Significant contributor to economic development in rural areas

Weaknesses

(1) Highly labour intensive operation leading to industrial relations problems

(2) Poor leadership by bureaucrats with limited knowledge of the transportation industry

(cont'd)

(3) Extensive number of different trade unions involved in the industry

(4) Lack of delegated authority and co-ordination between middle-level managers

(5) Overstaffing

(6) Lack of professional attitude about optimizing service quality and productivity

(7) Uneconomic fare structures

(8) Lack of investment in new technology

(9) Uneducated, poorly trained staff

Opportunities

(1) Ever-increasing demand for transportation services

(2) Opportunity to expand operations into new areas of the country

(3) Potential for diversification into related services (e.g. parcel delivery)

(4) Inadequacy of rail network in many areas of the country

(5) High train fares

(6) Ability to threaten privatization to gain management and employee acceptance of need for new strategy and revised operational processes

(7) High level of passenger loyalty and goodwill

(8) Highly available, well-trained managers could be hired from the private sector

Threats

(1) Impact of high inflation driving up operating and capital costs

(2) Increasing competition from private companies on STUs' more profitable routes

(3) Adverse climatic conditions

(4) Central Government may implement policy of widespread privatization of social support provision

(5) Lack of Government funds to support modernization of the STU network

(6) Political influence impacting inappropriate decision-making at a senior level with some STU operations

(7) STU assets are a prime target for attacks during periods of social unrest or rioting

(8) Politicization of the unions leading to greater workforce unrest and an increasing number of labour disputes

Scenario planning

One of the criticisms that can be applied to many strategic planning tools is they tend to be based on assessing the current known situation and then on extrapolating of current trends, which leads to a determination of appropriate future actions. This may be appropriate in a highly certain and stable world. Nevertheless, as environmental volatility increases, there is a need to widen the assessment to determine to what degree tomorrow's world will be significantly different from that which the strategic planner's organization is experiencing today. A well-established technique for stimulating the assessment of broader and more uncertain futures is 'scenario planning' (O'Brien and Meadows 2001). The first documented example of the utilization of scenario planning was by the major oil companies when developing revised strategic plans following the advent of the OPEC oil crisis which caused the industries to recognize that the world was approaching the point where all known, economically extractible, oil deposits had been identified. The companies examined scenarios of different levels of demand for oil to determine the scale of problems that emerges relative to the degree of imbalances in supply and demand.

In most cases, the uncertainty surrounding the nature of future environments causes the strategist to seek a variety of different opinions by drawing upon a diverse range of sources such as scientists and engineers from varied disciplines from outside the organization, employees from across the organization's operations, industry suppliers, intermediaries, and customers. These providers of input may, or may not, be instructed to adopt the same assumptions in the development of their personal scenario. Once all the scenarios have been accumulated, a group of individuals, usually drawn from inside and outside the organization, review the materials and seek to indentify some common perspectives. These viewpoints are then summarized and circulated to all contributors to gain their views about scenarios which the assessors believe are most relevant in describing possible futures. Once this second round of opinions has been acquired, the assessment team determine which scenario or scenarios deliver the most likely picture of the future. This description of future sector conditions can provide the basis upon which the organization can then begin to develop a future strategic plan.

Scenario planning first emerged as a planning technique in the public sector in the 1970s when it was adopted by the Public Agenda Foundation (PAF). This is a research institute which specializes in assessing future problems which may confront the public sector and seeks to identify solutions which might be implemented before a problem becomes so large that it grows unmanageable. In their technique, those from whom opinions are sought are briefed on the background of the organization(s) for which scenario planning might be beneficial. These individuals are not usually provided with any guidance on whether there is a perceived need for change or any statement defining 'what is the potential problem'. This then permits these individuals much greater freedom in the development of his or her personal vision of future environments. When using the technique, the PAF may or may not use the data from these individuals to develop a range of most probable future scenarios. This is because in some cases it is decided that a single scenario is an adequate vision. In other cases, it may be decided that multiple scenarios would complicate the planning process because then managers would have an excessively disparate range of scenarios and interacting variables which would need to be assessed.

Service Demand Analysis

8

The aims of this chapter are to cover the issues of:

(1) Reviewing factors influencing the demand for public sector services

(2) Examining the influence of socio-demographic trends

(3) Examining the influence of culture

(4) Political beliefs causing variations in the availability of services

(5) Influence of economics, technology, finance, and environmental responsibility on service demand

(6) Reviewing the nature of customer need

Market demand

A key driver influencing the current and future performance of any organization is the size of the customer base being served and the organization's share of the total service provision available within a market. The total size of financial demand is a function of the number of customers and the average expenditure per customer. In all cases the expenditure per customer is decided by the purchaser. A key difference between financial demands in the private versus the public sector is in the former the customer decides their level of expenditure. In contrast, in the public sector, a funding body such as the Government usually defines the number of customers and how much expenditure per customer is to be permitted.

In a mature market, the number of customers and the average expenditure have reached a maximum and hence no further growth in an organization's expenditure can be expected other than in those cases where customers switch their purchasing from one provider to another. This scenario can be contrasted with markets in the Introduction and Growth phase. Here new customers are entering the market, and in many cases, the expenditure/customer may continue to rise.

In business-to-business (B2B) markets, although customer numbers and expenditure influence market size, ultimately total market demand is derived from sales trends downstream in the consumer market(s) which the B2B organizations are supplying. Hence any change in future consumer expenditure is liable to impact all companies in the supply chain serving this market. For example, sales for the two major firms in the aircraft industry, Boeing and Airbus, are determined by the expectations of the world's airline industry over the size of travelling general public by aeroplane over the next few years. This effect was demonstrated in 2008/9 when the rising price of oil cost led to an increase in cost of jet fuel which, combined with the recession, caused a reduction in airline passenger numbers leading a number of airlines to cancel or postpone their orders for new aircraft.

A similar situation exists in public sector markets where one agency's products or services are purchased by another agency (i.e. public-to-public or P2P market) or when a private sector organization supplies goods to the public sector (i.e. business-to-public or B2P market). The purchasing agency's volume of service output will determine the scale of demand for the supplier's goods. Any variations in the demand for the products and services from the supplying agency or private sector organization will be determined by the changes in the service output activity of the purchasing agency.

Data on market size and forecasts on future size are usually widely available for many consumer markets. This is because Government departments, industrial trade bodies, and market research firms undertake in-depth studies to generate data which are used in national economic planning by economists and for strategic planning within large consumer goods companies. These data are assembled from sources such as sales by major firms, intermediaries, and market research studies of consumer usage and attitudes. The ability of consumer goods companies to develop more accurate, updated forecasts for market size has been greatly enhanced by the electronic capture of purchase information through data acquisition systems linked to retailers' electronic point-of-sale (EPOS) systems, loyalty cards, and on-line purchasing activities (Ogut et al. 2008). To extract data from these systems for determining trends and generating new forecasts, companies exploit a concept known as 'data mining'. This technique is primarily used by companies with a strong customer focus. It permits these companies to determine relationships between factors such as price, product positioning, economic indicators, competition, and customer demographics. By using sophisticated statistical tools, data mining permits firms to measure which customers are most likely to leave, the behaviour of loyal customers, and the purchase behaviour across different customer segments. The available evidence would suggest that few Governments or many public sector agencies have yet recognized the benefits of data mining to determine variations in nature of demand across populations and the ability of these systems to ensure that the supply of services can be rapidly adjusted to reflect situations where there is a major gap between service needs and actual service delivery.

Where projects have been implemented which exploit the processing power and low cost of modern software systems, as well as improving the accuracy of demand data by customer groups, the system users can also implement 'what if' scenario analysis. This technique assists planners develop more comprehensive plans and, even more importantly, permits both planners and line managers to gain a much better understanding of how the relative importance of different variables can result in significant changes in the demand for services. To illustrate the benefits of computer modelling in the public sector, Babington (1993) described a project in the United Kingdom where a model was developed for assisting the management of a regional health budget for the provision of hospital care. The developed system provided up-to-date output concerning where the money is being spent, the expenditure by treatment, the number of hospital admissions by medical specialty, and which geographic locations are the primary sources of patients. Once created, the model has assisted planners determine approaches for optimizing the allocation of resources across the hospitals in the area. The model also permits assessment of the potential impact on service demand of factors such as socio-demographic change, capital spending, and alternative health care treatments.

A resistance to widespread adoption of sophisticated computer-based needs analysis techniques among senior managers within the public sector is, in part, an outcome of an embedded, prevailing managerial philosophy of providers in the same sector and agencies in different sectors defending their budgets from any perceived threats that might be associated with a re-assessment of allocating scarce resources between different organizations. Hence, by not having access to accurate data on future need, these individuals are not faced with having to defend their position that they cannot sustain performance if resources are withdrawn from their operations. Thus, for example, in the armed forces, admirals, generals, and air commodores will fiercely defend any suggestion that the future nature of modern warfare should result in a reduction or re-allocation of their budgets. Similarly, one cannot expect a police force to be supportive of the idea that some of their budget currently allocated to catching speeding motorists should be diverted to the ambulance service on the grounds that faster response times would reduce death rates from road traffic accidents and the medical costs of treating accident victims.

Fiscal Responsibility

Case Aims: To illustrate that effective management of resources in order to meet the demand for public services requires a change in operational philosophy at the highest level.

Even before the onset of the 2007/8 banking crisis and the onset of the recession which demanded a further expansion of public sector spending in the United States, the head of the US Government Accountability Office, David Walker

(cont'd)

(2005), was already openly expressing concern about the state of the country's public finances. In his view, a 'crunch' was coming which would impact all government departments. He noted that in order to sustain spending on defence and homeland security, other areas of discretionary Government spending were already being cut. In his view, unless fundamental changes were made in fiscal policy, the United States faces decades of deficits. This situation infers that difficult choices are inevitable.

In his analysis of changes in federal spending, Walker notes that in1964, two-thirds of the federal budget was discretionary, and nearly half was spent on national defence. In 2004, less than 40 per cent of the federal budget was discretionary and about 20 per cent was spent on defence. This change reflects ongoing rises in entitlement programmes with 40 per cent of the federal budget being assigned to Social Security, Medicare, and Medicaid.

Of greater concern to Walker is his conclusion that the US Government is providing incomplete and misleading information on the country's real financial condition and fiscal outlook. This behaviour results in frequent misinterpretations concerning future federal budget outcomes. Worryingly he reports that in 2005 his agency, the US Government Accountability Office (GAO), was unable for the eighth consecutive year to express an opinion as to whether the US Government's consolidated financial statements were fairly stated. Two key factors influencing this situation were the GAO's identification of financial management weaknesses at the Department of Defence and inaccurate reporting of intra-Governmental transactions. In addition, the GAO was concerned that very few Government agencies were able to specify their spending commitments and define the scale of incurred liabilities. As a consequence, the implications for future budgets are that numerous unfunded commitments exist and no legislative actions are being taken to address these problems. Long-term computer simulations by the GAO suggest that by 2040 the Federal Government would have to cut federal spending by more than 50 per cent or raise taxes to more than 250 per cent in order to achieve a balanced federal budget.

The GAO believes that the Government must be more open about the long-term implications of current public sector spending policies. In their view, federal annual deficit forecasts and even 10-year budget projections do not accurately predict the real long-term costs of federal programmes. Such information would permit elected politicians to have a much clearer understanding of the implications of new policies before these are voted on. Additionally, all Government agencies need to undertake an in-depth review of their activities to ensure their relevance for the twenty-first century and also to determine how to free up scarce resources. Walker believes that senior public sector managers should play a much stronger role seeking to transform Government spending plans. He feels these individuals could do more to ensure that current programmes achieve stated objectives, that actions are taken to reduce waste, and that policies introduced to ensure mismanagement occurs much less often.

Demand forces

One of the complications facing the strategic planner is that customers do not exist in isolation and that demand for services is unaffected by external events. As summarized in Figure 8.1, there are a diversity of potential factors of influence. In developing an assessment of opportunities and threats, there is a need for any assessment of future trends by a public sector agency to extend well beyond the basic influencing variables of number of customers, expenditure/customer, and the current provision of services by alternative suppliers from either the public or private sector.

Socio-demographics

Socio-demographics provide a measurement of the nature of consumer populations in terms of variables such as age, education, income, and social class. As socio-demographic profiles undergo change this will impact the nature and scale of the public sector services sought by a nation's population. Accompanying the economic boom enjoyed by consumers in developed nations after World War II was a significant increase in the number of children being born. This population trend led to individuals being born during this period becoming known as 'baby boomers' (Stern et al. 1987). Although there is some dispute about exactly which individuals can be considered to be members of the baby boomer generation, most sociologists attribute the label to those persons born between 1946 and 1964. Academics have always been interested in the baby boomers because they were the first generation (a) where the majority of their parents enjoyed the benefits of secure, well-paid, permanent employment and (b) who themselves were the first-ever group in the world to be exposed to television

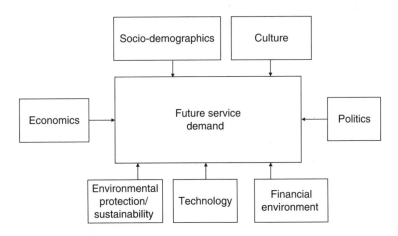

Figure 8.1   Forces influencing demand for public sector services

advertising from the day they were born. The massive buying power of households containing baby boomers explains why, even now, many large consumer goods companies still consider their primary target market is the 18–49-year age group.

Over the last 10 years, however, there has been a significant shift in the nature of the socio-demographic profiles within developed nations due to a decline in average birth rates and improving health care standards leading to greater longevity among older people. This effect, known as population ageing, has already been identified as representing a massive problem as Governments will soon be facing a potentially, massive fiscal crisis (Jensen et al. 1995). On average the cost of public pensions and health care benefits currently consumes 12 per cent of GDP in developed nation economies. The effect of population ageing is forecasted to cause spending on public pensions and health care benefits to rise to 24 per cent of GDP by 2040. However, what has received much less recognition is that accompanying population ageing is a significant shift away from the 18–49-year age being the largest potential source of taxable income. This change is because older people are increasingly the holders of the majority of wealth in developing nations. In the United States, for example, individuals aged 55+ comprise 35 per cent of the adult population yet control 70 per cent of the net worth of all household assets. Such a high level of wealth is the reason why older people in the United States feel able to spend over $1 trillion a year on goods and services. A similar scenario is to be found in the United Kingdom. By the beginning of the twenty-first century, the highest median income within the entire UK population has become those individuals in the 60–64-age group, whilst over the 50s now account for 60 per cent of United Kingdom's savings and 80 per cent of all personal assets. The existence of graduated income and capital gains tax related to size of income does mean that older people already represent the largest group of higher rate tax payers. This group will also increasingly be the dominant demand source for public sector services which may eventually cause politicians to have to think the unthinkable: namely move towards tax system based upon peoples' age (Chaston 2009).

Analysing Service Demand

Case Aims: To illustrate how economic and socio-demographic trends can influence the capability to deliver public sector services.

The nature of the interacting variables influencing strategic planning decisions over the future demand and supply of public sector services is illustrated by the issues covered in the State of Florida's mid-1980s Comprehensive Growth Plan (Kahley 1988). This plan was generated because state officials recognized the need to present for discussion by the legislative arm of Government the implications of an ongoing rise in Florida's population at much faster rate than

(cont'd)

most other states in the United States. The rise was caused not by higher than average birth rates but inward migration from retirees from elsewhere in the United States and younger people arriving to work in service industries associated with the retiree market and Florida's rapid expansion as a tourist destination following the opening of attractions such as Disney World.

Despite concerns that retirees can place added burdens on the state's health provision infrastructure this is more than compensated by the fact that retirees provide 35 per cent of the private sector consumer spending power (24 per cent from the retirees' savings and investments) and 15 per cent from Federal Government social security payments. Of concern is the issue that as the population continues to increase there is a requirement for significant investment in new infrastructure. The report estimated that an investment of $53 billion would be required in the 1990s, of which $16 billion would be spent on roads and $9 billion to fund an expansion in the number of school places for younger couples moving to the state seeking employment. In terms of such spending, the issue arises as which group should shoulder the increased tax burden, retirees, business, farmers (who consume a major proportion of Florida's scarce water supplies), or incoming young families. An added dimension of the debate is the proportion of infrastructure required to support the state's tourism industry. There have been suggestions of introducing a tax aimed at tourist visitors either collected directly or via adding a tax to private sector services such as accommodation. Eventually, it was decided this action had a potentially detrimental impact on tourism and that sales tax on products such as petrol and alcohol was already generating income from tourists, even though it was also accepted that these taxes also placed an unfair burden on lower-income Florida residents.

The other issue of concern is the potentially unstable nature of tax flows because economic downturns can massively reduce tourism numbers. An economic downturn can also lead to a collapse in apartment and house prices which in turn has a negative impact on the Florida's construction industry in terms of both a source of corporate taxes and providing employment for a large number of the state's younger residents. The risk of this latter outcome was validated while following the house price collapse in 2007/8 in the United States where Florida house prices, previously rising at an above-average rate due to private investors becoming involved in property speculation, fell by a much greater amount than most other areas in the United States. Concurrently, massive declines in share prices on Wall Street and associated events such as rich Floridians losing millions in the Bernie Madoff scandal severely impacted retiree spending power. Hence, the state Government is currently struggling with one of the most difficult budget management and allocation of resources across public sector service provisions facing any of the state legislatures in the United States.

Culture

This is a critical variable in terms of influencing market size in the private sector because culture determines the way consumers live and their behaviour in relation to product consumption patterns (Ford et al. 2005). Culture reflects the complex interaction of values, attitudes, and beliefs that influence peoples' opinions. Cultural attitudes will also influence a nation's requirements in relation to the Government's provision of services. This situation is illustrated by the differences in the structure and funding of health care systems in countries such as Canada, France, Germany, the United Kingdom, and the United States. In the first four countries the cultural values of society are orientated towards social equality. As a consequence, their Governments are major participants in the provision of health care in these countries. In contrast, in the United States there is a much stronger belief in the 'work ethic' and individuals being personally responsible for meeting the needs of the family. As a result there is a preference for the private sector to be the primary source of health care services with the Government involvement restricted to very specific activities such as the provision of health care for the elderly (Brown 2003).

A nation's dominant cultural values can change over time and culture also varies significantly between different countries. Politicians are extremely astute at reading cultural shifts in the population. This permits these individuals to modify their manifestos and their support for specific legislation upon seeking re-election or when in office. Possibly the most extreme example of exploiting differences in culture are the arguments politicians have used over the years to persuade their nation's inhabitants that declaring war on another country is a justified act because people in this other country exhibit totally unacceptable cultural traits (Huntington 1993).

To gain further understanding of the effect of culture shift on people's political preferences, McMann (2009) undertook an analysis of voting behaviour in the United States over the period 1946–1992. By the application of multi-variate analysis to a very extensive data set, he concluded that in periods when people feel under greater social or economic threat they exhibit a tendency to vote for Republican candidates. This occurs because people's concerns about protecting the more disadvantaged in society declines as their concerns for their own welfare increases. Apparently, the perception of the US electorate is the Republican Party that is more sympathetic to protecting the well-being of the average citizen, whereas the Democrats are perceived as biasing their policies towards increased taxation with the increase in public revenues being expended on helping groups such as the unemployed or single parents.

Economics

In most countries, consumer expenditure represents approximately 60 per cent of a nation's GDP. Hence, any change in consumer purchasing behaviour will have a major impact on the size of both consumer markets and B2B markets which constitute the supply chain supporting affected end-users markets (Bryant and Macri 2005). Important influencers of consumer spending are the proportion of the population in employment and the per capita earnings. An indirect, but additional important influence is the level of consumer confidence. In an economic downturn where unemployment is rising and earnings are falling, these trends are accompanied by a decline in consumer confidence as people worry about both job and financial security. This fall in confidence usually causes people to cut back on their levels of discretionary expenditure on items such as buying a house, new cars, or going on an expensive vacation.

The important role that consumer spending plays in the size of national GDP does mean public sector organizations do need to carefully assess tax revenue inflow implications associated with future economic trends in terms of whether a nation's economy can be expected to grow, remain unchanged, or enter a decline phase.

Sustaining a growth strategy during an economic downturn is a much more difficult task. Hence, one of the critical issues confronting the public sector strategist is to accurately determine the point at which economic growth has peaked and hence will soon be followed by an economic downturn. Prior to the 1980s, most economists viewed the business cycle as largely unsystematic and unpredictable. Since the 1980s, however, there have been numerous studies validating the predictive value of a number of leading economic indicators such as the Conference Board's Composite Index of Leading Economic Indicators in the United States (Navarro 2008) and the OECD's publication of their annual Economic Outlook which reviews probable economic trends on a global basis. Assuming a public sector organization understands that these key indicators are providing early warning of an approaching economic downturn, decisions can be made concerning how a public sector organization should revise future spending plans.

Navarro (2009) has concluded there is need for all organizations to focus on two major activities in relation to the management of strategy during the business cycle. These are (a) developing forecasting capabilities to anticipate key turning points in the business cycle and (b) acquiring the capability to implement revised business-cycle strategies and tactics across the organization. By achieving these two objectives the organization will be in a much stronger position to proactively respond to changing economic conditions. Navarro (2008) has also proposed that the success of an organization's business-cycle management system is determined by possession of the competences needed to implement key actions once economic indicators suggest a downturn is imminent. Although Navaro's proposals were designed for use in the private sector, certain of his ideas can be converted to the somewhat following more generic actions that are also applicable in the public sector:

(1) *Asset Management* – With a recession on the horizon the organization should begin to revise procurement policies to avoid acquisition and ownership of assets which will be in less demand.

(2) *Supply Chain Management* – Working with members of the supply chain to ensure suppliers or downstream customers are not left with stockpiles of assets for which demand will fall.

(3) *Marketing* – Expenditures would usually be reduced and the promotional message revised to reflect any change in service provision activity that the organization may implement during the downturn.

(4) *Capital Expenditure* – With indications of the onset of recession plans to acquire capital assets such as new building need to be reconsidered, especially where this expenditure is linked to the expansion of service provision that will be less in demand during a downturn should be cut back.

(5) *Staff Size Increases* – Usually these should be put on hold; thereby, the chances of permitting the organization to avoid the situation of rising staff costs at a time with revenue inflow are likely to be reduced.

Politics

Politicians, whether brought to power via the ballot box or through revolution, have long since realized that manipulation of their nation's economy is an effective mechanism by which to achieve their own personal motives and concurrently satisfy important groups within the population. In seeking to determine future market opportunities, the public sector strategist requires an in-depth understanding of prevailing political manifestos as part of determining probable demands to be expected from politicians because this will assist in prioritizing how resources can be allocated across the service portfolio.

At the end of World War II, across the world there was a polarization of philosophy into two very different political perspectives, namely democratic capitalism and communism. Originating in Russia in the early twentieth century as a political movement seeking to remedy the social wrongs of a repressive monarchy, one appeal of communism was that the nation's economic destiny would be placed in the hands of the people (Halal and Nikitin 1990). A fundamental economic principle of communism is the view that capitalism results in the exploitation of the worker. To overcome this problem, it is necessary for all economic activities to remain under the control of the state utilizing some form of centralized Government planning model. An unfortunate outcome of state control, however, is the political leadership may decide it is necessary to severely curtail individuals' personal freedom. Towards the end of the twentieth century the huge disparity in living standards between capitalist democracies and the communist states forced the political leaders in countries such as Russia and China to accept that to stimulate economic growth there was a need to move towards some form of free market economy.

Even within the Western democracies there are significant variations between countries and between political parties within countries concerning the most appropriate policies for managing a nation's economy. The high level of social deprivation which people faced during the 1930s' Depression meant that most post-war Governments accepted the need to utilize public spending policies to avert economic downturns. Politicians were also aware that electorates would favour political parties who were supportive of welfare systems providing free or low-cost access to health care, education, and other social benefits. The actual nature of welfare systems varies between countries. European politicians, for example, support the creation of wider, more inclusive welfare provision than their counterparts in the United States. Europe is also more supportive of the concept of national ownership of key industries such as utilities, the broadcast media, and telecommunications. One of the outcomes of this difference is that compared to the United States, the tax burden and employment legislation in EU countries means European firms, especially in mainland Europe, face extremely high on-costs. These added costs reduce their ability to compete on a cost-effective basis versus firms based in lower labour cost economies elsewhere in the world.

The other dilemma facing the public sector planner is determining how the political manifestos of different political parties (Persson and Tabellini 2000) may influence future Government spending. In the United States, for example, the policies of the Democratic and Republican parties are very different in relation to issues such as taxation and welfare policies. The same scenario exists in the United Kingdom in terms of differences between the policies of the Labour and Conservative parties. As a result, in terms of determining future market opportunities, the public sector planner needs to assess the probability of which political party is likely to be in power and also how this party's political manifesto will impact economic conditions and requirements over the nature of services which the Government will expect public agencies to deliver.

Poor Spending Decisions

Case Aims: To illustrate that public sector spending decisions may not always be in the best interests of a country's inhabitants.

Most inhabitants of a country will usually be supportive of public sector policies and spending in relation to needed services such as health care or education. However, in the face of rising public sector deficits and higher taxation, there will be growing concern among many in the electorate about the ability of their politicians and bureaucrats to make wise decisions over expenditure in certain other areas of public sector service provision. To assess how private citizens and business respond to new initiatives, Klerkx et al. (2006) examined the validity in the Netherlands of a Government's decision to expand expenditure on public sector agricultural advisory services in recent years. They examined the activities of the Nutrient Management Support Service (NMSS), a Government-funded

(cont'd)

support service designed to optimize the fit between the demand and supply of 'agricultural knowledge products' which the country's civil servants decided was needed to reduce nutrient emissions into the environment. The activities of the support service included distributing vouchers to farmers, establishing a certification system to improve quality control, facilitating systems for gaining a better understanding of farmers' needs, and investing in new communications technology such as the Internet to improve market transparency.

At the time the NMSS project was established there was already profound distrust between the farming sector and the Ministry of Agriculture. This distrust went beyond the validity of Government spending on what was perceived as an unwanted service on nutrient management policy. This was because farmers were already highly critical of the way the Government had handled recent crises such as swine flu and foot and mouth disease. The perspective of farmers was that they had been over burdened by a massive increase in administrative duties to complete new Government forms, contradictory policies over handling disease outbreaks, and the overall lack of Government vision concerning the future role of agriculture in the Dutch economy.

Klerkx et al. summarized the results of a study of dairy farmers' trust in the Agriculture Ministry. Over 90 per cent indicated that they did not trust the Government, 67 per cent did not agree with the aims of the public sector nutrient management policy, ranking this ninth in a list of the Government's top ten agricultural policies. This study also revealed that 89 per cent of farmers did not believe the Government had attempted to consider farmers' actual needs and interests when defining the standards to be utilized in the NMSS quality certification scheme. Another survey found that 76 per cent of farmers did not consider themselves as having a problem with nutrient management, and 80 per cent of respondents indicated that they already knew how to meet the nutrient norms for their stock without being provided with additional information from the Government.

In fairness to the NMSS shortly after their creation, the agency also concluded that a lack of knowledge on nutrient management was not the key problem among farmers. This caused the NMSS to make proposals to change the focus and future strategy of their organization. However, the Ministry was not in favour of making fundamental changes to the project and continued to emphasize the necessity of concentrating on delivering the original goals and targets which the Ministry had defined for the new agency.

In most of academic literatures on public sector advisory service, the conclusion is these services only deliver a positive cost/benefit outcome if the agency activities are 'demand-driven'. This means there must be a good fit between the knowledge desired by farmers and the services delivered by public sector agency. Klerkx et al. concluded that in the case of the NMSS, the project in many ways resembled a classic attempt to implement Government policy

(cont'd)

without any real understanding of client's actual needs. The authors further argue (Klerkx et al. 2006, p. 201)

> the concept of demand-driven public sector services in Western European agriculture is reflected in an ongoing fundamental difference of interests between Government and the farmers. This is because Governments are focusing on reaching societal goals with respect to ecology and the environment, which often run counter to the immediate economic interests of individual farmers.

Despite the farmers' objections to the benefits of the NMSS project, the Dutch Government spent over 60 million euros on the provision of nutrient-related advisory services to farmers. Throughout these activities the view of farmers and agricultural experts was that there were other issues such as pasture management and animal feeding which would have been a more effective point of focus and, furthermore, could have served as an entry point for discussing nutrient management issues in a broader context. Over time, the growing resentment of farmers can be further heightened when the issue arose of whether the Government's policy would be defended in the European court. Eventually the nutrient advisory programme collapsed towards the end of 2003 when the European court decided the Dutch Government's policy was not in line with European regulations over nutrient controls in agriculture.

Finance

Although most management texts attribute Henry Ford's success to his introduction of mass production into his Detroit car plant, few mention that the Ford Motor Company also recognized another critical way of influencing sales: namely a willingness to assist customers to buy the Model T motorcar by offering low-interest loans. The ability of the financial sector to provide consumers with access to credit facilities such as loans and credit cards has been a critical determinant in the rate of growth in consumer spending across the world. The issue of the availability and cost of funds is also critical in relation to the internal operations of public sector organizations. Few of these organizations are able to self-fund their operations from cash inflows from the customers to whom they provide services or the purchase of major capital assets such as the construction of a new office block. Hence, most need to engage in borrowing either from a Government source or by issuing interest-bearing bonds. Similar to assessing the influence of financial conditions on consumer behaviour, the public sector strategist will need to determine the probable nature of the future business climate in relation to persuading Governments to make funds available and the cost of raising funds in terms of the probable level of interest that will need to be offered to make a bond offering of interest to the financial markets.

In an increasingly volatile and economically uncertain world, the OECD has expressed the view that the traditional approach to public sector budgeting of merely setting spending levels for the next 12 months, and in some cases also providing a projection for the next 3 years, is no longer a viable strategy (Ulla 2006). Instead, there is a need to specify a sustainable fiscal position based upon avoiding debt consuming an increasing share of GDP. To achieve this goal, there needs to be a clear specification of future spending priorities. Governments and public sector organizations merely relying upon extrapolation of prior service spending are no longer viable concepts. Knowing that demographics will cause increase in expenditure and reduction in tax revenues, Governments and agencies must clearly accommodate these trends into their long-term plans.

The OECD believes that in the past many public sector forecasts have seriously underestimated the growth in Government expenditure. They consider the probable strategy for reducing public sector spending is to partially shift service provision (e.g. pensions, health care) back to the private sector. Underestimations of expenditures have usually been connected to benefit payments and health costs. To avoid such uncertainty in the future it may be necessary to specify the operations of entitlement programmes in such a way that unexpected changes in the assumptions do not increase public expenditures. One way this can be achieved is to decide that adverse financial outcomes are borne by the beneficiaries. For example, as is now occurring in many countries when forecasting public sector pension provision Governments are linking the initial entitlement of retirement age to increasing life expectancy. Thus, the initial entitlement age is being deferred and this is intended to ensure that although people are living longer, this should not result in an increase in the country's spending on the provision of state old-age pensions. Another method that has been proposed is to link the level of the monthly benefits to life expectancy on the grounds that the material needs of people decline as they move into their 80s and 90s. Thus, monthly payments would decline as people move from an active to a more sedentary lifestyle which would reduce the total level of spending on old-age pensions.

Ulla points out that one of the main uncertainties in public sector expenditure is future interest rates demanded by financial markets in order to purchase public sector bonds. To reduce this uncertainty, he posits it is necessary for public sector borrowing to place greater reliance on debt obligations with long durability and fixed interest rates.

Ulla also suggests that creating accurate long-term borrowing and interest rate forecasts is probably more important than the numerical data generated on current or near-term public sector spending. This is because these spending data do not accurately reflect what will happen in the future. By placing greater emphasis on longer-term forecasts, this would force politicians and civil servants to develop a more in-depth understanding of the future financial problems that can arise as a result of inappropriate fiscal decisions within the current financial year. By discussing how different actions can influence forecasted outcomes, policy makers would be in a much better position to make changes in their strategic thinking at an early enough stage that revised fiscal policies can be gradually phased in over time. This avoids the catastrophic economic and social impact that is being seen in countries such as Greece when a failure to take action at an earlier date means the country is forced to accept a decade of major austerity.

Technology

In today's rapidly changing world the most likely source of sustained performance in private sector organizations is the exploitation of new technology (Herps et al. 2003). Technological change can provide the basis for an entirely new product or service, improvements in current goods, upgrading the effectiveness of internal processes such as production, or enhancing any of the activities within a company's contribution to optimizing the effectiveness of the supply chain activities. Although given less emphasis by the strategic planner in many public sector organizations, new technology can also have a major impact on changing the nature of services provided or enhance the efficiency, effectiveness, and economics of service provision.

The entrepreneurial public sector organization will tend to be more aware of new opportunities offered by technology and incorporate these into the development of future strategies. More conservative organizations may place less importance on the role of technology in the development of new services or improving internal processes. Where there is an awareness of the importance of technological change in both the public and private sectors, this often tends to be focused on investment activity concerned with increasing productivity and replacing high-cost labour inputs with automated, machine-based processes (Jones 2002). Although this strategic orientation can significantly improve operational performance, there is the risk that excessive emphasis on process change will mean losing opportunities that might make new services available.

Evidence from academic articles, Government reports, and the media suggests that public sector organizations have a somewhat poor track record in correctly identifying the most appropriate new technology to incorporate into their operations. Frequently, the development phase often results in cost overruns or the technology not delivering expected cost/benefit outcomes specified when contracts with suppliers were originally agreed. In some cases, the scale of implementation problems prove to be so large that eventually the project is terminated before completion with a resultant major loss of public sector monies.

As noted by Goldfinch (2006), some of the most expensive failures associated with the introduction of new technology into the public sector involving the waste of vast sums of money in recent years have been IT projects. Commenting on the situation in the United States, in his view the majority of projects to significantly upgrade information management systems have been unsuccessful. Furthermore, the larger the project, the greater the probability that the project will be a failure by not delivering the cost/benefits which were believed to exist at the project outset. In 1994, for example, the US General Accounting Office reported that spending of more than US$200 billion in the previous 12 years had led to few meaningful returns. Such failures are not restricted to the United States. In the United Kingdom, the Wessex Health Authority's Regional Information Systems Plan was cancelled after spending what is estimated to be excess of £40 million for a non-functional system. The New Zealand Police abandoned an IS development in 1999 at a cost of more than $NZ100 million.

There are various reasons why such projects fail. In some cases, the system never performs at standards specified in the original contract, go drastically over budget, or completion deadlines are not met. Even when systems appear to be functioning correctly, the project may not generate productivity gains or deliver the benefits expected. Alternatively, the system never fully comes on-stream due to user resistance. This can be due to such factors as managerial recalcitrance, lack of staff training, and inability of the staff to cope with the complexity of the new system. Despite the accumulated evidence of numerous failures, enthusiasm for large and complex investments in the public sector remains unabated. For example, largest-ever public sector project was initiated in 2002 by the United Kingdom's National Health Service at an estimated cost of US$11 billion. The project hit numerous obstacles, actual spending exceeded estimates, and eventually the entire project has been redesigned and the overall aims for the project have been drastically reduced.

Goldfinch believes a key factor influencing poor project outcomes is knowledge asymmetry. This is because the public sector project manager usually has much less understanding of the technology than the suppliers' representatives. These latter individuals are thus in a position to possibly conceal from the client that the project is likely to face fundamental problems. Furthermore, it is often the case that the public sector project leader is reluctant to be the bearer of bad news and hence may downplay emerging problems when reporting to senior management or an independent public sector monitoring agency. Appointments in bureaucracies are often made on the basis of seniority and successful political behaviour rather than actual competence. As a result, senior manager placed in charge of a major project may lack the necessary skills to operate in highly complex fields such as IT development or alternatively may simply be afraid of asking basic questions for fear of losing face among more junior members of the organization's management team. Further, misunderstanding and miscommunication can occur because of professional jealousies resulting in enquiries over project progress from external bodies such as auditors because these entities are perceived as a source of unwarranted interference. Hence, responding to enquiries from external agencies is resisted in various ways, including restriction of information.

Goldfinch suggests that where the decision is made to consider a new investment in IT, the first question should be how this can be done with the least disruption, the least cost, the least risk, and the least uncertainty. The most dangerous course is to invest in high-risk, highly ambitious project involving leading edge technology or long development time frames. This is because the probability of failure is very much higher. In his opinion, a more sensible solution would be to examine what is currently working in the private sector and to buy an off-shelf system which has already been demonstrated to work. In those cases where such a system is not available, possibly the best option is to accept that technology is not yet widely available that can produce the IT solution that is being sought. At this juncture instead of the public sector organization listening to the potential suppliers of the management consultants hired to advise about proceeding with a massive, high-risk leading-edge development programme, a more appropriate decision is to postpone the proposed IT project until the necessary solution becomes more widely available. Given the rate that new IT systems are being developed by the today's computer industry, it is highly probable a viable and much more affordable solution will become available in just a few years.

On a slightly more positive note in relation to advances in IT, some public sector agencies have been able to exploit off-shelf technology and database management systems in what has become the 'digital age' of service provision. Costs have been reduced, speed of response increased, and new services created following the switch-over to e-mail systems, creation of Web sites, the growth of electronic procurement systems as the early phase in a fundamental transition from a paper-based to an electronic record-keeping and information management (Dunleavy et al. 2005). In commenting upon the benefits that digitalization has brought to the public sector, these authors feel it has been feasible to re-instate central processes which lead to economies of scale and scope, radically reduce operating costs, and exploit re-engineering to upgrade the effectiveness of back-office administration functions. Furthermore, as effective online systems are created, this permits integration of functions such that public sector agencies can genuinely act as a 'one-stop-shop' provider of services to numerous customer groups.

Dunleavy et al. also noted that of even greater appeal of digitalization is that the technology can be utilized to rapidly implement significant innovation at relatively low cost. The authors point to the example of when the transport authorities in London in 1998 decided to install charging technology in underground rail stations and buses for using a smart card (the 'Oystercard'). This allowed users to put credit on their card and then pay for any form of mass-transit journey by swiping the card past an automatic reader. Initially 350,000 existing holders of paper season tickets switched to the electronic card. As awareness of the benefits of the Oystercard became apparent, card usage grew to over 2 million people in less than 4 years. This expansion has led to large cost savings in ticketing staff, major reductions in peak-hour queuing times, and increased use of mass transit by passengers for whom ticket-acquisition is no longer a potential problem within the journey process.

Environmental issues

Rachel Carson's book, *The Silent Spring* published by Houghton Mifflin in 1962 is widely credited with helping to launch the 'Green Movement' by bringing to the general public's attention the hazards of pollution and the adverse ecological impact of uncontrolled use of pesticides. Most industries' initial reactions to concerns about pollution are to seek to avoid investing in upgrading their environmental management responsibilities unless confronted by tighter Government regulation. Towards the end of the twentieth century, this attitude has begun to gradually change. Factors contributing towards this shift in attitudes include (a) growing awareness about the risks associated with global warming, (b) growing evidence of the finite availability of the world's oil resources, and (c) some consumers indicating a preference to purchase goods from companies exhibiting an above-average level of eco-responsibility.

Initially, most organizations became concerned about the perceived threats associated with ignoring eco-responsibility when confronted with possibility that raw material resources may become constrained (Bekefi and Epstein 2008). One of the areas which has received greatest attention in both the public and private sectors is the need to reduce the energy costs associated with the operational processes of creating and delivering services. In recent years, public sector organizations within the European Union have been giving much greater priority to strategies for achieving cost savings by reducing the level of energy usage inside their buildings. More recently, the EU politicians' desire to provide leadership in the battle to reverse global warming has resulted in public sector organizations in the European Union face new statutory regulations in relation to being required to achieve specific reductions in their level of greenhouse gas emissions. Actions to achieve this goal include redesigning offices and revising travel policies to reduce employees' carbon footprint. A beneficial side effect of such strategies is these activities can be utilized by these agencies to present a public image of being committed to leading the trend towards creating greener, more environmentally responsible organizations. It may also be the case that some of these public sector organizations are able to generate new revenue streams by providing consultancy services to the private sector and not-for-profit agencies' customers about how to exhibit a higher level of environmental responsibility.

Understanding need

A fundamental driver influencing the strategic planning process is determining how an organization can satisfy customer needs more effectively. For this requirement to be fulfilled, the organization must have a detailed understanding of what are the real needs of both potential and existing customers. In reporting on the outcome of their research on the understanding of the customer need within the private sector, Ulwick and Bettencourt (2008, p. 63) concluded that

> Even thought here is broad agreement that innovation is the key to growth and that understanding customer needs is the key to innovation, not even 5% of the companies said there was agreement within their company as to what a customer need is.

These researchers have proposed that in order for all parties within an organization to fully comprehend their role in the provision of services, there should exist a statement of need which fulfils the following six requirements:

(1) The statement must reflect the customer's definition of value.

(2) The statement must have universal acceptance.

(3) The statement must be relevant now and in the future.

(4) The statement must prompt a course of action.

(5) The statement's meaning must not be open to misinterpretation.

(6) The statement must provide guidance on future organizational strategic priorities.

This type of advice is applicable in those cases where both the customer and the service provider have an informed understanding of future need. As summarized in Figure 8.2, there are four different options depending upon the degree to which either the supplier or the customer has an understanding of need. It is critical that the strategist is able to assess the degree to which information is available because this will significantly influence the approach taken in the development of the SWOT analysis.

Possibly, the most common situation concerning understanding of need is the one that is found in most private sector organizations: namely both the customer and the service provider have a clear understanding of the nature of market need. Under these circumstances, the strategist is able to undertake a 'Conventional SWOT' and be relatively confident of identifying the key opportunities and threats which might impact the organization in the future. In those cases where the service provider has a limited understanding of customer need, this will usually mean that the senior management have little faith in market research and tend to rely on their own knowledge of market circumstances to

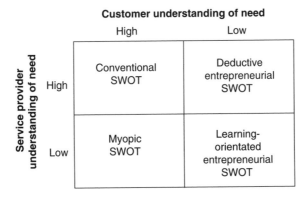

Figure 8.2   Alternative SWOT development options

define future opportunities. This orientation is not uncommon in many areas of the public sector. The potential risk in this scenario is the strategist may rely upon available information, not recognizing that it fails to incorporate detailed inputs from customers. As a result, this approach is labelled as a 'Myopic SWOT' because it will very probably lead to incorrect conclusions being made about the opportunities and threats which will confront the organization in the future.

Situations where the service provider has a more understanding of need than the customer tend to arise in those public sector organizations which are engaged in the provision of complex services such as health care. As a result, their perspective of opportunity may be more accurate than those of their customers. Some of these organizations may, however, seek to gain indications of possible customer response to innovative ideas by undertaking qualitative research studies or inviting key customers to become partners in the innovation process. This orientation towards generating more data from customers does reduce the risk of misidentification of possible future opportunities and threats.

The highest risk situation in terms of generating an accurate SWOT analysis is where neither the service provider nor the customer has any real understanding of need. This scenario arises in those cases where a new situation has emerged and nobody is really certain of the most appropriate action (e.g. the emergence of a new medical condition or social problem). Under these circumstances, it is likely that an effective solution will require the service provider exhibiting an intuitive entrepreneurial orientation. Nevertheless, the high level of uncertainty in this scenario about the accuracy of conclusions reached concerning future opportunities and threats will require the service provider to openly admit there could be inadequacies in proposed solutions. Assistance in achieving greater accuracy can often come from developing collaborative relationship with customers in order that both parties can jointly learn from the experience of testing the effectiveness of different solutions. This approach is reflected in the assigned label of 'Learning-Orientated Entrepreneurial SWOT'.

Technology

9

The aims of this chapter are to cover the issues of:

(1) The importance of technology as a source of opportunity

(2) The role of technology in relation to service innovation versus process improvement

(3) The factors influencing the successful introduction of new technology

(4) The S-curve and diffusion of innovation in relation to the speed of new technology adoption

(5) Disruption theory in relation to impact of new technology on organizational performance

Importance

Technological change is possibly one of the most critical of all of the meta-events that represent a future strategic opportunity or threat to any organization. This is because managed effectively technology has the potential to create totally new forms of service provision and permit changes in operational processes that can dramatically lower costs or significantly enhance service delivery. Alternatively, if ignored, a public sector agency may find that resources previously allocated to the organization have been transferred to another agency which has demonstrated a willingness to embrace new technology to achieve the three public sector mantras or objectives of economics, effectiveness, and efficiency.

Erikson et al. (1990) have proposed that technology can be divided into three types. 'Base' technologies which all organizations need to utilize because they are fundamental to the production or services. 'Key' technologies which are critical because they provide sources of delivering superior service relative

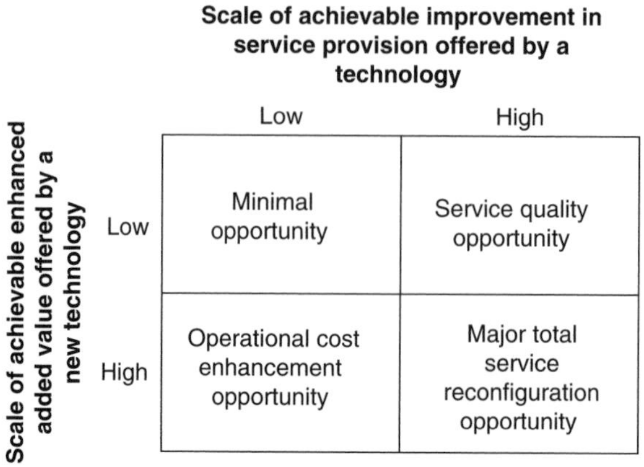

**Scale of achievable improvement in
service provision offered by a
technology**

	Low	High
Low	Minimal opportunity	Service quality opportunity
High	Operational cost enhancement opportunity	Major total service reconfiguration opportunity

(left axis label: **Scale of achievable enhanced added value offered by a new technology**)

Figure 9.1   Alternative service provision opportunities matrix

to other organizations competing for customers or resources (e.g. a University's ability to become a highly effective exploiter of e-based learning systems which leads to achieving lower operating costs than other colleges seeking funds from the Government). The third type of technology is 'pacer technologies' which can be expected to evolve into the key technologies of the future. Not every organization has either the skills or resources to be engaged in exploiting pacer technologies. However, for those public sectors operations which have these capabilities, exploitation of pacer technology may provide the future basis through which to sustain the long-term existence of the organization.

The importance of technology varies across different types of service provision. In part, this is due to the nature of the service offering. Opportunities to utilize new technology are significantly lower in service provision involving one-to-one provider/client–human interaction (e.g. social workers assessing child abuse cases). Hence, as illustrated in Figure 9.1, any analysis of future trends needs to take account of the degree to which technology permits the organization to (a) achieve a higher level of performance and (b) provide the basis for increasing the scale of added value activities that allow sustained levels of service provision even in the face of major reductions in Government funding.

In those cases where the technology neither permits achievement of superior service delivery performance nor higher added value, new technology offers minimal opportunity for a public sector organization to upgrade their service portfolio. Where there is low opportunity to add value, but significant opportunity to enhance service provision, this situation permits the organization to exploit technology to enhance service quality. In this situation, technological change will be important but the role of technology is to enhance customer satisfaction over the provision of existing services.

Some public sector scenarios involving the exploitation of technology do not permit any significant improvement in service provision but provide opportunities to achieve greater added value within an organization's operational processes. This usually involves the organization exploiting new technology to reduce operating costs. The most beneficial situation for any public sector agency is where there exists opportunities to both improve service provision and increase added value across operational process. An example of this scenario is provided by Governments which have moved to create Web-based tax return filing systems. The tax payer is provided with a faster, more convenient pathway through which to file their tax returns. The tax authorities receive the return in a form which can be processed and the tax liability calculated without the need for the involvement of large numbers of clerical staff.

Less, Not More, Public Sector Innovation?

Case Aims: To illustrate that the continued expansion on innovation to create new weapon systems may need reconsideration in the face of mounting public sector deficits.

The ending of World War II did not, as some expected, result in a downturn in public sector expenditure on armaments. Instead, the growing ideological confrontation between the major democracies and communism, especially in terms of being prepared for a war with Russia, sparked off a major arms race where vast sums of money were spent on R&D and subsequent production of ever more innovative, but ever more expensive, weapons system. Some experts predicted that the end of the Cold War in the 1990s would be accompanied by a major downturn in public sector expenditure in developed nations, releasing funds to use in delivering domestic social policies. Unfortunately, this outcome has not occurred. Observing the potential risk for defeat due to underfunding of the armed forces before World War II has caused military leaders in countries such as the United Kingdom and United States to retain the view that military spending must continue in order to avoid being unprepared for the next war which might break out somewhere in the world. In terms of a major war, military planners in the West now perceive China as a potentially much greater future threat than Russia. However, to use a potential event which is both not certain and if it occurred this would be many years in the future is possibly somewhat dubious logic. Hence, in commenting upon this scenario Betts (2007, p. 72) proposed that

> The correct way to hedge against the long-term China threat is by adopting a mobilization strategy: developing plans and organizing resources now so that military capabilities can be expanded quickly later if necessary. This means carefully designing a system of readiness to get ready – emphasizing research and development, professional training, and organizational planning. Mobilization in high gear should be held off until genuine evidence indicates that U.S. military supremacy is starting to slip toward mere superiority. Deferring a surge in

(cont'd)

military production and expansion until then would avoid sinking trillions of dollars into weaponry that may be technologically obsolete before a threat actually materializes.

The other justification for sustaining higher spending on defence was provided by 9/11. This led to an ongoing 'war against terrorism' such as intervening in the Middle East in response to the threat posed by Saddam Hussein. In seeking to gain acceptance of their view that spending should not be cut, the military is often assisted by the politicians' claim that the development of new weapon systems can generate significant export income and also spin offs from the technology can assist in the development of new products in civilian manufacturing industries.

Given the huge public deficits facing some developed nations, there could be benefit in revisiting the philosophy that speaks of the expenditure on innovation to develop the next generation of weapons. In relation to the issue of achieving savings in military spending, added understanding is provided in an interview in 2006 with Lawrence Korb, the former US Assistant Secretary of Defence. He described areas where in his view $60 billion could be saved in United States' defence budget without having any adverse impact on the country's national security (Anon 2006b). Korb estimated that the total military expenditure by the United States for 2006 would be $575 billion. This represents 50 per cent of the world's total expenditure on defence. In his view the military is spending funds on innovation for weapons systems which are probably inappropriate for the defence issues facing the country. These new systems have been initiated to deal with threats from a bygone era, but bureaucratic and political momentums sustain their existence. One is the F/A-22 fighter jet which costs over $300 million per plane. This aircraft is designed to deal with the next generation of Soviet MIGs, except there is no next generation of Soviet MIGs. Another project is the DD(X) Destroyer, which is designed to wage open ocean warfare. However, there is no blue water navy with whom such a confrontation can occur. In relation to $60 billion in annual savings, Kolb proposed these can be achieved (i) reducing nuclear weapons from the current 6000 operational nuclear weapons and reducing 6000 currently in reserve down to 1000, (ii) not deploying the proposed national missile defence system which does not actually work and cutting back the research programme, (iii) terminating projects no longer needed because the Cold War has ended, and (v) shutting down projects for weapons under development that are simply not performing (e.g. the V-22 Osprey project which has a record of accidents and an exponential increase in costs). In relation to why Congress does not appear to reduce defence spending, Kolb responded (Anon 2006b, p. 36) 'Now that we're in this so-called global war on terror, politicians are afraid to vote against weapons programs.

(cont'd)

I think that makes the influence of the military-industrial-Congressional complex even greater.'

A key aspect of managing excessive public sector deficits is to minimize waste within the sector. Similar to United States, over the years the United Kingdom's Ministry Of Defence (MOD) has faced great difficulty in achieving value for money in weapons procurement. Weapons systems have repeatedly been acquired late and over budget (Smith 2007). This author suggests a key reason for this situation has been an ongoing failure to spend appropriate monies up-front during the assessment phase on R&D and technology demonstrations before proceeding with a major project (e.g. 0.8 per cent of the £3.5nb budget for the Astute submarines was spent on assessment; the Nimrod patrol aircraft, 0.1 per cent of the £3.6bn budget). Additionally, because of the length of time defence procurement projects require, it is usually between 5 and 7 years into a project that the problems become apparent. As a consequence, some very expensive military equipment can be obsolete even before it enters service. For example, the Eurofighter is based on early 1980s' designs, and upon entering service it was without aircraft's missile, the Meteor. An additional spending problem is high ongoing expenditure on weapon support costs. In the private sector, new technology generates lower production costs and higher volumes, whereas weapons systems involve high production cost and lower production volumes. Then as much of the equipment is old before it is introduced, this causes problems over the availability of replacement parts. This outcome is particularly common in relations to electronics. This is because commercially available technology is based upon next generation designs. These cannot be used to repair weapons systems based upon old technology.

Focus

The potential for technology to dramatically enhance the capability of a public sector organization's service delivery capability provides strong justification for the strategic perspective that the long-term success will be driven by the organization's capabilities to exploit key and pacer technologies. Technological capability tends to be both a scarce and expensive resource. Consequently, in determining where these scarce resources should be allocated in terms of future activity, there is a need to determine which service provision activities represent the greatest source of opportunities and threats. In terms of assessing this issue, one approach is to assume there are two dimensions to be considered: namely the nature of services provided and service output in relation to existing or new scenarios. As illustrated in Figure 9.2, this approach results in an assessment being required in relation to four different service provision scenarios.

Service provision

	Existing	New
Existing	Technological change influencing existing service(s) performance or value	Technological change influencing existing service(s) adapted for meeting new customer needs
New	Technological change leading to a new generation of service(s)	Technological change leading to radically new service(s) and/or diversification

(Service output)

Figure 9.2   Service provision matrix

Another issue which will usually require assessment is the priority to be given to technological investment in relation to upgrading existing internal organizational processes versus activities directed towards developing new services (Fox et al. 1998). As summarized in Figure 9.3, to determine the nature of technological priorities, this will require an analysis of four different future scenarios. Where there is confidence that current service process production technologies are expected to remain appropriate for the foreseeable future, the organization can focus on enhancing service provision activities (e.g. serving more customers, providing services to additional groups of customers). In the case where new technology can result in the creation of a next generation of service output(s), actions will be necessary to implement a new service(s) development programme. This can be contrasted with the situation where the current service provision is perceived as adequate, but opportunities exist to upgrade an

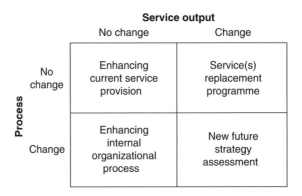

Figure 9.3   Focus of action matrix

area of service process production technology. Action in this area can lead to an enhancement of internal organizational activity that may reduce costs or improve service quality. Where there is a possible need for both service process production and service product to be changed, this more complex situation will usually require a consideration of the need for a possible future change in organizational strategy.

Health care Innovation

Case Aims: To illustrate how innovation has the potential to reduce costs in a major area of public sector spending.

Health care is becoming one of the largest and fastest growing areas of public sector expenditure which many political parties believe should be 'ring fenced' when consideration is given to planning national spending cuts. Nevertheless, unless new ways are found to deliver health care services, cuts will inevitably have to be implemented. Fortunately, healthcare is a sector where technologically based innovation can have massive impact on both reducing costs, enhancing health care service provision, and providing new ways of treating previously untreatable or terminal conditions.

One field of innovation is biotechnology which involves the application of scientific and engineering principles to the processing of materials by biological processes (Williams 1998). This relatively new science already supplies human health products (e.g. biopharmaceuticals, vaccines, and diagnostics). Recombinant DNA technology, or 'gene therapy', has been used to develop a number of therapeutic proteins, including antibodies, cytokines, hormones, and vaccines for use in tackling and diagnosing a range of disorders. Also, biotechnology has led to the development of hundreds of medical diagnostic tests that both lower the costs of diagnostics and detect medical conditions early enough to greatly increase the probability of a favourable outcome in patients responding to treatment.

Recent advances in online information and communication technologies have led to the development of innovations in the delivery of medical services. One example is provided by tele-radiology which can facilitate the delivery of radiological services across various time zones and geographical regions. Opportunities offered by this new technology include (Kalyanpur et al. 2007):

(1) Internet-based service delivery of radiological services to emergency departments, large hospitals, and remote rural clinics. Within the United States, this innovation has already led to the development of the 'nighthawk' service whereby a radiologist is able to simultaneously provide services to multiple hospitals via tele-radiology links to a central data analysis and diagnosis facility.

(cont'd)

(2) Optimization of workflow in which tele-radiology increases the efficiency of a radiologist by ensuring he or she spend his or her time delivering quality care to the maximum number of patients.

(3) Subspecialty consultations whereby tele-radiology enables images of a specific body region/modality need to be referred to the radiologist with expertise in the interpretation of specific medical conditions.

In recent years, medical researchers have recognized the benefits of working in partnership with engineers to develop new medical treatments. Examples of engineered devices include the heart pacemaker, the defibrillator, and the cochlear implant. Possibly the area of greatest potential is the use of robots in undertaking surgical processes. The first robot-assisted heart bypass occurred in Germany in 1998 and the first unmanned robotic surgery took place in May 2006 in Italy. Noor (2007) forecasts that in the future, surgical robots will be smaller, simpler, and cheaper to use. They will be integrated, with other smart instruments, into hospital operating theatres to form plug-and-play systems. Other applications include robotic legs, arms, and hands, both as prosthetic devices and as exoskeletons.

Since the early days of the computer, health care and IT experts have been forecasting that computer-based, centralized medical record systems (or informatics) will help in advancing the revolution of healthcare provisions. In some countries such as the United Kingdom the accepted approach to creating these systems is a central database management centre at which medical records can be stored for re-access by medical staff in the future. Unfortunately, due to problems over cost, lack of feasible technology, concerns over data security, resistance from some in the medical profession, and poor project management, this solution has yet to be established as a cost-effective solution. A feasible, lower-cost alternative solution which is emerging in the United States is to exploit existing technology from the credit card industry to embed medical information into an individual's data in a plastic card (Parente 2009) known as the Integrated Health Record (IHR). This is a patient- or family-centred technology which is designed to capture key data on the individual including their contacts with health care providers. Physicians can access the card to be informed of the patient's medical condition and then create a new personalized treatment plan. This plan can then be accessed by other medical staff with whom the patient may come in contact during the receipt of current treatment or at some later date.

Population ageing will be accompanied by an increasing number of people with health concerns visiting their doctors. This increase in demand for medical services could rapidly escalate unless alternative approaches to diagnostic

(cont'd)

medicine can be developed. Awareness of the need to handle this trend on a cost-effective basis has led in recent years to increased R&D to develop new biosensors (Newman et al. 2001). As evidenced by the success of glucose biosensors for self-testing of blood glucose by diabetic patients, technological advances have resulted in significant reduction in the cost of diagnostic services. The total world market for biosensors has more than trebled in recent years, with annual sales now over $2000 million. In 2000, one of the largest producers of sensors, Medisense manufactured 1 billion sensors per annum. This represents a usage rate of 2.7 million biosensor diagnostics being undertaken everyday.

Sources of influence

New technology has been a critical driver in terms of influencing the world economy ever since the early years of the Industrial Revolution. There is a good reason to believe that technology will continue to provide innumerable opportunities for the emergence of new sources of entrepreneurial activity throughout the twenty-first century. For the next generation of entrepreneurs with the same competences as Bill Gates, Richard Branson, or Steve Jobs have, identifying new opportunities or threats just requires an intuitive decision about where to focus their future endeavours. For less gifted individuals the task, however, will be more difficult. Hence, where insightful intuition is lacking, one approach available to the strategic planner is to evaluate influence of the potential factors which might determine whether a new technology will be adopted (Chaston 2009a). A summary of these key influencing variables are summarized in Figure 9.4.

At the core of the diagram in relation to the uptake of a new technology will be the customer (Ibrahim et al. 2008). The new technology must usually be capable of effectively satisfying existing customer needs. More importantly, however, in most cases the new technology will offer even greater opportunities for the public sector provider by also satisfying as yet, unidentified new customer needs. To survive, most new technologies have to successfully compete with existing technologies (Hoffman 2000). In most cases, these existing technologies will be utilized by individuals employed in public sector organizations who have a vested interest in ensuring the failure of new service provision. In maximum cases, this vested interest exists because the introduction of a new technology could reduce their ongoing security of employment. An example of this outcome might be provided by clerical staff in a Government agency where the current paper-based filing and data processing activities are replaced by the introduction of an automated Web-based system which permits customer to move to an online submission of required information. Another sorts of influencing variables are wild card events. These can sometimes occur because a completely

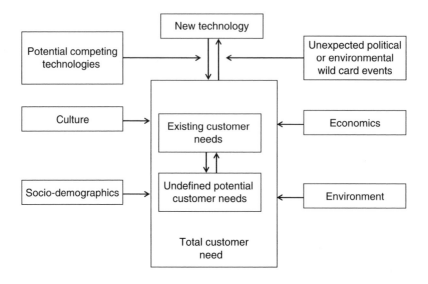

Figure 9.4   Variables influencing the adoption of a new service technology

unexpected event acts as a catalyst for increasing the market potential for a new approach or type of service provision.

In many cases, the first generation of products or services based upon a new technology will be expensive to purchase at the time of their initial introduction. Hence, during periods of weak economic conditions public sector agencies may feel unable to risk purchasing such a high price item. In some cases, low initial market demand means profits generated are insufficient to support the R&D activities required by suppliers that are necessary to drive down the costs to permit the new technology to become affordable to cash-constrained public sector customers. In contrast, during an economic upturn Government tax revenues usually support an expansion of public sector budgets which permits these organizations to more easily afford to purchase even relatively high priced new technology.

Customer acceptance for a new technology will also be influenced by prevailing cultural values. One of the key reasons, for example, for the unexpected, very rapid growth in market for the first generation of the mobile communications device, the BlackBerry, was the influence of the product being perceived as a 'must have' item to demonstrate personal status within among staff in both public and private sector organizations. Market penetration rates for subsequent generations of the product were also greatly assisted by the enthusiasm with which staff then moved into other activities such as data transfer and sending visual images via the Internet.

Socio-demographic change which results in the re-shaping of markets will strongly influence the demand for new products and services. In the Western world, the onset of population ageing has led to people aged 55+ becoming the dominant age group within society (Chaston 2009b). Many of these older people are now more financially secure and enjoy a higher standard of living than younger people, especially families with children. The implications of this scenario are that public sector organizations would be well-advised when assessing the potential for a new technology to enhance service delivery, to give greater attention to potential appeal of the service among older age groups instead of the traditional service provision group of 18–49-year-olds with families.

Over the last 20 years, there has been a gradual increase with the problems associated with population growth, pollution, and the earth's finite supply of key natural resources. Until recently, however, most citizens in developed economies were not too concerned about the impact of adverse environmental change on their lives. Now, however, all organizations need to be more concerned about eco-protection in terms of the potentially hazardous environmental implications that might be associated with existing and new service process technologies. Furthermore, in the last few years there has been growing awareness of global warming, with both politicians and citizens within nations now recognizing the need for a higher level of environmental responsibility in relation to greenhouse gas emissions. This attitude shift has implications in relation to the expectation of customers being more supportive of those public sector organizations which exhibit a high level of moral and ethical standards in relation to reducing consumption of non-renewable hydro-carbon resources and greenhouse gas emissions.

Reducing the Body Count

Case Aims: To illustrate how technological innovation can dramatically reduce public sector employee costs and concurrently enhance service provision.

The largest component of expenditure in most areas of the public sector is on people: paying their salaries, providing physical facilities in which to work, and then sustaining them in retirement by providing a pension, which in many cases in the public sector is a final salary, index-linked scheme. Hence, a very important focus in technological innovation is to replace people with machines in the public sector. The advent of the Internet has made this possible as demonstrated by the introduction of e-technology into the tax department in Singapore (Tan and Pan 2003).

In the past, the Singapore tax system was slow, suffering from manual tax processing systems, and an accumulation of paper documents. Further problems occurred due to a lack of experienced staff to process the tax returns. These problems, when added to others caused by a highly bureaucratic organizational orientation, created long delays in the country's tax collection operation.

(cont'd)

The first significant change to the tax filing process was the introduction of an imaging system to reduce the volume of paper files. The digitized images are stored in a centralized database that is accessible to all tax officers. This led to substantial cost savings as productivity was greatly increased. Digitization also provided a system that could efficiently process most of the country's tax returns without physical intervention. This is because 80 per cent of returns have found to be acceptable and do not require the involvement of a tax official to audit the data. A Workflow Management System was created for channelling unusual tax cases for inspection by a tax official. The system also selected to whom the file should be sent by using a rules-based system to match a case to the appropriate inspector.

Even with the imaging system, physical data entry was still unavoidable and hence a customer phone filing system was introduced. Despite the simplicity of the instructions provided to the caller, most taxpayers found it is uncomfortable to use the system. As a result, an e-filing system was launched, initially for salaried employees and subsequently for all taxpayers. The Internet filing system contains an Electronic-Filing Personal Identification Number (EF PIN) for authentication purposes. In seeking to make e-filing effortless for taxpayers, the tax department established computer-based links with a number of Government agencies and businesses organizations in order to have them transfer relevant information from their employee records directly into tax department database. Once the information for a particular taxpayer has been uploaded into the system, all the taxpayer has to do is submit a series of zero returns through the e-filing system. By 2003, this auto-inclusion scheme was acquiring data on approximately 550,000 citizens which represent 46 per cent of all employees in the country.

S-Curve

Not all customers or organizations respond at the same speed in terms of adopting a new technology. This behaviour, when analysed in relation to the percentage of customers or organizations adopting a new technology, results in an S-shaped curve (Ortt and Schoorman 2004) of the type shown in Figure 9.5. The shape of the curve is influenced by there being three different phases in the adoption process. Firstly, there is the 'Development Phase' during which the new technology is being identified, developed, and evolved into a feasible commercial proposition of appeal to potential users. This is followed by the 'Early Adoption Phase' during which the more innovative, risk-taking members of the adopting population are prepared to incorporate the new technology into their ongoing personal lives or business activities. Once the new technology has clearly demonstrated a benefit to the early adopters, the more conservative elements within

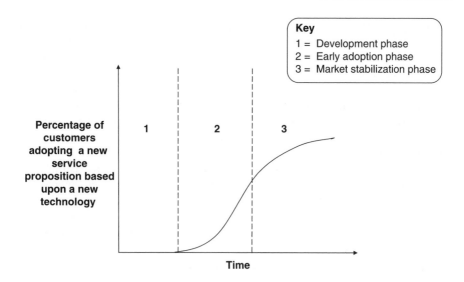

Figure 9.5   The innovation S-Curve

the adopting population will consider there are also few risks in becoming users. Ultimately, all of the later market entrants will be using the new technology and the proportion of users will plateau.

In assessing the scale of potential opportunities or threats associated with the expected S-Curve for a new technology an important issue is the speed with which the new customers opt to adopt the new technology (Brown 1992). One of the obstacles confronting a new technology is the cost of the new product or service relative to the price of goods available from suppliers based upon existing technologies. This is because new technology is often expensive to develop and will result in the first generation of new offerings being marketed at relatively high price. A very usual trend is that as supplier organizations gain experience of working with a new technology, this leads to a fall in production costs which is then reflected in declining prices. As prices decline this leads to the new technology becoming more affordable and new customers will enter the market. In those cases where it does not prove possible to reduce the cost of a technology, prices will remain high and the probable outcome is the number of customers will be much lower.

A long-established concept associated with the marketing of new products is the 'diffusion of innovation' curve. This proposes that potential customers can be divided into five groups known as innovators, early adopters, the early majority, the late majority, and laggards. The time taken for a potential customer to purchase a product will depend upon to which group an individual belongs. The first purchasers will be members of the innovator group. Having reviewed the launch of numerous high technology products, Geoffrey Moore (1991) proposed that the needs of each of these five groups are somewhat different. Innovators purchase the product because they wish to own the latest technology and are prepared to accept either performance problems with the new product. Early adopters will require to be persuaded that the product will work and thereby will offer a new way to fulfilling their vision of how to exploit technology. The early and late majority will postpone purchase until they are persuaded the product offers a functional benefit not provided by existing products. Laggards are price sensitive and hence wait until the product is virtually obsolete before entering the market.

Moore used case materials from a number of new technology launches to demonstrate that these different needs will require that the benefit which is offered to customers will need to change as suppliers seeks to 'cross the chasm' which exists between the different needs of each of the five customer types. As illustrated in Figure 9.6, Moore's chasm theory requires that unless the new technology delivers a benefit to reflect different market needs, at each phase along the diffusion of innovation curve there is the risk that new technology will not be attractive to a new group of customers. Most new technologies involve a very significant front-end investment and also expensive further investment to

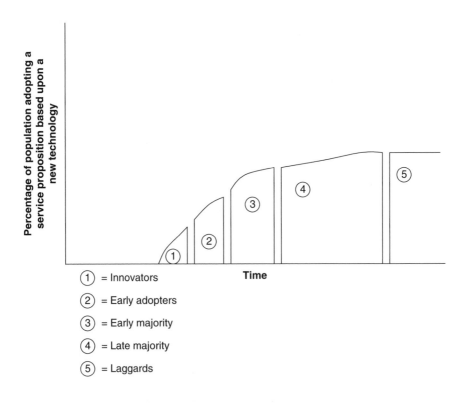

Figure 9.6   Service adoption chasms

scale up output whilst concurrently seeking ways of reducing the average cost of service delivery. This scenario represents both an opportunity and a threat for a public sector organization. The threat is that having invested in a new technology service demand is lower than expected and hence the cost of provision greatly exceeds revenue flows associated with service delivery. In contrast, the opportunity is that if the public sector agency develops a highly appealing, new, or improved service proposition, demand will increase leading to revenue flows well in excess of the cost of introducing the new technology.

Disruption

Throughout the twentieth century there have been a number of occasions when an entrepreneurial individual or organization has developed a new technology or perceived alternative application of an existing technology which eventually has severely impacted the performance of the current market leader(s) in a sector. As illustrated in Figure 9.7, in the majority of these cases highly destructive technological threats tend to originate from outside the current group of organizations which constitute the existing group of service providers.

New technology, if ignored by existing incumbent providers, provides an opportunity for new players to enter the market. This scenario was applicable in the private sector, for example, in case of digital technology being introduced into the world camera and photography market. From the invention of photography in the nineteenth century, the dominant players were organizations such as Eastman Kodak which specialized in the creation of low-cost, high-quality photography for consumer markets. Concurrently European firms such as Leica specialized in the use of high-level design and engineering skills to improve the quality of photographs by manufacturing better lenses and improving the internal mechanical systems through concepts such as the single and twin-reflex

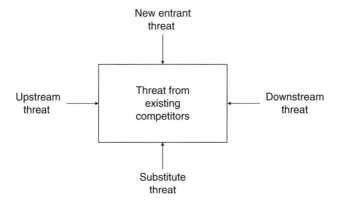

Figure 9.7   Sources of technological threat

cameras. By the 1960s, developments in the IT industry began to demonstrate that digitalization and reproduction of visual images offered new opportunities in relation to the future of the camera and photographic industries. Although Kodak recognized the threats posed by digitalization, their strategy seemed oriented towards protecting their dominance of the photographic film market and consequently led to poor performance in exploiting new technology. This apparent lack of interest by camera manufacturers in digital technology permitted Japanese firms such as Sony, Olympus, and Canon to launch digital cameras and eventually achieve market leadership.

In seeking to explain how apparently well-managed, large organizations permit competitors steal their business by exploiting a new technology, Christensen (1997) has used the phrase 'sustained innovation' to describe the orientation of most large corporations towards focusing their R&D efforts in introducing incremental improvements in existing products or organizational processes. The potential problem with this managerial philosophy is that the future performance of these firms is highly vulnerable to a new player entering the market offering a significantly different product or the introduction of a new, significantly more effective, organizational process (e.g. Dell's use of direct marketing of computers to US consumers while major firms continued to use a sales force or distribute their products through retail outlets).

The conventional theory of large firm failure is an event that occurs because an incumbent market leader fails to recognize the scale of the threat posed by a new firm entering their market and their speed of response is inadequate (Paap and Katz 2004). The alternative view posited by Christensen is that market leaders' desire to respond to changing market circumstances is often constrained by their existing major customers' insistence on key suppliers concentrating on further improvements being made to existing products. As a result, large firms may tend to focus on product or process innovation which can sustain the company's current market position in terms of staying ahead of other large organizations operating within the same market sector (Demuth 2008). Thus, for example, IBM did recognize the potential of minicomputers to provide smaller organizations with access to more affordable computer technology. However, the firm's existing large company clients articulated a desire for IBM to continue to develop the next generation of mainframe computers capable of offering even greater, more powerful, data processing capability. This behaviour permitted an MIT-trained entrepreneur, Ken Olsen, operating from an old textile mill in Massachusetts to launch the Digital Equipment Corporation (DEC). The new firm's success was based upon the strategy of making computers affordable to smaller organizations by supplying them with the first generation of minicomputers.

The implication of Christensen's theory in relation to the public sector is that an entrepreneurial service provider seeking to achieve significant growth in a sector where service provision is well-established should develop a very different service or revision of internal, organizational operational processes which would permit the offering of either superior or lower-cost service delivery. This approach is known as 'disruptive innovation'. The terminology is applicable to those situations where the new proposition is significantly different from the prevailing conventions being followed by other organizations such that the outcome is either the creation of a very different customer service usage pattern or the offering of a radically different service benefit proposition.

An emerging example of disruption is provided by the situation facing the public sector universities in the United Kingdom. These organizations are overtly focused upon managing the survival of their traditional classroom-based terrestrial operations in the face of Government cutbacks. As a consequence, they are tending to ignore the move by private sector organizations such as Kaplan and BPP. These firms are moving into the UK university markets and beginning to use online, distributed learning to offer lower-cost courses to students. This proposition is especially of appeal to those individuals who wish to study on a part-time basis because they are finding participation in full-time higher education unaffordable.

Christensen's concept of disruptive innovation being the primary cause of a major downturn in financial performance in the private sector is widely accepted by the academic world. Furthermore, there are a number of well-documented examples of poor organizational performance that exist which validate Christensen's viewpoint. Nevertheless, there is evidence to suggest his theory is not a universal explanation that can be applied to business failure in all industrial sectors (Cravens et al. 2002). For example, a review of case materials in most branded consumer goods sectors would suggest that only a minority of large company performance downturns can be explained by the advent of a disruptive technology. This is because the expertise which exists within these major corporations should permit an immediate response to a newly emerging market trend by utilizing their huge resources to mount a successful counter attack. This response may involve establishing of their own similar operation or alternatively, acquiring the entrepreneurial new market entrant before the latter organization can become a scale of threat sufficient to adversely impact future business performance. For example, when Canon first started to make inroads into the photocopier market with their lower price, desktop machine, Xerox clearly had both the technical expertise and dominant market position which would have permitted them to defeat their new enemy. Similarly, it seems inexplicable why the major firms in the branded foods and food service industries did not observe McDonald's early success and immediately opened their own chain of fast food outlets. Instead, they appear to have not only ignored the threat that posed by Ray Kroc, but also just remained on the sidelines as James McLamore and David Edgerton began to expand out from Miami with their Burger King operation.

Many examples of entrepreneurs defeating incumbent large organizations which did not involve disruption theory can be explained by the latter organizations having lost the flexibility and proactive culture upon which their global success had originally been based (Chaston 2009a). There appears to be no simple explanation of why a culture shift towards a totally conventional, passive, and non-innovative organization has occurred. One reason can be senior management apparently became fixated on believing that the strategy which was successful in the past will continue to serve the company well in the future, whereas in reality there is an urgent need to shift towards a more entrepreneurial organizational culture (Slevin and Covin 1990). Those leaders whose preference is to avoid implementing change would do well to reflect on Parnell et al.'s (2005) review of corporate failure and their observation that leaders 'should resist the notion that to-day's source of advantage will be eternal'. This type of leader as their organization moves from growth into market maturity seem to find both totally unacceptable and disruptive any actions by younger managers to persuade their organization to be more innovative. These younger individuals either then learn to accept the *status quo* to retain their jobs or alternatively quit and join a more entrepreneurial organization (Amabile et al. 1996).

Data Capture to Support Disruption

Case Aims: To illustrate how technology can be exploited to assist service provision productivity and identify new service provision opportunities.

In commenting upon the role of technology in the public sector, Mitchell (2001) suggests that with the growing need to 'do more with less' probably the only viable way of achieving this goal is through radical, usually disruptive, innovation. One opportunity is what he refers to as 'individual agility' which involves the wisest possible use of time by an organization's most expert staff and, where possible, developing new process implementation activities that can be utilized by less highly skilled employees. An example of using an expert's time efficiently is to use hand-held devices or digital camera that collect data from numerous field-level locations which can then be transmitted to a central hub where an expert can assess the nature of information received and determine appropriate next actions. This approach has very obvious and multiple applications by the police or other emergency services in the fulfilment of their assigned responsibilities. The same approach in health care, known as 'tele-medicine', permits a less qualified doctor to examine patients in remote locations and where a specialist second opinion is desired, the patient data can be sent via Web-streaming to a consultant at a major hospital hundreds of miles away. This same technology can also be used in a reverse sequence whereby the specialist can provide Web-based interactive training to numerous less qualified staff elsewhere within a public sector organization.

Ferguson et al. (2005) believe that the opportunity for all service organizations to identify new opportunities for technology-based innovation has been greatly enhanced by the advent of the Internet which permits access to huge volumes of data concerning new technological solutions from across the world and detailed breakdowns of customer service search and purchase behaviour.

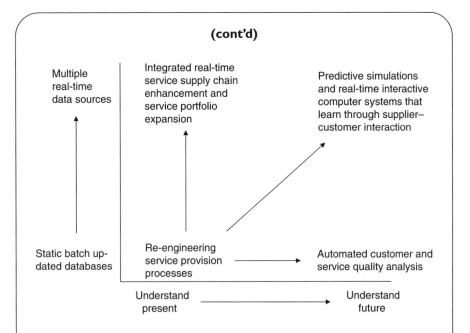

Figure 9.8   Managing service innovation

For public sector organizations to tap into this market does require an upgrading of the IT systems and staff's ability to utilize these systems to identify and implement new service provision offerings. There are two dimensions influencing the exploitation of data. One dimension is the degree to which the organization has moved from in-house, static database systems, to which only data from internal operations is added on a batch-processing basis, to a real-time knowledge management system which uses real-time access to multiple external databases to acquire new data. The other dimension is the degree to which data are used to analyse the past, review current operations, and assess future opportunities. As illustrated in Figure 9.8, the position of the organization on these two axes determines the degree to which highly innovative, possibly radical new service propositions can be identified and made available.

Once an effective real-time external data acquisition system is in place, the system can be used to direct questions towards potential and existing customers to determine their service needs and their perceptions of other, as yet, service requirements. Furthermore, by the use of remote sensors within the service provision process, the system can also track service activity in real-time. Subsequent computer-based analysis of these data can provide the basis for determining how the service delivery process might be enhanced (e.g. moving staff resources between areas of low- and high-service demand, identifying and correcting periods of service delivery downtime, etc.).

Internal
Competence

10

The aims of this chapter are to cover the issues of:

(1) Internal capabilities and the concept of RBV (resource-based view of the firm)

(2) The competences of an entrepreneurial organization

(3) The importance of the strategic competences

(4) Productivity and people management for enhancing performance

(5) Quality and TQM (Total Quality Management) into public sector organizations

(6) Managing knowledge and the utilization of new technology

Organizational capability

When one examines case materials about private sector service firms losing market share, what often emerges is customer needs have not undergone any real fundamental change. Instead, the organization has not remained alert to the need to continually seek ways of upgrading internal capabilities to sustain their strategy of superior service delivery of product based upon internal capability in areas such as productivity or quality. This failure to invest in a continuous search to improve organizational performance thereby provides other organizations with the opportunity to exploit their development of superior internal capabilities to deliver greater customer satisfaction (Chaston 2004).

The strategic philosophy concerning success based upon exploiting superior internal capability is known as the 'resource-based view of the firm' (or 'RBV'). Although the strategic importance of internal capability has been accepted by management academics since the 1950s, the concept gained much wider acceptance following Pralahad and Hamel's (1990) proposal that market leaders usually achieved and sustained their business performance by a strategy of consistently exploiting a 'core competence'. Their viewpoint is that exploiting a core competence provides the basis for supporting two possible strategic options. An organization can utilize a core competence to support the entrepreneurial activity of developing and launching new and/or improved products (e.g. Microsoft's original expansion into new areas of software such as their Access database system and regular updation of their existing portfolio of Windows products) and/or enter new market sectors (e.g. Honda's excellence in engineering capability to support their entry into the marine outboard engine market). Alternatively an organization may acquire a core competence in the entrepreneurial development and implementation of superior operational technologies which permits the organization to compete on the basis of price. This latter approach is the reason why major supermarket chains in the United States lost market share to Wal-Mart who exploited superior capabilities in the areas of procurement and logistics as the basis for offering much lower prices to the US consumer.

The role of most public sector providers is the provision of services. Unlike the private sector, unless there is pressure from Government for privatization or outsourcing, there is rarely a need for a primary strategic aim of outcompeting other organizations by achieving differentiation from other providers through superior service delivery. Nevertheless, a key strategic aim for most public sector agencies is to achieve Government-specified performance indicators in order to receive ongoing funding. Hence, in determining an organizational strategy related to this aim, the RBV view is an extremely useful managerial concept. This is because it permits the public sector strategist to determine which areas of organizational capability should receive priority in order to even more effectively meet Government service output and service quality targets in the future (Bryson et al. 2007).

Entrepreneurial competence

The RBV of the firm posits that superior performance is achieved by the organization implementing a strategy based upon acquiring unique capabilities that add value, are scarce, and difficult to imitate. Edith Penrose was one of the first academic researchers to identify the importance of the relationship between strategy, performance, and internal capabilities of the organization (Augier and Teece 2007). She perceived key internal capabilities available to an organization from its own resources, especially in service-based industries, are managerial expertise and experience. Her research was concerned with managers in general. In relation to entrepreneurial activities, she merely identified that certain leaders are more able to exploit new opportunities because they exhibit a greater level of 'dynamic capability'.

Droege and Dong (2008) have suggested that a unique competence of managers within entrepreneurial organizations is their ability to identify and exploit unique ideas. This is because these individuals are more able to recognize new opportunities either through intuitive assessment or by drawing upon their personal knowledge base. Individuals and organizations that exhibit an entrepreneurial orientation are more willing to act independently of prevailing sector conventions, explore new ideas, and seek to discover new ways of delivering customer satisfaction. Covin and Slevin (1989) have proposed that this orientation, which provides the basis for exhibiting unique competences, consists of five dimensions: autonomy, innovativeness, proactiveness, risk-taking, and competitive aggressiveness.

The attribute of autonomy refers to the ability to implement independent actions in the identification and execution of a new idea. Sustaining autonomy in large hierarchical organizations is often difficult. This is one reason that entrepreneurial behaviour occurs somewhat rarely in public sector organizations. Innovativeness describes the degree with which an organization utilizes a strategy of exploiting new ideas that can provide the basis for developing new products, services, and processes. Even when the specific actions needed to pursue an opportunity are not yet clear, inaction is to be avoided. This is because even in uncertain environments, action provides the greatest opportunity to achieve gains that ensure the ongoing survival of the organization. As identified by Covin et al. (2006), organizations exhibiting an emergent, less structured approach to defining strategy usually achieve better performance than those which follow a more structured, highly planned approach to strategic management.

Proactiveness is distinct from both innovativeness and competitive aggressiveness. It is a critical, core dimension of entrepreneurial competence because it reflects a willingness to seize opportunities well before these are apparent to other organizations. The proactiveness dimension can shape the organization's performance relative to external environment conditions, influence trends, and in some situations, create demand (Lumpkin and Dess, 1996). Proactive strategies focus on anticipating and acting upon opportunities. Proactive organizations are frequently the first to introduce new or improved services.

Virtually all strategic decisions involve uncertain outcomes. Some decisions, however, involve greater risk because the management may not yet fully understand the nature of an identified new opportunity or the scale of resources necessary to ensure a successful outcome for an innovative project. Entrepreneurial organizations are thought to be more prepared to take strategic risks because of a willingness to accept greater levels of uncertainty about the outcome of their actions. Competitive aggressiveness describes a firm's emphasis in responding to competitors' actions. Unlike proactiveness, competitive aggressiveness differs from the former because it usually involves reacting to an identified change. Additionally, competitive aggressiveness can be present in both conventional and entrepreneurial organizations. Hence, there is some dispute among academics about whether this organizational competence is unique or necessary for an organization engaged in implementing an entrepreneurial strategy.

One possible reason that some organizations fail to exhibit strong entrepreneurial competence can be explained in terms of the existence of 'resource stickiness' (Mishina et al. 2004). The commonness forms of resource stickiness are to be found in an organization's human and financial assets. Stickiness can arise for two reasons. In some cases, the organization lacks sufficient organizational capacity to re-allocate resources away from existing operational activities and re-assign these to more entrepreneurial endeavours. In order to overcome this obstacle, organizations wishing to sustain long-term growth through innovation do need to invest in the creation of a certain degree of 'organizational slack' to support the implementation of new activities when emerging entrepreneurial opportunities become apparent. The other cause of resource stickiness is that, although slack resources do exist within the organization, senior management lacks an adequate level of 'entrepreneurial ambition'. As a consequence, available spare capacity is not allocated to pursue innovation. Instead senior managers allocate slack resources to less risky activities such as improving the efficiency of existing organizational processes.

Key competences

Many of the published articles about the influence of internal capabilities on the strategic success of highly successful entrepreneurial firms tend to be based upon anecdotal, usually qualitative evidence, concerning observations of a very limited number of organizations. The risks associated with using such findings are the data may not have sufficient validity to provide the basis for generalizations that are applicable to defining which competences are fundamental key factors and critical to implementing an entrepreneurial strategy. To overcome this potential problem, Chaston and Mangles (1997) used a number of published studies on competences associated with business growth to evolve a composite qualitative model summarizing the key competences shared by these various research studies. The model shown in Figure 10.1 provided the basis for a large-scale quantitative study of UK firms in both the manufacturing and services sectors. Discriminant function analysis was applied to the survey data which permitted the creation of a quantitative model describing how variations in capability can be expected to influence performance. This model demonstrated that there are certain important internal capabilities, which are of either a strategic or operational nature, that strongly influence performance in entrepreneurial organizations.

The entry point of the model summarized in Figure 10.1 is the critical capability of the organization to be able to identify emerging opportunities and to evolve an effective strategic response. Day and Schoemaker (2005) have suggested that exploitation of this competence often requires an ability to identify weak signals in the external environment. In commenting on weak signal identification, MacKay and McKiernan (2004) posit that conventional strategic planning tools are somewhat ineffective. Furthermore, they feel that individuals who exhibit the skill of recognizing weak signals seem to exhibit an unusually highly developed intuitive ability to identify new opportunities and to

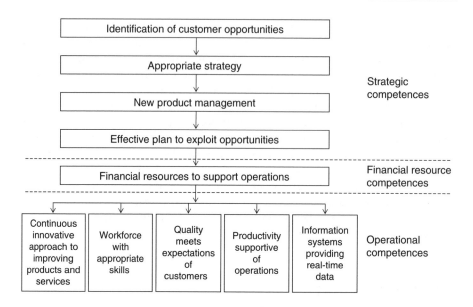

Figure 10.1   A qualitative model of organizational competences to support and deliver an entrepreneurial strategy

evolve entrepreneurial responses well ahead of more conservatively orientated individuals.

Exploiting a newly identified opportunity involves developing a strategic concept to service the opportunity in a way which will be superior to any existing service offering. The model shown in Figure 10.1 indicates the need for involvement in some form of planning activity to assist in the assessment of the validity of the actions is necessary to successfully exploit an identified opportunity. This conclusion is supported by Khan and Manopichetwattan (1989). These researchers found that in their large-scale study of manufacturing firms, non-innovative manufacturers exhibited a limited understanding of strategy, had poor planning skills, and lacked the ability to implement an integrated response to changing environments.

The degree to which service provision performance has actually been enhanced by innovation can range from announcing the launch of 'a new, improved service', which is essentially only marginally different from existing services, through to the development of a highly significant new proposition (e.g. the iPad). The scale of change and the frequency with which improved services are launched by organizations in the private sector vary between industries (Biggadike 1979). In mature, low-technology markets service change may be quite minimal. To a significant degree this situation reflects that there are few opportunities to radically alter the sector's base technology. This can be contrasted with growing, high-technology markets such as telecommunications and electronics where ongoing advances in technology lead to the frequent launch of the next generation of services (Montoya-Weiss and Calantone 1994).

The other critical strategic competence is having sufficient funds or access to adequate borrowing facilities to support innovation and change programmes. There is a common adage used by bankers and venture capitalist that 'actual plans take twice as long to implement and actual costs will be twice as high'. Parks' (1977) research supports this perspective. He found a very common scenario among entrepreneurial organizations is new product projects frequently encounter cost over runs, generate less than forecasted sales revenue, and take much longer than expected to progress through to market launch. Given this situation, there is a critical need for entrepreneurial organizations in both the private and public sector to have sufficient financial resources to be able to survive any problems which may emerge during the development of a new product (Hogarty 1993).

The source of the funds to support innovation in the public sector can come from various sources including retained cash surpluses, cash inflows from service provision, or external borrowing. Public sector bodies usually face certain constraints over achieving and retaining autonomous control over their financial resources. This is because in many cases, provisional spending plans are defined by the Government for the 3–5-year period that the elected party remains in power. Furthermore, actual permitted spending is often only specified for the next 12 months. Additionally, legislation often exists that restricts how funds can be utilized (e.g. the revenue from the sale of council houses not being permitted to be re-invested in building new public housing in the United Kingdom). In some cases, there is the added problem that year-end surpluses may be taken back by the funding body. This latter situation can lead to waste due to emergence of a managerial philosophy of 'buy anything you can now' to avoid funds having to be returned or alternatively the next annual budget being reduced by the amount equal to the balance of unspent monies at the end of the prior financial year.

Operational competences

Chaganti and Chaganti (1983) determined that the highest level of success among organizations is linked to the utilization of a strategy of offering a broad range of products or services, exploiting innovation to frequently update their product line, and responding positively to market demands for product or service customization. They noted, however, that innovation may have an equally important role in being used to implement improved process changes inside the organization that can result in improved productivity. The usual focus of process innovation will be to achieve one or more of the three key strategic aims of reducing costs, improving quality, and saving time. Although an entrepreneurial manager will probably act as project leader in guiding an internal process upgrade programme, ultimately success is critically dependent upon involvement of other members of the organization's workforce.

Laforet and Tann (2006) concluded that in relation to sustaining business growth in entrepreneurial UK companies, there was much greater reliance on process rather than new product innovation. Organizational activities they identified included the utilization of new computer-based technologies and the automation of process technologies. The conclusion about the dominant role of process innovation in this one sector, however, should not be considered as a generalization that can necessarily be applied to other sectors of industry. For example, in the case of the US timber industry, Wagner and Hansen (2005) posited that process innovation was more important among large firms and that product innovation was a more certain path for achieving business growth among smaller companies.

Fostering Employee Innovation

Case Aims: To illustrate the actions required to create a more innovative, results-orientated public sector workforce.

The Virginia Blood Services (VBS) collect, test, and distribute blood and blood components to the patients of the Richmond, Virginia metropolitan area. In the late 1980s, the Board recognized that changing technology and growing demand required new thinking about managing organizational processes in the future. A skills assessment programme was introduced to assist employees determine their existing capability gaps. Meetings were identified as being non-productive so a 'managing effective meetings' training scheme was launched. Team membership skills were also considered poor and hence training in this area was introduced. Key learning aims for participants included (i) adhering to established priorities, (ii) seeking others' opinions, listening, and then responding, (iii) using plans that makes employees part of the team (iv) taking responsibility for identifying and resolving problems, (v) prioritizing activities and focusing on those that will best achieve the organization's goals, and (vi) examining costs and the resulting financial impact of implemented actions on the organization (Bak et al. 1995).

New multi-functional teams were created to foster innovation and change. Achieving integration of perspectives required careful attention to the composition of each team. Examples of the interdepartmental teams are provided by (i) the blood supply team which had members from donor recruitment, blood collection, laboratory, distribution, and finance, (ii) the employee relations team that drew staff from a number of departments with the aim of assisting management in developing guidelines for improving rapport between employees and managers, and (iii) the hospital relations team which was constituted of individuals from blood collection, laboratory, and distribution to facilitate an effective relationship with client hospitals.

(cont'd)

The first year of team-based innovation at VBS demonstrated evidence of improved communication, an increase in morale, enhanced productivity, and more effective problem-solving capability. Hence, the team concept was widened in Year 2 and all were assigned a common objective of (i) Know your own job well, (ii) Know what 'quality' means in your job and department, (iii) Know more than your job, (iv) Know what other people in the organization do, and (v) Keep raising the standards.

The Board's assessment of the team-based approach led to the conclusion that to foster innovation and change there was the need to establish the following common, specific organizational aims:

(1) Smash the hierarchy and convince employees that their jobs are as vital as the chief executive's.

(2) Ask board members to help set goals and plot strategies. Teams are encouraged to utilize board members as resources.

(3) Tap the grass-roots knowledge by encouraging all employees to try new ideas and clear the way for ideas and changes to move up.

(4) Establish a sense of mission so that every decision flows from the viewpoint of delivering the organization's mission.

(5) Set goals and reward employees for progress in reaching each objective and focus the annual performance appraisal on an assessment of individuals' team membership skills.

Productivity

The primary role of any private sector organization is to convert inputs into outputs that can be sold for a profit. Survival can only be achieved when total output can be sold at a price that exceeds total operating costs. The difference between price and costs can be described in terms of the profit generated. This profit describes the 'added value' achieved by the workforce. Productivity is a measurement of added value. The importance of productivity is reflected by the fact that many Governments consider data on the productivity of firms in their country as a key indicator of the competitive capabilities of their respective economies (Mayhew and Neely 2006). One way of determining the effectiveness of a company is to compare productivity in relation to that achieved by other organizations (Lawton 1999). To permit comparisons between firms, productivity is usually expressed in terms of added value per employee. This figure is calculated by dividing annual profit by the number of employees.

Given the absence of the profit concept in most public sector organizations, the survival of these types of organizations is based upon the revenue received for outputs not exceeding cost of inputs. Under these circumstances, productivity can only be assessed in relation to fund inflows per employee. In terms of assessing public sector productivity in some cases the assessor can compare one unit with another in the same sector (e.g. comparing hospital productivity). In other cases this type of comparative data may not be available. In this situation, the researcher will be required to make comparisons with similar job roles or organizational service provision in the private sector. This potential drawback with this latter approach is that the researcher may encounter obstacles in making direct comparisons because of differences in the working environment between the two sectors (e.g. rule-based definitions of task and more hierarchical structures in the public sector). Haque et al. (2000) point out that this methodological problem requires great care when examining the results of their own and other academic's research studies on public sector productivity.

From their study, Haque et al. did conclude that the productivity of public sector workers does appear to be lower than their counterpart in the private sector. These researchers did note that one factor of influence was public sector employees work in a much less flexible environment which reduces their ability to introduce new approaches to enhance personal output. A second factor is that as public sector pay on average is lower than in the private sector this can mean public sector organizations may be unable to employ the most productive individuals. This is because these latter sorts of individuals will tend to prefer to work in the private sector. A third issue is that during economic downturns, Governments have a tendency to increase the public sector workforce as a solution for reducing unemployment levels. As a consequence, public sector organizations can become overmanned and also employ less competent individuals. Interestingly, Haque et al. (2000) did find evidence that when there are minor reductions in the size of the workforce in some public sector organizations, there is a tendency for productivity to rise. This outcome possibly reflects the departure of lower quality of employees and a reduction in the level of overmanning that has previously existed.

More recently, the UK consultancy company Know D'Arcy surveyed 1855 supervisors including in Local Government and also carried out observations in the workplace (Hope 2010). This study concluded that council staff spent 32 per cent of their time being productive whereas this figure rose to 44 per cent in the private sector. The reason for low productivity in the public sector organizations was attributed to poor supervision and unwillingness of managers confronting poor performers or even establishing what good performance actually means within the organization. Another identified influencing factor is public sector managers need to divorce themselves from the belief that significant improvements cannot be achieved without investing in IT. The view of the consulting firm is there is a greater need to review what people are doing and to develop higher levels of personal accountability for staff performance so that individuals know what is expected of them in the implementation of assigned job roles. The conclusions reached in the study were criticized by the General Secretary of the United Kingdom's largest public sector union, Unison. In his view, a fundamental flaw in the study is the assumption that one can compare productivity in the public sector with employees in a private sector such as in a manufacturing operation.

In many organizations, labour costs are often the highest single area of expenditure. For organizations seeking to achieve higher productivity, there are a number of capability enhancement options available which can save time or reduce direct costs. Gunasekaran et al. (2000) has proposed that in many cases, organizations can make very cost-effective productivity gains by focusing upon improving workflows. Typically this will involve simple actions such as improving procurement practices, identifying and removing bottlenecks in process operations, and investing in upgrading workforce skills. The researchers also reviewed the alternative solution of replacing employees with machines. Their conclusion is the approach should only be considered where the combined costs of purchase and operation of the new equipment greatly exceed the costs of continuing to use employees to undertake the task. Aris et al. (2000) reached the somewhat different conclusion about investing in advanced technology to reduce labour inputs. In their view, this can be an extremely effective strategy through which to improve productivity. These authors did note, however, that obstacles such as lack of awareness of the latest technology, an inability to select the best solution, or inadequate workforce skills can lead to actual cost/benefits achieved being much poorer than had been expected at the time of reaching the decision to invest in new technology.

People

Large private sector firms frequently claim their employees are the company's most valuable asset. This perspective relies upon the view that in an increasingly competitive world where most companies have access to the same available knowledge about customer needs and exploitable service delivery technologies, the only key difference may often be the superior intellect, work skills, and commitment of an organization's workforce (Hoffman 2000). Superior employee competence is considered as an especially valid perspective in the service sector. This is because in many of these markets there are minimal differences between the services offered by suppliers. Consequently, exploiting the skills of employees is often only way to ensure customers receive a service experience superior to that available from a competitor (Fuchs et al. 2000). An example of this approach to differentiation is provided by Singapore Airlines where the capability of their staff has helped the airline to be regularly rated as one of the world's best international carriers.

Another influencing factor in relation to greater reliance upon superior employee competence is organizations' increasing recognition of the strategic benefits of relationship marketing (Gupta and Singhal 1993). This strategic philosophy has emerged in B2B markets because factors such as shorter product life cycles, increasingly complex technologies, rapidly changing customer buying patterns, and increasingly sophisticated customers have necessitated that to survive the competitive aggressiveness of the market many organizations now need to work in close partnerships with both key suppliers and customers (Webster 1992). In more competitive and turbulent B2C markets, companies have recognized that the lifetime value of each customer in terms of their total purchases means there is a need to focus on customer retention. This new approach involves an orientation in which to create stronger customer loyalty employees have to redirect their efforts away from generating the next sale to focus on building a long-term relationship with the customer (Gronroos 1990).

In his assessment of marketing practices in the public sector, Laing (2003) concluded that in most cases PSOs were still exhibiting a transactional marketing orientation. Given that many of the services provided by the public sector involve repeat delivery of the same service to customers over time (e.g. health care, welfare payments), there clearly exists significant opportunity from adopting a relationship orientation. This shift in orientation has the potential to lead to much more effective interaction between the provider and the customer which in turn can enhance customers' perceptions over service quality. Although the outcome of relationship marketing providing closer, more effective interactions with customers seems intuitively appealing, PSOs do need to carefully assess the implications of this change in marketing orientation prior to implementation. This is because as evidenced by data from the private sector, inappropriate use of relationship marketing can tie the organization into unproductive, more expensive, or even damaging relationships (De Weaver et al. 2005).

A fundamental aspect of Human Resource Management (HRM) theory is that the capability of employees to fulfil their assigned job role is critically influenced by their level of job satisfaction, motivation, and commitment to the organization. In most of the studies which have been undertaken involving public sector employees, the available evidence would tend to suggest that most individuals achieve lower job satisfaction, are less motivated, and have a lower commitment to their organization than their counterparts in the private sector (Young et al. 1998). The majority of the studies which have reached this conclusion have been done in the United States, and to a somewhat slightly lesser degree in Europe. There has been discussion in the academic literature that these outcomes reflect the influence of the Protestant Work Ethic in which peoples' self-assessment of the superiority of work quality in the private sector is influenced by cultural values which focus on personal achievement such as income, ownership of material goods, and social status. Under these circumstances, one would expect higher job satisfaction in public sector organizations in societies exhibiting Confucian values. However, studies in Singapore (Aryee 1992) and more recently in South Korea (Kim 2005) provided data suggesting that even in these countries public sector job satisfaction and motivation are lower than in the private sector. These researchers concluded that public sector employees perceive their private sector counterparts in these two countries are better able to achieve their career ambitions and are engaged in much more interesting job roles.

In commenting upon conclusions reached in research on public sector employee job satisfaction, Aryee (1992) raised the issue that some studies have tended to focused solely on managerial and professional staff. He, therefore, examined the issues of employee attitudes of blue-collar public sector employees. His conclusion was that in many cases, the public sector employees were more or equally satisfied and more or as equally motivated as their counterparts in the private sector. One possible reason for this situation is most public sector organizations are more highly unionized than many modern day private sector operations. As a consequence, blue-collar public sector workers are able to utilize their membership of a union to ensure their work environment contains fewer autocratic managers, lesser threats over job losses, and more employee-friendly attitude towards behaviour such as taking sick leave or time off to handle personal or family-related problems.

Building Better Managers

Case Study: To illustrate the benefits of succession planning in public sector organizations.

Due to population ageing, the percentage of younger employees is decreasing while a large number of older staff are retiring. In Henrico, Virginia, the County Authority had 76 retirees in 2000 compared with only 46, one decade earlier in 1990. Furthermore, 44 per cent of senior management will be eligible for retirement by 2008. Hence, the County was forced to implement succession planning in response to (i) the loss of intellectual capital in key positions as upper managers become eligible to retire in the near future and (ii) an inadequate number of lower-level managers with skills necessary to move into higher-level positions (Holinsworth 2004).

Phase one of succession plan trained supervisors in how to guide employees through a professional development process using individualized learning plans. Phase two provided information to senior managers on strategies for developing subordinate managers for the purpose of succession planning. Senior managers were trained to understand effective succession planning in terms of (i) identifying key positions for succession, (ii) identifying key position competences, (iii) developing subordinates, and (iv) assessing subordinates' skills development needs. The timing of succession actions is critical because promoted managers need to become productive more rapidly than in the past. This is because managerial roles have grown more complex, thereby requiring individuals to have higher-level qualifications and a wider skills set.

Unlike some organizations that have a 'select then develop' system, the County decided it was important to make staff development available to all interested employees. Gap analysis was used to assist employees specify personal development goals. In terms of then assisting these individuals,

(cont'd)

fortunately the County had already established a Leadership Development Program Skills. This programme covers communication, conflict resolution/ negotiation, decision-making, customer orientation, employee development, financial management, interpersonal relations, organizational awareness, managing futures, performance management, accountability and integrity, strategic management, and team leadership. It was also decided that potential candidates for promotion needed to widen their experience and hence a learning programme was arranged to provide management experience of a different division within the County operations.

In the 2 years prior to the programme's implementation, there were 7 upper management openings but only two were filled with internal candidates. In the first 2 years of the new initiative, all 8 upper management openings were filled internally. Todate there have been 16 upper management openings, with 15 filled through internal promotions. A key factor for the programme's success has been the strong visible support of Henrico County's County Manager. He is committed to the importance of sharing knowledge and enhancing the organization's intellectual capital. This individual is also committed to closely linking HRM plans to the organization's overall strategic plan.

Quality

During the 1970s, many Western manufacturers, fighting to sustain profitability in the face of both inflation and refusal by militant unions to permit revisions in working practices, passively allowed the topic of quality to disappear from their organizational radar screens. Countries such as Japan, quick to realize the vulnerability that this situation created, moved into world markets offering higher quality, reliable products at reasonable prices. One of the critical competences developed within leading Japanese companies was the exploitation of the concept known as Total Quality Management (TQM). The essential basis of the competence is to reject the conventional perspective or retro-resolution of quality problems once these have become apparent in the finished product. Instead, TQM is based upon a commitment to identify and then resolve at source stage any problems that might cause a decline in quality standards. Such actions are not just implemented across the organization, but also within the component supplier organizations upstream in the supply chain (Anderson, and Sohal 1999).

It was only after inflation began to decline and unions began to adopt a more co-operative attitude, that European and US firms have been able to attempt to match the level of quality achieved in Japanese corporations. Despite well-documented evidence from the private sector that poor implementation of TQM can reduce staff morale, lower productivity, and even lead to a decline in quality, some public sector agencies embraced the philosophy as providing a certain and major improvement in their organization's operations. Their apparent lack of understanding of the complexities of implementation sometimes led to failure and highly adverse cost/benefit outcomes (Rago 1994). In reviewing the major problems in introducing orthodox TQM into government organizations, Swiss (1992) proposes that fundamental failures included (i) issues regarding customer identification, (ii) contradictions about customer expectations, and (iii) that although the general public receives the service, the Government departments who are the customers paying for services have very different expectations concerning the costs of service delivery. As a consequence, public sector organizations face the dilemma of needing to deliver satisfaction to two customer groups usually having differing expectations over service quality. As noted by Rago (1994), however, this is less of a problem in relation to the use of TQM inside the public sector organization. This is because both supplier and service users have an understanding of the issues of how budget constraints will serve to limit the feasibly achievable level of delivered service quality.

Another problem which Swiss feels may exist is that the major focus of TQM in the private sector is on the improvement of work processes in manufacturing environments. In the public sector, employees are attempting to apply TQM to the delivery of services. As the delivery of services is usually a labour intensive activity, achieving understanding and sustaining equality of service delivery across a large public sector organization may often prove difficult. In the private sector, the company that delivers superior quality may achieve a higher market share resulting in increased revenue and profitability. The degree of clarity provided by financial performance achievements is usually absent from public sector scenario. This may mean it is not clear to employees what are the ultimate goals of their organization's TQM initiative. A related issue is whether TQM should be used to improve the quality of service for existing customers versus utilizing improvement measures in overall organizational processes to increase the number of customers served. Rago has suggested that the issue of increased quality or expansion of services needs resolving by senior management before a TQM initiative is introduced into a public sector organization.

Radin and Coffee (1993) concluded there are a number of attributes of the US public sector that create pressures that prevent or at least complicate the implementation of TQM. These include:

(1) TQM places an emphasis on strategic planning and decision-making that have a proactive quality. Many public sector agencies live in a world of annual budgeting, time-limited spending authorizations, and frequent changes in political leadership. These conditions usually lead to disruptive environment which is not supportive of a successful, enduring TQM programme.

(2) Quality and the customer are two values that are crucial in the TQM perspective. For many public sector organizations, however, both of these values are problematic. This is because of the multiple accountability mechanisms that are at play within democratic political systems.

(3) Fragmentation which can arise within inter-governmental systems. Few national public agencies actually deliver services to individuals within the society. Instead, the national agency is a part of a complex product delivery chain that involves other national agencies, local agencies, charitable organizations, and in some cases, even the private sector. Hence, achieving a unified approach to goal determination and service quality standards is a much more complex task than in most private sector organizations. In some cases, fragmentation is heightened because some agencies within a delivery network have only adopted TQM as a mechanism to enhance image without having any genuine commitment to implement changes in their organizational processes.

Lesson from New Mexico

Case Aims: To illustrate some of the issues associated with enhancing the chances for the success of a public sector TQM programme.

Cox (1995) holds the view that TQM initiatives in the public sector can be successful as long as project leaders recognize the public sector is a more complex environment, that top-down initiatives will fail, and just developing a customer focus is not enough. In his view, the concept of quality must be redefined before it can be applied in many public agencies. These perspectives were developed from observing the implementation of TQM projects in the United States such as a state-wide initiative in New Mexico which commenced in the early 1990s.

At the outset, two critical decisions were made by the New Mexico Governor: namely pilot programmes will be used to validate process before any scheme is expanded into all major agencies and current budgets will be used with no additional monies being made available to support the pilot tests. In selecting agencies for the pilot, some of these entities (e.g. the state printing office) are very similar to private sector operations and hence definitions of desired quality were relatively simple. The issue of finding an appropriate agency where quality is more difficult to define was resolved by the Public Defenders Department volunteering to participate in the project.

Lessons learned from the pilot stage included enthusiasm and excitement generated by the introductory training began to fade as people realized how much work is involved in TQM programmes. Hence, sustaining motivation and employee morale requires senior managers who have above average leadership skills. Additionally, success will only occur when the agency is able to define 'quality' in a way which is acceptable and understandable among both customers and employees. The other lesson is the need to develop an effective system for monitoring the performance of a TQM-orientated organization. This is necessary in order to permit continuous assessment of performance and to ensure that where quality gaps would emerge employees would be able to determine the cause of the inadequate outcome.

(cont'd)

On the basis of observing projects such as the New Mexico project, Cox has concluded that TQM projects in the public sector are almost certain to fail if the following errors are made:

(1) Only a soft or imprecise definition of 'quality' is achieved causing a lack of understanding of the performance aims sought by a TQM initiative.

(2) The agency makes some initial improvements in organizational processes but fails to adopt a 'continuous process improvement' orientation and hence ongoing efforts to achieve further upgrades in service quality do not occur.

(3) Senior management fails to act as strong supporters of TQM.

(4) Impatience sets because the positive outcomes associated with TQM can often take a significant period of time to become apparent.

(5) Where possible TQM should be introduced by relying upon existing financial budgets. In those cases, where 'special funding' is made available to accelerate the project in order to claim immediate success, once this special funding comes to an end, there is a tendency for the ongoing TQM programme to be inadequately resourced.

Information management

Data stored in a person's mind are known as tacit information. Providing others with access to such knowledge usually requires a 1:1 interaction between individuals. This contrasts with explicit information which is stored in a form accessible to others (e.g. in a written report or computer file). The complex nature of operations in large organizations has long caused their managers to recognize the critical importance of ensuring information in an explicit form so that it can be accessed by others. Smaller organizations, however, tend to adopt a somewhat more cavalier approach to the management of information. Much is stored in a tacit form, which means employees may be forced to reach decisions without having an adequate understanding of the situation for which they have been assigned responsibility (Chaston 2004).

Kotzab et al. (2006) concluded that information management was critical to firms in B2B markets when seeking to exploit innovation within the supply chain of which they are a part. Tanabe et al. (2005) reached very similar conclusions about the critical importance of managing information as the basis for optimizing the performance of entrepreneurial service firms. The potential importance of effective information management as a key competence that can provide the basis for achieving a competitive advantage has been greatly assisted by the advent of ever more hardware and software systems that permit the high-speed analysis of large quantities of data. In recent years, this technology has led to the emergence of integrated Customer Relationship Management (CRM) and Enterprise Resource Planning (ERP) applications by firms such as SAP and Oracle to assist both faster understanding of customer needs and optimizing the efficiency of internal processes across the entire organization (Coltman 2007). One group of institutions in the private sector which have greatly benefitted from exploiting CRM systems is banking. This is because banks which have used CRM to compile data on customer expectations versus actual experience have been able to build stronger long-term customer loyalty than their less IT-orientated competitors.

The core function of a successful CRM strategy is to create a sustainable competitive advantage by better understanding and communication being exploited to deliver greater added value to existing customers and by attracting new customers. Organizations which have possibly benefitted the most from a key competence in exploiting CRM technology are those which utilized automated information management systems to warehouse and then analysed real-time data generated by the activities of their online customers (Thompson et al. 2003). Using segmentation tools, these organizations can analyse customer data in relation to dimensions such as socio-demographics, variation in demand for products/services, and pricing sensitivity as the basis for evolving more innovative approaches to presenting new, customized online offerings. Additionally, by analysing changing real-time purchasing patterns, these organizations are able to develop more accurate forecasts of future demand. This improved accuracy will reduce operating costs because the level of lost sales due to 'out-of-stocks' or not having sufficient staff to provide services during peak periods of demand scenarios can be avoided.

Amazon.com is a leading example of how CRM competence has assisted the company in building a globally successful online brand (Javalgi et al. 2005). Amazon achieves an additional sense of community with consumer by providing shared buyer experiences in the form of customer feedback and recommendations based on analysing individual customer's purchase behaviour. Furthermore, by Website customization, such as Amazon's One Click service, the customer is provided access to faster order processing based upon the retention of credit card and delivery information from prior purchases.

Canada is possibly the leader in electronic Government implementation followed by Singapore, the United States, Australia, Denmark, the United Kingdom, Finland, Hong Kong, Germany, and Ireland (Chen et al. 2007). Unlike the traditional bureaucratic model in public sector organizations where information flows only vertically and rarely between departments, electronic Government links new technology with internal legacy systems, and in turn links Government information infrastructures externally with everything digital. As a consequence, electronic Government offers a potential to dramatically increase access to information and services for citizens whilst in many cases also reduces operational costs. Nevertheless, it does need to be recognized that implementing successful e-government projects is not a simple task. Heeks (2000), for example, estimates about 20–25 per cent of such projects are either never implemented or abandoned immediately after implementation, and a further 33 per cent partially fail in terms of falling short of major goals or the emergence of significant undesirable outcomes.

In many public sector service delivery systems between the Government and the citizen there exist other agencies with delegated authority to deliver services on a geographically restricted basis. As noted by Michael and Taylor (2001), the degree to which timescales and service delivery targets set by Governments are actually met is often totally reliant on the e-capabilities of these second-tier agencies. For example, in 1997, the UK prime minister announced that 25 per cent of all government services in the United Kingdom would be delivered electronically within 5 years. To determine the degree to which this target would be met, Michael and Taylor researched e-government delivery among District Councils. In the United Kingdom, these organizations are responsible for delivering services such as education, policing, and social services. The researchers found that 4 years on from the prime minister's stated e-target aims, only about 50 per cent of the District Council had achieved a strategic integration of their IT and less than 20 per cent appeared to able to deliver online services. It appeared that outcome reflected an orientation within District Councils to concern themselves primarily with implementing internal electronic service delivery initiatives, such as e-mail and establishing Intranet sites. Only a very small minority of these organizations were engaged in externally focused developments, such as 'one stop' online service provision or the operation of call centres. Two probable causes of this outcome are (a) the limited level of incremental funds Central Government has prepared to provide the District Councils to cover the capital costs associated with creating e-government systems and (b) outside of major cities, the electronic communications infrastructure needed to provide citizens with high speed Internet access has still not been put into place.

Knowledge competence

A key driving force which has influenced performance of organizations since the beginning of the Industrial Revolution is the discovery and application of new knowledge as the basis for innovation in existing industries or leading to the creation of totally new industries. In the twentieth century, there was an exponential increase in the rate of new scientific and technological breakthroughs which occurred. Current evidence would suggest this exponential pace of new knowledge creation will be sustained in the twenty-first century. The implications of this scenario are that the exploitation of new knowledge will remain a critical competence within organizations seeking to sustain long-term growth (Sheehan 2005).

Syed-Ikhsan and Fytton (2004) proposed that management has the responsibility to identify where knowledge resides in the organization and also to design strategies that can promote the use of this knowledge. These authors believe management should allow employees to access all kind of knowledge, regardless of whether the knowledge is available in or outside the organization. They concluded from a study of knowledge management in Malaysian public sector agencies that the level of knowledge transfer is highly correlated with the existence of a sharing culture and the quality of knowledge assets available within the organization. Although they theorized that the behaviour of individual employees could act as a barrier to knowledge transfer, they were unable to demonstrate any correlation between the level of individualism within public sector organizations and knowledge transfer performance.

The researchers' conclusions are not compatible with other studies in knowledge management. For example, Riege (2005) concluded that the individual employees can help in successful knowledge transfer. Some of the barriers he identified included:

(1) Work pressures leading to a lack of time to share knowledge;

(2) Fear that sharing may reduce or jeopardize job security;

(3) Low awareness of the value and benefit of possessed knowledge to others within the organization;

(4) Preference for explicit over tacit knowledge sharing because the latter involves hands-on learning, observation, dialogue, and interactive problem solving;

(5) Insufficient capture, evaluation, feedback, communication, and tolerance of past mistakes that would enhance individual and organizational learning;

(6) Inadequate verbal/written communication and interpersonal skills;

(7) Retaining ownership of knowledge due to fear of not receiving just recognition and accreditation from managers and colleagues;

(8) Lack of trust in others because they may misuse knowledge or take unjust credit for it;

(9) Lack of trust in the accuracy and credibility of the source of the knowledge.

Riege also identified that other barriers exist at an organizational level in terms of limiting knowledge transfer and the exploitation of available knowledge to optimize organizational and individual employee performance. Some of the barriers to knowledge sharing he identified include:

(1) Lack of leadership in terms of clearly communicating the benefits and values of knowledge sharing practices.

(2) Lack of rewards and recognition that would motivate people to share knowledge.

(3) Ensuring acquisition and sharing of knowledge held by highly skilled and experienced staff are not a high priority.

(4) Inadequate resources for supporting knowledge acquisition, storage, and access by others.

(5) Communication and knowledge is restricted to a top-down, one-way information flow.

(6) Hierarchical organizational structures that inhibit or slow down knowledge transfer.

The key issue confronting public sector senior management is the degree to which their organization can rely on exploiting existing knowledge versus placing emphasis upon the importation of new knowledge to support innovation. This situation can subsist because existing knowledge is widely available and tends to be relied upon during decision-making. In contrast, few public sector organizations appear to appreciate the benefit of accessing new knowledge and as a consequence such organizations are less able to generate any really radical, innovative new ideas. Entrepreneurial organizations which seek to achieve growth through proactive innovative activities have long understood the critical importance of sustaining their competence in the application of new knowledge to enhance performance. The implications of existing versus new knowledge as sources of new opportunity are summarized in Figure 10.2.

Reliance on the exploitation of existing knowledge will usually only permit the organization to sustain current business strategies and in some cases, identify opportunities to utilize existing knowledge as the basis for output or market diversification. This does not mean, however, that organizations orientated towards implementing entrepreneurial strategies should ignore existing knowledge. In most cases, existing knowledge can provide a much lower risk source of future opportunity than that available from exploiting new knowledge. Hence, even entrepreneurial organizations should seek to achieve an appropriate balance of the degree to which resources are allocated towards utilizing existing knowledge versus acquiring new knowledge.

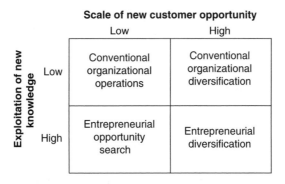

Figure 10.2   Opportunity/knowledge matrix

In some cases when new knowledge first emerges, there may be no obvious new opportunity application. For example, when first invented the laser was described as a 'solution looking for a problem'. The important issue where opportunities to exploit new knowledge are not immediately apparent is for the organization to permit a certain proportion of resources to be applied to look for new application opportunities. One company which has excelled at applying this philosophy is 3M Corporation where scientists and managers from different departments are encouraged to exchange information. This is because 3M has found that this interchange can often lead to new opportunities being identified which may lie outside of the experiences of the individual(s) who initially identified an area of new knowledge.

Organizations which base their strategy on exploiting new technology tend to be attracted to the leading edge core technology because this is seen as providing the basis for above average performance through the creation of new goods and even new sectors. Hence, in terms of analysing future opportunities or threats, it is necessary to assess how knowledge can be amplified by combining new knowledge with the current leading edge technology (Ohmura and Watanabe 2006). At the beginning of the twentieth century, the two leading edge technologies were electricity and the internal combustion engine. These were then overtaken by electronics which as this technology generated solid state devices provided the foundations for IT to become the current leading edge core technology. The degree to which organizations exploit new knowledge in relation to advances in IT does vary across both the public and private sectors.

Organizations need to be very aware that the interaction between new knowledge and a leading edge core technology is a dynamic process. Those organizations engaged in the provision of services delivered by expensive professional staff should continually be seeking ways of replacing these individual with machine-based solutions. An example of this scenario is provided in the health care sector where surgeons having evolved a new surgical technique which use computer-based systems to undertake part or all of the medical treatment. As technology-based solutions become widely understood, the techniques will become adopted by more conservative organizations. This outcome means that the entrepreneurial organization has to continually strive to identify and exploit new approaches for utilizing knowledge in order to remain the leading organization in their respective sectors of activity.

Based upon the benefits achieved through CRM in the private sector, both academics and consultancy firms are highly supportive of the concept being introduced into the public sector. Certainly on the basis of various Government tax departments across the developed economies, CRM can lead to enhanced customer satisfaction, improved speed and quality of service provision, and reduced operating costs. Nevertheless, there is a need for a certain degree of caution. Experience from the private sector shows that CRM projects can often prove to be expensive failures due to problems caused by factors such as actual project costs much greater than estimated at the outset, technology failing to deliver promised capability, inability to integrate existing and new databases due to software incompatibility, unwillingness of departments to share data, and resistance of staff to being required to change their assigned job roles. These same problems can certainly be expected to be duplicated in public sector CRM initiatives. In commenting upon CRM utilization in the public sector, Pollard et al. (2006) also noted other additional obstacles will be encountered. These include inappropriate organizational culture, hierarchical structures impeding decision-making, and a preference for autonomy which will frustrate data sharing between departments in the same organization and, just as importantly, between different Government organizations.

Issues and Objectives

11

The aims of this chapter are to cover the issues of:

(1) Prioritizing external versus internal issues when determining strategic actions
(2) The use of decision matrices in determining priorities
(3) The role of gap analysis in determining performance goals
(4) The specification of single versus multiple strategic objectives
(5) Consideration of stakeholder priorities in the setting of strategic objectives

---

Key issues

Upon completion of the analysis of the external and internal environments, the organization is in a position to undertake a SWOT analysis. The classification of a variable as an Opportunity or Threat and Strength or Weakness will influence how the managers subsequently interpret the nature of the variable and the actions to be implemented. This effect is an important aspect of 'categorization theory' in that an incorrect classification of a variable can lead to errors in the way the variable is handled in any subsequent business plan (Dutton and Jackson 1987).

Specifically categorization of a variable as an opportunity or a strength will be perceived as implying a positive situation over which the individual or organization has a significant degree of control. In contrast, a threat or a weakness will be perceived as a negative situation over which the individual or organization has little or no control. In those cases where a variable has been labelled but further information is seen as being required to enhance decision-making, the nature of the information sought will be biased towards acquiring data which are of a positive nature in terms of an opportunity or strength. The opposite scenario is applicable in the case of a threat or weakness where the tendency is to select data that provide additional negative information.

In most cases, the labelling of a variable occurs early in the planning process and involves individuals with specific areas of managerial responsibility. Thus, service providers such as doctors whose orientation is directed towards external environments are likely to be initiators of classifications related to opportunities and threats. As far as initial classifications related to strengths and weaknesses (internal issues) are concerned, this task is usually undertaken by line managers, drawing in some cases on the knowledge of members of other departments such as finance and HRM. Senior managers do need to be aware of the orientation of those engaged in the classification process because potentially their personal view points and attitudes can bias their perspectives. Entrepreneurs, for example, tend to be orientated towards positive, proactive scenarios and hence may underestimate the real magnitude of the threats facing the organization. This can be contrasted by many finance managers whose more conservative attitudes may lead to identification of a variable as being a much greater threat than it actually is.

Very few public sector organizations can ever aspire to have access to a scale of resources so that response can be determined for every variable identified in the SWOT analysis. Consequently most organizations will need to examine their SWOT results to prioritize variables as the basis for deciding which should be classified as 'key issues' requiring urgent attention in any subsequent business plan. The issue of prioritization will be influenced by the orientation of the analyst. Individuals who are strong advocates of RBV will tend to identify internal competences as key issues. This outcome can be contrasted with externally orientated individuals who will probably determine that events outside of the organization should be selected as the most important key issues.

Drug Issues

Case Aims: To illustrate how changing market conditions are creating issues which will require re-evaluation of their health care strategies.

The second half of the twentieth century was a 'golden age' for the large, multinational pharmaceutical companies. Innovations in areas such as antibiotics, vaccines, and drugs for the treatment of specific medical conditions such as depression or blood pressure permitted these organizations to develop highly successful product portfolios. A critical influence over total sales during this period was Governments and private health insurance companies' ability to fund the purchase of these drugs for the majority of Western nation inhabitants. An added stimulus to revenue generation for the suppliers is the 15-year protection provided by patents for new formulations. During this period, the only major constraint these major firms faced were the rising costs of

(cont'd)

responding to Governments imposing increasingly restrictive testing regimes to ensure that only entirely safe new products are approved for market introduction (Anon 2007a).

In recent years a number of key issues have emerged which are beginning to dramatically alter the market scenario facing Governments concerning their ability to sustain a strategy of purchasing ever latest drug treatment. Probably the issues of greatest concern are population ageing and the huge costs associated with many new specialist drugs in areas such as cancer treatment. This means that Governments are facing the need to cap total spending on health care provision leading to proposals for health care reforms and demanding lower prices from the drugs firms. The issue over the high price of many drugs has caused developing nations to begin to demand that the major 'pharmas' lower their prices if they wish to be permitted to continue to market their products in these countries.

The other key issue is the inability of Governments to continue fund rising health care budgets causing a move to purchase lower priced, generic drugs. The early generic drugs were manufactured by smaller companies which were able to copy existing formulations where the patent period had ended. For a long time the large firms refused to become involved in generics because they perceived this would make them vulnerable to pressure from Governments to also reduce prices on their newer products still protected by patents. This situation underwent dramatic change, however, when the Indian Government passed a law protecting the country's drug industry from infringing patents on imported drugs. Through techniques such as reverse engineering the Indian drugs industry began to develop drugs which duplicated those being produced by the big 'pharmas' which they then sold at much lower prices.

An inability to afford any increases in public sector health care spending and the success of producers based in countries such as India means that developed nation Governments are beginning to apply pressure on the major 'pharmas' to convince them that their existing business model of developing and launching extremely expensive patented new drug formulations is no longer a financially viable proposition (Anon 2009a). Pressure is also being applied to persuade the large companies to direct a greater proportion of their expertise and capabilities towards exploiting emerging new technologies (Rothman and Kraft 2006). The human genome project has provided the basis for greater understanding of how manipulation of DNA molecules can provide a whole new type of medical treatment. Interest in exploiting the opportunities offered by genome technology was relatively low in many of the large drug companies. In part this was due to the US Government's decision that the specific knowledge concerning the human genome could not be patented. This raised questions within the drugs industry of how companies could retain control of new genome-based products which they might develop. To a certain degree this apparent

> **(cont'd)**
>
> lack of interest was due to the fact that many of the companies engaged in biotechnology and genome development programmes were expending huge sums on R&D with little evidence that developing any products offered real commercial potential. This latter situation has begun to change in recent years and some companies are beginning to generate a profit. This outcome can be used by Governments, when determining about funding university research and seeking universities to form new public/private sector research partnerships to require the big drugs firms to become more heavily involved in funding this area of medical research instead of apparently remaining focused on trying to develop yet another monopoly for another patented, financially rewarding new drug formulation.

Issue prioritization

No doubt there are cases of public sector organizations where focus should be biased towards either internal or external key issues when formulating their strategic plans. In most cases, however, it is possibly wiser that organizations allocate attention to both external events and the internal capability in order to effectively optimize service provision. One technique whereby internal and external issues can be simultaneously assessed is through the use of a modified version of the GE–McKinsey Matrix to develop Opportunity Response and Threat Response Matrices (Rowe et al. 1994; Hatten and Rosenthal 1999).

The shared aspect of both matrices is to assess the importance of different scenarios in the external environment in relation to the organization's level of relevant internal competences. In order to classify the scale of identified opportunities and threats, it is necessary for the organization to determine which key variables are critical contributors to events in the external environment. These variables will usually exhibit a certain degree of sectoral and organizational specificity. In many cases, however, key influencers common to most scenarios will be variables such as customer demand, customer loyalty, customer price sensitivity, complexity of technology, rate of technological change, sustainability, environmental protection, and economics.

Each variable to be used in the analysis is assigned a score on a simple 1–10 scale where the higher the score, the greater the contributive influence. The scores are summed and the total divided by the number of variables to convert the overall measurement back to a number between 1 and 10. Scores between 0–3, >3–7, and >7–10 are considered to respectively indicate a scenario is a low, average, or high importance. A similar analysis is undertaken in relation to relevant competences. Again some variables will usually exhibit a certain degree of sectoral and organizational specificity, whereas other key influencers will be common to most scenarios. Examples of this latter type of variable might include workforce skills, age of assets, process capacity, financial resources, R&D capability, service provision ability, access to key input resources, information management ability, service quality, and logistics management. The same scoring and analysis system as used for the external environment analysis is utilized to permit competences to be assessed in relation to being rated low, average, or high. The scores combined with the relevant scores for opportunity or threats for each scenario are then entered onto the respective matrices of the type shown in Figures 11.1 and 11.2.

Future service provision opportunities

	Low	Average	High
Low	No future	Limited future	High-risk future
Average	Limited future	Ongoing stable future	Internal competence upgrade
High	Withdraw resources to create cash cow	Diversification	Entrepreneurial emphasis to sustain future leadership position

(Level of relevant internal competences)

Figure 11.1   Opportunity response matrix

Future threats

	Low	Average	High
Low	Ignore	Monitor situation	Crisis scenario demanding immediate containment
Average	Monitor situation	Implement appropriate actions utilizing current resources	Transfer of resources to upgrade competence
High	Transfer most resources to other areas of activity	Release some resources to other areas of activity	Immediate action to implement viable solution

(Level of internal competences)

Figure 11.2   Threat response matrix

As shown in Figure 11.1, the location of a specific scenario on an Opportunity Response Matrix will determine priorities in relation to the future allocation of organizational resources. Specifically the nine different actions are:

(1) Low Opportunity/Low Competence: This scenario indicates there is no future for this kind of activity and hence ongoing activity should be terminated in this area of service provision.

(2) Average Opportunity/Low Competence: The organization lacks the competences to exploit this situation and hence there is a limited future in relation to exploiting this opportunity.

(3) High Opportunity/Low Competence: This is an area of critical concern and high risk. This is because examples of high opportunity are extremely rare but in this case the organization currently lacks the required competences to be successful in the provision of services. A priority action is to determine the viability and scale of investment required to acquire appropriate competences. This will be followed by a determination of whether the level of associated risk justifies such an investment.

(4) Low Opportunity/Average Competence: The organization lacks the competences to exploit this situation and hence there is a limited future in relation to exploiting this opportunity.

(5) Average Opportunity/Average Competence: In most cases, this scenario is likely to be an important contributor to the organization's primary core activities. Hence, the opportunity should continue to be seen as sufficiently important so that the existing allocation of resources will be sustained in the future.

(6) High Opportunity/Average Competence: Given the high level of opportunity, this means the scenario can make a very important contribution to the organization's future overall performance. Hence, priority should be given to upgrading the organization's level of competence in this area of activity.

(7) Low Opportunity/High Competence: Relative to the scale of opportunity, the organization is over-resourcing this area of activity. Resources should be allocated elsewhere which will then permit this scenario to be more economically serviced.

(8) Average Opportunity/High Competence: The organization has achieved a level of competence greater than that is required by the identified opportunity. Hence, a diversification of resources should be implemented whereby some resources are transferred across into other, similar types of opportunity.

(9) High Opportunity/High Competence: This is likely to represent one or more areas of opportunity where acquired competences have permitted the organization to achieve a leadership position. In order to sustain superiority of performance, priority should usually be given to entrepreneurial endeavours that permit the organization to exploit innovation as a path by which to remain the leading service provider.

As shown in Figure 11.2, the location of a specific scenario on a Threat Response Matrix will determine priorities in relation to the future allocation of organizational resources. Specifically the nine different actions are:

(1) Low Threat/Low Competence: This scenario can be ignored for the foreseeable future. This is as because the analysis reveals a minimal threat, this lack of the competences to respond effectively is not a problem.

(2) Average Threat/Low Competence: The organization lacks the competences to effectively respond to this threat. However, given the scale of the threat is assessed as average, the scenario should be monitored to ensure no deepening of the threat levels goes unnoticed.

(3) High Threat/Low Competence: This is an area of critical concern and high risk. This is because although the scale of the threat is very significant, the organization lacks the required competences to respond to the situation. An immediate priority is to put a threat containment plan in place while the organization examines how appropriate competences can be put into place to resolve the threat over the longer term.

(4) Low Threat/Average Competence: The organization has the competences necessary to handle this threat. The low threat level suggests that the only action should be to monitor the situation to ensure there is no worsening of this situation in the future.

(5) Average Threat/Average Competence: In most cases, this scenario is likely to have a reasonably significant potential impact on future operations. However, the organization has the necessary competences to handle the situation. Hence, a threat management plan should be implemented which only draws upon the organization's existing capabilities without additional resources being allocated.

(6) High Threat/Average Competence: Given the high level of threat which this scenario represents but the average level of competence, priority will have to be given to injecting the additional resources required to achieve and upgrade the organization's level of competence.

(7) Low Threat/High Competence: Relative to the scale of threat, the organization is over-resourcing this area of activity. Resources should be allocated elsewhere which are in greater need of upgrading competences to handle identified threats.

(8) Average Threat/High Competence: The organization has a level of competence greater than that is required to manage the identified threat. Hence, resources should be transferred across to similar areas of threat which could benefit from an enhanced level of competence.

(9) High Threat/High Competence: This level of threat will be of concern and priority should be given to overcome the identified problem(s). Fortunately, however, this is an area where the organization has already developed the necessary level of competence to handle the situation.

Gap analysis

In addition to identifying the key issues which will need to be managed to ensure ongoing organizational success, it is usually beneficial to determine whether the probable future performance will meet the organization's planned expectations. This knowledge can be generated by implementing a 'gap analysis' which involves plotting planned and probable performance over a medium-term period such as the next 5 years (Guo 2002). As illustrated in Figure 11.3, the difference between probable and planned performance provides the organization with an understanding of the scale of the problem concerning inadequate future performance. The gap analysis in Figure 11.3 is concerned with service provision (e.g. demand for medical services).

The advent of increasingly sophisticated data analysis and statistical software packages provides the forecaster with a wide range of different tools for examining future trends. It is extremely rare for any of these forecast techniques to provide a certain, totally accurate estimate of future performance. This is because future performance can be influenced by a multitude of variables, many of which cannot be sufficiently accurately interpreted in order to be included in the forecast equation. However, experienced executives can often make reasonably accurate guesstimates of probable performance in relation to different scenarios. This capability can be exploited by using managers' perspectives on the probability of alternative scenarios as the basis for constructing a decision tree of the type shown in Figure 11.4.

The example presented in Figure 11.4 is concerned with forecasting total future service provision. The methodology used is based upon dividing the service provision portfolio into four groups: namely mature/declining services, growth phase services, introduction phase services, and near-to-launch new

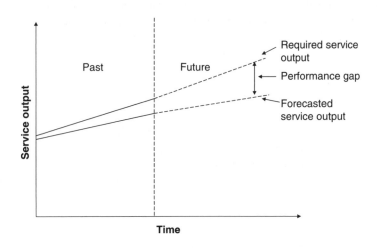

Figure 11.3   A service output gap analysis

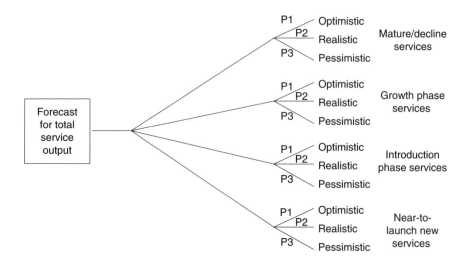

Figure 11.4   A decision tree forecasting technique

services. For each service category, three forecasts are required to cover optimistic, realistic, and pessimistic scenarios. The forecast for each service group is calculated by multiplying the sales forecast scenario with the probability of occurrence for each scenario.

Although a gap analysis will provide data on the scale of any expected shortfall in performance, the analysis has the drawback of not providing any information which diagnoses the reason(s) for the gap. As a consequence, some organizations will seek to identify which factors are key influencers of performance and then implement further gap assessments to gain understanding of how these are contributing to performance shortfalls. This additional knowledge, when combined with the prioritized opportunities and threat analysis, can add further clarity to the future actions required to deliver the organization's desired performance objectives (Carpinetti and M de Melo 2002).

Terwiersch and Ulrich (2008) have proposed that one typical area which is the cause of a gap is the performance of one or more items in the organization's service portfolio. They propose that the nature of this gap can be identified in one or two ways. One approach is to identify any product performance gap by assessing services in relation to (a) customer attitudes concerning their desired performance for services and/or (b) the performance of similar services such as those offered by major private sector providers. One technique illustrated in Figure 11.5 for undertaking this type of evaluation is to measure customer requirements in relation to the key dimensions of service and price. As shown in Figure 11.5 the example of public sector organization's service lies along the performance/price line for meeting customer needs. In contrast, competitor A from the private sector is delivering

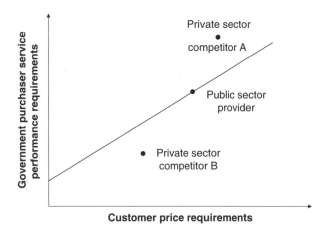

Figure 11.5   Government–customer requirements and product assessment

superior performance relative to price. This situation may represent a future threat if the private sector provider acquires the abilities to reduce the future cost of his or her offering and the Government purchaser is prepared to out-source service provision to the private sector. In contrast, competitor B from the private sector is not a threat because his or her product underperforms relative to the needs of customers. This situation could change, however, if the Government purchaser in response to financial constraints decides to accept lower quality and a lower price. In this situation, the public sector provider would need to assess internal ability to rapidly offer a lower price service.

The alternative approach to identifying performance gaps is to evaluate the effectiveness with which the organization exploits technology to deliver the specified performance of a provided service relative to the technological achieve-ments of competitors. Terwiersch and Ulrich (2008) recommend that a parallel evaluation be undertaken in relation to the position of services on the service product life cycle curve. At the Introduction stage, the organization needs to determine which is the probable dominant technology which will emerge within a sector and the ability of the organization, relative to other potential service providers, to exploit the technology. In the Growth stage the dominant technol-ogy will become more obvious and again the organization needs to determine whether there is a gap between themselves and other providers in the use of this technology. At the Maturity and Decline stage, the critical focus will shift to process efficiency and capacity utilization. Hence, the gap assessment for these types of services will need to switch towards assessing organizational process competences relative to other providers.

Ultimately the aim of any organization is to ensure that expectations about any key area of performance are matched by actual achievements. Where it

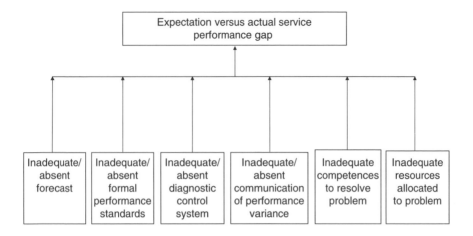

Figure 11.6   Potential causes of service performance gaps

becomes apparent that one or more areas of the organization's operations are experiencing performance gaps, there is a need to implement an assessment of why this is occurring. Any evaluation will need to be extended beyond just the issue of inadequate forecasts. This is because as summarized in Figure 11.6 there are a number of different factors that can result in expectations not being matched by actual outcomes.

In his review of the strategic planning process in the public sector, Plant (2009) notes that performance gaps are more likely to emerge in the public sector than in private sector organizations. One potential gap he identified is that forecasted performance will be modified by new legislative requirements that demand a change in operational processes. This outcome will add costs, thereby reducing the total volume of services that can be delivered in the future. Another cause of a potential performance gap is those cases where a reduction in Government funding requires the prioritization of the services to be delivered in the future. During this assessment, it may become apparent that one or more low priority services will have to be removed from the organization's service portfolio. In recent times, public sector organizations have faced a massive increase in legal action from dissatisfied customers seeking compensation for physical or mental damage which they perceive as the outcome of a poorly performed service. As a consequence, Governments have been forced to require public sector organizations to be competent at risk assessment and in some cases the outcome is the decision to withdraw a service. For example, many schools in the United Kingdom ceased to organize field trips for students following a number of high-profile cases of students being injured or killed. Thus, where a service termination decision is made on the basis of greater awareness to reduce operating risks, this can lead to a service gap in the organization's future provision activities.

Sustainable Energy

Case Aims: To illustrate how a future opportunity exists to exploit new technology to overcome the performance gap which currently exists between conventional and sustainable electricity generation.

One of the fundamental dilemmas facing Governments seeking to promote a sustainable energy generation policy is the inability of sustainable technology to match the lower costs associated with power generation using hydrocarbon fuels. Even though sustainable energy has gained from more Governments committing to adopt alternative energy solutions to reduce greenhouse gas emissions, expansion of programmes based upon exploiting sustainable energy sources such as wind or wave power faces major problems. Government may be prepared to offer either capital investment grants or subsidize ongoing energy generation. With Governments increasingly being faced with growing public sector deficits, this situation may result in public sector policies based upon subsidizing sustainable energy projects being withdrawn unless ways are found to overcome the technology gap so that costs of production are still much greater than the alternative of using hydrocarbons fuels.

One possibility on the horizon that may eradicate this technology gap is the concept of locating solar power generators in an area of the world which enjoys a higher than average level of sunlight and exploiting a technology known as Concentrated Solar Power (CSP). This involves using directive mirrors to generate heat that is used to run steam turbines that generate electricity (Jansen 2009). Added efficiency is achieved by storing spare heat in tanks containing melted salts that can continue to power the turbines at night. The concept known as 'Desertec' is being promoted by a European network of scientists who are beginning to attract serious interest from both European financial institutions and large engineering companies. In theory one system based in the Sahara could meet the European Union's entire demand for electricity. A massively upscaled version could deliver the world's entire supply for electricity. Currently the estimated costs of CSP are about 0.15 euros per kilowatt compared to 0.06 euros for coal or nuclear stations. Desertec members believe this performance gap could be reduced assuming public sector funding will be made available to support commercialization of the technology and the construction of power lines to distribute the electricity generated in the Sahara to customers in Europe and/or elsewhere in the world.

Strategic objective

The purpose of defining a 'strategic objective' is to provide the organization with a specification of future performance which can be used to guide the selection of

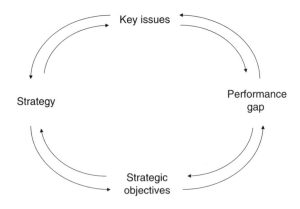

Figure 11.7 Process iteration

an appropriate strategy. As illustrated in Figure 11.7, specification of objectives also permit assessment of actual performance versus forecast upon implementation of the strategic plan. There is some debate in the academic literature concerning the nature of the objective(s) to be specified and whether there is a need to specify multiple objectives (Denton 2006). In terms of the nature of any objective, given the requirement to assist assessment of progress being achieved upon implementation, any specified aim must meet the parameter of being measurable. In most cases, the measurability criteria will mean that there will be a preference for an objective to be quantitative.

Other key requirements of a strategic objective are achievability, sustainability, and universality. The purpose of achievability is necessary because there is no purpose in setting a performance target which employees or Government funding agencies perceive to be impossible. The former will become de-motivated and the latter will become sceptical about making funds available to the organization. Sustainability is an essential dimension for management seeking to construct an enduring organization because it represents the critical requirement that the organization continues to perform well over a very long period of time. Universality refers to the need for the strategic objective to be perceived as applicable across the entire organization. This is because all employees must be able to relate to the organization's strategic objective so that this overall umbrella aim can assist them in assessing their personal effectiveness in fulfilling their own job role or the task role of the department in which they are based.

In relation to the use of just a single strategic objective, one possible generic statement of aims for a public sector organization is long-term maximization of customer service expectations at the lowest possible cost through the optimal utilization of available resources. As senior management need to focus on constructing enduring organizations, the phrase 'long-term', is a critical aspect of a public sector organization's strategic objective. This is because even the incompetent managers can find a way of achieving a short-term goal of utilizing current financial budget over the next 12 months to deliver a level of services capable of meeting immediate customer expectations. This aim can be met by implementing actions such as reducing expenditure on equipment maintenance, not updating key capital equipment, and terminating all employee training programmes. The reduction in operational costs will usually permit sustaining delivery of services for a short period of time. Beyond this point in time, however, actions associated with reducing all but the most immediate areas of expenditure will usually lead to the outcome of increasing customer dissatisfaction, declining service quality, and lowering employee productivity. In some cases, the scale of damage to the organization may be irreversible, thereby leaving the operation in a permanently weakened position relative to other public sector organizations that have rejected the concept of managerial short-termism.

In seeking to gain further understanding of the issue of the dilemma of setting long-term versus short-term objectives during the planning process in public sector organizations, Johnston and Pongatichat (2008) acquired data in the form of case studies on public sector agencies in the United Kingdom. They concluded that managers found measuring long-term strategic objectives was often difficult to achieve. This is because these have originally been specified in this form by previous managers who were uncertain about what was required by the agency's funding body. The outcome is the previous and current incumbent managers tend to use existing short-term measures as proxies for their long-term objectives. This is despite the known lack of cause-and-effect relationship which exists between short-term measures and the long-term strategic objectives. Furthermore, since strategic objectives related to fundamental social change often take years to accomplish, these aims tend to be subject to uncontrollable factors such as the election of a new government or access to available resources. In contrast, shorter-term objectives are perceived as more achievable because these are aims over which managers feel they have some degree of control.

The fundamental purpose of commercial organizations is to achieve an adequate return on investment from the assets utilized in the company. Public sector and not-for-profit organizations' fundamental purpose is somewhat different in that most exist to deliver services which cannot be provided by the private sector. Nevertheless, the public sector organizations need to have specified strategic objectives concerning the long-term provision of an appropriate quality of services to a maximum number of clients within the target group(s) in the sector(s) where the organization operates. In those cases, where the PSO is facing resource constraints, a strategic decision needs to be made in terms of defining an objective of either (a) the long-term provision of an average quality of services to the maximum number of potential clients or (b) delivering superior quality services to a restricted number of clients.

Multiple objectives

A key reason for reliance on a single strategic objective based upon financial performance in many private sector organizations is that financial measurement systems are usually much more accurate and can provide real-time permit data.

This latter attribute is rarely feasible with most non-financial monitoring systems. This is because accounting systems have been developed which have the capability of meeting demands to provide specific financial information on a timely basis to stakeholders, financial institutions, and public bodies such as the financial regularity authorities and Government departments.

The 2008/9 banking crisis among many of the world's leading financial institutions re-enforced existing concerns, which have been expressed by both academics and management practitioners, that restricting performance goals to only financial performance targets can cause managers to limit focus on 'hitting the numbers'. This behaviour can in turn lead to short-term strategic thinking (Mailliard 1997). This has led to questions about whether organizations should continue to base their strategic objective on simple, short-term financial performance targets. The alternative perspective which is gaining support among academics and practicing managers is the concept of multiple strategic objectives. This approach is based upon the organization seeking to achieve additional aims such as customer satisfaction, productivity, and product/service quality when defining future long-term strategic goals.

One of the more widely used multiple objective definition techniques is the balanced scorecard concept developed by Kaplan and Norton (1996). Their idea was to combine financial and non-financial issues into a systematic approach that covers four different areas of an organization's operation, namely financial, customer, internal business operations, and innovation. The purpose of the scorecard approach is to translate the organization's strategic intent into measurable units of information which can be evaluated and compared. As well as defining financial aims such as ROI, concurrently non-financial data such as the customers' perspectives and process productivity are included in the specification of long-term strategic objectives. The system has been adopted by some public sector organizations. It should be recognized that the system is somewhat complex and that to be effective there will usually be the need to significantly upgrade performance data acquisition and analysis capabilities within the organization.

Stakeholders

Organizations do not exist in a vacuum. Each entity is a member of a specific sector and also a member of the socio-political system of each country in which the organization has operations. As a consequence, each organization is involved in the management of a complex web of relationships with individuals and other organizations which have a vested interest in current and future performance. The participants in these relationship, which exist both inside and outside of the organization, are stakeholders. It is crucial that the organization recognizes the importance of stakeholders because they often have the ability to influence the future existence of the organization. Consequently, in determining strategic objectives, the organization does need to ensure that where possible these aims will be acceptable to the majority of stakeholders (Atkinson et al. 1997).

External stakeholders in public sector organizations include customers, Government funding agencies, other members of the organization's supply chain, politicians, the financial community, and society in general. Internal stakeholders are the current and retired employees, plus their families, who rely upon the organization to provide an ongoing source of income. It was proposed earlier in this chapter that the primary aim for a public sector organization is to seek for the longest possible duration to fulfil customer service expectations at the lowest possible cost through the optimal utilization of available resources. Where the public sector organization seeks to expand strategic objectives to reflect meeting the broader needs of society in general, a secondary objective might be defined, namely seeking to concurrently meet the performance expectations of the organization's other stakeholders. Some performance expectations of stakeholders can be defined in formal contractual terms (e.g. the salary scales agreed with the workforce). However, other performance expectations are implicit promises contained within strategic objectives which have been adopted to retain the ongoing support of specific stakeholders (e.g. prioritizing service needs to ensure emphasis is given to caring for the most disadvantaged in society, assisting local communities to be environmentally responsible, etc.).

The debate often arises within organizations about seeking to satisfy stakeholder needs whether any one group should be given priority over others. Harari (1992) expressed the view that private sector organizations must identify the customer as the priority stakeholder. This is because he believes that greater priority given to other groups such as the organization's management team or the financial community may result in excessive emphasis being placed on short-term profits. This latter focus on immediate profits may be detrimental to product performance or sustaining service quality. Applying Harari's concept to the public sector raises a dilemma, namely how to handle the fact that there are two customer groups, the purchaser and the consumer of services. Thus, for example, a Government agency may only be prepared to provide a budget to a small local hospital that permits the Accident and Emergency (A&E) department to be open during the day, whereas the hospital's potential patients want an A&E service which provides 24 hours cover. Under these circumstances, the hospital will be forced to decide which customer should be given priority. Under most circumstances, the decision will be determined by the source of funds to operate the PSO. Thus, in the case of the hospital, the probable outcome will be acceptance of the Government agency's demands even though potential A&E patients in the local community will be dissatisfied by the subsequent time constraint placed upon service provision.

In the face of rising public sector spending constraints there will be times when long-term survival of an organization may require hard decisions being made that are detrimental to one or more of the organization's stakeholder groups. For example, a Local Authority may have been forced to close their residential nursing home because the building no longer meets health and safety standards and no funds are available to modernize the facility. In this instance equality of treatment does not apply because one group of stakeholders, the residents of the home and their families, will be disadvantaged. In terms of how best to resolve the dilemma of stakeholder inequality, it is perhaps best to assess any major decision in relation to the overarching primary objective of sustaining the long-term service expectations of the majority of the organization's customers. In terms of the closure of the residential home, regretfully although some of the residents and their families will be disadvantaged, by closing the home resources might be released to expand the Local Authority's support services for elderly people still living in their own homes or by expanding the provision of day care services for pensioners.

Accountability

Case Aims: To illustrate the issues concerning the division of responsibility between politicians and civil servants.

A major focus in the assessment of public agency performance in New Zealand has been about senior management accountability. Managers were perceived to face scrutiny over procedures and processes, but not the outcome of their activities. Concurrently public managers are excessively subject to political accountability from elected politicians who are willing to intervene in any administrative act in response to political problems. The problem with political accountability is it focuses public attention in a way such that public managers are distracted from their key tasks and may become risk averse. The probable solution is to rely on fewer politicized mechanisms such as independent regulators and auditors or alternatively create systems whereby public agencies are made directly accountable to members of the general public.

The New Zealand approach to public sector reform adopted a multi-dimensional approach to accountability in relation to specifying who is to be accountable to whom, for what, and how. Agencies were to be held accountable in terms of detailed agreements negotiated with government ministers which set out these agencies' respective duties. For core government departments, the central strategic mechanism is a formal annual purchase agreement between ministers and departments.

Mulgan (2008) concluded that new output-based framework has failed to deliver clarity of accountability. Outputs were preferred over outcomes as accountability targets because they are less ambiguous, more easily specified and measured. However, outputs are uninformative guides to what the public can expect from their public servants. Furthermore, ministers, the media commentators, or members of the public rarely resort to output statements or output measures as the basis for holding governments to account. This is because outputs are too unspecific when seeking to assess an agency's performance. Furthermore, making agencies accountable for a set of specified outputs encourages a 'check-list' mentality. The separation of outputs from outcomes

(cont'd)

whilst restricting public servants for responsibility only for outputs theoretically implied outcomes which were the sole responsibility of ministers. Furthermore, in parliamentary committees, questions about the impact of departmental policies could be deflected by civil servants on the ground that outcomes are the responsibility of ministers not the public sector agency.

Specification of outputs has proved vital for independent auditors seeking to determine whether an agency is delivering value for money. Additionally, amendments to the output/outcome framework have been made to attempt to remedy identified deficiencies in the system. Nevertheless, Mulgan has concluded that separation of output from outcomes does not appear to have delivered any major accountability dividend to either politicians or the general public in relation to ensuring the more effective delivery of services. The convention that only ministers are answerable to the public while public servants remain anonymous has changed. The introduction of an ombudsman, parliamentary select committee investigations, and Official Information Legislation has assisted in exposing public servants to direct public accountability. As a result, senior public servants have become more visible and sometimes been forced to accept responsibility for their more politically controversial decisions.

Nevertheless, despite the fundamental reforms of the public sector in New Zealand, the convention of ministerial responsibility still remains. In commenting on this situation, Mulgan (2008, p. 31) suggested that 'So long as elected governments retain overall control through their extensive executive powers, they will be held accountable for government policy. The public, including the media, will not easily surrender a mechanism that provides the most reliable means of placing the government under pressure to be publicly accountable.'

Non-executive boards

Agency theory refers to the concept of defining the role of managers in professionally managed and publicly owned companies being responsible for acting in the best interests of the shareholders. Where senior executives in private sector organizations have minimal equity holdings, agency theory suggests that the number of non-executive board members should be increased in order to ensure the company executives are fulfilling their obligations to meet the best interests of the shareholders (Johnson 1993). An accepted converse of this concept is that where top management has a significant equity stake, there is less need for the involvement of non-executive board members in the company's decision-making. The sub-prime mortgage debacle, the collapse of major financial institutions, and the huge bonuses being paid within the financial community, however, would seem to raise questions about the validity of prevailing theory concerning the effectiveness of non-executive board members to protect the long-term interest of shareholders (Anon 2009b).

It seems reasonable to suggest recent events, especially in the financial services sector, are reflective of a prevailing attitude among senior managers, who may or may not be owners of significant equity, of supporting strategic short-termism in which these individuals are prepared to put increasing amount of their own personal wealth ahead of the rights of either shareholders or other stakeholders. It would also appear to be the case that the presence of non-executive directors on the boards of major financial institutions did little to prevent senior executives ignoring their responsibility to act in the best long interests of the shareholders. In fact, one is not unreasonable to wonder whether some non-executive board members are prepared to be complicit in supporting short-termism and questionable lending practices because they might use their knowledge of internal events within organizations to greatly increase their own personal wealth. This perspective was recently highlighted by Ross (2010, p. 14) in an article about the behaviour of non-executive members on the boards of investment trusts. She notes that these individuals are increasingly being perceived as 'being more keen to hold onto their jobs that doing what is best for the company'. The author points there is a significant problem over the behaviour of non-executive directors which she illustrated by quoting one board member who commenting on the potential bias in their role responded with the question 'Do turkeys vote for Christmas?'

In the context of who fulfils the non-executive role in providing strategic oversight of public sector organizations engaged in the delivery of services, there is some variation in the approaches used to achieve this aim. In some instances such as schools or hospitals, individuals from outside these organizations are either recruited or elected to serve on a Board constituted of themselves and senior managers from the public sector organization. In the United Kingdom, for example, the primary functions of the Board overseeing a NHS trust such as hospital, the role of the Board members includes (Cray 1994):

(1) Assisting in defining and assessing the trust's long-term vision.

(2) Assisting in defining and assessing the creation of a clear strategy for realizing the specified vision.

(3) Assessing the chosen strategy is being implemented.

(4) Monitoring whether financial, contractual targets and health care provision targets are being met.

(5) Monitoring whether the needs of stakeholders are being met.

(6) Ensuring that within the trust ethical standards of behaviour are being maintained.

A service provision model widely adopted by the UK Government in the 1990s was to transfer the responsibility for the oversight or management of service delivery from a public sector agency to a quasi-autonomous, non-governmental organizations, or 'quangos'. The logic behind the creation of quangos was that these entities would exhibit the characteristics of private sector organization and thereby enhance the effectiveness and efficiency of service delivery (Bertelli 2005). Typically these organizations' only customer is the Government and when engaged in actual service delivery their primary source of revenue comes from contracting to deliver specific services. Examples of this model include the provision of training programmes for the unemployed or delivering support services for small businesses. In terms of establishing an oversight system to ensure quangos are fulfilling their assigned roles, Governments tend to rely upon (a) formal audits and performance reviews by civil servants and (b) the appointment of a non-executive Board member with senior management experience of working in either the public or private sector organizations.

In some cases, the oversight system can be very complex involving both national and local agencies. For example in the United Kingdom, overall policy for education is provided by the Ministry of Education and performance assessment is in the hands of an external body Ofsted. Funding of schools is provided by the Government which allocates these monies to Local Authorities who have day-to-day responsibility for the schools in their area. This function is discharged by employees working in the Local Authorities Education Departments. The oversight of these departments is provided by the Audit Commission reviewing actual expenditure and elected officials serving on Education Committee monitoring the activities of Education Department staff. In addition to this two-tier system, further oversight at the level of each individual school is the responsibility of a Board of Governors who are local volunteers, usually parents of children attending the school.

Societal stakeholders

Down through the ages there have been numerous examples of industrialists whose desire for profit and personal moral values have led to abuse of their workforce, mistreatment of customers, or being prepared to pollute the environment. However, over the last 50 years factors such as the emergence of a consumer society, citizens' use of the legal system to challenge the behaviour of large organizations, and an increasingly borderless world have all contributed to major organizations facing greater pressure to exhibit a high level of social responsibility. As a consequence, major corporations now need to give much greater priority to the views of society in defining the performance objectives of their different stakeholders. Furthermore, in many Western nations, consumers are now tending to include the issue of the level of social responsibility being exhibited by major companies as a factor which can influence their purchase decisions. This trend is illustrated, for example, by the pressure that consumer groups brought to bear on the athletic shoe manufacturer Nike in terms of abolishing the use of child labour in their suppliers' manufacturing operations located in developing nations.

Stakeholder theory proposes a fundamental principle that should be accepted by all organizations is that all individuals should be treated with respect. It is important to note that this principle supports the philosophy that everyone should have the right to express their own opinions when their personal interests are adversely affected by the behaviour of an organization. The relationship between a doctor and a patient's family regarding the best available treatment for a patient needing immediate emergency surgery is one scenario where this philosophy might be applied. In recent years a culture shift has resulted in an increasingly proportion of the general public having adopting the view that as stakeholders their views should possibly be of greater consideration by public sector agencies than has been in the past (Ihlen 2008). To enable public sector organizations to monitor and respond to changing stakeholder expectations there is a need to acquire some form of understanding of the society of which they are a part and the nature of possible events that might change relevant publics' perception of the organization's activities. Should this occur, then members of society might decide to actively pursue the aim of ensuring that a public sector organization should be held accountable for what are perceived as unacceptable behaviours.

In terms of how public sector agencies should monitor stakeholder attitudes and behaviours a widely accepted approach is the use of a social audit. This activity can be a vital tool for assessing the success or failure of public sector organization to be aware and responsive to changing stakeholder needs. In commenting on the benefits of social audits, Ghonkrokta and Lather (2007) proposed that these should permit the following outcomes:

(1) Improve the social, ethical, and environmental knowledge within the organization such that amendments and corrections can be made in the execution of future activities.

(2) Build awareness among the general public that by PSOs undertaking social audits this will create an atmosphere of greater trust, acceptability, credibility, and mutual respect.

(3) Makes administrators appear more transparent and accountable. This assists these individuals when seeking to justify their future actions as members of the organization because the audit creates an atmosphere of co-operation and co-ordination.

(4) Knowledge generated by the audit can enhance actions of a PSO to achieve greater social inclusion, partnerships, and participation.

(5) Data from the social audit will support and define a process by which the organization more effectively identifies, measures, assesses, and reports on performance.

The publicity over global warming and depletion of natural resources has caused the general public in developed nations to have matured and heightened awareness about organizations needing to become more environmentally responsible and to demonstrate this through revised operational processes. To gain further understanding over the degree to which UK public sector agencies are implementing such changes, Walker and Brammer (2009) undertook a study to determine the nature of sustainable procurement in Local Authorities. They found that the most important factor influencing procurement decisions was an aim to maximize purchases of procurement from small and local companies, followed by concerns related to the health, safety, and labour practices in suppliers and the management of incoming supplies. The least embedded practices were those relating to environmental issues such as recycling and reducing greenhouse gas emissions. This result suggests that contrary to the current national policy emphasizing the importance of environmental responsibility, Local Authorities may be risking alienating some stakeholders by focusing on social and economic, rather than environmental factors when making procurement decisions. Most Local Authority respondents, however, held the view that in the prevailing economic climate the general public would prefer procurement orientation giving priority to supporting local economies and communities by buying from small and local suppliers. This is because most staff believe sustaining economic well-being is more important than environmental responsibility. This attitude is similar to that found in relation to consumers' attitudes towards seeking to purchase green products or organic foods. Such items are popular during periods of economic growth. Once an economy downturns, however, the fall in consumer confidence is accompanied by a move away from concerns about environmental issue because 'value for money' becomes the dominant factor in reaching a purchase decision.

Strategy

12

> The aims of this chapter are to cover the issues of:
>
> (1) Definitions of 'strategy' and competitive advantage
> (2) RBV theory in relation to identifying strategy
> (3) Alternative strategic positioning options
> (4) Assessing the need for strategic defence options
> (5) The importance of strategic flexibility

Definition

Even a cursory review of management texts and academic journal articles will reveal that there are significant differences of opinion among academics about precisely what is a strategy. In commenting upon this situation Markides (2004, p. 6) noted that:

> *the confusion is not restricted to academics. If asked, most practising executives would define strategy as how I could achieve my company's objectives. Although this definition is technically correct, it is so general that it is practically meaningless.*

The confusion which exists over defining 'strategy' is not a new issue. Almost 20 years ago, the editors of Planning Review explained that 'nobody seems to know what is strategy anymore'. In an attempt to clarify the situation, the journal asked the MIT Professor Arnolodo Hax to present his perspective in this matter. Hax (1990) posited that a strategy embraces all of the key activities of the organization and hence should be required to be constituted of the following 6 specific elements:

(1) Provides a coherent unifying and integrative pattern of behaviour.
(2) Determines organizational purpose in terms of long-term objectives, actions, and resource allocation priorities.

(3) Selects the areas of activity the organization is in or is considering entering.

(4) Attempts to achieve a long-term sustainable advantage by responding to the opportunities, threats, strengths, and weaknesses of the organization.

(5) Engages all the hierarchical levels of the firm.

(6) Defines the economic and non-economic contributions the organization intends to make to the stakeholders.

Most management texts contain similar expositions when defining 'strategy' as that presented by Hax. The length and complexity of this type of definition are probably a primary reason for the confusion which exists in the minds of both students and management practitioners. Hence, to overcome this problem, perhaps it would be wise to develop a simpler definition. One approach is to draw a lesson from a UK advertising claim for Ronseal's range of wood treatment products, namely 'it does what it says on the tin'. Assuming one is prepared to accept this perspective, this suggests a definition that:

> *Strategy is a statement which specifies the nature of the competitive advantage to be utilised to achieve an organisation's strategic objective(s).*

It might be argued that this definition, by inclusion of the concept of competitive advantage, is not applicable to public sector or not-for-profit organizations. However, consideration of the activities of these organizations will usually lead to the conclusion that competition is an element present within their external environments. Charities, for example, compete with other charities for donations. Different areas within the public sector such as education, social services, and health care compete for resources both between each other and between the various agencies charged with delivering a specific aspect of welfare state provision.

Identifying and sustaining a competitive advantage are also becoming more important as public sector agencies seek to ensure their ongoing existence in a world where Governments are being forced to make massive cuts in public sector spending. In such circumstances those organizations capable of demonstrating a competitive advantage of superiority in the fulfilment of their assigned roles are less likely to be the focus of budget cutbacks. Whereas organizations perceived to be performing poorly and unable to demonstrate any advantage over other organizations in the same and different areas of the public sector can expect to have their budgets severely reduced. In some cases, perceptions over inferior performance may result in the decision to close the organization as it is seen as unable to fulfil the service provision role which had been assigned in the past.

Competitive advantage

The term 'competitive advantage' first came to the fore in the 1980s in large part due to the Porter's (1985) text on the subject. As noted by Klein (2002), however, neither Porter and subsequently nor some other academics have been willing to offer a definition of 'competitive advantage' which provides sufficient clarity such that, similar to the definition of 'strategy', the concept is totally understood by students or management practitioners. For example, as pointed out by Klein, even Porter (1985, p. 32) in his seminal text on the subject was not prepared to go beyond the statement that 'competitive advantage grows fundamentally out of the value a firm is able to create for its buyers that exceeds the cost of creating it'. Klein expressed the opinion that most people, upon being asked to attribute this definition to a private sector scenario, would probably not perceive that statement as applying to competitive advantage but instead assume it is a description of the activities associated with the generation of profit.

In terms of creating a link between competitive activity and the management of strategy, a simple definition applicable to both private and public sector organizations is hereby proposed, namely:

competitive advantage is the long term tactical philosophy adopted by the organisation through which to outperform other organisations serving the same customer(s) and market sector(s) or competing for access to the same source of financial resources.

One possible reason for the confusion which may exist in the literature about competitive advantage is that in an earlier text on strategic management Porter (1980) proposed there were four alternative generic strategic 'competitive advantage' options through which a firm could achieve market success. His model has subsequently been widely accepted by academics. One wonders whether confusion over the term 'competitive advantage' would have never emerged if only Porter had referred to his four proposed options as 'alternative strategies through which to gain advantage over competition'.

The basis of the Porterian generic alternatives is based upon the two dimensions of (i) basis of performance and (ii) degree of market coverage. In relation to the latter, Porter proposed that an organization could opt to offer products or services to the majority of the market or alternatively, adopt a 'focused' approach of only meeting the specific needs of a small group of customers. In relation to performance, Porter proposed the choice of 'cost leadership' or delivering superior performance (or 'differentiation'). In his view, 'cost leadership' was a low-scale advantage because over time it is probable that eventually another provider will enter the market offering a product or service at an even lower price. This scenario can emerge because organizations may no longer have access to the resource which provided the original cost advantage. For example, in the private sector, low labour costs may disappear in a developing nation as the country implements modernization and industrialization of the nation's economy. Alternatively, a company may have access to a highly accessible mineral but extraction activities over time may cause this resource to become depleted and costs will rise.

Although an elegant, simple tool which has been extremely useful to students and management practitioners over the years, the Porterian model does

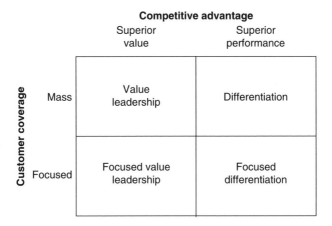

Figure 12.1   A customer-orientated competitive advantage matrix

suffer from a potential defect in the typology proposed for defining 'alternative sources' of competitive advantage. The defect is that the terminology of 'cost leadership' tends to place too greater emphasis on offering the lowest possible price. This may cause users of the tool to believe unless an organization can sustain a low price, this option will only provide a short-term advantage. Hence, a recommended alternative as illustrated in Figure 12.1 is to use the terminology of 'superior value'. This term will assist organizations to recognize there are other options available in addition to competing purely on the basis of low price. In the public sector, for example, a public sector agency facing rising labour costs which is causing the Government to consider outsourcing service provision to the private sector might adopt an entrepreneurial orientation and seek ways of adding value to service output by using new technology to automate service production and delivery processes. Alternatively, a university might reduce operating costs associated with employing a large number of academic staff by investing in the creation of an online, computer-based course delivery system. This alternative approach would permit certain aspects of teaching delivery costs to be reduced because an online system will reduce the need to rely on the extremely expensive process of delivering learning using terrestrial, classroom-based interaction between students and faculty.

A second potential defect in the Porterian model is some users may adopt a literalist application of the concept in terms of all strategic positions being mutually exclusive. As a consequence, there is the risk that a belief will develop that one cannot adopt a combined competitive advantage approach (Reitsperger et al. 1993). In the United States and Western Europe a standard response to the emergence of price competition from lower cost, Asian suppliers in the 1980s was to assume that survival could only be achieved by adopting the competitive advantage of superior product performance. To achieve and sustain superior performance usually requires R&D and investment in new technology. In some markets these higher costs can be recovered from customers who are prepared to pay a premium price in return for superior performance. However, one nation which recognized the fallacy associated with a literalist interpretation of the Porterian model was Japan. Entrepreneurial manufacturers recognized that an even stronger competitive advantage can be achieved by offering a superior product, but through the application of appropriate process technologies, also add value by making the product available at a lower price. One of the first examples of 'blended advantage' was Toyota who launched their range of luxury vehicles under the Lexus brand name. These cars were hugely successful because they offered consumers the same standard of quality as the world's leading brands such as Mercedes and Cadillac, but at prices approximately 25 per cent lower than competition.

The third potential defect with the model is the assumption that once an organization has determined the best source of competitive advantage, this advantage must be sustained for ever more. Examination of case materials of highly successful private sector organizations that have survived over long periods of time will reveal the fallacy of this managerial concept. What these case materials indicate is that over time, in response to emerging changes in external environments, to remain successful organizations must retain the ability to be flexible over the their choice of competitive advantage. This ability is necessary in order that the organization retains an appropriate fit between what the market needs and what a firm can supply (Markides 2004). This perspective suggests there is the need to slightly revise the earlier definition of strategy as follows:

Strategy is a statement which specifies the nature of the entrepreneurial competitive advantage to be utilised to achieve an organisation's strategic objectives.

The addition of the term 'entrepreneurial' will ensure that the organization remains committed towards recognizing early signs of environmental change and has the competences, flexibility, and internal culture to respond by using innovation as the basis for evolving a revised competitive advantage more suited to future environmental conditions. In order to overcome some of the criticisms of the Porterian model, Treacy and Wiersema (1995) proposed that the changing nature of markets meant that the two dimensions of market coverage and product performance were no longer adequate in the determination of strategy. In their view the key issue which required recognition is the growing importance of relationship marketing which was causing some organizations seeking to build long-term customer loyalty to move away from their more traditional philosophy of transaction marketing. This concept was subsequently expanded by Chaston (2009b) who felt the Treacy and Wiersema model gave insufficient attention to the option of competing on the basis of price. He proposed this potential weakness can be overcome by using the four dimensions of transaction, relationship, product performance, and price. The features associated with a strategy are associated with these dimensions:

(1) *Transactional Excellence*

Price/quality/value product or service combinations superior to that of competition.

Standardized products or services.

Excellence in managing conventional production and distribution logistics.

Information system designed to rapidly identify production and/or logistic errors.

(2) *Relationship excellence*

Product/service combination which delivers complete customer-specific solutions.

Product/services solution based on conventional specifications appropriate for the sector in which an organization is located.

Employee obsession with finding even more effective conventional solutions to customer problems.

Information systems which rapidly identify errors in solution provision.

Culture of all employees committed to working closely with counterparts within customer organizations.

(3) *Product Performance Excellence*

Product/service propositions offering outstanding superior performance versus competition.

Orientation towards always seeking to extend the performance.

Boundaries of existing products/services.

Excellence across the entire workforce in understanding how the latest advances in technology might be incorporated into products/services and/or production processes.

Culture of employees always striving to apply conventional approaches to finding new market opportunities for exploiting identified product/service performance improvements.

(4) *Price Performance Excellence*

Product/services prices significantly lower than the rest of the market.

Skilled in the production of 'no frills' products\ services.

Excellence in acquiring prior generation technology and capital equipment at either zero or low cost.

Information system designed to rapidly identify adverse cost variance trends across the areas of procurement, production, and distribution.

Culture of employees always striving to find ways of applying conventional thinking to further reducing operating and/or overhead costs.

Most organizations having analysed customer need and the behaviour of any competitors will probably determine that it is feasible to exploit internal

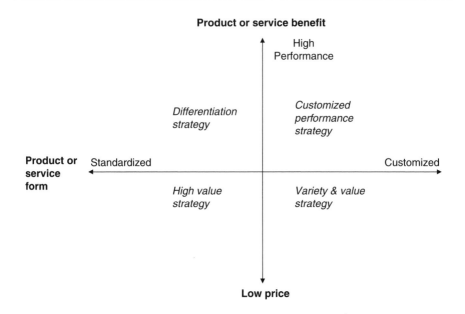

Figure 12.2   Strategic innovation options

capabilities to develop a strategy which would represent a combination of two of the four dimensions available. The outcome will then result in the selection and implementation of one of the strategic positions type shown in Figure 12.2.

Alternative Strategies

Case Aims: To illustrate the different strategies which might be adopted by a Government department.

Charhi (2000) posits that the identification of an appropriate strategy in the public sector is more complex than in the private sector. This is because public sector planners need to take account of factors such as the views of politicians, the existence of legislation defining or limiting the nature of service provision, pressure from the general public, and, because the public sector entity is often the sole provider, the inapplicability of concepts such as how costs or pricing need to be taken into account. As a consequence, Charhi has proposed that academic texts proposing direct transfer of strategic models without any revision to reflect differing circumstances from the private sector are possibly presenting inappropriate ideas.

   To acquire data to assess the validity of his perspective, Charhi undertook an analysis of the strategies adopted by ten different departments in the Canadian Federal Government. From this study he concluded that the following strategies were being utilized:

(cont'd)

(1) Internal or Revitalization Strategy

- improvement in managerial processes and systems
- improvement in operational processes
- improvement in organizational structure
- further development of HRM policies and culture

(2) Service Improvement Strategy

- Improve service quality
- Develop new services
- Engage in research on service development and enhancing internal operational processes

(3) Re-Orientation Strategy

- Redefine field of activity and levels of service provision
- Examine the option of privatization
- Opt out or withdraw from some areas of service provision

(4) Political Strategy

- Seek to defend current sectoral role
- Persuade politicians of the benefits of retaining current role
- Seek to have strengthened existing legislation influencing the current service provision role
- Seek to have new legislation introduced that adds more mandatory tasks for overseeing sector activities

(5) Environmental Strategy

- Focus on conservation/environmental/resource protection
- Engage in more education and awareness building in relevant sector(s)

(6) Partnership Strategy

- Develop collaborative relationships with other agencies/organizations
- Exploit the relationship to expand 'one stop' service delivery
- Exploit the relationship to achieve cost reduction through economies of scale

(7) *Status Quo* Strategy

- Retain current role and service provision portfolio
- Make no changes in nature and volume of service provision
- Focus on maintaining current budgets and make no changes to operations processes

(cont'd)

In terms of popularity, Charhi concluded that the two dominant strategies were Revitalization (28 per cent) and Service Improvement (26 per cent). The other five strategies tended to be more rarely adopted, all at a level in the region of 10 per cent of respondents. The selection of strategy appeared to be influenced by a department's perception of the future external environment, internal capabilities, and ability of the workforce to accept and implement change. It also appeared that only five departments felt they could survive by focusing upon implementing a single strategy. Four other departments felt there is a need for a dual strategy and just one department decided there was a requirement to utilize a multiple strategy.

Sustainable survival

For most organizations, a very critical objective of the selected strategy is to ensure the long-term survival of the organization. There is the risk that a poorly defined strategy may only provide a temporary market advantage. This view is supported by Mintzberg (1994a, p. 15) who concluded in relation to the Design School approach to strategic planning there is 'the danger that the strategy will be outdated within 3 months. If you go back to that strategy you may be focusing your attention on the wrong areas in the business'. To overcome this criticism and thereby avoid the risk of short-term organizational thinking, perhaps a slightly expanded definition is required. One suggestion is that:

Strategy is a statement which specifies the nature of the entrepreneurial competitive advantage to be utilised to deliver long-term strategic objectives associated with the construction of an enduring organisation.

The pace of technological change when coupled with an increasing number of countries engaged in industrialization now entering into world markets means that few private sector organizations can expect to survive without continually assessing the need to implement fundamental strategic change. The emergence of fiscal crises in many developed nations also means the issue of fundamental strategic change, usually achieved by exhibiting entrepreneurial behaviour, is now just as relevant in the public sector. This is because delivery of change is probably virtually impossible without relying upon exploiting innovation as the basis for updating the service portfolio, identifying opportunities to create new services, enter new sectors, develop new internal processes, or/and in some cases, discontinue certain areas of the organization's current operations.

Failure to recognize the importance of entrepreneurship as a key element of strategy will eventually lead to the demise of the organization or alternatively, leave the organization as a shadow of its former greatest. Sadly the world of business is littered with such examples (e.g. in the United States the airlines, Pan

Am and TWA, in the United Kingdom the car companies Rover and Morris car companies and Triumph motorcycles). The responsibility for such outcomes must rest with the leadership, often across a number of generations, who decided that life would be much easier if their organization totally ignored innovation and instead focused on short-term activities to maximize sales and profits from the existing product portfolio. During the early phase of ignoring the strategic importance of entrepreneurship, the high short-term profitability of the organizations in the private sector will often cause the leadership to be held in high esteem by their peers, the business press, and the financial community. What these leaders are prepared to ignore is their long-term responsibilities to stakeholders such as loyal customers, sustaining the existence of other members of their supply chain(s), creating employment opportunities in the communities where there operations are based, and the ability to generate the corporate taxes needed by Governments to meet the social welfare needs of future generation of less advantaged citizens where the organization is based.

In an increasingly uncertain world, leaders of public sector organizations also need to adopt a more realistic and long-term perspective of the risks posed to ongoing survival as Governments act to reduce huge public sector spending deficits. In the past there may have been a tendency for some leaders to adopt the view that Governments would not be prepared to let major public sector operations go bankrupt. This attitude is an increasingly dangerous perspective in today's world. For example in the United Kingdom, the Government has recently commented that some Universities may have to be closed having exhibited an inadequate degree of fiscal responsibility. Should this occur, sustaining student needs will be achieved by the delivery of their programmes being transferred to other, more effective Higher Education providers.

There is increasing recognition of important role of innovation that can play in terms of offering the most appropriate strategic philosophy through which to ensure the long-term survival of PSOs (Osborne and Brown 2005). These authors have proposed that innovation is necessary in order to respond to both 'planned' and 'emergent' change. The former involves the public sector manager determining that changing external or internal circumstances will require the crafting and implementing of a new or revised strategy. An example would be the senior management in a hospital determining the increasing exploitation of 'key hole' surgery will require changes in the structuring of physical facilities, treatment provision, and the skills of hospital staff. More difficult to manage are emergent strategies because these are caused by some form of significant change or the onset of crisis and typically demand a fundamental re-evaluation of future strategy within a PSO. The impact of major cutbacks in public sector spending being currently evoked by Governments is an example of an emergent scenario.

In terms of senior management being able to determine the role of innovation as a key component of future strategy, there is the need to determine what will be required in terms of PSO's future role as a service provider. A typology which can be utilized is to assume there are two dimensions associated with innovation: namely focus internal processes versus service outputs and new service provision

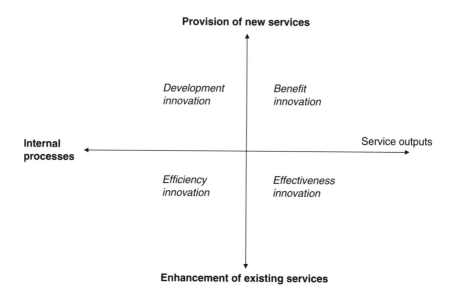

Figure 12.3   Strategic positioning options

versus sustaining the delivery of existing services. Both these dimensions can be treated as being continuums. This approach generates the typology illustrated in Figure 12.3. This typology suggests there are four different potential areas of focus in determining how innovation will influence future strategy in a PSO. These are:

(1) Efficiency innovation which focuses upon innovation in relation to the internal processes that can enhance the future delivery of existing services.
(2) Effectiveness innovation which focuses on innovation in relation to enhancing the provision of output for existing services.
(3) Development innovation which focuses on innovation that utilizes changes in internal process that can support the development of new services.
(4) Benefit innovation which focuses upon innovation directed towards the creation of new services that enhance the organization's future service provision portfolio.

The other aspect of innovation management in the public sector is the degree to which the activity is an identified fundamental aspect of strategy definition and implementation or an unplanned and unmanaged process (Veenswjik 2005). In the case of the latter situation innovation is an unexpected outcome from an interaction of factors and activities which have occurred within or impacted a public sector organization. For example, a group of individuals in a Local Authority might develop a computer-based information management and decision system for enhancing the effectiveness and efficiency of the Authority's handling of planning applications. Contacts from other organizations following media coverage about the success of the proprietary software might cause the Authority to establish a new revenue generating consultancy service advising other PSOs on the design and operation of computer-based decision-support systems.

Incorrect Assumptions

Case Aims: To illustrate how incorrect assumptions may cause a public sector organization to misread the strength of politicians' commitment towards achieving change.

It is not uncomment for public sector senior managers to assume the survival of their organization is a certainty. One justification is that the unions can force Governments to reverse closure decisions because these organizations are capable of causing economic damage, civil unrest, and even bring down Governments. As a result public sector unions can be expected to force politicians to back down from proposed changes in the public sector designed to resolve a fiscal crisis.

There is some anecdotal evidence that this attitude exists among public sector managers in countries such as Greece and Spain about relying the activities of the unions supporting their workforce causing Governments to reverse their decision to reduce public sector spending. Such individuals, however, do need to reflect upon the scale of the fiscal crisis facing their respective countries and how this will influence the level of civil unrest Governments are prepared to accept in order to be successful in reducing public sector spending.

An example of the resolve of political leaders is provided by the national strike by workers in the United Kingdom's state-owned coal mining industry during the 1970s. The mineworkers' union, having used the weapon of a national strike to force earlier Governments to back down over proposals for change, assumed they could achieve the same outcome when the Conservative Party Prime Minister Margaret Thatcher decided to reduce public sector spending by returning the coal industry to the private sector. In this case the resolve of the country's leadership was greater than that of the unions. The prime minister was prepared to live with months of civil unrest and economic disruption caused by a miners' strike in order to achieve her goal of fundamental economic and social change. The miners' union assumed media coverage of violence between the police and the mineworkers could achieve a reversal of the Government's privatization decision. Instead the media coverage heightened the general public's support for Mrs Thatcher's policies. Eventually the growing adverse mood among the UK general public caused the mineworkers to decide to return to work. Soon afterwards the industry was returned to the private sector.

Entrepreneurship

Higgins (1995) posited the long-term survival of existing major organizations in the twenty-first century is critically reliant upon a strategy which is based upon exploiting entrepreneurship to sustain long-term, competitive advantage. It is often dangerous for academic researchers to identify the latest firms that are global exemplars of innovative behaviour and to utilize their strategies as the basis for defining 'best managerial practices'. This is because even some of the world's most successful firms do seem encounter periods when senior management seem to forget the importance of innovation.

Even over the last 20 years, there are a number of examples of companies identified as 'excellent' which subsequently exhibited a downturn in performance, thereby contradicting the claim of being named as innovative organizations. Higgins provides a number of examples of the risks associated with claiming a company have demonstrated undisputed excellence. Two of the companies he identified as excellent were GE Corporation, which has filed more patents than almost any other firm in the United States, and the US computer company Hewlett-Packard. In recent years, however, both companies have encountered their fair share of problems. During the late 1990s, with growth slowing for many of the company's older product lines via their GE Capital division, the company massively expanded involvement in the financial services industry through their provision of loan and leasing facilities to customers (Anon. 2009d). Initially this expansion was hailed by industry observers as an outstanding strategic move by the company. Increasingly, however, as GE became obsessed with always hitting quarterly profit forecasts, GE Capital was used to implement last minute financial activities such as the sale of assets to close any emerging profit gap. Not surprisingly this behaviour trait led to the same bad habits that also existed in the wider US financial community emerging within the GE Capital operation. By 2007, GE Capital was equal in size to some of the world's largest banks, providing 67 per cent of GE's total sales revenue and 55 per cent of total profits. When the global financial meltdown commenced, GE Capital was found to be the owners of some extremely high-risk, toxic debt in sectors such as property, credit cards, and loans to emerging economies in Eastern Europe. To recover from this highly dangerous position, GE was forced to implement actions such as reducing annual dividends by over 65 per cent, raising $15 billion in new capital, and drawing upon low-cost loans being offered by the US Government.

In case of Hewlett Packard, Higgins (1995, p. 97) stated the company 'continues to dazzle the industrial world because, it continues to grow at a staggering pace, launching successful new products at a rate few competitors can match'. Unfortunately, again in the face of slowing sales for existing products, the company decided to de-emphasize innovation and instead decided to acquire Compaq, a major manufacturer of IBM PC clones. The strategic rationale was this would provide a new platform for growth by helping Hewlett Packard gain entry into new market sectors. As was obvious to many people in the computer industry, at the time of the Compaq acquisition, the US manufacturers of PCs were already rapidly losing market share to lower priced Asian-based producers. Hence, it soon emerged that the price of the acquisition was much higher than the business was worth and as a consequence, Hewlett Packard struggled to remain a healthy company. Eventually recovery was only achieved by a return to the company's prior long-standing strategy originally defined by the organization's founders of exploiting expertise in innovativeness to deliver better solutions to customers by exploiting new technology.

The competence debate

In part because of academics' enduring desire to challenge established ideas, Porterian theory has been criticized by adopting an excessively market-orientated approach to defining competitive advantage. Some of these leading critics such as Pralahad and Hamel (1990) are strong supporters of the RBV concept. They presented the alternative perspective that RBV theory is a more realistic rationale for explaining success. In their view this is because exploitation of a superior key competence provides the basis for the competitive advantage which permits the organization to outperform other organizations serving the same customers. Pralahad and Hamel supported their view about the critical importance of acquiring a core competence by drawing upon examples such as Honda. They posit that this company's superior engineering capability in the field of designing and manufacturing vehicle drive chains is the reason why the company has achieved a leadership position in the global car industry.

Examples such as Honda do appear to be a valid reason for supporting the RBV concept in the case of firms operating in highly stable, unchanging mature, low technology B2B and B2C markets. In this environment widespread understanding of markets and process technology means that companies face huge difficulties in achieving any significant tangible differences in product performance. Under these circumstances, a focus on identifying a core internal operational competence that might provide the basis for a competitive advantage that differentiates the company from competition possibly can be a feasible strategic philosophy (Hayes and Upton 1998). Service industry markets are probably the most difficult in which to achieve the aim of providing a tangible, perceivable difference in the services made available to customers. Hence, a highly successful alternative strategy is to identify a set of organizational competences which permit the organization to defeat competitors by offering greater value through the exploitation of competence in reducing operating costs.

Hamel and Prahalad (1994) proposed the view that RBV theory is also validated by examples from high technology industries where the key competence is contained within an organization's ability to assemble a bundle of skills and technologies which permit the organization to develop a unique new technological platform. These authors suggest an example of this perspective is provided by the case of Microsoft. The company's core competences in the development of new software platforms have permitted the company to become the dominant provider of software installed in both business and home PCs. Furthermore, the authors posit that the firm by having achieved market dominance for a specific business platform greatly increased the probability that acquired internal competences will provide the basis for further market growth and the launch of new products (Wonglimpiyarat 2004). In the case of Microsoft, their platform dominance in Windows operating systems for PC provided the springboard from which to launch a whole new series of products such as Windows 95, 97, 98, 2000, NT, and their Internet Explorer Web browser. Additionally, in order to acquire the technical competence to enter new areas of the software industry, Microsoft has pursued a strategy by acquiring other software firms such as Forethought, Fox Software, and Visio Corp.

A more balanced approach to the issue of the importance of key competences is that proposed by Kay (1993). He posited that distinctive competences are a potential source of competitive advantage, but only if applied to appropriate external environmental situations. The approach exhibits certain similarities with the views expressed by Porter. Kay proposes that strategy is about relating the organization's core competences to external environments and that to be successful competitive advantage must be sustainable and, where feasible, also be unique. Kay suggest that there are four major sources of strength available to the organization, namely reputation, innovation, internal, and external relationships and organizational assets. He proposed that the importance of these sources of strength will vary between sectors and between organizations operating in the same sector. Thus, for example, it can be argued that in the case of Microsoft, the company's competitive advantage was a combination of internal competences that led to the creation of their MS:DOS and Windows platform linked to their external relationship with IBM whereby this company adopted Microsoft technology as the core software to drive their new generation of PCs. It seems reasonable to suggest that without this unusual market relationship between the two companies through which to expand participation in the IT industry, Microsoft would have faced a much harder battle to become the global leader in the world software industry.

The idea of linking internal competence to external relationships leading to the delivery of greater customer satisfaction is probably a more secure strategic philosophy in most cases than reliance on a purely internal source of competitive advantage. It is also a valid perspective that to rely on an entirely market-orientated strategy without regard to having created the internal competences that support delivery of superior quality or service can also risk the organization being overtaken by competitor. This latter perspective is especially valid in those cases where a competitor has developed more advanced internal competences permitting the offering of an upgraded benefit proposition.

Figure 12.4, by using the two dimensions of core competence and market understanding, summarizes the implications of failing to develop a more

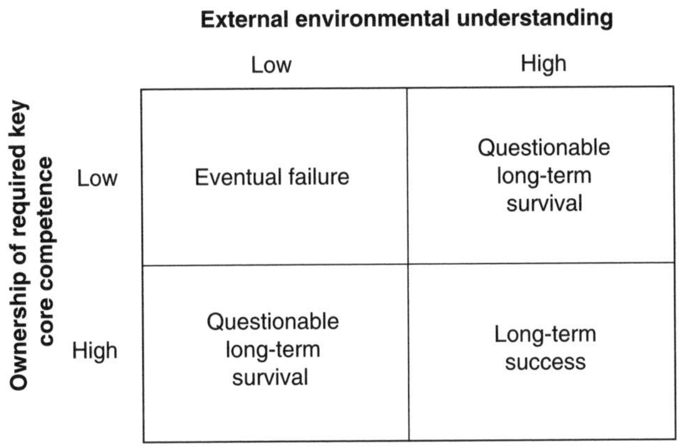

External environmental understanding

Figure 12.4   Outcome options matrix

balanced view of how to achieve and sustain an effective strategy. A lack of ability along both dimensions will inevitably lead to failure. However, a weakness along even one dimension suggests the organization has a questionable long-term future. More certainty over long-term survival is more likely to be achieved by combining both market understanding and ownership of appropriate key competences in the creation of a sustainable competitive advantage.

Factors Influencing the Planning Process

Case Aims: To illustrate how differences in operations give rise to the need for public sector entities to act differently than their private sector counterparts.

One of the most extensive attempts to examine strategic planning in the public sector was Bryson (1995). In his text he examined the nature of the differences which exist between public and private sector organizations in relation to how these could influence the planning process. Some of the more important differences he proposes are the role of politicians as a source of influence, the degree of public scrutiny to which public sector bodies are exposed, policy ambiguities, and the degree of attention and influence of multiple stakeholders. Goals tend to be less specific and more complex. Extensive interaction with external bodies is often required to achieve the effective provision and delivery of services. A key internal difference is public sector organizations tend to be much more bureaucratic and hierarchical which can be a major influence over decision-making and create greater complexity when seeking to identify issues and reach consensus during the development of the strategic plan.

In commenting upon the existing literature, Hendrick (2003) felt there was also need to focus on the very significant differences in the external and internal

(cont'd)

environments in private versus public sector situations. In her view the external environment facing the public sector strategic planner is made more complex by the stronger influence of outside parties, many of whom held very diverse views about the role and responsibilities of specific public sector agencies. There can also be the problem that public sector organizations can face significant hostility from external sources over the scale and availability of resources that should be made available. She also felt that inside public sector strategic management is made additionally complex because within these organizations there tends to be greater centralization of control and significant resistance to change.

In order to generate empirical data on the influence of identified differences, Hendrick undertook a study of the strategic planning process within departments in the City of Milwaukee administration following the administration's decision to introduce 'System 94'. This programme required all departments to submit a strategic plan with the aim of linking all these departmental inputs together to develop a city-wide strategic plan. Prior to this time, the planning process was based upon departments developing a 'bottom-up' specification of required financial budgets which were then assessed by the mayor who determined what funds each department would receive. Under the new system, central administration informed each department of the budget they were to receive and to use these data as the basis for initiating a 'top-down' planning approach.

Her analysis revealed that the strategic planning capability was strongest in those departments that had already established effective monitoring systems, where there was the greatest need to adopt a co-ordinated approach to service provision and actual performance is relatively easy to assess. There were also some surprises in the data. For example, the Treasury Department ranked high on planning capability but scored poorly on their implementation of the System 94 approach. Further investigation revealed that this was probably caused by the City Treasurer refusing to participate in the System 94 programme and instead continuing to use the department's own planning system which he perceived as more effective. A similar outcome was found for the Port of Milwaukee. Both departments scored highly, however, on the innovative nature of their plan in relation to responding to changing external environmental circumstances. This suggested that although a different planning model was being used, extensive experience with in-house systems permitted these two departments to become more effective in developing and implementing strategic plans. Those departments which had a large number of staff or were involved in multiple interactions with external bodies encountered the greatest problems in developing an effective plan. Of these departments, those which had fewer problems with the planning process were those which already had an effective monitoring process in place or were able to use a small number of indicators to assess performance.

> **(cont'd)**
>
> Although Hendrick's hypothesis was that the complexity and uncertainty of a department's external environment would influence the planning process, the results did not support this perspective. This is not a unique conclusion, because other writers such as Bryson have posited that the complexity of managing internal relations in centralized, hierarchical organizations will mean the orientation of the planners will be towards overcoming internal obstacles and achieving adequate internal co-ordination of service process provision activities. As a result, the planners have less time to be concerned with external issues than their counterparts in private sector organizations. Hendrick, although accepting convergence of her study and other writers in relation to this aspect of the public sector planning process, expressed concern that it appears public sector bodies tend to give insufficient attention to external environmental issues. In her opinion in an increasingly turbulent and volatile world, such an orientation could place public sector departments at increasing risk in developing strategies capable of sustaining successful performance in the future in relation to delivering an optimal service portfolio.

Strategic defence

For a private sector organization which is reliant upon revenue generated by sales from products or services which have entered the maturity phase of the life cycle curve, possibly one of the greatest sources of potential threat is the entry of a firm, usually from a developing nation, offering the same benefit proposition at a much lower price. Unless the existing incumbent firm has a new range of products or services positioned on the growth phase of the life cycle curve, senior management will be under extreme pressure to respond to the new threat by also reducing prices. Although such a move may be perceived as a tactical necessity, in reality the company is usually discarding the business strategy which has been the basis of past success. As a consequence, management may be guilty of repositioning the company in such a way as to destroy all ability to sustain the long-term strategic aim of building an enduring organization.

For an incumbent established firm whose market position is based upon offering low prices, the preferable response to the emergence of a lower-cost competitor is to identify a way of dealing with this threat without making a fundamental adjustment to the organization's existing long-term strategy. In support of this perspective, Morehouse et al. (2008) have proposed that the affected organizations should examine short-term tactics to minimize the impact of price competition while concurrently determining how changes in products or markets served can permit retention of the firm's existing long-term strategy. In relation to the effective management of a tactical response to price competition, the authors recommend that the firm should carefully monitor new potential sources of low-cost competition. This is because the earlier a potential threat recognized, the greater the time period available to the firm to evolve an effective response.

Once the price threat has been identified, further analysis is advisable to determine how the competitor has achieved their cost advantage. Potential sources can include access to lower-cost labour, raw materials, a different production technology, or an alternative channel management strategy. In some cases, the incumbent firm may be able to duplicate the same technique as the new competitor as a way of also being able to reduce operating costs. More usually, however, the incumbent firm will not be able to duplicate the competitor's operational processes. Hence, a search will need to be instigated to identify other potential pathways through which to reduce costs. This activity may identify that past market success has caused the company to have become somewhat complacent. As a result operational inefficiencies and slack business processes may have been permitted to develop. In this situation, emphasis on tightening of operational procedures and making the workforce aware of the need to focus on implementing efficiency upgrades may create the cost savings being sought. Should it be apparent that the level of price competition will be very intense, then the firm will probably need to introduce more drastic actions to introduce new economies into the operation. These could include relocating operations to a new country where labour or raw material costs are lower, sub-contracting or outsourcing certain areas of the business, or introducing new more advanced technology that can reduce production costs. In those cases, where no significant cost savings can be found that would permit profits to be sustained following a reduction in prices, the alternate option is for the firm to seek to strengthen customer satisfaction over their perceptions of the superior value offered by the existing product or service portfolio. This might be achieved, for example, by increasing the level of advertising expenditure which can increase customer awareness of the product benefits being offered. Other opportunities may exist by upgrading the range and quality of complementary services offered alongside the core product proposition (e.g. a machine tool company offering a free production line design and machinery installation service).

Assuming a company is able to mount an adequate defence in the face of increased price competition, this outcome will hopefully provide the window of time needed in order that innovation can be utilized to develop higher profit margin solutions involving new products or entry into new markets. Hopefully these new solutions will be compatible with the organization's existing long-term strategy. Occasions may emerge, however, when retention of the old strategy will not provide the basis for the ongoing generation of an adequate level of profits. In these circumstances the organization will be forced to implement a fundamental review of the organization's long-term future to identify what are the viable strategic options which remain available.

Until recently many public sector organizations have not been concerned about the emergence of lower-cost competitors. In the face of large fiscal deficits it may be necessary to re-visit this operating philosophy. This is because in the face of the need to reduce public sector spending even Governments which pre-viously considered the use of lower-cost private sector providers as breaching prevailing political philosophy may now be open to the idea of permitting ser-vice provision to be handed over to the private sector. This potential outcome means that similar to the private sector, public sector agencies now do need to be aware of service provision costs of private sector operations because these entities may soon become a new source of competition for Government funds. Where the private sector appears to have lower operating costs, the public sec-tor operation will need to examine strategic options for lowering internal costs through mechanisms such as enhancing employee productivity or implementing process re-engineering initiatives.

Strategic flexibility

A critical factor influencing the sustained success of organizations is their abil-ity to consistently implement an effective long-term strategy. Consistency is an important philosophy because it avoids the company initiating actions in response to short-term changes in market conditions that might divert the com-pany away from focusing on entrepreneurial developments designed to ensure fulfilment of long-term organizational goals (Hax 1990). In seeking to ensure consistency, the organization must also avoid becoming so rigid in its thinking such that fundamental shifts in environmental conditions are ignored. By being prepared to implement actions in response to environmental change, this will permit avoidance of a major decline in organizational performance. To be able to make such a response, however, the organization must retain a sufficient level of cognitive flexibility to permit strategies to be modified, thereby more effectively equipping the organization to handle external environmental change.

Hitt et al. (1998) have proposed that an emphasis on strategic consistency was relevant when most organizations operated in a world of gradual change and where the same strategy could be expected to remain effective for many years. In the past market boundaries were well-defined, appropriate market data were readily accessible, and there were few variations in the utilization of operational processes in different parts of the world. Over the last 25 years, however, external environments have increasingly become more unstable. New entrants have emerged, new technologies have fundamentally changed existing markets or spawned entirely new sectors, and the intensity of competition has increased. In the face of these changes to survive organizations must develop a higher degree of strategic flexibility. This will permit exploitation of techno-logical advances and the ability to survive in economic conditions which are increasingly becoming affected by global level events.

In reviewing the options of how organizations can sustain their performance, Hitt et al. (1998, p. 24) posited that 'Strategic flexibility, then, is the capability of the organisation to pro-act or respond quickly to changing competitive con-ditions and thereby develop and/or maintain competitive advantage.' In their view a critical aspect of achieving flexibility is the existence of a leadership team that has the vision to comprehend how the organization can best exploit new opportunities and threats that emerge in the external environment. A fundamental aspect of this strategic vision must be to identify ways to manage existing operations while concurrently developing new product or service opportunities which are compatible with the organization's long-term strategy. This type of visionary thinking is necessary in order to sustain the organization's financial viability such that it remains possible to invest in the new resources that will be required to achieve long-term aims associated with innovation and change.

An organization must ensure that where possible, revisions in future plans continue to exploit the core competences upon which the entity has achieved current success. This will not happen unless the organization has developed existing competences which are flexible and dynamic, thereby permitting rapid identification and implementation of new, entrepreneurially orientated, business activities. Without ensuring core competences exhibit a dynamic dimension, there is the risk that these competences may become outdated. This outcome will limit the future strategic options available to the organization. There is also the risk that as competences become inflexible this also will restrict the breadth of potential opportunities that can be considered as viable strategic options by the organization. As core competence rigidity develops, this increases the risk of capabilities becoming internally institutionalized, thereby narrowing the potential strategic opportunities available to the organization.

A key aspect of strategic flexibility is the willingness of organizations to monitor their external environments to determine whether existing competences will sustain future performance or whether actions should be implemented to develop new competences. The implication of this perspective is that the long-term viability of organization is dependent upon continuous assessment of the advisability of resources being assigned towards supporting existing competences or re-allocating resources to support development of new internal capabilities. The elements and process which underpin strategic flexibility are summarized in Figure 12.5.

Although strategic flexibility is accepted as a critical factor in sustaining the long-term successful survival of organizations, embedding the philosophy into public sector organizations can be difficult. This is because there exist a number of barriers which can severely constrain the aim of providing public sector employees with greater freedom in the self-determination of decisions and implementing more effective or efficient ways of working (OLooney 1992). One of the major constraints is that process activities and outputs are defined either by Government legislation or strict guidelines issued by senior managers over procedures that must be followed. Additionally, there is usually less freedom than that encountered in the private sector in relation to HRM policies. For example, public sector managers are usually required to follow an inflexible set of procedures when seeking to discipline a poorly performing employee or in reaching the decision to dismiss an individual. Also managers have less freedom over delegating tasks. This is because in many cases there exist strict rules governing at

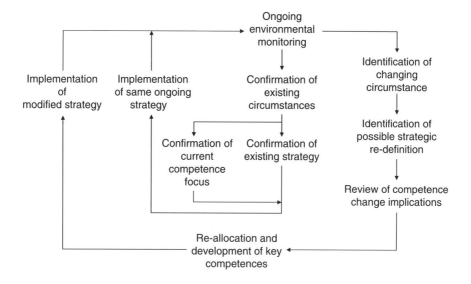

Figure 12.5   Circle of continuous strategic re-evaluation

which level within the hierarchy decisions over issues such as approving expenditure or purchasing supplies can be made. It is also often the case that managers are not permitted the flexibility to propose alternative actions. Instead, what are perceived as being important decisions are made at a senior level within the organization. These decisions are then imposed on lower-level managers without permitting these latter individuals to negotiate alternative, possibly more effective actions. Another constraint within the public sector relates the rigidity of time frames in relation to both when decisions can be made and actions implemented (Ring and Perry 1985). A key factor influencing this latter situation is many public sector budgets once defined will remain fixed for a 12-month period. Once a budget has been set for a specific action then implementation of expenditure must occur within the same financial year. This severely restricts managers from actions such as deferring decisions while awaiting the availability in the market of a preferred technology or item of capital equipment. Hence, the manager may be forced to purchase an inferior solution because there is the risk that the area of expenditure may not be included in next year's budget.

Significant additional understanding of strategic flexibility was generated by research by Miles and Snow in the 1970s. This led to the identification of a strategic typology in which organizations could be classified as Prospectors, Defenders, Analysers, and Defenders (Miles et al. 1978). These researchers proposed that the changing nature of external environments caused organizations at certain points in their life history to confront the need to reconsider future strategy and internal operations. This activity was labelled as an 'adaptive cycle' in which the organization examine the need to adopt a more entrepreneurial strategy and make revisions to the two internal domains of process technology and administrative systems in relation to key issues such as structure, departmental roles, and employee skills.

Within the Miles and Snow typology, Prospectors are those organizations which are orientated towards identifying new external environmental and product/service opportunities. Having selected a new opportunity, the organization has sufficient flexibility in relation to technology and administrative processes to implement appropriate actions to exploit their entrepreneurial orientation. Defenders focus on retaining control over their current business and attempt to sustain financial viability by exploiting high levels of efficiency in managing technology and administrative processes. To avoid encounters with other potential suppliers, Defenders usually attempt to occupy a small, narrow market domain where their expertise permits delivery of a superior product or service offering with little risks or threats from competition. Reactors are the least responsive type of organization. Management is fixated on sustaining the organization's existing strategy and internal processes. The usual outcome is that as external environments change this rigidity eventually leads to the demise of the organization. The fourth strategic typology, which lies halfway between Prospector and Defender, is the Analyser. These latter organizations monitor environmental trends but will not consider development of new products/services or moves into new areas of customer provision until there is solid evidence that real opportunities exist. Once the organization is convinced of the need for entrepreneurial action, adequacy in relation to internal flexibility permits an effective re-allocation of resources to support revisions in technology and administrative processes.

Charhi (2000) has expressed the view that despite the different nature of the external environments confronting public sector organizations, the Miles and Snow typology is an applicable typology for analysing the strategic behaviour in the public sector. He proposes that Prospector organizations will tend to favour a re-orientation strategy involving the identification and introduction of new or improved service portfolios. Defenders will favour actions such as internal revitalization of service process systems and focusing upon specialist service provision in order to avoid confrontations with other service providers that could risk a loss or transfer of hard-won resources. Analysers are entities which will base their strategy on a mix of re-orientation and revitalization activities. Reactors will favour sustaining a *status quo* position and seek to use political influence to defend claims concerning the need to retain their current resource base.

Although the Miles and Snow typology provides an effective paradigm through which to classify organizations in relation to their capability to exhibit strategic flexibility, by the late 1990s the model seems to have become less popular among academics. As a consequence, there was a significant decline in the frequency with which the concept was used as a research model to analyse organizational behaviour or to receive as mentioned in many of the more recent management texts. To a certain degree this reflects the increasing interest among academics about the role of organizational learning and knowledge management in assisting organizations evolve new or revised strategies (Chaston 2004).

Another key influence for decline in interest in the typology was the problems researchers encountered in reaching definite conclusions about the relationships which exist between the Miles and Snow typology and the performance of organizations in different sectors. Zahra and Pearce (1990) in their review of research methodology problems associated with the use of the typology noted that a very critical issue was the variation between researchers concerning their approaches to classifying organizations and in the application of scales to achieve an empirical basis for determining which fitted into the four different organizational types. Other problems which these authors identified included the tendency of some researchers to examine the nature of the environments confronting organizations in a specific sector without engaging in the longitudinal data acquisition process which is needed to identify how the behaviour of organizations within a sector has changed over time.

Sanchez (1997) has subsequently posited that effective management of strategic change is critically reliant upon the degree to which an organization is able to transfer resources between different areas of activity. He proposed that resource flexibility will be greater in those cases where there is a large range of alternative uses to which a resource can be applied. Further enhancement in resource flexibility will occur when switching from one use of a resource to an alternative use is a relatively simple activity and does not incur high costs. The other influence is the time required to move a resource from one application to another within the organization. The level of strategic flexibility will also be reduced where a resource to be transferred is in short supply. Although this situation could be avoided through the ownership of slack resource capacity, this solution is somewhat inefficient and may also be quite costly. The alternative to retaining excess levels of a key resource is to wait until an early indicator of the need for future strategic change has been identified. At this juncture, the organization can assess the implications of change and begin to invest in the acquisition of the additional resources which will soon be required.

In terms of embedding a philosophy of strategic flexibility into an organization, the issue arises of which approach to strategic planning is appropriate for achieving this aim. A 'deliberate strategy' is one which is carefully planned and then implemented. An 'emergent strategy' is a strategy that is not deliberately planned but instead develops over time through a series of activities aimed at finding ways for improving future performance. The deliberate approach to strategic planning runs the risk of being excessively rigid and mechanistic. In contrast, the emergent process is both informal and flexible. It also offers the advantage of involving employees at all levels of the organization and permits the strategy to evolve as everybody gains further understanding of changing external opportunities and threats facing the business.

Dibrell et al. (2007) examined planning philosophies within the US timber industry. Through analysis of qualitative and quantitative date they concluded that there existed three different approaches to planning within the industry. Rigid firms are those which use a deliberate approach to planning. Exploration firms use an emergent approach. Dynamic firms adopt a blended approach of both deliberate and emergent decision-making. The conclusion from their study was that Dynamic group of firms were the most successful. Within these firms the orientation is towards deliberate planning until monitoring of the external environment indicates the possibility of major change. Their response is then to draw upon the cognitive flexibility which exists within the organization to identify a new, more appropriate strategic solution. Within the Rigid firms there was much slower reaction to changing events and an unwillingness to move away from the strategy which has proved successful in the past. The Exploration firms were likely to recognize signs of external change but it appeared their informal approach often led to a failure to develop a coherent viable strategy for responding to these different market conditions.

Strategic complexity

As environmental systems become more complex, making sense of futures becomes more difficult and adaptation to the changing environment becomes more problematic. Mason (2007) has proposed that as a result of increasing levels of environmental turbulence there has been the reduction of orderly competition, this has caused more difficulties in predicting customer, product, and service requirements. As a consequence, organizations are faced with requiring increasing need for information which can support strategies based upon innovation and quicker new product development cycles. An example of increased levels of competition in global markets is the emergence of new players from China and India. Such events mean that organizations are now facing more complex, rapidly changing external environments. As a consequence, managers may perceive effective exploitation of speed of response as a potential source of competitive advantage. One way of conceptualizing this new view of markets is to adopt the Schumpeterian perspective that there now exist increasingly turbulent events which can be considered as either opportunities or threats. To survive and prosper in the face of such environments organizations need to be increasingly vigilant and develop greater capability in relation to being more effective in implementing rapid responses to the face of environmental change. This new orientation has become known as strategic complexity theory (Cunha and da Cuhna 2006). This new perspective on strategic management posits that organizations are complex adaptive systems that to be successful must learn to align their strategies with their rapidly changing externals environments utilizing interaction and response rather than analysis and planning (Eisenhardt and Martin 2000; Eisenhardt 2002).

In relation to adopting a complexity orientation, simplicity becomes a major feature of new organizational forms (Child and McGrath 2001). This new orientation is achieved by permitting organizational operations located near to market to adopt a more simple structure and to be granted semi-autonomous control over their strategic response to environmental change. The role of head office in this situation is to act as a co-ordinating mechanism which ensures retention of an overall common purpose and to ensure learning through knowledge transfer occurs within the organization. Rindova and Kotha (2001) have proposed that complexity theory also encompasses the need for organizations to maintain an ability to evolve, a process which they describe as 'continuous morphing'. Structural simplicity is an important facilitator of rapid response because employees are free to tackle problems at the local level. These empowered employees can respond more rapidly to new challenges simply because they have to seek permission from head office before implementing actions. Nor do the employees have to wait for actions to be taken by others elsewhere within the organization.

In relation to the application of strategic complexity theory in the public sector Ferlie (2007) suggests that organizations are also facing rapid environmental change which is causing the need to reject a Weberian managerial philosophy. Instead, public sector organizations are also accepting the need for decentralization, individualization, and support for employees exhibiting entrepreneurial behaviour. An additional source of complexity facing PSOs is that some Governments' desire to enhance strategic decision over service provision is the trend towards involving an increasing number of external stakeholders in decisions concerning the management of service delivery (McAdam et al. 2005). White (1989) in her review of the increasingly popular philosophy of involving external stakeholders in the determination of future public policy aptly referred to this new environment as 'public management in a pluralistic arena'.

To assess the degree to which strategic complexity theory was applicable to public sector situations, Bakir and Bakir (2006) adopted a grounded theory approach. They determined that managers in Local Government were beginning to drop the concept of seeking to define and meet strategic goals. Instead, the orientation of managers was shifting towards 'gazing and envisioning'. In the face of more uncertain futures and ambiguous data these individuals engage in coordinating with the aim seeking to 'interconnect and interrelate' across their organization. This approach appears to enhance the capability of the organization to find ways of aligning future strategies with contexts identified from an assessment of internal and external futures. The approach was very different from that proposed by the Design School's sequential rationality model of strategic planning. Instead, managers used dialogue and intuitive thinking as the basis for achieving internal consensus over strategies most appropriate to perceptions of the changing world being faced by the organization. During the planning phase, managers reflect on events and actions, engage in sense-making as basis for new learning, and through the exploitation of learning, create new knowledge.

Implementing Strategy 13

> The aims of this chapter are to cover the issues of:
>
> (1) Ensuring effective implementation of the strategic plan
> (2) Utilization of a deployment phase to define implementation requirements
> (3) The importance of achieving unified actions across the entire organization
> (4) The benefits of operational management and customer focus
> (5) The benefits of adopting a supply chain orientation

Achieving purpose

One way of avoiding excessive emphasis on merely meeting annual performance targets is to create an environment where managers recognize the importance of adopting a much broader, longer-term perspective in relation to reviewing corporate performance. As illustrated in Figure 13.1, this involves assessing the potential impact of proposed actions and the actual outcomes of implemented actions in relation to the SWOT analysis, the key issues which require consideration during strategy implementation, and the impact of possible action plans in terms of their compatibility with the organization's overall strategy. In those cases where this analysis leads to the identification of dissonance between long-term strategy and planned actions to achieve current year financial targets, this should immediately indicate to senior management that a more careful assessment of proposed actions associated with strategic plan implementation should be instigated.

Implementation is the phase during which employees become involved in executing the actions to deliver the strategic plan which has been formulated. In most cases, and most especially in the public sector, the process of executing the organization's strategy involves people who are required to deliver

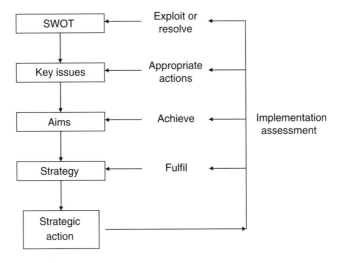

Figure 13.1   Implementation assessment model

a plan that has been formulated by somebody else. Implementation involves translating strategic goals into performance objectives, ensuring these objectives are relevant, understanding the plan exists across the entire organization, the allocation of resources, and motivating employees. In commenting on the strategic implementation process, Hacker et al. (2001) posit that successful strategic implementation will often require fundamental changes within the organization. In their view inadequate management of change is often the reason why so many implementations fail. These authors suggest that implementation problems can be reduced if more organizations inserted a 'deployment phase' in between the two phases of planning and implementation.

The concept of a deployment phase within strategic management is relatively new in the academic literature. It first appeared as a distinct component of strategic management of the total quality movement in the 1980s. Managers found a deployment phase assisted in creating more effective links between strategic objectives with staff's everyday tasks. Referred to as 'critical deployment processes' (or CDPs) these activities include:

(1) Ensuring that the proposed future strategic direction for the organization is effectively communicated to all employees such that they understand what are the future strategic objectives and how these fit with the assigned responsibilities of the departments in which they work.

(2) Ensuring that organization infrastructure is 'fit for purpose'. It may be the case that certain objectives will require the formation of specifically tasked improvement teams. Should this be necessary, these teams must be provided with clear expectations of their assigned goals and the processes to be utilized for achieving these goals.

(3) Determining which are the key drivers influencing achievement of strategic objectives. Lower-level units within the organization although provided with strategic direction, also need to be given flexibility in terms of their ability to self-determine appropriate actions to achieve specified performance goals. Permitting these operating units certain degree of decision autonomy is likely to increase commitment to strategy, stimulate the emergence of highly entrepreneurial solutions, and thereby improve overall implementation effectiveness.

(4) Permitting departments and work groups to develop strategic action plans relevant to their assigned roles and responsibilities. This requires that strategic objectives are translated into viable and measurable actions.

Hacker et al. believe by defining deployment as a distinct component of strategic management and identifying the critical processes required during deployment, the complexities and problems which are inherent in the strategic implementation phase could be lessened. This is because as actions are clearly defined and understood, employees can focus on executing the strategy without having to refer back to management for direction or needing to terminate an action because appropriate resources have not been made available. The authors note that in public sector organizations barriers often exist which result in poor execution of a deployment phase. Some of these forces are the same as those encountered in any change programme such as resistance to new ways of working, poor leadership focus, employee insecurity, and lack of co-operation. In their view, an additional unique force in the public sector is the tendency of leaders to focus on planning and to give insufficient emphasis to the importance of effectively managing the strategy implementation phase. This attitude is probably due to the fact that planning is interesting, mentally stimulating, and intellectually rewarding. Implementation of the plan requires attention to detail and the resolution of differences between departments or lower-level work teams. Hence, this latter phase often only invokes a limited degree of interest among senior management.

Another problem is some leaders seem to believe that good strategic plans can be implemented with little additional direction and input from them. In reality leaders must do more than just communicate the basic components of the strategic plan to middle-level managers, lower-level managers, or work groups. Instead leaders must become directly involved in ensuring that all employees are fully appraised of the purpose and nature of the organization's strategic plan. Leaders should also become involved in the deployment and implementation phases by meeting with departments and work groups as often as their other managerial responsibilities permit. A probable cause of this weakness in leadership skills in the public sector is many current leaders have risen through organizations based upon their skill in maintaining current operations and promotion on the basis of age-based seniority. These leaders now find themselves leading organizations in the midst of changing external expectations which include Governments requiring the ability of their organizations to develop and execute new strategies. This requirement is often a totally new experience for individuals who in the past merely concentrated on using the same strategic plan year after year.

In a relatively early assessment of the impact of introducing strategic planning into public sector organizations, Montari and Bracker (1986) concluded that two key influences in relation to successful implementation are (a) the degree of control that senior management exerts over the organization's decision-making and managerial task definition and (b) the competence of the workforce. The interaction of these two factors creates the four alternative organizational environments illustrated in Figure 13.2. A high level of senior management control is relatively common in public sector organizations. This results from the creation of multi-layered hierarchical bureaucratic systems where middle- and lower-level managers are permitted little or no freedom to reach or implement a decision without firstly gaining approval from their respective line managers. It can also be the case that because in the past, lower-level employees have clearly defined work roles and have been granted no discretion on how to undertake tasks different from that laid down by detailed, written procedures, these individuals lack the competences necessary for independent innovative thought or being able to act without being closely supervised. As proposed in Figure 13.2, unless senior managers are willing to relinquish some degree of control and also to introduce training programmes to develop problem-solving skills across the workforce, a rigid bureaucratic environment will prevail. This environment is totally unsuited to the effective implementation of a strategic plan, especially if this plan involves a fundamental shift in the organization's strategy and strategic aims. Where such fundamental change is necessary, senior managers must be prepared to delegate authority down through the public sector entity whilst concurrently implementing an employee development programme across the entire organization.

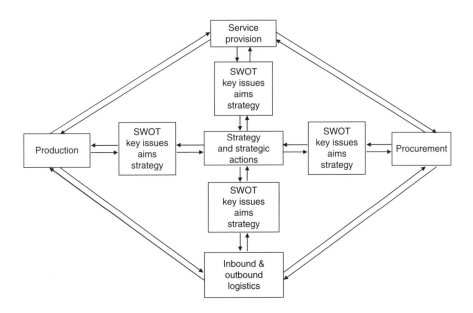

Figure 13.2   Departmental integration of strategic actions

Deployment in Action*

Case Aims: To illustrate the benefits of a deployment phase to more effectively link strategic plans to plan implementation activities.

Following Federal Government policy changes the US National Aeronautics and Space Administration (NASA) was directed to return to the original mission which involves re-establishing NASA as a research-focused organization. This required both NASA and the Kennedy Space Center (KSC) to change from undertaking essentially operational roles and becoming more involved in R&D. This revision in strategic direction demanded significant cultural change for the Centre's workforce.

KSC now uses a formal strategic management system to manage organizational activities. Following formulation of a new strategic plan by senior management, the director delivers centre-wide presentations. The purpose of the presentations is to create a shared understanding of previous year accomplishments, the current situation facing the organization, proposed future strategic direction, vision, and strategies. Following the presentations, the Centre directors met with each unit leader to discuss proposed future strategic direction in greater detail. The aim of these meeting is to ensure understanding of strategic direction and to discuss expectations which exist among unit leaders. Following these meetings, the unit leaders translate the Centre's strategic direction into specific objectives for their respective units.

Execution of certain aspects of the strategic plan usually requires the formation of cross-functional, strategic initiative teams to manage centre-wide projects. The activities of these teams have been to cause significant performance changes to occur across the entire organization. For example, KSC has deployed a strategic initiatives team to develop and deploy an information acquisition and feedback process by designing tools and processes for more effectively collecting and addressing customer feedback.

KSC uses a formal agreement procedure to document and agree specific objectives with each unit. The Business Objectives Agreement contains seven elements: namely, organizational responsibilities, mission, mission objectives, support agreements, procedure list, performance indicators, and external agreements. The mission objectives and performance indicator define the specific annual objectives for each area of responsibility within the organization. Unit objectives are linked to the Centre's overall strategies that are defined in the strategic plan.

Departments and cross-functional teams use a goal-performance-evaluation system to report on the execution of the action plans associated with each strategic objective. The action plans specify all the key activities required to achieve agreed objectives. Those individuals who have accepted responsibility for implementing a key activity are identified within the action plan.

(cont'd)

These action plans are reviewed regularly throughout the implementation phase.

The United States Postal Service (USPS) provides an example of a public sector organization which utilizes a formal strategic planning process followed by a deployment phase to optimize plan implementation processes. The USPS senior management annually identifies national objectives and strategies during their strategic planning sessions. Objectives are identified for the Voice of the Customer (e.g. customer service goals), Voice of the Business (e.g. revenue and internal effectiveness goals), and Voice of the Employee (e.g. training and safety goals). National and area objectives are communicated to distribution centre (P&DC) executives during annual strategy meetings.

Distribution centre managers are then accountable for communicating and achieving assigned objectives for their area of responsibility. Each manager is given significant autonomy in the processes used to deploy and implement the actions required to achieve specified performance objectives. A recognized problem within the P&DCs has been the absence of action plans specifying activities at lower levels within these operations. The P&DCs receive mail from other USPS processing and distribution centres as well as the general public. Most P&DCs operate on a 24/7 basis. The management structure is hierarchical consisting of three or four levels. First line supervisors are usually internally promoted. A recognized cause of poor performance is that in the past joint involvement of supervisors and employees in identifying actions to achieve strategic objectives and goals has been limited. Traditionally lower-level management and employees have been task-oriented, operating within a daily or weekly planning cycle with no obvious linkage between their activities and the organization's strategic goals.

To overcome this problem annual planning meetings were modified to include time for the lower-level managers to discuss how each unit within the P&DC facility would be expected to support the annual objectives and goals. These activities provide a much clearer understanding of the need to link daily activities to the strategic goals. Where fundamental changes were identified as being required this has led to the formation of specialist cross-functional and cross-shift teams. Through both analysis of prior performance and critical assessment of current activities, an improvement objective would be selected and critical drivers identified that require attention in order to improve future operations. The team also determines what appropriate actions are needed for implementation such as revising employee training, increasing maintenance activities, or revising operating procedures.

(cont'd)

Each team develops a written action plan documenting when, how, and by whom identified actions are to be implemented. These formal action plans are discussed with senior managers whose role is to ensure that proposed actions are compatible with the organizations overall strategic plan. Following implementation of approved action plans, formal reviews are held within teams and between teams and managers. A key dimension of these discussions are assessments of performance in relation to (a) performance compared to other P&DC sites, (b) actual performance improvements within the P&DC, (c) the trend in the pace of improvements, and (d) determination over whether implemented actions have made a real difference in relation to the effectiveness and efficiency of the P&DC.

Source: Hacker et al. (2001)

Unified purpose

In the early years following the launch of a successful, new entrepreneurial business, the usual organizational structure created by the founder and sustained by any successor was the 'functional' business model (Miller 1986). This structure followed the logical concept of employees fulfilling their assigned common tasks working together in specific departments such as operations, service delivery, or finance. Although this structure can be effective, there may be a tendency for employees to perceive their primary role is to ensure the optimal performance of their own department, even in those cases where this can be detrimental to the performance of other areas of the organization. Such selfishness can be massively damaging to long-term performance in seeking to successfully deliver the organization's overall strategy.

In relation to departments exhibiting excessive insularity, Miller and Warren (1989) posit that in the private sector a key reason for the failure of Western companies to compete effectively with new entries from Pacific Rim nations is the common occurrence of senior management failing to ensure a philosophy of strategic alignment is embedded across their company's entire operations. These authors contrasted this situation with Japanese multi-location manufacturing firms, where all departments at each location and management across all locations are focused on ensuring their actions underpin and support the organization's overall strategy.

Achieving a high level of strategic alignment requires that all departments fully understand their role in terms of prevailing current key responsibilities and what actions would fruitfully contribute towards delivering the organization's performance goals and strategy. To effectively fulfil this role does require, as illustrated in Figure 13.3, that all key operational departments interact with each other to orchestrate and co-ordinate their activities. This is necessary in order to achieve effective and optimal interaction across the entire organization.

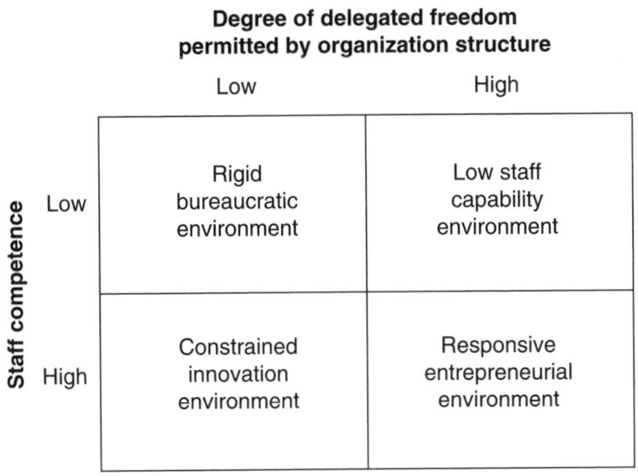

**Degree of delegated freedom
permitted by organization structure**

	Low	High

	Low	Rigid bureaucratic environment	Low staff capability environment
Staff competence			
	High	Constrained innovation environment	Responsive entrepreneurial environment

Figure 13.3   Organizational environment matrix

The failure of organizations to ensure there is a common focus leading to implementing of aligned strategic actions is not restricted to the manufacturing sector. Evidence of similar problems is also apparent within service sector companies. Inter-departmental variance in this sector can be even more of a problem than in tangible goods operations. This is because the inability to differentiate service products means that in most cases market performance is determined by service quality. Where departments have different views and priorities this will inevitably lead to the emergence of gaps in the delivery of high-quality services.

Factors of Success

Case Aims: To illustrate some of the factors that can influence success and failure during the implementation of a strategic plan.

On the basis of involvement in facilitating the successful utilization of strategic planning in public sector organizations, Bunning (1992) proposed that it is critical for plan implementation to be seen as a learning process. This is achieved by ensuring employee involvement creates opportunities to acquire new understanding, knowledge, and skills as a result of interacting with each other in a synergistic way. The consequence is that strategic planning is perceived as personally beneficial and provides the basis for experience gained being translated into new knowledge that can be utilized by the organization as a basis for future actions. Recrimination when things go wrong must be avoided. This is because such activity merely leads to a culture where people will hide mistakes and the emergence of an unproductive blames-shifting culture where staff seek ways of diverting attention onto others within the organization. Success demands a degree of humility among managers in admitting to employees that they do not

(cont'd)

know all the answers and in some cases errors have been made in the incorrect formulation of some of the proposed actions in the plan. Success demands the existence of a collaborative learning culture where everybody in the organization is committed to learning from experience and sharing their learning with others. Bunning posits that for these aims to be achieved it demands senior management in public sector organizations:

(1) Are committed to success and fully understand the overall thrust and purpose of the strategic plan.

(2) Initiate a communications programme so that everybody understands the rationale and need for strategic actions that are proposed.

(3) Define and communicate performance objectives related to roles and tasks across the organization.

(4) Ensure that detailed operational plans exist for guidance of staff at the lower levels of the organization.

(5) Ensure that all the plans are closely linked with the organization's financial budget and resources actually follow specified action pathways.

(6) Ensure that the organization's culture is compatible with the proposed operational plans.

(7) Ensure any new behaviours required by the strategic plan are understood and staff's appropriate behaviours are acknowledged and celebrated.

(8) Ensure that a staff development programme is in place so that staff have the knowledge, skills, and attitudes required at various levels for the successful implementation of proposed operational plans.

(9) Ensure an effective, non-burdensome monitoring system is in place that permits both staff and management are able to assess progress in implementing operational plans and use the system to diagnose reasons for variance in a way that can provide the basis for implementing actions to invoke actions that can lead to ongoing learning to avoid repetition of operational errors in the future. The performance measurement items should all meet the criteria of being SMART, that is Specific, Measurable, Achievable, Realistic, and Time-based.

Barriers to gaining advantage and benefit of the strategic plan will occur if:

(1) The operational plans fail to provide the framework and mechanisms to support staff's activities for 52 weeks of the year.

(2) Staff fail to achieve a sense of satisfaction with the operational plans and their involvement in implementing these plans.

(cont'd)

(3) Management expect all aspects of proposed areas of organizational change are to be achieved within 12 months.

(4) The staff are overburdened with an excess number of actions that involve fundamental shifts in organizational and personal behaviour.

(5) Change programmes are poorly understood by staff and they are de-motivated by either the complexity or excessive number of change programmes.

(6) Progress reviews only occur at the end of the year and fail to permit staff at all levels to achieve learning in relation to how to further enhance their own personal contribution towards gaining overall organizational success.

Operations management

In the face of increasing global competition, the tendency of many Western nation firms in the latter part of the twentieth century was to implement strategies focused on sustaining profitability by reducing costs. These cost savings were usually achieved by strategic actions aimed at revising internal processes, downsizing, and improving workforce productivity through task automation. One of the most popular approaches for achieving these types of cost reductions was Business Process Reengineering (BPR). The concept received widespread support and attention following the publication of Hammer and Champy's (1993) best seller entitled 'Reengineering the Corporations'. Unfortunately there was a tendency of some firms to be so enthusiastic about reducing operating costs when introducing techniques such as BPR that strategic focus was entirely directed towards activities only concerned with what was occurring inside the organization. Little or no thought was given to whether these internal organizational changes might be detrimental to the strategic goal of continuing to satisfy the needs of the customer (Sehgal et al. 2006).

Operations Management (OM) is concerned with systemic transformation process to convert a set of inputs into outputs. Inputs include labour, equipment, raw material, information, and other capital resources. This management discipline provides the basis for achieving continuous improvement in operational processes that can enhance quality, productivity, and customer satisfaction. The advent of the computer has dramatically enhanced the capabilities of OM to handle complex, previously unsolvable problems. Many of the current applications such as Material Requirement Planning (MRP) and Manufacturing Resource Planning (MRP II) were first developed to achieve integration of processes and supply chains in manufacturing industries. Unfortunately although attempts were made to introduce these systems into other private and public sector organizations, their complexity, development costs, and inability to handle the greater volume of highly diverse data sets in service environments meant that such projects usually failed. In the case of public sector projects the cost of failure ran into millions, and often left the Government organization with a non-functional solution. Over the past decade, however, developments based on Internet-based technologies have created a new, more effective platform to permit OM concepts to connect organizations with their customers and other supply chain members in a seamless, real-time information acquisition networks. This has led to new concepts such as automated CRM systems which have proved extremely effective in improving service quality and reducing operational costs for Government departments engaged in activities such as managing tax assessments and tax collections (Bayraktar et al. 2007).

These recent advances in IT means that even public sector operations are now able to use OM techniques to reduce operational costs, to enhance speed of customer response, and to customize service provision to meet the differences in need which often exist within a nation's population. Furthermore, public sector organizations can join the private sector in offering 24/7 service response. These new systems mean that tasks previously requiring large numbers of clerical and administrative personnel can now be automated. This reduces the organization's labour costs whilst permitting retained staff to spend more time analysing data as the basis for creating ever more entrepreneurial approaches to future service portfolio provision. Given these advantages, it seems reasonable to posit that computer-based OM solutions will provide the most effective strategies through which public sector organizations can survive Government cutbacks whilst concurrently fulfilling Government demands for enhanced quantity and quality of service provision.

In order to optimize the exploitation of OM techniques and better fulfil stakeholder expectations, public sector organization will need to enhance the effectiveness and efficiency of their internal operations by moving away from hierarchical structures and placing greater dependence on cross-functional, cross-department teams. This perspective is based upon Hammer and Champy's analysis of organizations which caused them to conclude that successful operational process re-design will usually necessitate fundamental changes within organizations such as altering job specifications, managerial roles, performance measurement systems, and corporate culture.

Process Innovation

Case Study: To illustrate how process innovation can enhance the performance of a public sector organization.

Rivenbark (2006) proposed that organizational evolution in the public sector will begin with process innovation. This activity evolves upgrading the organization's current routines. Process innovation is ongoing and dynamic as a result of the emergent internal and external problems. The author suggests

(cont'd)

that process innovation should start with an analysis of the base routine(s) associated with service production and delivery. Success in implementing process change usually results in innovation being given greater priority. At this point process innovation becomes a fundamental component in the formulation of new strategies which are designed to enhance future long-term success of the organization.

To increase the probability that such strategies are implemented and improvements are achieved, the organization's leadership have to ensure that the management of existing routines is altered to accommodate the new strategies for process improvement. This will often require that employees change their routine habits and such actions will require a change in the organizational culture. Rivenbark (2006) proposed that in public sector process innovation necessitates information flow from the bottom upwards and from the top downwards because only in this way can performance measures in public organizations be effective. Behn (2003) believes there are eight managerial purposes of performance measurement: namely, evaluate, control, budget, motivate, promote, celebrate, learn, and improve. When public organizations adopt well-designed performance measurement systems, performance measures fulfil their intended purpose of monitoring service delivery.

Merely introducing a measurement system cannot be expected to improve service delivery or service quality. To deliver this aim requires that the strategic plan provides guidance over actions required to achieve for performance, financial, and strategic goals. Strategies aimed at stimulating innovation usually require a front-end investment Hence department heads must have the capability to analyse the resource implications of strategy change and communicate their requirements to senior management. Success in the public sector is likely to be enhanced when department heads interact with senior management in the formulation of a strategy, especially where this strategy involves innovation. Department heads must use the new strategies as the basis for their annual action plans for providing guidance to their work teams. This requires decisions in relation to cross-functional activities and the selection of current routines needing re-configuration that are achievable in those cases where the department is facing any budget constraints. In this way action plans are compatible with budgets and this emphasizes to the workforce the relationship which exists between available resources and the implementation of innovation programmes. Successful innovation requires the leadership to ensure that the current routines are changed and new routines actually enhance service delivery and service quality. In addition, successful implementation management must accept that it does not always guarantee improvements will be achieved.

The City of Asheville, North Carolina, provides a case example of the effective implementation of a process innovation programme. Each functional unit develops a mission statement, service delivery goals, quantifiable objectives, and

(cont'd)

performance measures which were compatible with the City's overall strategic plan. The mission of the sanitation function, for example, is that of 'providing quality services to all customers through on-schedule collection of municipal solid waste and to efficiently carry out every task, special project, equipment operation, and customer request' (Rivenbark, 2006, p. 234). The budgeting process of the sanitation department was required to be linked to overall strategy in the development of action plans for the workforce. Some of the identified strategies were specifically designed to expand the capacity of service functions, while others were intended to address council priorities.

The cost per ton of refuse collected increased from $98 per ton in 1998/99 to $106 in 2000/01. The sanitation department decided to alter the base routine of residential refuse collection by changing from three-person collection crews working on rear loading trucks to one-person crews working on automated trucks. The strategy of automation expanded the operational capacity of the sanitation function as evidenced by tons collected per full-time equivalent position to $76 in 2002/03. The annual budgetary savings achieved by process innovation were approximately $500,000. This achievement supported the overall organizational goal of enhancing the fiscal responsibility of the city.

Systems theory

One approach for seeking to understand and then to implement appropriate strategic actions is to consider a public sector organization in the context of systems theory (Scott 1985). The appeal of systems theory is that it defines certain rules of operation which appear to have validity in relation to complex organizations such as those commonly encountered in the public sector. One example of this concurrence in theory and reality is provided by the concept that systems are considered to be goal-seeking and seeking to achieve equilibrium via adjustment, control, and learning. Additionally, the 'law of requisite variety' suggests that there must be enough variety in a system to absorb the variety in the environment if it is to be able to respond and deal with the challenges posed (Wilkinson 1997).

In their review of how an organization (which can be considered as an 'open system') can achieve equilibrium with their environment, Dixon (1994) suggested the following systems theory principles can be applied:

(1) All variables must be considered as a component of a whole system and not analysed as a separate and distinct variable which has no interaction with other variables.

(2) The ultimate aim of the system is to achieve the point where the interaction of variables leads to system equilibrium.

(3) Synergy exists in that the whole is greater than the variables (or 'parts') which are constituent components of the system.

Dixon and Perry also proposed that to achieve these outcomes there are certain guidelines that should be followed by the organization. These include:

(1) Utilization of data collected from all parts of the organization, including the views of users, customers, and other stakeholders.

(2) Decisions should be based upon input from all interested internal parties.

(3) Decision-making and evaluation of outcomes provide the basis for organizational learning that generates new knowledge that will enhance the effectiveness of future decision-making.

(4) Once strategies are determined and implemented, there is the need for continuing support to ensure learning occurs within the system that may eventually lead to the identification of new ways of delivering services.

Yoon and Kuchinke (2005) posit that rational and natural systems are useful in understanding how to reduce uncertainty within an organization to enhance internal efficiency. In open-systems theory, it is assumed that boundaries between organizations' input and output are distinct. When environments are volatile, organizations run the risk of becoming too rigid for future changes by trying to stabilize current activities. Systems theory proposes that open-systems evolve and develop through the acquisition of new data. This suggests that in considering organizations as open-systems, their survival in today's more volatile world is critically influenced by the degree to which new information and knowledge is acquired and exploited. This need for new knowledge will often result in the organization adopting a new form through seeking to become members of learning networks. In this new world of networked forms, organizations can be described as 'operative complex' systems in which systems are of different sizes with organizations utilizing self-organization in order to move towards achieving equilibrium with their external environments.

Customer focus

Evidence concerning major firms which continue to thrive and prosper in global markets despite increasing competition from the Asia-Pacific region suggests their ongoing success is closely linked with their emphasis on strategies based upon being highly 'customer-centric'. In his analysis of this trend, Day (2006) concluded that in both B2B and B2C markets, successful companies were engaged in a strategic re-alignment concerned with moving away from an orientation involving optimizing internal processes and instead seeking to identify new, entrepreneurial strategies that delivered the goal of working more closely with their customers. Effective execution of a customer-centric philosophy will require that all departments concerned with the production and delivery of output are focused on the priority aim of meeting customer needs. Additionally, there is a critical requirement for effective knowledge sharing between key departments. Concurrently, for all of the organization's support service departments such as finance and HRM are also committed to contributing to a strategy which is aligned to the primary aim of satisfying customer needs.

Day identified that not all major organizations which he researched were at the point where strategic re-alignment had achieved the goal of totally fulfilling the needs of customers. Even more importantly many of these organizations, especially in the case of public sector operations, were failing to proactively revise services in response to indications of changing external environmental requirements. On the basis of his research, Day proposed that the realignment process is composed of the following favour phases:

(1) *Phase 1 Silo Recognition*: This is the point where the organization recognizes that departments are focused upon achieving their own goals such as reducing costs. There is no real attempt to respond to changing external environments. More importantly, knowledge acquired about changes in the external environment is retained within departments (a process known as 'silo thinking') and not shared with others within the organization.

(2) *Phase 2 Informal Change*: Senior managers and departmental heads primarily remain concerned with internal issues, but certain individuals, usually entrepreneurially orientated sales staff responsible for managing major customer groups, begin to work with colleagues across the organization to develop a more proactive orientation towards serving customer needs.

(3) *Phase 3 The Awakening*: Eventually senior management begin to realize that the move to developing closer relationship with key customer groups is reflected in increased customer loyalty and profitability. In some cases, this outcome is brought to their attention by customers expressing their satisfaction about the level and quality of service they are receiving. At this juncture, senior management recognizes that to achieve the strategic aim of sustaining the long-term existence of the organization there is an urgent need to align internal and external activities in such manner that the primary strategic focus remains on becoming a customer-centric organization.

(4) *Phase 4 Achieving Customer Focus*: The final phase in changing the orientation of the organization involves identifying actions that can ensure closer relationships with customers. Equally importantly, senior managers must orchestrate the strategic actions required to ensure optimizing knowledge exchange activities inside the organization such that all areas of the operation are aligned to meeting the needs of customers. Alignment actions to achieve this goal will vary between organizations. This variation will reflect

differences such as the complexity of the technology, market structure, the closeness of the relationship demanded by the customer, and the location of service provision sites.

Performance Alignment

Case Aims: To illustrate the problems that can occur when there is a lack of alignment between strategic goals and performance assessment systems.

In order for a strategic performance monitoring system to be effective, Johnston and Pongatichat (2008) have proposed it should fulfil the following criteria:

(1) Provides the organization with confirmation that performance is moving in the direction proposed in the strategic plan and can assess progress against specified strategic priorities.

(2) By monitoring the implementation of strategy this ensures short-term actions are being aligned with long-term strategy by encouraging behaviour consistent with strategy. This ensures goals and planned process activities are being achieved.

(3) Shows clear links between the performance of individuals, sub-units, and departments, thereby establishing a shared understanding of progress against the plan across the entire organization.

(4) Assists in limiting overemphasis on local objectives, in reducing overlapping of process activities, and by focusing on the outcome of change actions and supports and encourages organizational learning.

Melnyk et al. (2005) concluded some monitoring systems can create tensions within the organization. This is because top-line strategic metrics may not be in alignment with bottom line operational metrics created to guide the efforts of the workforce in fulfilling their roles during strategy implementation. Hence, there is a need for mechanisms that organizations can utilize to deal with the tension between the lack of alignment in between overall strategy and measures of operational performance. To gain further understanding of the issues associated with misalignment, Johnston and Pongatichat (2008) undertook a study of strategy implementation in Government departments in Thailand. To assess misalignment between strategy and performance measures, they compared statements of strategic aims with Key Performance Indicators (KPIs).

In terms of the link between strategy and KPIs, their analysis showed very few KPIs which corresponded with the departments' strategies or strategic goals. Although operating plans and resultant employee actions should be derived from the strategy, many respondents in the study explained that their plans were rarely derived from their organization's strategy. Instead, operating plans, more concerned with ensuring activities that had gone on in the past, remained

(cont'd)

effectively and efficiently implemented in the current financial year. Furthermore, managers indicated paid little attention to strategy and instead focused on operational issues and objectives associated with optimizing the day-to-day performance of their work groups.

Managers in these Government departments felt that assessing long-term strategic objectives was often difficult because these were often vague and take a long time to achieve. Hence, they tended to rely on short-term measures as an indication that long-term objectives were being met. This was despite the fact that these managers acknowledged there was no empirical evidence to suggest that any cause-and-effect relationship existed between short-term performance measures and the long-term strategic goals. These managers felt that they had control over their department's immediate outputs which could be used as metrics to guide employee performance. They had decided that long-term performance outcomes were of little benefit in optimizing departmental performance. Additionally, most respondents felt that by demonstrating success in achieving short-term performance goals, senior management would not be too concerned over failures to achieve long-term objectives. These managers' experience from working in the organization had shown them success in short-term objectives was the key criterion used in their annual appraisal and determination of their suitability for promotion or to qualify for a salary increase.

The researchers concluded that their study confirmed a prevailing opinion among many public sector managers that although academic strategic management theory specifies the critical importance of performance measures aligned with strategy (e.g. Neely et al. 2001), in the vast majority of organizations this rarely happens. Nevertheless, even where misalignment exists, these short-term measures do assist managers and their teams (a) achieve greater understanding of performance problems, (b) have greater control over activities, and (c) can be used to justify the need for more resources.

In terms of achieving greater alignment in public sector organizations, Johnston and Pongatichat believe there are a number of actions that can be considered. Firstly, senior managers need to implement programmes and provide the strength of leadership that convinces lower-level managers of the critical importance of delivering the organization's strategy because this is fundamental to the long-term existence of their organization. Secondly, managers at all levels need to co-operate in developing a portfolio of measures which fulfil the dual purpose of assessing both performance against strategy and performance in relation to shorter-term operational issues. For this to be achieved requires removing the asymmetry common to public sector organizations whereby virtually all power and authority is vested in the senior management accompanied by lower-level managers' perceptions being that they have no control over their assigned roles or the assigned roles of their work groups. Hence, senior managers must move from being autocrats and become transformational leaders seeking to build more flexible and participative organizations.

Externalizing strategy

In the 1990s, shorter product life cycles, greater product variety, increased pressure to reduce operating costs by reducing out-of-stocks through speeding up order–delivery cycles, and a move towards the globalization of supply sources all combined to require private sector organizations to rethink their way of working with other members of their supply chains. This led to the emergence of supply chain management becoming an important strategic issue in terms of optimizing organizational performance and process efficiencies.

There is growing evidence to suggest that similar strategic opportunities in relation to supply chain optimization also exist in the public sector. To achieve strategic goals by enhancing supply chain management does mean public sector organizations can no longer merely consider their own plans in determining appropriate strategy implementation actions. Instead there is a requirement to extend their vision outside of the organization in order to achieve compatibility with the strategies of other key members within the supply chain. Kopczak and Johnson (2003) in reviewing trends in the increasing importance of supply chain management concluded that a number of fundamental changes in organizational behaviour are required to exploit the benefits of working more closely with other organizations within a supply chain. These include:

(1) *Cross-Organizational Integration* This involves going beyond achieving strategic success by merely ensuring integrated actions inside the organization and adopting a philosophy of achieving integrated actions with other members of the supply chain. Achievement of this goal demands that supply chain members discuss strategic objectives and reach consensus on the optimal approach for ensuring convergence in strategic actions across all participating organizations. In many cases, achievement of this goal can be greatly aided by organizations agreeing to share information on a real-time basis by creating automated, computer-based data exchange systems.

(2) *Mutual Cost Savings* In the past most organizations concentrated on actions to minimize their own internal costs and gave little concern to whether this created problems or inefficiencies for others with whom they trade. At times this inward looking attitude can be to the detriment of others within the supply chain. Optimization of a supply chain operation requires members to examine costs across the entire system and to determine what operational changes can be made to achieve a net reduction in overall costs, even though in some cases this can lead to an increase in cost for one or more supply chain members.

(3) *Optimal Service Design* In the past most organizations concentrated on developing new or improved services that offered them the greatest cost/benefit outcomes. Little consideration was given to whether revises of service concepts increased the operational costs to others within the supply chain. In order to optimize service provision costs for all supply chain operation members, there is a need to examine all aspects of organization's

service portfolio specifications to determine whether redesigns can be implemented to achieve a net reduction in overall production costs across the entire supply.

(4) *Improved Demand Management* All members of a supply chain from customer through to raw material suppliers can encounter problems due to fluctuations in demand. Unfortunately many of these fluctuations are caused by actions such as suddenly changing strategic direction, revising the service portfolio, announcing sudden cost increases, and forecasting errors. The scale of fluctuations can be reduced by actions such as real-time exchange of operational activity information between supply chain members to improve forecasting accuracy. Where possible this activity should be accompanied by agreements to provide longer lead time over any announcements concerning revisions in service portfolios or cost increases.

(5) *Increasing Customer Value* This activity involves members of the supply chain examining how by collaborating over identifying new innovative approaches to the operation of communications and distribution channels the final customer receives additional value from the service(s) provided. For example, a supplier may develop an online order and advisory system that can be used by public sector customers to move towards automated, computer-based purchasing, thereby reducing both time and human resource utilization in the organization's procurement department.

In relation to the growing importance of enhancing supply chain performance, Morash and Clinton (1998) have proposed that integration of purpose between members tends to start with operational co-operation such as sharing information, for example, the monitoring of the progress of delivery for goods which have been despatched. Having been persuaded of the benefits of working more closely in this way, this can then lead organizations to examine other opportunities in which collaboration can offer added value to the services being produced. The next stage in the development of the relationship is where members of a supply chain seek to further optimize end user customer satisfaction by achieving cross-organizational integration of their individual strategies.

In considering the benefits of becoming involved in the creation of a supply chain, the public sector manager is cautioned against believing that all such systems are reflective of a commitment to co-operation based upon all members exhibiting a relationship marketing orientation. In most supply chains there exists a power asymmetry in which one member has the capability to enforce their requirements upon others. Greater power is usually vested in the organization which links the supply chain to the final customer because their refusal to purchase products or services will mean market access by the upstream supply members can be blocked. Hence, in determining both the benefits and operational realities of participation in a supply chain, members do need to assess factors such as the rational for chain formation, the authenticity of claims made by other potential members, the expectations of benefit each member uses to justify their role within the supply chain, the probability that an adequate degree of trust exists at the outset, and whether the level of trust can be expected to strengthen over time (Vanger and Huxham 2010). Where the public sector manager determines that a review of these factors raises doubts of the efficacy of supply chain participation, it would probably be advisable to sustain the convention 'arms length' orientation when working with these other organizations.

Inter-Organizational Co-Operation

Case Aims: To illustrate some of the variables which will influence the effectiveness of co-operative relationships in the public sector.

The nature of the public sector is such that in many cases a national agency contract with local agencies to deliver a service portfolio to the country's citizens across the entire country. For this type of provision to be viable, there is an implication that some form of co-operation is involved in achieving the defined strategy for this type of service provision portfolio. This strategy is made viable because by working together rather than by working separately means some form of synergy is achieved or the costs of service provision are reduced.

Given the importance and common occurrence of co-operation between organizations within the public sector in the provision of services, the issue arises concerning what factors are critical in ensuring effective implementation of the chosen collaborative service delivery strategy. Lundin (2007) suggests that to be successful the most important factor is the need for mutual dependence over resources. The implications associated with this scenario are that one organization needs the involvement of one or more other agencies in order to optimize fulfilment of the specific service delivery responsibility. Supporting evidence for this perspective is provided by the fact that in most public sector situations where organizations are mutually dependent upon resources they tend to interact more effectively and have fewer disagreements than in those cases where local agencies are less resource dependent upon each other.

Another factor of influence is the degree to which the organizations' collaboration over strategy implementation has congruent goals for the service to be provided to the final customer. Where this does not occur due to the existence of differences of opinion over service portfolio priorities between national and local agencies, service quality is likely to be poorer and resource utilization will be less efficient. Further enhancement in co-operative service delivery relationships can be expected to occur if the participants trust the motives and expected future plans of the other participant agencies.

To gain further understanding of these factors of influence, Lundin examined the provision of services for the unemployed in Sweden. This programme involves a co-operative alliance between the National Labour Market

> **(cont'd)**
>
> Administration which is a national government authority and local outlets of the service provider, PES. There is a PES office in nearly all Swedish municipalities, and in the larger cities, there is often more than one office. The municipalities themselves are also collaborative partners in this network of national and local provision of services for the unemployed. From his study Lundin concluded that one of the critical factors influencing the success of this programme is that the national and local agencies are mutually dependent upon each other both in terms of service provision and availability of required resources. He also believes that a key reason for the success of programmes for the unemployed is the existence of congruent aims and strategic actions across the network of collaborating agencies. In his view the achievement of a high level of trust is not critical in this specific scenario. This is because resource interdependence and congruent aims are such that these factors are more critical in determining that effective co-operation between agencies will occur.

Networks

A major obstacle to entrepreneurial activity in the public sector is that various stakeholder groups have different views on what should be achieved and how outcomes should be resourced. This is very evident in the case where a PSO wishes to implement change which some members of the general public consider is unacceptable for reasons such as an adverse impact in local environments. One possible solution to this dilemma is to create policy networks in which all interested parties can exchange ideas and as a result of informed debate hopefully reach a consensus over what is the most appropriate action to be implemented. This philosophy, for example, was the underlying influence behind the UK Labour Government's decision to promote the idea of 'local partnerships' to handle issues such as regional economic development or the resolution of local social problems (Martin 2010).

The concept of using networks to ensure interested parties reach consensus is probably intuitively appealing to both politicians and social scientists (Skelcher et al. 2005). Unfortunately the behaviour of humans in their desire to achieve their own personal agendas may result in networks being faced with value conflicts and complex interactions between members seeking to create alliances to strengthen representation of their specific views. A possible outcome is that in order to reach a decision acceptable to all, the PSO may be faced with implementing a strategy based upon compromise which is neither appropriate nor effective.

This risk of member dissent within policy networks is illustrated by the case of the network established by the Dutch Government when seeking to identify an appropriate strategy for the future development of Amsterdam's Schipol Airport

(Huys and Koppenjam 2010). Included within the network were representatives of local communities whose primary interest was to minimize the impact of airfreight operations disturbing their day-to-day lives. These aims were in direct conflict with other members of the network such as the airlines and the airfreight management companies for whom commercial viability was of more importance than concerns over environmental issues. The Government created the Alders Group as a policy network constituted of all the major parties who were considered as having a vested interest in any future operational strategy for operations at Schipol. Local residents were represented by a collection of different resident groups who organized themselves under the collective name of VGP. In 2008, the Alders Group presented their report on the future development of Schipol. At this juncture the VGP group claimed they had been blackmailed into agreeing with the Alders' submission by being told their disagreement would result in their exclusion from involvement in any future decision-making. This outcome forced the Government into having to initiate three further rounds of discussion in which the number of stakeholders was expanded to involve provincial and local government organizations.

Expansion of the policy network further exacerbated the differences of opinion among members over the issue of identifying an acceptable trade-off concerning growth of the airport versus fulfilling demands over environmental issues such as the management of noise pollution. In commenting upon the difficulties in identifying an acceptable compromise over these two mutually exclusive strategies, Huys and Koppenjam concluded that although the Alders network had the appeal of involving multiple stakeholders in defining and implementing strategy, the probability of success was always extremely low. This was because from the outset a complete lack of trust existed among some of the network members. These authors also suggest that unless there is a way for members to evolve a win-win solution, it is very probable that public sector networks will typically fail to assist in the identification of a feasible solution based upon the formulation of a consensus-based opinion. Assuming this observation is relevant to other public sector scenarios, it might be argued that PSOs seeking to identify and implement strategies based upon innovation would be well-advised to avoid strategic implementation plans that are reliant upon inputs from local communities under the auspices of using a network designed to utilize partnerships as a path through which to create greater social cohesion.

Sustaining performance

As evidenced by examples of highly successful entrepreneurial organizations, such as Southwest Airlines and Dell, a successful strategic positioning can sometimes sustain an organization for many years without the need for change. The same situation, however, is rarely applicable in relation to the actual implementation of strategy. External environments are continually changing, customers are exhibiting new needs, and new threats over the availability or cost of resources will emerge. Under these circumstances, to create and sustain an enduring organizational demand for ongoing investment in promoting entrepreneurial behaviour can provide new, innovative products, services, and production processes (Stonich 1990).

Bird (1988) has proposed that sustaining entrepreneurial behaviour to support implementation of new, innovative strategic actions depend upon the organization sustaining an 'entrepreneurial intention'. In support of her perspective, she notes that organizations enjoying a period of success are often led by entrepreneurs. Hence, it is critical that after their departure, the entrepreneurial spirit which provided the basis for the period of success is sustained by subsequent senior managers. Achievement of this goal requires that the organization remains focused on responding to the changing needs, habits, and beliefs of potential and existing customers. This knowledge provides the basis for strategic actions that fulfil the aim of exploiting innovation as an ongoing pathway through which to achieve success whilst concurrently delivering the organization's strategy.

The success of entrepreneurs is rooted in their ability to rapidly respond to newly identified external opportunities, to overcome threats, and to develop even greater operational service provision capabilities inside the organization. Bird noted that as organizations become larger and more complex, speed of response in relation to reaching at decisions and implementing actions may decline. She posits that it is critical, therefore, that senior managers continue to place emphasis on retaining a philosophy of being able to implement rapid and flexible decision-making in responding to new ideas. This orientation should be accompanied by a willingness to delegate authority to lower-level managers to implement actions who are nearest to the external environment where entrepreneurial actions will benefit customers.

As most organizations, especially in the public sector, can expect to encounter resource constraints, decisions will often need to be made about whether entrepreneurial activities associated with strategy implementation should be focused on service provision or internal process innovation. An empirical analysis by Athey and Schmutzler (1995) sought to achieve clarification over this issue. Their results supported the generalization that where customer needs are stable and the important requirement is to add value or reduce the cost of services provided, process innovation is probably a lower risk and hence, more advisable priority. This can be contrasted with situations where the changing nature of the external environment requires the supply of new or improved services. In these scenarios customers tend to be revising their needs based upon experiences acquired by exposure to available services. These situations usually means the organization should give priority in the allocation of scarce resources towards focusing upon developing the next generation of services to be made available.

Successful innovation is more likely to occur in those organizations where there is a culture which is supportive of identifying and exploiting new ideas as a key mechanism to enhance ongoing performance. This is because successful innovation usually depends on horizontal co-operative interactions

Source of idea

	Internal	External
Process	Operational productivity opportunity	Quality/service improvement opportunity
Service	Intuitive entrepreneurial opportunity	Customer driven entrepreneurial opportunity

Idea focus

Figure 13.4   Source innovation matrix

between departments and vertical interactions between management levels in order to gain access to required resources. As illustrated in Figure 13.4, the original source of ideas will also influence the most likely primary focus of the innovation activity.

Ettlie and Reza (1992) undertook an empirical study to determine which factors most influenced the probability of successful innovation in organizations in the United States. Their conclusion was that possibly the most critical factor was effective co-operative interaction between departments in terms of sharing information about identified opportunities and problem/resolution activities. The study did not reveal a statistically significant correlation between the strength of vertical relationships inside the respondent firms and the level of successful innovation inside the organization. Ettlie and Reza concluded that in organizations which are more internally orientated the tendency is to place greatest priority on actions concerned with improving internal process flows and resolving problems in the 'design through to production phase' during the development of new products. This is contrasted with organizations which place emphasis on sustaining close links with sources external to the firm. These latter firms tend to have a much broader perspective on opportunities for innovation, gaining their ideas from sources such as customers, intermediaries, and suppliers.

The search for ideas

The adage that 'travel broadens the mind' is probably at its most applicable in the context of the entrepreneur. This is because visiting different countries can open up completely new opportunities and ideas for new products. As a consequence, multinational corporations which focus on innovation as the basis for sustaining long-term strategic performance often have a significant advantage over competitors who only operate in a single domestic market. The advent of the global corporation has further increased the ability of entrepreneurial employees to tap into new overseas sources of ideas.

In their review of the entrepreneurial benefits of being a global organization, Santos et al. (2004) provide the example of Nokia. Although this company was a late entrant into the mobile telephone market, the organization's broad expertise of global markets permitted identification of new opportunities which rapidly permitted the company to overtake their US competitor Motorola which had minimal experience of markets outside the United States. Two key reasons why operating on a global basis enhanced Nokia's entrepreneurial activities were that the organization had (a) access to a much larger, more diverse pool of knowledge and (b) greater exposure to different factors influencing customers' usage of mobile telephones.

In knowledge intensive industries global firms are able to rapidly identify the geographic location of different pools of knowledge and gain insights into a much broader range of research which is being undertaken across the world. In many cases, having identified an especially important knowledge pool, global firms are increasingly opening new R&D facilities at these specific locations. In commenting upon this trend, Santos et al. (2004, p. 33) noted that:

> *Companies such as Novartis AG and GlaxoSmithKline Plc now realize that the knowledge they require extends far beyond traditional chemistry and therapeutics to include biotechnology and genetics, and the use of advanced computers and robots in drug discovery. Much of this new knowledge has emerged from diverse sources away from the companies' traditional R&D labs in Basel, Bristol or New Jersey. Instead, it is often located far away in California, Tel Aviv, Cuba or Singapore. As a result, these pharmaceutical giants have learned that globalization of their innovation processes is no longer optional; it has become imperative.*

In order for an organization to exploit new knowledge from an overseas source as the basis for supporting entrepreneurial activities involves the two activities of prospecting and accessing. There are a variety of techniques which are available when prospecting for new ideas. The advent of the Internet has greatly assisted the prospector because an online search will rapidly provide information on topics such as new product launches, new technologies, and the latest scientific advances. Many private sector organizations have now implemented automated key word and phrase searches in order to monitor the emergence of potential new opportunities on a 24/7, 365-day basis.

Seeking to gain new understanding from observing practices elsewhere in the world is not a particularly common activity in most public sector organizations. To a large extent this is because the high costs that are associated with managers spending time in other countries. The advent of automated search systems clearly overcomes this problem but to date there is little evidence that many public sector organizations have begun to exploit this approach to solving problems by using new knowledge acquired from elsewhere in the world.

There is a risk in accessing new knowledge from another area of the world where the organization has very limited experience or understanding of local culture. This is because the organization is less able to use personal contacts and personal networks to determine the real capability of an overseas public sector organization to have evolved a solution which is transferable to another country. One way to minimize this risk is for the public sector managers to spend time in the country in question to carefully assess the viability of solution transfer. This is, however, an expensive solution. Consequently, it is usually only very large Government departments which have the resources to implement a strategy of acquiring an in-depth understanding of public sector processes being used in other countries.

To date many public sector organizations have tended not to actively participate in learning networks consisting of other organizations interested in sharing knowledge and assisting each other develop cost-effective solutions to commonly encountered problems. Given the proven benefits that private sector organizations have gained from participation in learning networks, it is apparent that public sector organizations do need to implement an attitude shift in relation to this issue, especially in terms of gaining access to solutions already in existence in public sector operations elsewhere in the world. There is evidence that in recent years some public sector organizations are beginning to appreciate the benefits of exchanging knowledge about the resolution of operational problems. In the UK example the Association of Local Government Authorities is exploiting the learning network philosophy to assist members identify new approaches for enhancing organizational productivity.

Implementation Errors 14

The aims of this chapter are to cover the issues of:

(1) Poor leadership creating barriers in the implementation of the strategic plan
(2) How abuses by leaders can impact organizational performance
(3) The detrimental influence of focusing on achieving short-term targets
(4) Inappropriate organization structures and control systems
(5) Failures in not utilizing knowledge to create more informed organizational practices

Poor leadership

One common reason to explain a failure to successfully implement a strategy is the shortcomings in the capability of organization's leadership. The Harvard Professor Barbara Kellerman (2005, 2004) has proposed that there exist a diverse range of different forms of bad leadership. These include the following:

(1) *Incompetent leader* who lacks the skills, willingness, and ability to make effective decisions.
(2) *Rigid leader* who may be competent but unable to accept new ideas or proposals to change future activities.
(3) *Intemperate leader* who is unable to control their anger or emotions causing the organization's working environment to be both unbearable and unpredictable.
(4) *Callous leader* who ignores the needs, wants, and wishes of everybody else.
(5) *Insular leader* who ignores the needs, wants, and wishes of everybody except the close group with whom they work on a day-to-day basis.

278

(6) *Corrupt leader* who is willing to lie, cheat, and steal to achieve any objective.

(7) *Evil leader* who is a psychopath willing to consider any possible action to achieve an objective without any regard to prevailing society values and morals.

Dotlitch and Cairo (2003) posit that even very effective leaders can terminate their run of success in their careers by exhibiting flawed behaviours. These flaws are often closely related to the factors that made them successful in previous managerial roles. These authors concluded that leaders fail because of who they are and how they act when they are placed under exceptional stress. They identified the following traits which can lead to strategic failure within the organization for which these individuals are acting as the CEO:

arrogance – everybody else is wrong;

melodrama – the need to be the centre of attention;

volatility – extreme mood swings;

excessive caution – unable or unwilling or afraid to make key decisions;

habitual distrust – a belief that 'others are out to get you';

aloofness – impersonal, cold behaviour;

childish – rules are unnecessary and can be ignored;

eccentricity – being different just to annoy others;

passive resistance – not revealing what one thinks to avoid arguments;

perfectionism – excessive emphasis on minor, unimportant details;

eagerness to please – putting popularity ahead of the right decision.

Fulmer and Conger (2004) in their book on best practices in succession planning also identified the following similar factors which they feel can result in a failure by leaders to ensure the successful implementation of a new strategy:

(1) *Failure to deliver results*:

- Blames others for a failure to achieve promised results.
- Makes excessively optimistic promises and then fails to deliver.

(2) *Betrayal of trust*:

- Undertakes to do one thing and then does something completely different.
- Makes excuses about outcomes accompanied by blaming subordinates.
- Hides or modifies key information which is damaging to personal reputation or the organization's market reputation.

(3) *Resists change*:

- Unable to adapt to new ideas, plans, or priorities.
- Excludes consideration of any opinions other than their own.
- Fails to understand or accept alternative perspectives.
- Rejects or belittles the opinions of others.
- Fails to engage in discussions when alternative opinions are presented.

(4) *Failure to take a stand*:

- Indecisive when an urgent or immediate key decision is required.
- Listens to the last opinion expressed by another individual who they perceive has influence over their future with the organization (e.g. the company chairman).

(5) *Inability to become involved*:

- Considers information which contradicts their view as unimportant when making a 'big decision'.
- No interest in being involved in day-to-day activities within the organization.

Unsupportive Leaders

Case Aims: To illustrate how leaders can frustrate entrepreneurial initiatives in public sector organizations.

As part of the US Government's attempts to improve leadership within the public sector the Ford Foundation and Kennedy School of Government (Ford-KSG) sponsor the annual Innovations in American Government Awards Programme. Borins (2000) utilized case materials from the programme concerning potential candidates to receive the awards as the basis for identifying problems that cause significant obstacles for individuals wishing to introduce entrepreneurial ideas into their respective organizations.

   In terms of their position within their organizations seeking to implement innovative solutions, 85 per cent of these public sector entrepreneurs were either middle managers or front-line staff. The focus of their entrepreneurial ideas includes use of new, usually operational process improvement (35 per cent), computer-based technology (30 per cent), and private sector management concepts to achieve public sector purposes (30 per cent). The primary obstacle acting against being more entrepreneurial is the leaders of their respective organization continuing to support retention of a highly

(cont'd)

bureaucratic culture. As noted by Schultz (1992) the characteristics of bureaucratic leaders include (a) a belief that their position and title gives them legitimate authority to act autocratically, (b) an insistence that the hierarchy provides an effective definition of authority in relation to only leaders being permitted to make major decisions, (c) a lack of leadership skills because these individuals have progressed up through the organization on the basis of promotional process that emphasizes seniority level of education or technical skills over managerial capability, and (d) an implicit faith in the philosophy that successful organizations are those run using strict adherence to restrictive and inflexible rules and procedures. As a consequence the public sector entrepreneur will often face problems achieving co-ordination between departments, low enthusiasm at all levels within the management hierarchy and amongst employees, an unwillingness to adopt difficult new technologies, and the actions of the unions interested in defeating the introduction of change. A second, slightly less frequently encountered, obstacle is that of the leadership resisting the allocation of needed resources to support the project and not being prepared to assist the entrepreneur find ways of overcoming legislative or regulatory constraints. A third obstacle is the unwillingness of the leadership to assist in the process of overcoming opposition from external stakeholders such as the recipients of the services provided by the public sector agency, the general public, or adversely affected private sector interests.

Leadership abuses

A not unusual reason for the poor performance of an executive in a senior position is the individual abuses the powers that are vested in their job role. One example of this type of behaviours is forcing subordinates to execute orders that over time will inflict long-term, lasting damage on the organization. Vredenburgh and Brender (1998) have proposed the primary causes of the abusive exercise of power derive from an individual's personal motives. These motives can include fast achievement of task to impress superiors, a desire for absolute control, and demanding unquestioning loyalty and obedience from subordinates.

Personal motivation is only part of the reason why abuse of power can exist within organizational hierarchies. This is because certain prevailing conditions can contribute to emergence of actions involving the abuse of power. These conditions include ambiguity or discretion about how decisions are to be made, a lack of openness between managers, and excessive pressure by senior managers to improve performance or rapidly resolve problems. The presence of any of these conditions can divert an organization away from the goal of attempting to achieve long-term success. In organizations where there is a preference for secrecy such that managers avoid sharing key information with subordinates, this will further increase the risk that abuses of power are likely to occur.

In reviewing the behaviour of leaders who fail, Burke (2006) proposed they could be classified into three basic types, namely incompetent, ineffective, and evil. Incompetent leaders lack the technical competences needed to fulfil the role of being a visionary and strategist. Ineffective leaders may have the technical skills to analyse complex situations but limited interpersonal skills. This means they will fail to motivate subordinates to implement changes that are necessary to improve organizational performance. Evil leaders are individuals who are unethical and cannot distinguish between right and wrong. As a consequence, decisions tend to be made to suit themselves (e.g. firing the finance director who questions instructions to implement illegal accounting practices) or to maximize self-gratification (e.g. awarding themselves huge bonuses). In the event individuals exhibiting these types of poor leadership skills do not inflict such serious damage on the organization before being replaced, then a competent successor will usually be able to reverse an adverse performance trend.

Burke also raises the issue of whether certain deficiencies are important at different stages in an executive's career or when confronted with different managerial challenges. For example, a strength in being willing to take a tough unilateral decision in terms of closing a failing organizational unit could become a weakness when there is a need at a later date to listen to the views of others who are more informed about a specific situation. He also proposes that flaws such as emotional instability, arrogance, or abrasiveness may be more critical among senior managers than among middle managers. This is because at the upper levels of an organization job roles are larger, more complex, the stakes higher, and the costs of failure are greater.

Given that a leader in a large organization is usually surrounded by highly competent subordinates, the question arises about why these individuals do not provide feedback concerning errors of judgement being made by the leader. This situation is not uncommon in hierarchical organizations in public sector organizations where the prevailing culture is often that decision-making is the preserve of senior managers. The absence of criticism is also likely to arise when the leader is known to be arrogant, resistant to criticism, or has a reputation for acting vindictively against those who question their decisions.

Learning from a Private Sector Example

Case Aims: To illustrate how leadership behaviour can eventually cause the total collapse of an organization.

The first major financial scandal of the twenty-first century involving the Enron Corporation. This company was a major, diversified US corporation based in

(cont'd)

Houston, Texas, in which failure was in large part due to decisions made by the organization's leadership. Following some years of manipulation and distortion of the firm's financial data to convince the financial markets that the company was profitable when in reality the operation was incurring huge losses, the company was declared bankrupt in December 2001. The ensuing scandal led to the dissolution of the company's auditors, Arthur Andersen, who were one of the world's top five accounting firms. The accountancy practice was found guilty of obstruction of justice in 2002 for destroying documents related to their annual audit of Enron. The conviction was overturned in the US Supreme Court in 2005 but by then the Andersen name had been irrevocably damaged.

In commenting upon the leadership issues associated with the Enron case, Fernández-Aráoz (2005) noted that in many cases this type of outcome can be attributed to failing to undertake an effective search and recruitment process when appointing a new leader. He posits that the 'deck is stacked' against the selectors because there is only a limited number of outstanding individuals available who can actually lead a modern organization in a rapidly changing, increasingly technologically complex world. Another problem is for the organization to what degree it can be totally certain about the skills and attributes required of their next leader. This is because the competences appropriate for current situation facing the organization may suddenly be dramatically altered as the result of macroeconomic, political, competitive, or technological change. Furthermore, in today's business world there is frequently pressure from stakeholders, such as major investors, to make a rapid appointment to replace the current incumbent who they believe is performing poorly. Under these circumstances, mistakes can be made, and in the face of time pressures, selectors may discount or ignore any negative signals associated with their most favoured candidate. A tendency also exists among most people to base their selection decision using criteria with which they are most familiar. This occurs because decisions based upon familiar issues such as the attributes exhibited by a popular, previous leader are perceived as offering the safest and least risky basis upon which to make a decision. Unfortunately in many cases, the move to appoint a new leader is necessary because an individual with a very different perspective on future strategy and management is required to reverse poor organizational performance. The impact of an incorrect selection decision can be further amplified when a totally unsuitable leader brings with them a management team with whom they have worked in the past. This can result in the organization now being staffed with an even larger number of individuals capable of impeding the effective definition and implementation of an appropriate organizational strategy.

Driven by numbers

The purpose of a strategic plan should be to define how the organization intends to achieve the aim of creating an enduring organization. Unfortunately, in large part due to the standard accounting systems which are based upon the performance over the previous 12 months, there is a strong tendency among managers to focus on meeting the near-term quantitative performance objectives such as annual output or total annual operating costs. This situation is exacerbated in the public sector because many organizations can only be certain about their allocated budget for the current 12-month financial year. This is because Governments and their Treasury departments have a preference for retaining fiscal control by not making financial commitments over longer periods of time. This can lead to the situation in the public sector of managerial decisions being made which completely ignore the long-term strategic goals.

In the public sector following unexpected fall in the demand for services, senior management have a tendency to put on hold any agreed strategy based upon investing resources behind innovation and further enhancing the quality of services. Instead senior management are more likely to instruct staff to find ways of reducing costs by lowering quality or postponing certain upgraded service delivery actions until a later date when stability between demand and supply of services has returned. These actions will probably result in the annual budget being met, but at the cost of failing to introduce new services accompanied by damage to organization's perceived image before the general public about being committed to delivering high-quality services.

An example of this scenario occurred following concerns in 2009 over the potential scale of the global swine flu pandemic. The swine flue outbreak caused many Governments to purchase large quantities of anti-viral drugs and vaccines. In some cases, the scale of expenditure resulted in patients facing cutbacks across other areas of health care service provision. These cutbacks had an adverse impact on the general public's perceptions of service provision capabilities of public sector health care providers. This adverse opinion was subsequently further damaged when it became apparent there had been an overreaction to the assessed medical impact of swine flu, leaving Governments owning massive unused, unneeded stocks of vaccine.

One of the key influences on the priority given to 'make sure we make the numbers' in the private sector in recent years has been the pressure placed on CEOs by major shareholders such as the pension funds. These organizations want ongoing year-on-year increases in both dividends and share prices. Another factor influencing an orientation towards actions to achieve short-term performance targets is the popularity of paying large bonuses to managers based upon simplistic targets such as achieving an agreed level of annual sales. In an article by Guerrera (2009a) discussing the excessive emphasis on short-term bonuses in relation to the world banking crisis, she quotes the Yale Professor Jeffrey Sonnenfeld at Yale University who commented that 'Immediate shareholder value maximization by itself was always too short term in nature. It created a fleeting illusion of value creation by emphasising immediate goals over long term strategy.' His view was supported by Jack Welch, the previous CEO of the American conglomerate GE Corporation. His apparent hindsight opinion in relation to his role of placing emphasis on always being able to report quarterly profit increases for GE was this 'was the dumbest idea in the world. Shareholder value is a result, not a strategy. Your main constituencies are your employees, your customers and your products.'

Public Sector PRP

Case Aims: To illustrate the potential problems that can arise from the use of PRP to enhance performance of public sector employees.

The advent of NPM was accompanied by proposals from some management experts that delivering performance targets and strategic aims would be more likely if PRP was introduced into the public sector. The rationale behind this decision was that PRP will result in public sector managers becoming more performance-orientated.

There are three theories about how PRP can motivate managers that are utilized to explain and justify the impact of pay-for-performance (Risher 1995). The equity theory argues that people tend to compare their input or effort with that of their co-workers and use that as the basis for evaluating merit increases and bonus awards. Expectancy theory contends that people behave in ways that they expect will be rewarded. Re-enforcement theory makes use of the recognized behaviour that rewarding a specific outcome reinforces the likelihood that the same behaviour is likely to be repeated.

This move to PRP was seen by many politicians as a significant step in introducing proven private sector employee motivation practices into the public sector. What seems to have escaped these individuals' notice is the fact that most of the evidence on PRP in the private sector suggests that paying a bonus rarely results in raising the probability that a performance target will be met (Martin 1995). This perspective was validated in a very extensive study of PRP in the private sector by Daily and Dalton (2002). Their study supported the view that in many cases, performance bonuses which are orientated towards rewarding achievement of financial targets create the added risk of distorting organizational performance. This is because the existence of an annual bonus, as demonstrated by the behaviour of some bankers during the recent financial crisis, can actually lead to unethical, sometimes illegal, behaviour. Supporters of PRP may argue this problem can be overcome by paying bonuses in the form of stock options or shares because this will create a longer-term performance orientation. Daily and Dalton found that even in these where these alternative rewards systems are used some managers will continue to act in ways that are too beneficial to themselves in terms of enhancing near-term share prices. Such behaviour can ultimately damage long-term organizational performance.

(cont'd)

By the end of the 1990s, even Governments were beginning to accept that PRP in the public sector was in hindsight an idea which had either no or a negative impact on managerial behaviour (Anon 2000b). An evaluation for the UK Government, for example, concluded that PRP schemes in the public sector record fewer positive outcomes and create more problems than similar schemes in the private sector. In many cases, the introduction of PRP did not increase employee motivation and the study concluded that at best productivity increased by about 18 per cent versus 36 per cent in private sector.

In an attempt to determine how successful companies reward their employees for effective implementation of organizational strategies and achievement of strategic aims, Martel (2003) undertook a study of HRM practices within some of the world's top companies such as Cisco, Intel, and Wal-Mart. A common attribute shared by the companies surveyed was their strong preference to avoid reward systems that recognized the achievements of specific individuals. These organizations all believe there is a need to recognize achievement, but this recognition should focus on groups of employees such as all members of a work team or a department. The other critical factor is that these firms focus their reward system on recognizing the achievement of non-financial goals such as customer satisfaction, quality, and effective implementation of specified actions contained within the strategic plan.

Obsolete conventions

In their analysis of why entrepreneurial activity is critical to the ongoing success of private sector organizations, Miller and Friesen (1980) posited that delivering the same product or service proposition over an extended period of time was no longer an option in an increasingly volatile world. Their formula for organizational survival was re-investment in continuous innovation, accompanied by ongoing internal adaption in order to prepare the organization for the next shift in external environmental conditions.

Despite this perspective, it is not unusual to find organizations in both the private and public sector which appear to be utilizing the same strategies over many years to achieve their performance goals even when environmental trends indicate there is a need to change (Huff 1982). It may be the case that this has occurred because senior managers have learned through common experience that no other product or service provision strategy is likely to succeed. A more likely explanation, however, is that many senior managers have a tendency to remain faithful to winning strategic actions which assisted them in achieving promotion into the upper levels of management in their current organization. Unfortunately, the major risk in this situation is these individuals may continue to support operational conventions which have become obsolete and that continued use will be detrimental to future organizational performance.

Another common view held by many senior managers is the concept that 'big is beautiful'. This perspective can cause them to be supportive of a strategy to continue to keep higher a share for existing products or services even if those goods may have already entered the maturity stage on the Product Life Cycle curve. Alternatively when this option is perceived as non-viable, senior managers may opt to implement an aggressive acquisitions policy to increase company size taking over other organizations. Although size can confer certain advantages such as negotiating lower prices for raw materials and exploiting economies of scale, as Drucker (1985, p. 38) noted over 30 years ago 'absolute size is by itself no indicator of success, let alone evidence of managerial competence.'

Another group of academics who posited that seeking to become an even larger organization was often detrimental to long-term financial viability were Dalton and Kesner (1985). In reviewing the available evidence on private sector 'growth through acquisition' strategies they were unable to identify any merger aimed at providing scale advantages which over the longer term generated a genuinely significant improvement in financial performance. In many cases the combined financial results of these new larger entities either remained flat or declined. As a consequence, these authors concluded that the only real beneficiaries of growth through acquisition were the senior managers engaged in the activity. This is because their salaries usually rose dramatically following an acquisition and they also enjoyed enhanced status within their respective business and social communities.

Structure and control

Most new start-up organizations utilize a loosely defined organizational structure in which the founder(s) acts/act as the locus of control. Typically, organizational growth is accompanied by an evolution into a more formalized structure. In most cases, this structure will be based upon the allocation of specialist tasks to specific departments. For many organizations this functional (or 'U-form') remains an appropriate system. In these structures, senior management retain their locus of control but in most cases the specialist knowledge and interaction between managers responsible for each department, plus an effective vertical communication system, will ensure the organizational focus remains on implementing actions that support the selected strategy.

The effectiveness of the U-form structure can be downgraded, however, where one department is perceived as more critical to success than others. This is because there is a tendency of this department to abuse their power in achieving resolution of their own short-term internal problems without consideration of the potential impact of their actions on long-term corporate goal. Sources of power refer to specific base of capability to provide some performance or resource considered important to the organization. Individuals or units will possess power to the extent that they are able to address important problems facing the organization, control resources valued by others, are timely in bringing problems and resources together, are not easily substitutable, and have successfully used their power in the past. Yukl and Falbe (1990) established the distinction between position sources and personal sources (i.e. sources of power derived from organizational position versus those based on an individual's attributes). Power sources usually involve role autonomy and the opportunity to instil dependence upon others, thereby permitting groups or departments to be able to impose their will over others who have less influence inside the organization.

Hoskinson et al. (1991) have proposed that an ability to retain a commitment to delivering strategy, especially where an entrepreneurial orientation is deemed critical to achieving long-term performance goals, often begins to diminish as organizations seek to diversify into new areas of activity or begin to focus resources on process improvement activities. This occurs because diversification is usually accompanied by the move to the independent subsidiaries (or 'M-form' structure) and decentralization of controls as individual divisions are each granted greater control over managing their own operations. Unfortunately, because senior managers tend to wish to remain involved in situations where complexity and information flows are increasing, decentralization is usually accompanied by the imposition of tighter financial controls from the centre. This move can cause lower-level managers to become averse to making mistakes or taking risks. Emergence of this behaviour trait will probably be accompanied by a decline in entrepreneurial activity because maximizing the performance of existing products or services is perceived by these managers as a much safer risk proposition. Over time should the level of performance in these units continue to decline due to a lack of innovation, the usual outcome is the centre will seek to impose even tighter financial controls and set increasingly non-achievable performance targets. This move will further accelerate the downward spiral in organizational performance.

The basic decision model of define an aim, implement an appropriate action, and then utilize a control system to monitor actual outcomes is a concept which is practised in the majority of both private and public sector organizations. The simplest and easiest control system is to compare actual versus forecast for variables such as revenue and costs. These data provide the basis for undertaking an analysis which determines the degree to which actual results are at variance with the planned objectives. Unfortunately it would seem that the majority of organizations perceive that this approach, albeit in a possibly more sophisticated form, is also an appropriate mechanism by which to monitor overall strategic performance (Preble 1992).

The drawback of financial variance control systems are these typically only provide limited historic knowledge about past events. The purpose of strategy selection followed by appropriate strategic actions is to define the long-term pathway for the construction of an enduring organization. Unfortunately although organizations may appreciate this fact, the orientation towards using variance-based monitoring, especially when accompanied by an organizational culture in which managers focus on 'making this year's numbers', often means that effective strategic control systems are never established. As a result in many organizations there is no system to (a) identify weak environmental signals which might indicate a need to a review strategy viability or (b) assess emerging environmental data that might suggest one or more assumptions made about the key issues during the planning process are invalid. Preble concluded that without such knowledge it is usually the case that no review is ever undertaken concerning the ongoing validity of organization's long-term strategy.

Another failure of many control systems is the tendency to generate extremely detailed information about every aspect of the operation. This trend has been accelerated by the advent of computer-based financial and operational management systems. At the 'click of a mouse' managers at all levels can be overwhelmed with data giving rise to 'analysis paralysis'. In commenting on this scenario, Slater et al. (1997) have proposed that organizations need to focus on a small number of key measurements that are critical to successful implementation of strategy. Their proposal was based upon the three core strategic options model proposed by Treacy and Wiersma (1995) of customer intimacy, product leadership, and operational excellence. In relation to customer intimacy, the primary focus should be upon monitoring that the organization is continuing to develop an even deeper understanding of existing and potential customers needs concerning providing highly customized products or services. Product leaders' primary focus should be on monitoring markets in relation to ensuring innovation continues to deliver an ongoing superiority over competition. Operational excellence is concerned with sustaining internal capabilities that ensure excellence in productivity and efficiency. Hence monitoring in this case should focus on analysing data on key internal performance variables.

Most KPI-based control systems in the public sector have the primary goal of assurance-focused performance indicators that verify improvements in areas such as service quality and productivity. In his review of the performance audit systems which have been introduced into the NHS in the United Kingdom over recent years, Freeman (2002) suggests that politicians and senior civil servants' faith in the effectiveness of these new measurement systems may be misplaced. He suggests that the introduction of structured KPI systems may displace more effective existing informal modes of quality assurance. In his view, it is often the case that new structures by displacing these long-standing, highly effective informal internal systems with an externally imposed, formalized system can lead to suspicion or fear, thereby undermining the conditions of trust required by staff to continually strive to enhance productivity or quality.

Freeman accepts that the use of performance measures is appropriate for monitoring compliance with regulations or comparing actual financial outcomes in relation to an original plan. In his view, however, many of the current KPI systems in use in the United Kingdom are of little or no use in understanding how interventions or implementation processes have contributed towards improving organizational performance. His perspective is based upon the belief that

KPIs are rarely capable of explaining why a particular outcome has occurred. Without such knowledge then managers and staff are unable to determine what policies and programmes need modifying in order to improve performance.

As pointed out by Smith (1995) another problem of KPIs is that even where data are available and reliable, they may be potentially misleading and easily misinterpreted. In his opinion measurement validity should reflect the extent to which indicators represent what is usually a more abstract variable. Hence, for example, valid measures of health care quality need to reflect attributes of the health care system instead of measuring patient data or of other non-health care issues. Thus one might conclude that re-admission rates are a valid indicator of quality of care by assuming that re-admission is solely due to deficiencies in the quality services delivered during the previous admission to hospital. This conclusion, without examining other variables, such as the nature of the treatment, the socio-demographics of the patient population, and quality of post-operative care in the local community, could lead to an erroneous conclusion about the quality of health care service being delivered. Thus it is imperative that when indicators are utilized to manage public sector service provision these should only relate to factors that are under the control of the public sector staff being scrutinized by the indicator.

Freeman concluded that a fundamental problem with many of the KPI systems which exist in the public sector exhibit is the lack of clarity in relation to the aims of the control system. This situation has inevitably led to problems over ownership of the data and disputes over their meaning and proper use. He stresses, therefore, the important objective is that all participants must agree on the use of indicator data and the design of the best measurement system to assess specific task outcomes. The other critical issue is there is little point in using KPIs which provide data that relate to situations over which the service provider has no control. For examples, Freeman has concluded that in the case of UK health care some of the KPIs defining medical service provision cover areas over which clinicians have no control over either process or outcomes. Not surprisingly this has led clinicians to perceive these indicators are redundant even though they are required to utilize scarce resources in order to generate the data required by hospital administrators.

Gaming Instead of Delivering

Case Aims: To illustrate the problems that can arise when KPIs lead to unwanted behaviour within public sector organizations.

The UK's Public Administration Select Committee (2003) was appointed by the House of Commons to examine the reports of Parliamentary Commissioners about matters relating to the quality and standards of administration provided by civil service departments describes the difference between a 'measurement culture' and a 'performance culture'. The former being described as one of

(cont'd)

tracking quantitative achievement in the public service, whereas the latter is concerned with building organizational capacity. The report outlines the danger of a measurement culture is that excessive attention is given to what can be easily measured at the expense of what is difficult to assess. This is despite the fact that the difficult measurement may be more appropriate for assessing service provision. Furthermore, in some cases there is also a danger of meeting targets being seen to be more important than delivering high-quality services. An example of this latter scenario reported by the committee is the case of the ambulance service where the focus is on meeting response times and the use of 'lay responders' to hit targets even though these individuals may not be appropriately trained in meeting the needs encountered upon involvement in a medical emergency.

Radnor and McGuire (2004) used the framework developed by the Public Services Productivity Panel to undertake a case-based assessment of KPIs in the public sector. The Productivity Panel framework is based upon five building blocks of performance management, developing a bold aspiration, measures that needed to be SMART (Specific, Measurable, Accurate, Realistic, and Timely), ownership for every target, delivery of targets to be regularly and rigorously reviewed, and success in delivering targeted performance by reinforcement through incentives. The researchers concluded from case studies that the role of the leadership in the public sector was more about being administrators than leaders, particularly in relation to overseeing performance outcomes. In order to achieve or respond to the various stakeholder demands, leaders required their staff to spend time on form filling and chasing information rather than changing or managing process. The researchers provided the example of a call centre which was given a target based upon 'number of calls answered' in any given week. This resulted in staff when being asked questions by callers that they could not answer, the staff terminated the call, and moved onto the next call.

This study supports the findings of the 2003 Select Committee which concluded KPIs in the public sector have clearly led to 'perverse consequences' of organizations attempting to meet whatever are the specified targets and not exhibiting any degree of concern that this resulted in these organizations becoming totally unconcerned about their primary role of providing an adequate volume and quality of services to the general public.

Increasing evidence is emerging that suggests KPIs based upon targets and league tables have led to leaders wishing to avoid external criticism are condoning the emergence of an organizational culture based upon lying about results or even cheating by misreporting data which have been acquired. Hood (2006, p. 518), for example, reported that when asking central government officials about gaming, they separated cheating from gaming and acceptable from unacceptable gaming with one respondent describing 'outright falsification or

(cont'd)

making up of numbers as cheating, but creative classification or interpretation considered gaming'.

Radnor (2008) posits there is a need to understand the gaming culture which senior managers have permitted to develop in public sector organizations. This is because when permitted to emerge it can significantly reduce productivity and at the extreme have unintended, often adverse, consequences in relation to the quality of services delivered. In her view there is the need to answer the fundamental question of why do some leaders feel there is a need to promote and support a gaming culture? Probable answers include the personal values of these leaders and fundamental weaknesses in the KPI system designed to assess the performance of public sector organizations. Given this conclusion, it would appear there is an urgent need to ensure leaders in post are committed to ensuring that where gaming remains in place ways are found whereby the energy used by staff in engaging in this activity is diverted towards improving service delivery not just meeting a specific number defined by a KPI. Only once this has occurred is there any chance the performance regimes imposed by Governments can actually achieve what they were originally designed to do: namely provide the framework whereby leaders create a culture in which driving improvements in service and productivity lead to achievement of value for money in the provision of public sector services.

Learning problems

Senge (1990) proposed that a clear relationship exists between the failure of organizations and their inability to learn from experience. Hamel and Prahalad (1993) have extended this perspective by proposing the learning process must be translated into the acquisition of new knowledge that can be used to upgrade core competence, thereby permitting organizations to be more effective in responding to environmental change. They concluded that learning by understanding the nature of changes in customer behaviour is an important feature in ensuring the successful ongoing implementation of new or revised strategic actions. These authors have proposed that market-orientated organizations tend to more biased towards the behavioural characteristic of seeking to exploit new sources of knowledge.

Drawing upon the ideas of Argyris and Schon (1978) concerning alternative learning, Chaston (2004) proposed that poorly performing organizations tend to exhibit a 'single-loop' or lower-level learning style. The consequence is virtually no new learning occurs because of a tendency by management to place reliance upon utilizing existing knowledge in the problem solution process. As illustrated in Figure 14.1 this style can be contrasted with 'double-loop' or 'higher-level' learning commonly encountered in more entrepreneurial

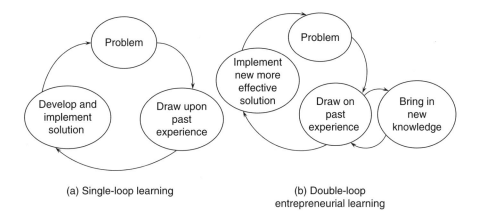

(a) Single-loop learning   (b) Double-loop
                                            entrepreneurial learning

Figure 14.1   Alternative learning styles

organizations which permits these entities to be more versatile, flexible, and adaptive than single-loop learners.

The preference for a specific learning style has no real benefit to the organization unless appropriate internal structures, policies, and processes exist to exploit the knowledge available to the organization. To gain an understanding of the nature of learning systems in conventional versus entrepreneurial firms, Chaston et al. (1999) undertook a survey of knowledge management practices within UK manufacturing companies. This study revealed there are very distinctive differences between the learning systems used in conventional, conservative companies when compared to their entrepreneurial counterparts. The study provided the basis for proposing that the factors leading to the operation of an effective learning system permitting the implementation of innovative, proactive strategic actions would exhibit the attributes shown in Figure 14.2.

In relation to *knowledge sources*, conventional organizations are biased towards drawing upon existing information from within their organization. This contrasts with entrepreneurial organizations who are biased towards exploiting knowledge sources external to the organization. Conventional organizations usually seek ways of using existing knowledge to further upgrade internal organizational processes. Bias in entrepreneurial organizations is towards using new knowledge to support ongoing development of products or customer services. On the issue of *documentation mode*, entrepreneurial organizations adopt a somewhat informal approach to knowledge storage, whereas conventional organizations tend to create a highly formalized, central record system to act as a repository of key information critical to the effective operation of the organization's memory system. In the case of *dissemination mode* entrepreneurial organizations seek to ensure that information is shared between all employees. In contrast, conventional organizations appear to adopt a somewhat informal

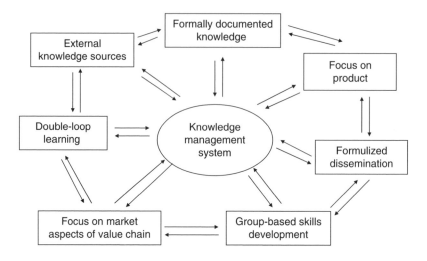

Figure 14.2   A knowledge management system

orientation, apparently assuming individuals will share knowledge with each other on an 'as needed' basis.

In relation to *value-chain focus*, conventional organizations focus their attention on activities associated with further improving the efficiencies of internal organizational processes. Entrepreneurial organizations appear to be biased towards seeking to add value to those dimensions of the value chain concerned with offering greater value to customers. Management of *skills development* in entrepreneurial organizations is centred around improving the competencies of work teams. This is contrasted with the conventional organizations where training is directed towards upgrading the capabilities of individuals within the workforce.

Knowledge Management Barriers

Case Aims: To illustrate the barriers which can exist to the effective exploitation of knowledge management within public sector organizations.

As with other managerial innovations, theories concerning knowledge management first emerged in the private sector. The public sector, reflecting the traditional much slower willingness to embrace innovative management practices are now only beginning to recognize the importance of knowledge management. Taylor and Wright (2004) pointed out that Government policy requiring partnership between purchasers and providers of health care services to provide integrated health and social care to each patient as a unified service provides an obvious opportunity through which to enhance service provision

(cont'd)

through adoption of a knowledge management orientation. This is because a partnership approach to optimize service delivery is best achieved by the sharing of information and knowledge across organizational and professional boundaries.

To assess the utilization of knowledge management practices within the NHS in the United Kingdom, Taylor and Wright (2004) utilized in-depth interviews to examine health care service provision for (a) the elderly, (b) children with severe disabilities, (c) food and nutrition initiatives, and (d) developing community policies. Their conclusion is that knowledge sharing is shaped by wider organizational issues which extend well beyond the dynamics of interactions between the provider and user of information. In their view knowledge management represents a significant challenge due to the interaction of certain key variables. The research demonstrated that managers must create effective systems which can handle external data and encourage knowledge sharing. There is also the need for an innovative climate where new ideas are welcomed, accepted, and people feel motivated to become involved in performance enhancement projects.

The study revealed an important barrier to knowledge management in the public sector is that although organizations are happy to reveal successes, there is a strong tendency to avoid actions that might identify and publicize mistakes. This is a major problem because a recognized aspect of successful knowledge management is that only by the recognition of mistakes can employees acquire the learning necessary to ensure that a mistake is not repeated in the future. Unfortunately the researchers concluded that public sector employees are usually averse to admitting things have gone wrong because of the cultural stigma which is associated with failure. Public sector senior managers need to establish an organizational culture where staff can be confident that admitting mistakes will not automatically result in career prospects being damaged. Government has a key role in addressing this problem by ensuring senior civil servants moderate their prevailing preference for punitive reactions followed by even closer oversight when a PSO admits that problems have occurred.

Another issue is effective knowledge sharing is dependent upon the quality of the information generation and analysis infrastructure. In order that employees can engage in an organization's decision-making processes to capture knowledge and new ideas generated from reflective learning, there needs to be an appropriate information management system that can be accessed and utilized by all employees (MacDonald 1998). It appears that although public sector organizations are being pressured by Governments and civil servants to improve their decision-making in many cases senior managers in public sector organizations engaged in service delivery have not created the internal systems required in order that information can be made available to staff in a timely and meaningful form. Taylor and Wright posit a major reason for this situation in the health care sector is senior managers are preoccupied with the need for external

(cont'd)

performance reporting to Government. As a consequence, insufficient resources are directed towards ensuring that information provision systems also address the data needs of staff inside their organizations. Without the existence of high-quality information systems, it is not surprising to find that employees in many PSOs struggle to execute assigned tasks effectively and are not provided with access to knowledge that could stimulate innovation and learning.

Performance improvement through knowledge sharing usually requires changes to working practices, measurement systems, and to peoples' behaviours. Hence, senior managers need to assess the overall level of change that is being demanded of their staff. As pointed out by Lawrence (1998) if numerous changes are introduced in quick succession, staff will become disenchanted or over-stressed. This outcome occurs because frequent policy changes are perceived by employees as evidence of a lack of purpose or direction within their organization. In many cases, these changes are beyond the control of the organization's senior management because they have been mandated by politicians. In the face of this situation senior managers need (a) to seek to persuade politicians of the need to provide longer periods of stability, (b) where change is necessary to seek to create systems whereby employees remain focused in knowledge management programmes designed to assist in optimizing the delivery of customer-focused performance improvement, and (c) exhibit sympathy over the stress being created by frequent changes in Government policy.

In commenting about the failure of knowledge management to provide systems for assisting public sector employees develop and implement ongoing improvements in service provision, Taylor and Wright concluded that the four greatest barriers in the way of achieving this outcome are:

(1) Governments seem to wish to engender a rule-based culture within the public sector that seeks compliance rather than stimulating innovation and performance improvement.

(2) The pressure to achieve actions required by KPIs erodes the willingness of staff to reflect upon and learn from mistakes.

(3) With policy changes predominantly being caused by revisions imposed by changes in Government policies, employees perceive they are facing excessive levels of unnecessary external interference.

(4) With the focus of most KPIs being concerned with the performance of individual organizational performance there is no incentive for public sector organizations to exploit inter-agency knowledge systems which would ensure optimal use of scare resources and delivery of services that fulfil customer expectations.

Governance 15

Private sector governance

The early forms of corporate entities emerged during the early seventeenth century in Europe. Most of these entities were created to serve the common good, such as building hospitals and universities. In the United Kingdom trading companies existed on the basis of being granted charters by the Government or the Crown. The concept of a commercial corporation in the United Kingdom was defined by an Act of Parliament in 1844 which permitted corporations to define their own purpose and activities, including trading to generate a profit. A second Act in 1854 gave shareholders limited liability that protected their personal assets from the consequences of the financial failure of a corporation. This stimulated the emergence of business corporations in both England and Holland in which trading company partners combined their personal assets and exchanged them for company stock in return for receiving relief from personal liability. This form of organization gave corporations the advantage of unlimited life, easy transferability of ownership, in addition to the benefits of limited liability for the shareholders (Grant 2003).

The emergence of the corporate entity in the United States occurred between 1880 and 1930 as manufacturers began to move from private ownership to bring in outside new stakeholders in order to raise additional capital. At the beginning of the twentieth century company expansion via mergers became popular, usually being often financed by public offerings of corporate stock. Business consolidations triggered a move in business whereby professional managers were employed to run the company while the owners as shareholders were no longer involved in the day-to-day running of the business. This situation led to dispersed ownership among a wide range of investors, and created changes in business structures. As a company continues to trade, capital comes less from investors and more from the profits generated from sales, and in some cases, also through borrowing from financial institutions. The corporation is the legal owner of capital assets with the management acting as trustees of the company assets. Stockholders become less able to claim significant share of the residual profits of a company (Cheffins 2001).

The separation of management and organizational ownership resulted in the twentieth century in a series of legislative changes and legal actions involving court battles in order to protect shareholder rights and to instil the concept of corporate governance into individuals responsible for managing companies (Wootton and Roszkowski 1999). These events led to greater acceptance of the concept of corporate governance which is concerned with seeking to achieve alignment of management and shareholder interests. Financial events such as the 1929 stock market crash and the subsequent Great Depression acted as a catalyst for further legislative change. For example, in the United States, the Federal Government passed the Securities Acts of 1933 and 1934 in an attempt to more closely regulate the behaviour of firms involved in the securities markets and to reform corporate behaviour.

The focus of any new legislation is often determined by well-publicized examples of what is considered to be inappropriate behaviour. Since World War II, these areas of concern have included issues such as the scale of pay and bonuses for senior managers, abuse of employee pension funds, and involvement in illegal actions such as paying bribes to obtain new business. Even though proponents of new approaches to improving governance usually claim their solution will provide an effective solution, it nevertheless does seem that the same management misbehaviour problems seem to re-occur on a regular basis.

Changes in governance legislation are usually accompanied by revisions in the accounting principles to be utilized by the accounting profession when reporting on the financial performance, cash flow, and the asset situation of public and private sector which they audit. The degree to which these rules are effective in terms of providing a genuinely transparent description of the real financial state of an organization, especially in relation to the private sector, has proved to be inadequate on a number of occasions. In the United States, for example, the collapse of Enron and the Worldcom Corporations led to the passing of the 2002 Sarbanes–Oxley Act. This legislation requires firms and their auditors to move away from a rules-based approach to audit towards a financial reporting system based upon a principles-based philosophy. The legislation also introduced new requirements in relation to ensuring the independence of internal audit committees accompanied by mechanisms to ensure this group is protected from unacceptable pressures from a company's senior executives or non-executive board members.

Whether any legislation will eventually result in an improvement in corporate governance remains somewhat questionable. Corporations usually respond by announcing they have been forced to take a serious look at their governance structure. Unfortunately, as demonstrated in the 2008 crisis in the world's banking industry, history in relation to the emergence of declining integrity among senior executives does have a habit of repeating itself on a regular basis (Wells 2006). Hence it is certain that some time in the future, senior managers in one or more organizations will again find a way of circumventing legislation and governance guidelines in order to deliver high annual profits or to cover up the probability that the organization will soon be forced into bankruptcy. This is because there will always be individuals prepared to place their self-interest in relation to personal wealth, career success, and public image ahead of adhering to any existing governance regulations (Leung and Cooper 2003). Such individuals can always be expected to find another way of exploiting legally acceptable, but morally questionable, financial practices, in order to sustain or even grossly exaggerate near-term profitability. For example, a major cause of the financial crisis on Wall Street was those financial institutions who used off-balance sheet transactions to cover the scale of these organizations' mounting liabilities. In view of this conclusion, possibly the best solution to ensuring high standards of corporate governance is that prescribed by the highly successful American investor Warren Buffett. His suggestion was that 'To clean up their act, CEOs don't need independent directors, oversight committees or auditors absolutely free of conflicts of interest, but simply need to do what's right' (Buffett 2002, p. A19).

Influential reports

An outcome of concerns about whether company directors are providing transparent and reliable information on the financial performance of their companies has led to various attempts to improve the financial aspects of private sector corporate governance in countries such as the United States and United Kingdom. The Treadway Commission in the United States involved participants from the American Accounting Association, the Institute of Internal Auditors, the Financial Executives Institute, and the Institute of Management Accountants. Chaired by James C. Treadway Jr, in 1987 the Treadway Report informed about some of the recommendations to enhance the effectiveness of company audit committees included (Vinten 2001):

(1) Having adequate resources and authority to discharge their responsibilities.
(2) Being informed, vigilant, and effective overseers of the company's financial reporting process and its internal control system.
(3) Should review management's evaluation of the independence of the company's public auditors.

(4) Should oversee the quarterly as well as the annual reporting process.

(5) Along with top management, the committee should ensure that internal auditing involvement in the financial reporting process is appropriate and properly co-ordinated with the independent public accountant.

(6) Annually, committees should review the programme that management establishes to monitor compliance with the company's code of ethics.

One of the most well-documented and influential examination of the need to improve corporate governance was the Cadbury Report in the United Kingdom. This report was commissioned because of a number of well-publicized failures of UK companies which recently had received a clean report from their external auditors. These included the collapse of British & Commonwealth Bank, BCCI, and the Maxwell Group. These corporate failures were attributed to the looseness of accounting standards and the lack of effective board-level accountability (Hemraj 2002). The Cadbury Committee, which consisted of 14 members, was set up in 1991 by the UK Stock Exchange, the Financial Reporting Council, and the accounting profession.

The conclusion of the committee was that there existed a need to remove the perceived weaknesses in the UK corporate governance system. It proposed a 19-point definition of principles of good governance. The main issues covered in the report included setting fair remuneration for directors, defining the responsibilities of the board, required qualification of directors, audit rotation, audit committees, and auditor liability (Forbes and Watson 2003). In relation to financial reporting and accountability the committee commented upon (a) reporting and control functions of the boards, (b) the role of the auditors, and (c) the role of shareholders. In relation to accountability it was recommended there was a need for a two-tier system of executive and non-executive directors and that senior executive directors should be barred from the membership of the company's audit committee (Boyd 1996). The code of conduct proposed it was the role of both non-executive directors and shareholders to protect ownership rights of the shareholders. Unfortunately the UK Stock Exchange refused to de-list companies that failed to comply adequately with the code, thus removing the strongest deterrent measure. Additionally, the Cadbury Committee did not call on the Government to introduce wide-ranging new legislation. The Cadbury Code was presented as solution based upon the exhibition of trust and honesty by company executives. As such the solution is based upon avoiding the creation of new laws and bureaucratic systems to improve corporate governance.

Some of the more important specific details in the report proposed the following approaches to improving governance (Mitchell 1993):

(1) Listed companies to state in their future annual reports whether they comply with the code.

(2) The company's Auditing Practices Board to comment on the adequacy of the auditors' annual report.

(3) Where possible the role of chairman should be separate from the chief executive.

(4) The calibre and number of non-executive directors should be such that their views will carry significant weight.

(5) The majority of non-executive directors should be independent of any business, or financial connection, with the company.

(6) Boards should have a formal schedule of matters reserved to them for their collective decision.

(7) The directors in their report should make a statement on the effectiveness of their system of internal controls and that the auditors should report thereon.

(8) The membership of the Audit Committee should be a minimum of three members and membership should be confined to the non-executive directors.

(9) The finance director, the external auditors, and the head of internal audit should attend meetings, but not as committee members.

(10) The committee should have explicit authority to investigate any matters within its terms of reference and should have the resources to do so, including obtaining external professional advice.

(11) Disclosure of the directors' total emoluments including the criteria for calculating any performance-related element.

(12) A remuneration committee consisting of non-executive directors should be appointed.

(13) The board should present a balanced and understandable assessment of their company's position.

(14) Interim financial reports to be expanded.

At the time, the Cadbury Report was considered to provide a global benchmark against which other countries could assess whether their corporate governance standards required upgrading. The United Kingdom's Auditing Practices Board in 1997 supported a proposal by the Hampel Committee which was subsequently incorporated into the Combined Code of the London Stock Exchange. These included (Vinten 2001):

(1) The board should maintain a sound system of internal control to safeguard shareholders' investment and the company's assets.

(2) The directors should, at least annually, conduct a review of the effectiveness of the group's system of internal controls and should report to shareholders that they have done so.

(3) Internal control and risk management should be connected with the achievement of business objectives, and securing shareholder investment and company assets.

(4) Internal controls should respond to significant business, operational, financial, compliance, and other risks to achieving objectives, ensure the quality of internal and external reporting, and comply with relevant laws and regulations.

(5) Disclosure and evaluation of significant business risks which has been present throughout the year.

Public sector governance

Politicians seeking to modernize their countries' public sectors have tended to advocate an NPM model which is based upon market-led reform of public services. The aims of NPM are to produce greater financial transparency, linking performance indicators to outputs, and attributing costs to outputs. The actual structural nature of NPM reforms varies both by the nature of services delivered and by country. A common aim across this diversity of action is to enable competition, minimize size of operations, and provide adequate quality to markets served (Budd 2007).

Commonly associated with reform are actions intended to achieve 'debureaucratization' of the public sector through actions such as functional decentralization, creating *quasi*-markets, workforce empowerment, and privatization. The proposal of such actions is often the cause of concern because senior civil servants and some politicians believe these changes will lead to reduced accountability, misuse of resources, loss of control, and, at the extreme, provide opportunities for fraud. This situation has led to examination of whether the nature of governance in the public sector needs to be revised to be more compatible with the new operational structures and processes.

This debate on the need for revisions in public sector governance is often based on a discourse about the nature of private sector governance in terms of the links which exist between organizational culture, managerial behaviour, and ethics. This has led to acceptance that any new public sector governance model should reflect the traditional public administration values of public interest, service, honesty, integrity, fairness, and equity combined with the new corporate (or professional) culture values of innovation, creativity, and continuous improvement (Kernaghan, 2000). Embedding this revised governance model into public sector operations is not a simple process. This is because the mindset of the public servant has been formed by generations of managers and employees operating within the context of powerful, rigid, hierarchical, and standardized organizations. Constructing a new organizational philosophy based on greater personal freedom, flexibility, greater self-authority over resources, emphasis on customers, creativity, innovation, and entrepreneurship requires inspirational leaders who have capability to implement a massive shift in organizational culture.

In commenting upon the introduction of private sector methods into the public sector, although the OECD (1999) believes this has enhanced the efficiency and effectiveness, in their view this trend can be accompanied by an erosion of traditional public servant cultures, standards, and operational processes (Bertok 1999). In recognition of this situation the OECD feels there is a need to ensure that while permitting public servants to exhibit greater flexibility, concurrently new governance mechanisms for safeguarding values need to be introduced in order to protect the general public's interests. This view is expressed because greater freedom of action within PSOs can sometimes risk individuals acting in a corrupt way.

In seeking to strengthen public sector governance systems ultimately the critical issue should be to focus on ensuring public servants continue to act in a professional way by adhering to the ethical values expected of employees in the public sector and to sustain the existence of a public sector environment which encourages the highest standards of behaviour. Guidance over ethical values should be provided by political leaders exhibiting high moral values when in office, showing some form of conformity with organizational statement of values such as codes of conduct, and emphasizing the need for all employees exhibiting professional standards of behaviour in fulfilling their assigned roles. It may also be the case that acceptable levels of governance will require the creation of a specialist body external to the organization responsible for auditing service conditions, management policies, and employee practices. To fulfil this role the external auditor must be able to rely on a legal framework that enables independent investigation and prosecution such that the general public can be reassured that transparency ensures close scrutiny of all public sector activities.

In response to concerns about governance in the public sector in 1998, OECD members expressed their commitment to regularly review policies, procedures, practices, and the activities of institutions that encourage high standards of conduct, prevent misconduct, and avoid the occurrence of corruption. The Council recommended that member countries take action to ensure well-functioning institutions and systems for promoting ethical conduct in the public service by:

(1) Developing and regularly reviewing policies, procedures, practices, and institutions influencing ethical conduct in the public service.

(2) Promoting government action to maintain high standards of conduct and counter corruption in the public sector.

(3) Incorporating the ethical dimension into management frameworks to ensure that management practices are consistent with the values and principles of public service.

(4) Combining judiciously ideal-based aspects of ethics management systems with rule-based ones.

(5) Assessing the effects of public management reforms on public service ethical conduct.

The issue of public sector governance has also been influenced by the emergence of 'Third Way' politics. This new political philosophy placed emphasis on the importance of 'joined up Government', collaborative interaction between private and public sector organizations, and the desire to achieve greater participation by the general public in public sector policy (Giddens 1994). As noted by Kooinman (1993), the new orientation did mean that no single governing agency is able to claim a legitimate right to determine its own rules of governance. Instead there is a requirement for politicians and PSOs to recognize that there exists a complex interaction between public and private sector actors in determining the most acceptable form of governance to be exhibited by public sector employees.

Osborne (2010) in summarizing the emergence of new perspectives in public sector governance proposed that there exist the following distinct strands:

(1) *Socio-political governance* which is concerned with the overarching institutional relationship within society.

(2) *Public policy governance* which is concerned with how policy elites and networks interact to influence and determine public policy and public policy implementation practices.

(3) *Administrative governance* which is concerned with the effective application of public administrative activities in relation to the role of the public sector as a constitute component of a nation's activities.

(4) *Contract governance* which is concerned with the actual processes associated with NPM with especial reference to the fulfilment of the contractual aspects of service delivery.

(5) *Network governance* which is concerned with the organization and effective operation of networks involved in the provision and delivery of services.

The Canadian Solution

Case Aims: To illustrate the actions of one Government to improve public sector governance following a financial scandal.

Similar to most developed nations the introduction of NPM in Canada resulted in greater focus on public sector accountability based upon moving away from inputs and processes and towards accountability for results. As noted by Free and Radcliffe (2009, p. 196)

> *the imprecision of most public sector objectives and the shortcomings of many of performance measures have had important implications for the nature of accountability . . . . . . Financial accountability with its prime emphasis on monitoring and controlling inputs – on how much was spent by whom and when – has become the bulwark of discharging accountability. . . . It is usually easier to understand and criticize how much has been spent on a given program or policy, such as a social welfare programs, than how effectively the funds have been spent.*

(cont'd)

What caused the Canadian Government to reconsider the whole issue of public sector governance was that in February 2004 Canada's Auditor General released a report alleging that senior officials from the governing Liberal Party had channelled at least $100 million from a $250 million government programme into a network of advertising and communication agencies with ties to the Liberal Party. After receiving the Auditor General's report, Prime Minister Paul Martin established a Royal Commission of Inquiry. The head of the inquiry Justice Gomery identified what he perceived as unchecked executive power within Government and made recommendations aimed at holding the executive branch to account by actions which included transferring more responsibility to Parliamentary committees, providing stiffer penalties for violations in public spending legislation, the de-politicization of civil service, and greater transparency over funding PSOs and a ban on the destruction of documents.

In response to these recommendations the Government decided to re-establish the Office of the Government Comptroller (OCG). Specific roles were created to ensure differentiation of task between the OCG and the Office of the Auditor General. The role of the Auditor General is to aid accountability by conducting independent audits of federal government operations. The Auditor General is an independent officer of Parliament and reports to Parliament, not to the Government. The audits are intended to provide members of Parliament with objective information to assist them examine the government's activities. In contrast, the Comptroller General is an office within the Treasury Board of Canada Secretariat, a government department. The Comptroller General is employed by the federal government and is responsible for overseeing the financial management practices within the Government of Canada.

The assigned role of the OCG is to perform specialist types of auditing and assessment of accountability in relation to internal departmental accountability and financial control procedures within Government departments. Instead of auditing accounts, the OCG examines departmental accounting, control, financial administrative procedures, management accounting, and financial information systems in terms of their adequacy, reliability, and timeliness. It also formally evaluates senior departmental management functions in relation to activities such as internal audit, financial planning, and programme evaluation. The Comptroller General also has authority over auditing standards within the Government of Canada. Additional aims of the OCG include (a) nurturing and managing the professional development of the financial and internal audit communities, (b) leading the introduction of modern, timely, enterprise-wide' financial information systems to track all spending, and providing appropriate tools for effective scrutiny and decision-making, and (c) oversee Government spending, including review and sign-off on new spending initiatives, monitoring, and reporting on how well financial management and internal audit are being managed in departments and agencies.

Governance obstacles

Heath and Norman (2004) have raised the issue that in some cases, the unique nature of many public sector organizations will create problems when one attempts to import governance models from the private sector without attempting to revise these models to reflect the different external and internal environments which exist within the public sector. For example, as the state is the owner of any public sector asset, one cannot give the public sector managers an ownership stake in the operation for which they are responsible. A public sector manager is also usually more immune to actions to have them removed for having exhibited poor managerial capability. This can be contrasted with the private sector where shareholders are a very credible threat to managers who fail to achieve the performance outcomes expected of them. On the other hand, politicians would rarely be prepared to permit a major public corporation to go bankrupt. Hence, managers in these organizations have fewer fears over making bad decisions, creating major financial deficits, or losing their jobs.

Another major difference between the two sectors is public sector managers usually have to take into account the demands of a larger and more diverse group of stakeholders. This will require careful assessment of which aspects of governance behaviour will be seen as more important across these different stakeholder groups. Furthermore, some of these stakeholders such as politicians will have significantly greater powers to influence decision-making within PSOs. This can lead to the situation of managers being less concerned about fulfilling certain governance criteria in order to 'play politics' over issues such as persuading politicians to approve a budget increase even though prior results for the PSO provide little or no justification for such an approval.

Following a report on the financial aspects of public sector governance by the Audit Commission (1996), the UK Government as part of their NPM strategy accepted the Commission's recommendations concerning ways of improving the standards of governance in Local Authorities through requiring these organizations to establish audit committees. These proposals were designed to bring into the public sector private sector governance changes that had been proposed in the Cadbury Report. Similar to the private sector these audit committees have the basic function of providing a system of oversight concerning the organization's internal audit staff's abilities to provide effective financial reporting systems. In addition, however, the public sector audit committee is required to undertake other tasks such as risk management, control, compliance, and to instigate special investigations. As noted by Davies (2009) because members of committees in Local Authorities are drawn from the elected representatives, this can lead to the emergence of two potential problems. One problem is finding elected representatives who have the necessary skills and experience to serve on these committees. The second problem is that committees are usually controlled by the political party in power and hence there is the risk that decisions are made for political instead of financially appropriate reasons.

To determine the effectiveness of the audit committee approach Davies (2009) undertook a study of Local Authorities in Wales. She found that in general the system was perceived as effective. Only in a minority of cases was the Committee Chairman perceived as either biased or not sufficiently qualified to fulfil their assigned responsibilities. Interviews with heads of internal audit in the Local Authorities revealed the majority felt the committee structure was of assistance in supporting their organizations' overall standards of governance. However, there was a feeling that the workload was causing some committees to not allocate sufficient time to issues beyond assessing audit effectiveness. These other issues included matters such as risk assessment and investigating possible departmental-level accounting irregularities within the Local Authority. The other issue she identified is that internal auditors recognize the difficulties which exist in assessing the level of value-added outcomes that are created by the creation of an audit committee. As a consequence, achieving appropriate status or reputation for the committee can take an excessively extended time to achieve. All respondents did feel that should mis-management and fraud come to light this could have the adverse outcome concerning the perceived effectiveness of the internal audit, the audit committee, and the reputation for adequate levels of governance within the organization.

Evidence of major success in establishing this new form of public sector governance is not widely available. Pedersen and Hartley (2008) propose that a key reason why reforms are not delivering the gains originally claimed by politicians is there are increasing signs of tension within the governance regimes of public services. In the United Kingdom, for example, over time politicians and Central Government departments have increased their level of intervention through mechanisms such as tighter financial controls, performance-based contracts, assessment of outcomes based upon a very high number of key performance indicators (KPIs), and an expansion of inspection bodies. As a consequence, public sector managers are being forced into what can be seen as a governance paradox. The paradoxical nature of this new governance philosophy is public sector service leaders are expected to exhibit entrepreneurial strategic thinking, have been granted a high degree of managerial autonomy but at the same time are fully aware that their organizations face even more intensive controls through inspection and supervision by central bodies. Furthermore, these central bodies have the power to act in a coercive manner when they deem that the provision of services is inadequate or insufficiently cost-effective. Not surprisingly, this increasing level of uncertainty and complexity which public sector managers face in relation to multiple, often competing expectations, demands, and strategic dilemmas is causing them to re-adopt old styles of governance which the NPM reforms were designed to abolish.

The reduction in public sector spending which developed nations will be forced to implement over the next few years will further adversely impact managers who will be expected to achieve ever-improving performance targets while concurrently being faced with a reduction in the available resources made available to them. In assessing the implications of the increasing difficulties created by the public sector governance paradoxes, Pedersen and Hartley (2008, p. 338) concluded that:

> *The challenges for leaders and managers are considerable. Not only do they have to address the inherent policy tensions... but also they have to work in an increasingly fluid and ambiguous set of inter-relationships between the state, the market and civil society orga-nizations. There are different paradigms of public governance at work at the same time, with confusing demands from the institutional landscape. Requirements for accountabil-ity, control and risk management mean that elements of bureaucracy remain and must be enforced.*

In order to gain further understanding of the leadership skills required of effec-tive leaders in the changing world of public sector management, Hind et al. (2009) undertook a large-scale study of individuals working in the European public sector. From this study they identified the set of 'key competences' summarized in Table 15.1 which they see as critical influencers of performance.

Table 15.1   Competences that constitute responsible business *behaviour*

Knowledge:
- understanding the competing demands of different stakeholder groups
- understanding how the core business activities create opportunities for other actors in society and how the company can make a contribution to society
- understanding the social and environmental risks and opportunities of the company and its industry sector
- understanding the institutional debate on the role and legitimacy of the firm

Skills:
- balanced judgement
- critical thinking
- team player
- creativity, innovation, and original thinking
- communicating with credibility
- business acumen
- listening skills
- managing stakeholder relationships

Attitudes:
- honesty and integrity
- long-term perspective
- open-mindedness
- appreciating and embracing diversity
- conviction and courage
- the drive to contest resistance
- the capacity to think outside the box

* *Source:* Modified from Hind et al. (2009).

Hind et al. concluded that public sector leaders need to be 'systemic thinkers' in order to be able to deal with complexity, think strategically, understand the bigger picture, and appreciate the diverse networks in which an organization is involved. Systemic thinking requires a deep understanding of both internal organizational relations and external social interactions accompanied by an appreciation of economic, environmental, and cultural dynamics.

Public sector organizations are usually constituted of heterogeneous groups of employees (e.g. gender, race, culture, and ethnicity). This situation demands that leaders are capable of embracing diversity in areas such as building corporate teams that reflect the diversity of the societies in which they operate. The key outcome of success in relation to this issue is organizations are able to respect diversity by recognizing the benefits that are provided. This can only occur if the leadership is able to ensure that close links are created between different groups, thereby permitting identification of commonly accepted goals and actions.

Leaders also require the ability to appreciate the impact of local-level decisions of national or international public sector strategies and policies. This is necessary in order that their organizations are able to operate using values and beliefs that are compatible with broader aspects of the public sector in which an organization operates. Effective leaders are those who understand that autocratic decision-making and issuing mandatory policies are an ineffective approach to developing and implementing strategies. A more effective approach is usually one based on meaningful dialogue, resolution of differences, and selecting the optimal decision to be implemented. This approach does not just apply to employees but should also encompass all interactions with key stakeholders outside the organization.

Another key capability is for leaders to exhibit empathy, perception, curiosity, and creativity when developing decisions and actions that will impact others both inside and outside the organization. This capacity permits more accurate identification of the thoughts, behaviours, and the emotions of others. As a consequence, there emerge more effective, collaborative working partnerships both inside and outside the PSO. Accompanying this capability is a requirement of being able to accept that it is not always possible to be in control or to have perfect knowledge of the outcomes of changing the fundamental nature of any of an organization's activities.

Unclarified Risks

Case Aims: To illustrate some of the problems that can arise when utilizing public–private sector partnerships to enhance service provision activities.

A popular concept introduced within the context of NPM models is the creation of 'public–private partnerships'. These are usually long-term contracts between

(cont'd)

public sector organizations and private sector companies. Politicians when supporting this type of venture will typically claim these initiatives are innovative solution offering substantial public benefits such as improved service quality, risk-sharing, and cost savings. As noted by Bloomfield (2006, p. 402)

> *In practice, however, the challenges posed by long-term public–private partnerships can undermine local governments' efforts to capture the hoped-for benefits of these arrangements. In several cases reviewed by the author and her colleagues at an independent state oversight agency over the last decade, long-term public–private partnerships that were reported and promoted as low-risk, cost-saving initiatives have saddled taxpayers with high-risk, costly obligations for decades to come.*

It is not unknown for the business arrangements which form the basis of these partnerships may be incompatible with existing legislation concerning the procurement processes to be utilized by public sector organizations. It could be the case, therefore, that a partnership in which a private company finances, designs, builds, and operates a public facility over an extended period may be impossible to award within the existing framework of legal requirements governing designer selection, construction bidding, and financing of capital projects. As a consequence, it can be the case that the unique structure of the public–private partnership relationship may require the politicians to permit a special waiver of existing procurement legislation. The justification for such an action is that legislation is preventing a public sector organization from exploiting the benefits of an operational model which due to the influences of 'market forces' offers new cost saving opportunities. Thus the act of exempting public–private partnerships from prevailing legislation is justified as providing an exemplar of a government's commitment to innovation, efficiency, and accessing the managerial and commercial knowledge benefits which exist within the private sector partner.

To illustrate the risks associated that can exist in the creation of public–private sector partnerships, Bloomfield points to the example of county officials in Plymouth, Massachusetts, persuading the state legislature to enact special legislation permitting the County to enter into a long-term financing lease for a new prison. The legislation exempted all project-related expenditures from the state bidding and oversight laws that normally applied to publicly funded construction projects in Massachusetts. Although state taxpayers were contractually obligated to pay the entire cost of financing the facility, an obligation totalling more than $303 million over the 30-year financing period, the legislation gave the County wide latitude to negotiate no-bid contracts relating to the project. The County allowed the team of private firms that had developed and successfully lobbied for the project to devise a complex series of non-competitive contracting arrangements to finance and build the project.

(cont'd)

The exemption permitted the private sector group to invent their own billing rates and rules. As a consequence, within the $4 million project management fee, the private sector firms included payments for recovering their development and of a failed bid proposal to the federal government several years earlier.

In theory public–private partnerships enhance Governments' capabilities to deliver major infrastructure projects through risk-sharing agreements that allocate significant project risks to the private sector. It would appear, however, in some partnership contracts executed by public sector agencies that this benefit is not always achieved. Forrer et al. (2002), for example, concluded that many public–private partnerships in the United States involve negotiated arrangements without competitive bidding and that as a consequence the outcome is the private sector participants have used the partnership as a means of transferring investment risk from themselves to a public sector agency. In addition, there is evidence that although the capital costs of the project are understood by the public sector negotiators, the complexity of the operating contracts upon which these partnerships are based may not really reveal the true costs of the operation until the new facility has been up and running for some years. It is at this juncture the public sector organizations may start receiving bills from their private sector partner for facility operations, servicing, and repair costs significantly greater than those which the public sector partner thought had originally been agreed.

Similar cases of PFI contracts not yielding the benefits promised have also surfaced in the United Kingdom. In 1997, for example, the UK Government awarded Siemens Business Services a PFI contract worth £120 million pounds over 10 years to install new computer systems at the Passport Agency. Siemens claimed that its digital scanning technology would cut costs, improve security, and shorten the time taken to process passport applications. In May 1998, before the new technology was introduced, the average waiting time for a passport from the Liverpool office was 11 days. By March this year, with Siemens's system in operation, it was 24 days. To reduce the backlog, the agency hired another 120 staff and offered hefty bonuses to persuade existing employees to come in at weekends. In desperation, the agency quietly relaxed security procedures allowing out-of-date passports to be extended without special checks.

Far from being a lone aberration, the passport fiasco is a rerun of many other Whitehall computer disasters such as the £77m 'Casework' system for the immigration service. As with the Passport Agency, this PFI contract was won by Siemens Business Services promising to cut costs, improving efficiency, and reducing the waiting times for applicants. Siemens failed to deliver the IT system in 1997 and then missed its revised target delivery date of July 1998. The National Audit Office was critical of the contractual arrangement whereby

(cont'd)

most payments to Siemens depend only on cutting costs and there was no direct contractual requirement to meet the Governments Directorate's objectives for the programme to improve the effectiveness of immigration controls and the quality of services delivered.

By 1999, the level of concern about PFI contracts in the United Kingdom led the Institute for Public Policy Research to establish a Commission to examine the scale of problems which have arisen with this approach to funding public sector infrastructure and updating computer systems (Pike 1999). One area of concern was that the Government had signed 14 PFI contracts to construct new hospitals. This is despite the fact that the medical profession were opposed to many of the projects, claiming they will lead to substantial reductions in the number of hospital beds within the NHS. In addition the British Medical Association argued that these PFIs do not provide any savings because the costs will equal or exceed the costs associated with traditional methods of public sector capital funding. Earlier in the same year the Commons Public Accounts Committee criticized the profoundly unsatisfactory performance of the National Insurance PFI computer project. At the time this was the largest civilian computer project in Europe being managed by Andersen Consulting. Also in the same year, the £1bn Horizon PFI project led by ICL to computerize Post Office counters and pay benefit claimants through post offices collapsed when the Benefits Agency withdrew from the project following problems over contract implementation and delivery.

Medical governance

In both public and private sector health care organizations, there is always a tension between administrators seeking to balance costs against revenue and the medical profession who perceive the activities of administrators as seeking to infringe on their rights to make decisions which only they, the doctors, consider that they are professionally qualified to make. As a consequence, an ongoing contention in relation to public sector governance is that which applies in the field of health care, especially in those countries such as the United Kingdom where the public sector is the dominant provider of health care is who should determine the nature of the services to be provided. The perspective of the medical profession is that their behaviour should be determined in the context of guidance specified under the terms of framework of rules which provide the basis for determining health care governance.

In examining the problems facing the United Kingdom's NHS, Storey and Buchanan (2008) have concluded that a number of barriers exist that can be to the detriment of delivering an effective and efficient service which is designed to fulfil the best interests of the patients. These authors propose that the nature of these barriers is as follows:

(1) *Performance and productivity*: These can exist because of a conflict between achieving the best possible outcome and risk in terms of patient safety. The problem is that excessive emphasis on minimizing risk may cause doctors to avoid developing more innovative solutions. This is because during the development period there may be a rise in the number of patients who have to be re-admitted to hospital for additional treatment.

(2) *Professional autonomy*: Within the NHS there already exist a number of national guidelines which can curtail the medical profession's professional autonomy. One such example is the guidelines issued by NICE which prohibits the use of certain drug treatments on the grounds that a drug has failed to demonstrate an adequate cost/benefit relationship compared to other drugs which are available. Cases do arise where doctors who believe the new treatment is superior to other existing treatments understandably feel that their clinical judgement is being ignored. Any attempt to appeal a national body's decision is often problematical because of the limited availability of statistics that can be used to support the clinician's opinion.

(3) *Craft mindset*: Health care professionals have a tendency to believe their skills are often unique and are the primary reason for successful medical outcomes. This attitude militates against standardized service provision and thereby permits individuality and idiosyncrasy which can be to the detriment of the overall standard of care delivered. When this issue is raised doctors will rely on the classic 'professional model' which claims the profession's code of conduct is sufficient to ensure they are working in the best interests of their organization and the patients.

(4) *Complacency*: Health care professionals often find that standardized systems are a barrier to freedom. Furthermore, fulfilment of required activities can become so routine that staff perceive them as burdensome ritualized procedures which over time lose relevance. As a result staff may neglect to complete forms properly or individuals using these forms fail to implement the actions that are required. The risk of these outcomes will tend to rise as the number of regulations increases and in some cases actually result in conflicting rules being put in place. The potential outcome is that layered safety systems become unwieldy and so potentially ineffective.

(5) *Accepted legitimacy*: Across many areas of the NHS staff working in the roles of service improvement through the creation of more effective governance often report difficulties in gaining acceptance of new administrative procedures. Instead of the medical profession seeing clinical governance as a system through which to optimize the quality of patient care, they may adopt the attitude that these systems represent excessive policing and interference with their perceived right to self governance. To a certain degree there is probably some validity in this viewpoint. There is a

growing feeling among many doctors that although clinical governance is an excellent concept it has evolved in practice into a hugely cumbersome, time-consuming, and non-productive system. Ultimately, therefore, unless changes are made to this type of governance system, non-acceptance can result in the imposition of a highly regulated environment leading to a decline in the level of individual self-governance exhibited by medical professionals.

In commenting upon the possible barriers to effective medical governance, Storey and Buchanan note that in the United Kingdom there is the increasing number of external monitoring bodies such as the Healthcare Commission, the National Litigation Authority, the General Medical Council, and Primary Care Trusts. In their view this explosion in the level of external scrutiny does risk the emergence of a minimalist, ritualistic, conformance-oriented approach amounting to little more than box-ticking by public sector employees. To a certain degree this new scrutiny systems have often emerged as a result of politicians implementing a reactive, fire fighting approach by passing new legislation without anybody being given an opportunity to evolve into a more effective solution to a newly identified healthcare delivery problem. In assessing whether medical governance practices can be enhanced, these authors have concluded that unless Hospital Boards are prepared to adopt their own governance model of giving less priority to meeting financial targets and instead focus more on patient safety and quality of service then it is unlikely that health care professionals can be expected to fulfil the rules laid down by their employers in relation to clinical governance.

Corporate social responsibility

The primary focus of Government legislation over the years has been to create new company laws and statutory requirements designed to avoid cases of misbehaviour and fraud re-occurring in the future. As such this perspective of corporate governance can be considered as somewhat narrow. More recently, Governments, various statutory authorities, investor groups, professional bodies, and academics have sought to broaden the concept to encompass other stakeholders such as customers, suppliers, and the general public.

In the United States, the director of the Good Governance Program within US Department of Commerce, Ivor Abramov (2007), proposed that common to every successful public and private sector organization is integrity, respect, and honesty. In his view best practices of corporate institutions and governmental organizations need to evolve into new global standards. In order for companies to survive in world markets, there is a need to embrace concepts such as shareholder value, more transparent accounting systems, and business integrity. For this to occur, however, businesses must avoid the philosophy of generating high short-term profits no matter the subsequent cost of either business failure or creating an adverse impact on the environment. Building sustainable long-term organizations demands that profit generation must be balanced against strategies related to meeting obligations to other stakeholders such as customers, employees, suppliers, and communities impacted by their business activities. The implications of this latter scenario are that major Western businesses, especially those involved in the extraction of natural, non-sustainable resources such as oil or minerals need to be accept their responsibilities to improve the quality of life of the world's poorest communities in the developing nations. Furthermore, these companies need to extend their governance to include assisting in meeting the basic needs of these communities, such as food, clean water, housing, and education.

This broader view of governance, known as CSR, has provided the basis for a new approach to managing the relationship between the organization and its stakeholders. Pressure to adopt this view has come from various sources. These include customers who might object to an aspect of the company's production processes (e.g. inadequate animal welfare in food processing), investment pressure groups who want the company to act with integrity, social pressure groups (e.g. those concerned about the implications of global warming), Governments, and international bodies such as the United Nations. The implications of CSR for senior managers seeking to create an enduring organization is to identify a strategy that continues to ensure leadership in the face of changing industry or market structures whilst concurrently fulfilling higher public expectations about the company's social and ethical performance.

Wilson (2000) has proposed that in evolving a strategy that is reflective of a CSR-orientated philosophy there are a number of factors which need consideration. Legitimacy of activity is a crucial factor in relation to whether corporation is fulfilling the role of providing society with needed goods and services instead of focusing upon the maximization of near-term profits. Governance is a core aspect of CSR because this provides the guidelines through which the company adopts a balanced perspective in seeking to meet the needs of shareholders and not, for example, attempting to maximize the earnings of the current senior management team. This is an issue of equity in that the organization does not act in a way which is detrimental to one or more stakeholder groups. An increasingly important issue is environmental responsibility. This is because recognition of the scarcity of certain resources and the potential damage which can be caused by an organization's activities has brought the issue of sustainability to the forefront of concerns expressed both Government and their citizens. Another issue is the degree to which the company exhibits a genuine responsibility for the security and well-being of their workforce. Although in some countries Governments have introduced legislation to protect the rights of employees, organizations that recognize the key role of their employees in delivering competitive advantage will usually go much further in terms of equality and further development of their workforce than is specified in any existing labour laws.

In reviewing the relationships between strategy and CSR, Katsoulakos and Katsoulakos (2007) concluded that self-regulation can only be effective where the organization by evidence of appropriate actions has established mutual trust and reciprocity with key stakeholders. For this to be achieved, the organization and the stakeholders must establish commonly held goals and values. Furthermore, in an increasingly resource-constrained world, where protection of the environment is fundamental to the long-term success of the organization, there is a requirement for strategic actions to be assessed in terms of stakeholders acceptance of the company's economic, social, and environmental impact. Molteni (2006) has expressed similar views in relation to the need for strategy to be reflective of a commitment to CSR that results in mutual trust between the organization and stakeholders. As summarized in Figure 15.1, he proposes that the organization should seek to strike a balance between the variables of stakeholder satisfaction, competitive advantage, and financial performance. This is unlikely to be a simple process and compatibility between variables is only likely to occur where the organization has adopted a culture based upon social entrepreneurship. In this way the organization will have the capability to identify and implement new unconventional actions that fulfil both the organization's and the stakeholders' performance expectations.

In terms of seeking to increase the level of CSR in the private sector, Governments are increasingly attempting to influence this by promoting the benefits of the philosophy to private sector organizations and through 'leading by example' in terms of CSR becoming a fundamental aspect of operational policies within public sector organizations. Albareda et al. (2006) have suggested that European Governments' perspectives on CSR reflect the relationships between welfare state policies and desired collaboration between private and public organizational actors in each country. In the United Kingdom, for example, with the state heavily involved in the delivery of welfare policies, national, regional, and local governments should all be involved in the implementation of their own CSR policies.

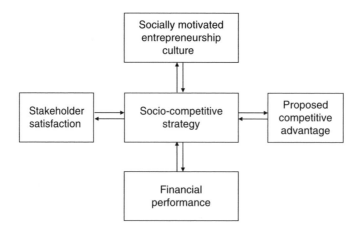

Figure 15.1   CSR and strategy interactions

Albareda et al. have observed that across the EU where there has been a great public recognition of the value of social capital in some cases this has led to PSOs incorporating such values into their governance policies. Pressure from the general public has also caused the private sector to be supportive of Government CSR policies by exhibiting greater commitment to working in partnership with public sector agencies in order to implement CSR programmes. In Italy, for example, the Government-civil society perspective has resulted in the Government providing financial support to organizations in civil society to implement CSR activities whose ultimate social beneficiary is society in general. The identified objectives of CSR public policy include (Albareda et al. 2006):

(1) The promotion of a CSR culture and exchange of best practices

(2) A guarantee to citizens that reporting of CSR commitment by companies is true and not misleading

(3) Defining a list of key performance indicators that firms can adopt on a voluntary basis

(4) Assisting support (SMEs) in developing their CSR strategies and policies

(5) Fostering experience exchange between countries in order to identify and implement the best practices at international level

In the United Kingdom the aim of the Government is to foster the idea that CSR is good for long-term business success as well as good for wider society (DTI 2001). This perspective has led the Government to present the aims of CSR implementation as including competitiveness, poverty reduction, community investment, environmental responsibility, better governance, and creating the most appropriate workplace conditions. To achieve these aims, the Government strategy includes:

(1) The promotion of business activities that bring simultaneous economic, social, and environmental benefits

(2) Working in partnership with the private sector, community bodies, unions, consumers, and other stakeholders

(3) Encouraging innovative approaches and continuing development and application of best practice

(4) Ensuring adequate minimum levels of performance in areas such as health and safety, the environment, and equal opportunities

(5) Encouraging increased awareness, open constructive dialogue, and the building of trust between public and private sector organizations to enhance collaboration over implementing CSR programmes

(6) Creating a policy framework which encourages and enables responsible behaviour by business

Public Sector CSR

Case Aims: To illustrate the issues associated with the need for public sector organization to exhibit a CSR orientation.

The World Bank (1997) notes that the introduction of CSR into the public sector is in some cases aimed at achieving reforms for reducing corruption and increasing transparency. This organization expressed the view that decentralization which often accompanies the introduction of NPM can lead to an increase in corruption at local or regional government level. This is because the restructuring can create more opportunities to carry out fraudulent activities due to the utilization of less constrained audit systems. In the Bank's view the fundamental role of CSR is to strengthen basic governance principles, thereby enhancing transparency, accountability, and responsiveness to stakeholder interests in the public sector.

Langseth et al. (1995) categorize organizational reforms around the four principles of awareness raising, institution building, prevention, and enforcement. The role of adopting a CSR orientation is this can lead to activities such as the implementation of codes of conduct, integrated financial management systems, and promote transparent procurement practices. Adoption of a citizen's charter will assist if defining the expectations by service users as well as a performance aim declaration by the provider. In many cases, acceptance of the prevention approach by public sector employees will require the creation of stakeholder institutions which can oversee strategic decisions and operational activities within the public sector. Examples of such bodies include supreme audit institutions, the judiciary, appointment of an ombudsman, and a focus of attention from the media and oversight processes by the legislature.

To provide an example of implementation of a CSR philosophy Bryane and Gross (2004) presented case materials on Tempe, Arizona in the United States. Like many local government operations in the United States, the city utilizes a model charter format in which there is a division of power between a city manager and the city council. The council sets policy and the manager administers the city. As elected officials, city council members belong to an extended information network comprised of citizens, businesses, city employees, and other elected officials who provide information, viewpoints, and analysis on city issues. Any of Tempe's 160,000 citizens, thousands of businesses, or 1600 employees can contact a council member by phone, e-mail, and/or personal visit.

All city government decisions are made in public, and the city government has to abide by both open meeting and public records laws that are mandated by the state government. The state's open public meeting law requires that a public body may make an open call to the public during a public meeting, subject to reasonable time, place and manner restrictions, to allow individuals

(cont'd)

to address the public body on any issue within the jurisdiction of the public body. Council activities are also monitored by the mass media channels. Council meetings are televised and the television broadcast can be accessed through the city's Internet site allowing anyone in the world with broadband access to watch the Tempe City Council's decision-making activities.

Assessing Futures 16

The aims of this chapter are to cover the issues of:

(1) The uncertain world environment
(2) The implications associated with continuing world population growth
(3) Resolving the problem of rising health care costs
(4) The growing demand for greater environmental responsibility
(5) The future utilization of robots to fulfil certain key activities and roles
(6) Strategic opportunities and associated managerial perspectives

Uncertain futures

The twenty-first century was welcomed in around the world by people exhibiting a high level of the 'feel good factor' and the organization of celebrations to welcome in the new millennium. Less than 10 years later, however, the world has faced a financial crisis at least equal to that which occurred during the Great Depression. Hence similar to the beginning of the twentieth century, when none of the century's subsequent major political or economics events which shaped world history were accurately forecasted, it is very unlikely politicians and economists will be able to accurately forecast the impact of current events on either the world economy or the precise nature of the services provided by the public sector over even the next 25 years, let alone the balance of the century.

Recent economic events were initiated by excessive borrowing by both consumers and entire nations. This error was then compounded by the decision of the financial community to sustain profitability by creating complex instruments which, by shifting liabilities out of their balance sheets, created the mirage that Government regulations over asset/lending coverage ratios had not been breached (Aldrick and Conway 2008).

An inability to accurately forecast meta-events that lead to fundamental shifts in the future nature of the world economy represents a major headache for public sector managers, PSOs, and Governments. This is because such shifts are usually accompanied by fundamental changes in customer behaviour and alter the availability of access to financial resources such as tax revenues or the ability to issue Government bonds. Either of these events will significantly impact future organizational service provision activities. Hence, Governments and the leadership in PSOs do need to promote the concept that in addition to developing a clearer understanding of near-term future trends, a greater proportion of organizational resources do need to be allocated towards identifying and responding to very weak signals which indicate fundamental change is likely to impact organizations within the foreseeable future. To successfully implement this task, assessments of opportunities or threats will need to encompass an evaluation of the factors of influence such as those of the type illustrated in Figure 16.1.

Assessors of future opportunity should recognize that factors shown in Figure 16.1 do not merely have a direct impact on the future (Chaston 2009a). This is because interaction between variables can be the cause of even larger fundamental change. For example, population ageing will place a greater tax burden on those still in work, many of whom are parents with children. As higher taxes reduce this latter group's spending power, fewer will be able to afford to fund college education for their children. As many Governments will be forced by population ageing to reduce their scale of subsidies made available for education, this will probably mean fewer children from poorer families will be able to enter Higher Education. This outcome has the potential to lead to growing a social divide in terms of career opportunities available to middle- and upper-class families versus working-class families.

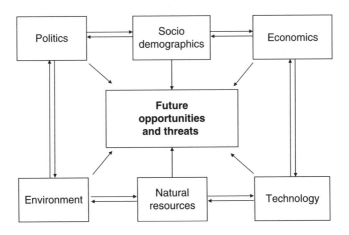

Figure 16.1   Forces of change

Population growth

Even as recently as the late 1990s, international organizations such as the United Nations Food and Agricultural Organisation (the FAO) and the World Bank were supporting the view that ongoing improvements in food technology would mean that by 2010 the world's food supply would be growing faster than demand (Schieb 1999). This forecast caused some experts to predict an easing in the incidence of famine because excess supplies would be accompanied by falling prices, thereby making food commodities more affordable. There was also a perspective that although the world has a finite supply of oil, improving extraction technologies and alternative energy sources would avoid extremely major increases in energy prices. Unfortunately what these experts ignored is that increasing per capita income due to economic growth in China and India means these nations will be able to bid up the price of food and oil, thereby further reducing the poorer nations' abilities to feed their populations and to provide affordable sources of energy.

Since 2003, the trend of rising oil and food prices in response to economic growth has clearly become apparent by a massive increase in world food prices. In theory growing demand for food shortages in the world will lead to higher prices that will be beneficial to nations engaged in sufficiently large-scale agriculture because output can be exported. Similarly developing nations such as South America and Africa will enjoy additional revenues as newly discovered oil fields are brought on-stream. Nevertheless, for the poorest nations in areas of the world such as Africa, the poorly developed nature of agriculture and the national infrastructure associated with food storage and distribution means these countries will probably remain net importers of even basic food stuffs. These countries will also face the need to consider increasing the level of Government subsidies for petrol and other energy sources in order to avoid civil unrest. As a consequence, in these poorer nations a greater proportion of public sector spending will need to be allocated to support food and energy subsidies. This will have a detrimental effect on the magnitude of funds available to support the provision of other public services such as education and health care. Hence, as world prices rise, this will reduce the proportion of available public sector budgets that can be spent on other aspects of welfare service provision.

In relation to food supplies, Pimental et al. (1999) posited that the twenty-first century represented an era of increasing levels of crisis in the face of greater constraints over available agricultural resources. Their analysis of the required cropland needed to support the population in various countries revealed that more and more developing countries would face problems as their populations continue to grow. One of the reasons for the scale of the problem is poor land management leading to major soil erosion at a rate never previously observed since data began to be collected in the nineteenth century. Of even greater concern is the future availability of adequate supplies of water for human and agricultural use. Although the world's water supplies are probably adequate, the locations of such supplies are extremely unbalanced (Coles 2003).

The Hazards of Vested Interests

Case Aims: To illustrate that support from a politically powerful group can result in decisions which may not be in the best interests of society as a whole.

The US Government has passed legislation that 15 per cent of all vehicle fuels should be made from converting corn into ethanol. A key factor influencing the Government was the fact that in the face of declining farm incomes, there has been strong lobbying by the farming community for legislation that would mandate increased production of ethanol from corn crops (Gresser and Cusumano 2005). In support of their claims to justify this move, the US farm lobby has pointed to ethanol being a better fuel in that as well as reducing country's dependence on oil imports from unstable regions of the world ethanol will also contribute to reducing green house gas emissions.

Unfortunately a closer examination of the claims being made for the move to ethanol in the United States are beginning to reveal this policy may not be as beneficial as was initially claimed (Patzek et al. 2005). In terms of energy efficiency it appears that to manufacture 1 gallon of ethanol requires an energy input equal to 1 gallon of petroleum products. Additionally the energy content of ethanol means that a vehicle will consume twice as much ethanol compared to petrol in order to travel the same distance. Added to these problems are the huge amounts of water that are required in the production process. Also there are indications that the waste products from the manufacture of ethanol could create significant new pollution problems as these enter the water table. To these concerns can be added the contamination of the water table caused by using nitrogen fertilizers to maximize the productivity of the corn crop.

Of even greater concern among some academics and agro-business experts is that as United States' corn crop is diverted into ethanol production, this will reduce the amount of corn available as a foodstuff. This in turn will drive up world commodity prices. These prices are likely to rise even further because if predictions about global warming are correct, United States can expect climate change will reduce the country's total corn production during the first half of the twenty-first century.

In defence of these criticisms, ethanol producers in the United States are pointing to the rapid advances that are being made in enhancing the efficiency of their manufacturing operations (Marshall 2006). Water usage has already been reduced and work is at an advanced stage in the development of high temperature heat treatment that improves the ratio of corn input to ethanol output in the production process. Nevertheless, a view which is being expressed by individuals outside the farming industry is that conversion of corn to ethanol is a much less efficient process that growing other faster growing cellulose-rich crops such as switchgrass can then be used as a fuel in conventional power stations. This alternative technology, known as biomass conversion, offers the added advantage that these cellulose-rich crops would be a major appeal to

(cont'd)

the poorer nations in the world. This is because these crops can be grown on very marginal agricultural land, can be tended by low-skilled labour, and do not require the use of fertilizers. This would then leave better agricultural soils to be used for the raising of food crops such as corn, thereby reducing pressures on world commodity prices.

Health care

Commercialization of scientific discoveries such as sulphonamides and penicillin in the 1930s revolutionized the effectiveness of medical treatments. These breakthroughs also demonstrated the vast sums of money which could be made from inventing new drugs. This led to the emergence of the global pharmaceutical industry at the end of World War II. In the 1950s and 1960s, the focus of these drug companies was to discover new anti-bacterial drugs (or antibiotics) that would treat conditions that did not respond to penicillin. In order to ensure that the vast sums of money invested in R&D could be recovered from the sale of new products, the pharmaceutical companies patented their new discoveries in order to avoid the drug being replicated by a competitor. As the number of new antibiotics increased, prices began to decline along with the drug industry profitability. In their ongoing search for new drugs which would confer a virtual global monopoly for the treatment of a specific illness, the European and US companies invested vast sums into R&D such that by the late 1980s, annual industry research expenditure was estimated to be in the region of $30–$40 billion. The reward for such expenditure was in the 1980s when a whole range of new drugs was introduced such as serotonin inhibitors to treat depression, beta blockers for heart conditions, and blood pressure reduction medications. The major drug companies claimed the high prices being charged for these drugs were necessary in order to recover their huge investment in research. Meanwhile as the global drugs companies prospered by developing new drugs, surgeons were developing ever more sophisticated techniques which both increased the costs of surgery (e.g. kidney transplants) and created new market opportunities for the pharmaceutical industry (e.g. the need for immune response suppressant drugs for use after organ transplants) (Benner 2004).

The market reality behind the drug industry's success is their sales could only be supported by developed nation economies' employers funding health insurance for employees and the ability of Governments to cover a large proportion of their nation's health care costs through the creation of the welfare state. Hence, over 90 per cent of the sales of branded pharmaceutical goods are restricted to the world's top 20 economically successful democracies. The growing inability of developed economy nations to fund their welfare programmes and private sector employers needing to cover ever increasing medical insurance premiums has caused Governments and the insurance industry to question the ongoing affordability of buying ever more expensive new drugs from the major pharmaceutical firms (Marmor 1998). In United States, for example, the annual spend on prescription drugs is in the region of $4000 per capita and about $2000 capita in Europe. The huge cost of these drugs bills is why in both Europe and North America politicians are being forced to consider legislative actions in order to stop what seems to be an ever increasing upward trend in the proportion of total health care budgets being spent on the purchase of drugs and medicines.

Only to a limited degree can Governments reduce their expenditure on drugs by refusing to authorize the use of new, more expensive treatments and by demanding that doctors prescribe generic drugs which are older formulations and no longer controlled under patent by the originating pharmaceutical company. The importance of this latter solution is evidenced by the fact that by the year 2000, the size of global generic drug market was already in excess of $30 billion. To date the country which probably has most benefited in economic terms by the trend towards increased use of generics is India (Malhotra and Lofgren 2004). Savings from such actions, however, will in no way close the increasing gap for demand for health care services relative to the public sector funds available to deliver these services. To a certain degree this gap will be reduced as Governments impose means testing when determining what services are to be made available to the general public. There will also probably be an expectation by some Governments that a larger proportion of the general public will be required to purchase private medical insurance. Nevertheless such moves are at best only a partial solution. Thus Governments will need to find for new solutions to overcome this huge fiscal problem and if these prove unavailable or non-viable, then very difficult choices will have to be made concerning whether budget cuts will have to be made in this or in other areas of public sector spending.

Breaking the Big Pharma Stranglehold

Case Aims: To illustrate how new solutions might be able to reduce the costs of medical treatments in the future.

The large pharmaceutical companies have enjoyed immense success during the second half of the twentieth century by inventing new blockbuster drugs which by being patented are then protected from competition. In the last 20 years using existing R&D techniques finding new blockbusters has become increasingly difficult. The solution which seems to appeal to the incumbents is to place greater reliance on M&As as a way of achieving growth through sustaining the monopoly over treatment provision (Cortada and Fraser 2005).

(cont'd)

One solution for Governments seeking to reduce health care delivery costs is to work with industry in the more rapid development of new, lower-cost treatments based upon exploiting new technologies. One area of opportunity where Governments could provide assistance is seeking to stimulate expansion of the countries' biotechnology industry. This opportunity exists because to a certain degree the large conglomerates seem to be less interested in future market opportunities arising from the exploitation of advances in biotechnology (Baker and Gill 2005). The scale of opportunity offered by biotechnology is illustrated by the fact that in 2000 the cancer drug market was still dominated by the large pharmas supplying chemotherapeutics and hormone modulators with 90 per cent of all drug treatment sales coming from these two classes of drugs. Within less than a decade this situation has radically changed. Small biotechnology companies have developed new, more specifically targeted therapy concepts such as monoclonal antibodies, signal inhibitors, or active immunization strategies which already account for almost half of the sales in this sector of the cancer drug market (Behnke 2005).

Biotechnology is still an industry at the introduction stage of an industrial life cycle. Scientists are only just beginning to understand the potential in terms of new health care treatments offered by the ability to modify matter at a molecular and even sub-atomic level. Biotechnology also offers an ability to begin to alter production costs by the exploitation of self-sustaining, low-energy input culturing processes. What is potentially interesting in terms of breaking the big pharmas' stranglehold over the health care industry is much of the knowledge required to develop these new manufacturing techniques lies outside their industry, being held by companies in the brewing and food manufacturing industries (Oliver 1999).

Another technology which Governments could support which has potential to radically alter future health care treatments is human stem cells. The initial interest in stem cells providing a solution to a huge range of medical conditions was triggered by research using Human Embryo Stem Cells (HESC). These are totally undifferentiated cells which just after the human egg has been fertilized have the ability to evolve into any form of human tissue. Concerns over the ethics of harvesting human embryos as a source of these cells has been reduced as advances have been made in persuading some cells from humans to revert to an undifferentiated status for use in the culturing of specific tissues. The potential of stem cells is huge. They can be used to repair tissue damage such as that caused by serious burns and over time can probably be utilized to grow complete new organs such as liver or kidney. Another area of growing interest is the use of stem cells to assist in brain cell regeneration as a cure for mental health conditions associated with the ageing process such as Alzheimer's and dementia (Salter 2007).

The Next Upwave?

Case Aims: To illustrate how genetics may provide solutions for many of the world's growing population and health care problems.

In view of combined threats of population growth, natural resource shortages, global warming, and ever-increasing rising health care costs, it would seem probable that the technology which can contribute to reducing these threats will provide the basis on the twenty-first century's first economic up-wave will be genetics. The important action required of Governments is to find ways of promoting this up-wave because this strategy offers both a way of reducing public sector costs and stimulating economic growth.

In relation to population growth and available food resources, genetics can play a central role. Plants can be developed which give higher yields and be more resistant to disease, frost, drought, and stress. Genetically engineered resistance to pests will be common through such techniques as inducing the plants to produce their own protective or repellent compounds. Insects that carry disease can also be targeted through genetic engineering to control their populations. Genetics can also be used to enhance the use of animals in areas of food production and the production of pharmaceuticals.

Unfortunately the scale of opportunity for the exploitation of genetics to develop Genetically Modified (GM) has been constrained by some Western nations being highly vocal about the dangers associated with the technology and have rejected the introduction of GM crops into their countries. The decision to ban GM foods in such nations is not a problem because the wealth of their inhabitants means these individuals can afford to purchase product produced by non-GM crops. In the future, however, sustaining this moral stance will increase the cost of food and thereby create a drain on consumer spending power. An even greater problem is that vocal rejection of GM technology by countries within the EU is disrupting the technology being made available in many developing nations. In Kenya, for example, production of maize which is the country's staple diet item has fallen by 18 per cent over 10 years, in large part due to pest infestations. This problem could be overcome by the introduction of pest-resistant GM hybrid maize varieties. But due to the well-meaning activities of Greenpeace and concerns about upsetting key European markets, these new varieties are not being used. Similarly in India, where the cotton crop is being destroyed by a worm infestation which has become resistant to insecticide sprays, activists have blocked the Government from distributing new, worm resistant, GM seeds to the nations thousands of small subsistence farmers. In Brazil, the national consumer federation has through action in the courts ensured it remains illegal for farmers to plant the GM varieties which could significantly improve the productivity of the nation's key food crops. Additionally these and many other developing nations have been told if they start

(cont'd)

planting GM crops, their agricultural output will be barred from sale in markets in Europe, Australia, and Japan.

In the near future manufacturers will be able to use genetically engineered micro-organisms to produce commodity and specialty chemicals, as well as medicines, vaccines, and drugs. They will also be widely used in agriculture, mining, resource upgrading, waste management, and environmental cleanup. The technology is likely to be particularly useful in the bioremediation of solid and hazardous waste sites and in agricultural applications such as fertilizers.

Another area where Governments seeking to reduce health care costs and stimulate economic growth is to focus their support for research associated with genomic medicine. This technology offers a vital opportunity in terms of finding ways of replacing expensive drugs (Benner 2004). The technology is based upon exploiting the knowledge which has become available from deciphering the DNA sequencing of human genome. This new understanding will permit new approaches using molecular biology to treat a diversity of medical conditions. By working at the molecular level, scientists are beginning to understand how to develop new solutions such as blocking molecule synthesis within cancer cells and using recombinant DNA to produce drugs such as human insulin. Genomics also has the potential to more effectively control disease vectors such as the mosquito. Although it is still too early to accurately predict the influence of genomics in the twenty-first century, there are indications that the impact will be even greater than twentieth-century discoveries such as vaccines and antibiotics. There is also growing evidence that genomics will provide the basis for the creation of new firms across the world which over time will overtake the existing huge global pharmaceutical companies as the new market leaders in the health care industry (Hammond 2002).

Possibly genomics' greatest potential will be in enabling doctors to identify, treat, and prevent the 4000 or more genetic diseases and inherited disorders. Genetics will become central to diagnosis and treatment, especially in testing for predispositions and in therapies. Within 20 years, there will likely be thousands of diagnostic procedures and treatments for genetic conditions. Genetic diagnostics can detect specific diseases, such as Down's syndrome and behavioural predispositions such as depression. Treatments include gene-based pharmaceuticals, such as those using DNA formulations that block the body from transmitting genetic instructions associated with a specific disease. In future, preventive therapies will involve removed, turning off, or blocking the activities of harmful genes. In some cases, healthy replacement of genes will be directly inserted into foetuses or will be administered to people via injection, inhalation, retroviruses, or pills. These therapies will reduce health care spending by permitting the abolition of adverse medical traits and by the prevention of certain diseases.

The environment

In the 30-year period, 1950–1980, only a minority of individuals and politi-cians in the Western world were concerned about the potential adverse impact of uncontrolled consumption on Planet Earth in relation to either environmen-tal damage or the exhaustion of natural resources. Even the advent of the OPEC oil crisis in the 1970s, which signalled an end of the era of low cost-energy, had minimal impact on Governments' or consumers' actions to conserve energy. By the 1980s, however, higher oil prices and impact of events such as acid rain, Chernobyl, and Three Mile Island did cause some changes in opinions concern-ing the need to protect the natural environment and finding alternative solutions to counteract the declining availability of key, non-renewable, natural resources.

The degree to which there has been an increase in environmental awareness has varied by both industry and countries (Mitchell and Dupre 1994). Indus-tries with a poor track record in areas such as dumping industrial effluent into lakes and rivers have often only been forced to change their ways as a result of adverse public opinion eventually causing Governments to invoke legislation that required industrial polluters to reduce the environmental impact of their operations. Within mainland Europe, the level of the general population's con-cern over environmental issues has traditionally been as much greater than, for example, in countries such as the United Kingdom or United States. Within some EU countries, heightened awareness over environmental issues led to the election of the world's first ever 'green' parties. These new political parties have manifestos concerned about the need for greater environmentally responsibil-ity. Their primary message is aimed at persuading private sector, public sector, and consumers of the urgent need to accept the '3Rs' of reduce, re-use, and recycle.

The dilemma facing firms located in countries that have introduced new, tighter environmental regulations is how to compete against firms located in developing economies where looser industrial regulations provide these com-panies with much lower operating costs and hence lower prices (Fisk 1974). The solution adopted by some Western firms has been to use 'green' marketing strategies to convince their customers that paying a premium price, in some cases to purchase inferior quality goods, was an appropriate behaviour shift because they as individuals would be reflecting a greater sense of personal environmental responsibility (Bonini and Oppenheim 2008).

The ability of organizations being able to ignore both Government and con-sumer concerns about environmental damage has been radically altered in recent years, however, by widespread acceptance of the existence of global warming (Dyson 2005). In large part this has occurred due to the activities of certain politicians such as Al Gore in the United States and the efforts of the United Nations' Intergovernmental Panel on Climate Change (IPCC). In order for countries to concurrently reduce carbon dioxide emissions yet avoid making fundamental changes in the lifestyle of their inhabitants, there is an urgent need for the planet to find alternative, cleaner sources of energy to replace oil.

Even at the beginning of the new millennium, some writers such as Jaffe and Manning (2000) were still expressing concerns that the price of oil relative to other cleaner, sustainable energy sources will mean Governments can expect to encounter a lack of urgency among consumers, industry, and many PSOs in relation to the need to find greener alternatives to burning fossil fuels.

In terms of the fastest source of growing demand for energy, China's industrialization policies are far outstripping the need for more oil than any other emerging economy. Assuming that the Chinese economy continues to grow at current rates, the country's increasingly wealthy consumers will buy even more cars and the level of oil consumption/capita will approach that of the United States. The implications of this outcome are that by 2030 it is estimated that China will need 99 billion barrels of oil per day (Brown 2006). Although in 2009 important new oil and natural gas finds have been announced in the offshore in the Gulf of Mexico, Brazil, West Africa, and Australia and onshore in North and South America, it will take some 10–20 years to bring many of these fields into full production. Hence energy prices, although probably on average still remaining lower than during the energy price spike in 2007/08, can be expected to remain high for the foreseeable future (Vaitheeswaran 2007). What is less certain, however, is the degree to which high oil prices will make a shift to more sustainable energy sources such as wind power of a commercially viable proposition, thereby leading to a reduction in greenhouse gas emission. Experts are split over the viability of this solution in relation to reducing world emissions. However, there is consensus that only by imposing lower emissions targets can Governments force their respective societies to change. The dilemma of such actions is that they will cause further rises in energy prices, thereby dampening economic growth, reducing consumer spending power, and increasing the costs of welfare service provision.

Strategic opportunities

Given the nature of problems confronting Planet Earth such as the need to reduce greenhouse gas emissions without causing huge rises in the cost of energy generation, it is apparent that current technologies are unlikely to generate completely adequate solutions. As a consequence, major new opportunities exist for those Governments which are prepared to assist individuals and organizations within both the private and public sectors to exploit science and technology to develop radically new products and processes. In order to illustrate the opportunities for new solutions, Constable and Somerville (2003) prepared their analysis of innovation issues based upon comparing the twentieth and twenty-first centuries. As summarized in Table 16.1, it is apparent that most of this century's innovation opportunities are related to environmental and health care issues.

A very similar perspective on the opportunities for using technology to generate innovative solutions has been generated by the National Academy for Engineering (2005) in the United States in a project entitled 'Grand challenges

Table 16.1 A comparison of innovation issues

20th-Century Innovation Issues	21st-Century Innovation Issues
1. Electrification	1. Energy conservation
2. Automobile	2. Resource protection
3. Airplane	3. Food and water production and distribution
4. Water supply and distribution	4. Waste management
5. Electronics	5. Education and learning
6. Radio and television	6. Medicine and prolonging life
7. Agricultural mechanization	7. Security and counter-terrorism
8. Computers	8. New technology
9. Telephone	9. Genetics and cloning
10. Air conditioning/refrigeration	10. Global communication
11. Interstate highways	11. Traffic and population logistics
12. Space flight	12. Knowledge sharing
13. Internet	13. Integrated electronic environment
14. Imaging	14. Globalization
15. Household appliances	15. AI, interfaces, and robotics
16. Health technologies	16. Weather prediction and control
17. Petrochemical technology	17. Sustainable development
18. Laser and fibre optics	18. Entertainment
19. Nuclear technologies	19. Space exploration
20. High-performance materials	20. 'Virtualization' and VR
	21. Preservation of history
	22. Preservation of species

for engineering'. Some of the key problems and proposed potential solutions which will impact the future operation of both private and public sector organizations that are covered by the Academy's report include:

(1) *Solar Energy*: Commercial solar cells typically convert sunlight into electricity with an efficiency of 10–20 per cent. But new materials can be expected to exceed this limit. One area of opportunity is to exploit nanotechnology which may permit engineering of structures on sizes comparable to those of atoms and molecules. The other issue in relation to solar energy is the storage of the energy generated. It may be the case the science will mimic the biological capture of sunshine by photosynthesis in plants, which stores the sun's energy in the chemical bonds of molecules that can be used as food. The plant's way of using sunlight to produce food could also be duplicated to produce fuel.

(2) *Nuclear Fusion*: This approach to energy generation is based upon the same process that generates the sun's energy. Human-engineered fusion has already been demonstrated on a small scale. The challenges facing the engineering community and Governments who are willing to support this industry is to find ways to scale up the fusion process to commercial proportions, in an efficient, economical, and environmentally benign way.

(3) *Carbon Sequestration*: This technology is concerned with capturing the carbon dioxide produced by burning fossil fuels and storing it safely away from the

atmosphere. One approach is for the smokestacks at coal-burning electric power plants to be replaced with absorption towers. It is also possible that engineers will be able to develop new techniques for sequestering carbon dioxide that are based upon natural processes or by pumping carbon dioxide into the ocean in ways that would lock it eternally into rock. Based upon experience gained from pilot programmes for the foreseeable future this approach is only commercially viable if Governments are prepared to offer the private sector players some form of financial incentive such as grants or tax breaks.

(4) *The Nitrogen Cycle*: Nitrogen fixation by micro-organisms is the only way in which nitrogen made its way from the environment into living organisms. Ammonia factories supplement the enzymatic magic of microbial nitrogen fixation with the brute forces of temperature and pressure, extracting close to 100 million metric tons of nitrogen from the atmosphere each year. Nitrogen removed from the air by human activity adds seriously to a number of environmental problems. Agricultural fertilizers, for example, are a major source of nitrous oxide, a potent greenhouse gas. Hence the engineering challenge is to develop ways of capturing those gases for useful purposes or alternatively significantly expand the generation of nitrogen using genetically engineered microbial organizations.

(5) *Clean Water*: Given that 7/8th of the planet is covered by sea water, desalination offers an obvious solution for resolving the world's water crisis. However, desalination plants are expensive to build and require lots of energy to operate, causing desalination to have limited value for developing countries, where water supply problems are most serious. Hence, new technologies are needed to lower energy use in these plants. One potentially useful new approach, called nano-osmosis, would filter out salt with the use of tiny nanotubes of carbon. Additionally, improved technologies could permit the more efficient use of water utilized for crop irrigation.

(6) *Health Informatics*: Enhanced capture, exchange, and analysis of patients' medical data could greatly enhance the diagnosis and treatment of illnesses. Some of the new technologies will involve gathering medical data without a visit to the doctor, such as wearable devices to monitor such things as pulse and temperature. Monitoring devices might even come in the form of tiny electronic sensors embedded in clothing and within the body. Such devices when linked with electronic health records could alert health professionals when a patient needs attention, or even trigger automatic release of drugs into the body when necessary.

(7) *Genomics*: Each person's DNA is basically the same, made up of about 3 billion 'letters' of code, each letter corresponding to a chemical sub-unit of the DNA molecule. But subtle variants in about 1 per cent of our DNA give humans their individual identities. Such differences sometimes predispose people to particular diseases, and some dramatically affect the way a person will respond to medical treatments. By developing understanding of the human genome, doctors should be able to diagnose and treat people based on those individual differences, a concept commonly referred to as 'personalized medicine'. The core benefit of personalized medicine is the potential to combine genetic information with clinical data to optimally tailor drugs and

doses to meet the unique needs of an individual patient. Thus the technology could, for example, be used to have patients' bodies automatically release insulin when the blood's glucose concentration becomes too high. Another new field is 'synthetic biology' whereby novel biomaterials are being engineered to replace or aid in the repair of damaged body tissues. Mastery of synthetic tissue engineering could make it possible to regenerate tissues and organs

(8) *The Human Brain*: Despite the huge advances which have been made in computing, the human brain still remains capable of undertaking tasks which are beyond the machines created by man. By understanding how the brain works may offer the best guide to building more effective Artificial Intelligence (AI) systems permitting the creation of 'smart computers'. A fuller understanding of the human brain will also permit the development of biotechnology solutions to brain disorders, such as drugs or neural implants. Neurological disorders may be circumvented by technological innovations that allow wiring of new materials into our bodies to do the jobs of lost or damaged nerve cells. Implanted electronic devices could help victims of dementia to remember, blind people to see, and crippled people to walk.

Machines replacing people

Since the early days of the Industrial Revolution the private sector has accepted that employees are often an expensive element of operational costs. In addition employees can become ill, wish to work in safe environments, and can only work for some hours before requiring a rest. Machines, on the other hand, can be employed on a 24/7 basis and do not expect to receive fringe benefits or go on vacations. Not surprisingly in developed economies as wage rates and the costs of providing welfare benefits have continued to rise, private sector organizations have sought ways of replacing people with machines.

Given that in the public sector employee costs can represent in excess of 80 per cent of total operating costs, it is somewhat surprising that less emphasis has been given to substituting machines for people as a path to cost reduction. However, in recent years the pressures to reduce costs and advances in technology are beginning to be reflected by greater reliance upon substituting machines for people in the public sector. Possibly the greatest area of impact has been the exploitation of computers. These machines have long exceeded human's capacity to store, process, and analyse data. As a consequence, they already play a critical role in public sector service activities in areas such as taxation, pension payments, and managing welfare benefits for the socially disadvantaged.

Another area of technological opportunity which is also just beginning to be exploited in the public sector is robotics. The term 'robot' was first used by the playwright Karl Capek in his play R.U.R. (Brown 2006). If one uses the term robot, most people have the image of a biped machine which exhibits human attributes. In fact, the first robots which were developed in the private sector in no way fitted this description. Instead, they were basically a mechanical arm programmed to undertake tasks such as welding or spraying cars on highly automated production lines. Hence, a somewhat more appropriate description of a robot is of being a machine that is programmed to undertake specific tasks which previously used to be assigned to a human. In some cases, the programming permits the robot to work autonomously, whereas, in other cases, the robot receives some degree of instruction by being remotely linked to a human operator.

Research into developing more advanced robots for use by public sector organizations has primarily focused on two issues, namely creating machines that can operate in hazardous environments (e.g. the robots used in bomb disposal) and machines that can undertake tedious, highly repetitive tasks (e.g. replacing hospital cleaners). Not surprisingly the hazardous environment issue has meant the majority of R&D in this area has been undertaken by the military. The growing problems associated with terrorism such as suicide bombers have accelerated interest in replacing humans with machines. The US Air Force has, for example, already demonstrated the benefits of using drones in the place of manned aircraft. Initially these machines fulfilled the role of undertaking reconnaissance but more recently by being fitted with missiles, have become capable of being used in an attack role. The pace of ongoing development has now reached the point where US Army has expressed a high level of confidence about being able to deploy robots in the place of humans on the battlefield. One example is the US MAARS machine which is a terrestrial armed robot that can be either used in highly dangerous combat conditions or to supplement the activities of troops. Another machine being tested is the Battlefield Extraction Assist Robot (or 'Bear') that can rescue injured soldiers. Also at an advanced stage of development is BigDog which is mule-sized four-legged robot designed to carry cargo over rough terrain (Smith 2010).

The area which appears to be generating greatest interest among scientists and engineers engaged in non-military projects is the development of 'service robots' which can operate in a broad range of environments (Ranky and Ranky 2005). Examples include working alongside humans in situations such as being a domestic servant, child minder, or assisting health care professionals. A major stimulus to advances in this area has been the advent of more powerful microchips to increase data processing speed and development of more effective sensors that can interpret visual and auditory signals. An example of a service robot is that developed by Fujita Corporation for use by the emergency services (Kusuda 2003). The robot was developed in response to the fact that Japan suffers from numerous natural disasters such as volcanic eruptions, earth quakes, and landslides. In many cases, human access to the disaster site is often restricted because of concerns about safety. The solution of building fully automated machines was rejected for both cost and logistics reasons. Instead Fujita's solution was to use standard construction equipment but to replace the human operator with a robot. The robot is transported to the disaster site in seven easily handled packs. Technicians then assemble the machine and install it in the cab of the construction equipment to be used such as an earthmover or backhoe. The human operator receives pictures via cameras mounted on the robot and then utilizes wireless transmissions to instruct the robot on how to handle item of construction equipment in which it has been located.

The development of service robots created a whole new set of programming problems for scientists (Gomi 2003). Industrial robots operate on a control programme specifically written for a specific situation in which there is minimal variation in the environment in which the machine is operating. In the case of service robots developed to undertake even the apparently simplest of tasks such as that faced by robot vacuum cleaner, the machine will encounter uneven floors, irregular distribution of dust, and irregularly shaped rooms. To handle these problems, the programming will require that data from sensors are processed through some form of Artificial Intelligence software. This is necessary in order that the robot can handle ambiguity in the data being acquired. Gomi posits that the differences between industrial and service robots are summarized in Table 16.2.

Once some of the early problems associated with developing robots to operate in a service-orientated role were overcome, the first commercial applications focused upon replacing humans undertaking repetitive, low-skill tasks in environments such as hospitals and public buildings (Larsan 1998). One of the first product launches in the United States was by the Kent Company in Illinois, United States in 1991, which introduced a robot floor scrubber. Initially each machine was programmed onsite by walking them along the corridors where it was to be used. Clearly this was both a time-consuming and expensive process. Hence, the company developed software known as AutoLearning. This system permits the robot to self-learn the layout of the area where it will be working.

The area where robots are likely to have a major impact in both the private and public sectors is their use in the provision of health care services. By undertaking repetitive or even hazardous tasks this then releases highly trained, expensive human professionals to spend more time undertaking analysis, diagnosis, and determination of appropriate treatment. One example of this scenario has been the development of robotic systems for managing the taking of X-rays and development of films. Robots are also moving into the operating theatre. The Penelope Surgical Instrument Server (SIS) uses machine vision, voice recognition, and AI to act as a robot assistant able to anticipate a surgeon's needs for a specific surgical instrument (Kochan 2005).

Table 16.2   Factors of difference in industrial versus service robots

	Industrial Robots	**Service Robots**
Usage	Manufacturing	Service, tending humans
Aim	Accuracy, precision	Quality of service
Operation	Repetition	Constant change
Objectives	Definable	Hard to define
Adaptability	Pattern recognition	Evolutionary learning
Co-ordinates	Defined, fixed	Undefined

The machine looks nothing like what many would expect of a robot because the main component of the machine is a robotic arm mounted on a mobile platform. Penelope is programmed to recognize specific instruments, picks these up, and positions them correctly when handing each instrument to the surgeon. The other invaluable ability of this robot is to check that all instruments have been returned to the surgical tray at the end of an operation. This capability ensures that no foreign objects have been left behind inside the patient. Even if only part of an instrument has remained within the patient (e.g. a piece which has broken off a scalpel blade), Penelope's vision system will immediately recognize that the instrument on the tray is no longer complete and can alert the medical staff.

As time goes on, especially in areas of very accurate surgery such as that under-taken by neurosurgeons operating inside the patient's brain or in non-invasive surgery where a probe is inserted into the patient, it is expected that robots will play an increasingly important role in undertaking tasks which previously were the sole preserve of highly trained surgeons. Concurrently, further develop-ment is expected in the use of robotics to assist people with disabilities. Mobility devices such as robot wheelchairs already exist. Work is also well-advanced in the use of prosthetic limbs which can interact with the human brain by being linked to the patient's own nervous system.

Innovation strategies

As in the prior millennium, during the twenty-first century there will be oppor-tunities for individuals or small group of like-minded developed to discover new ideas that will lead to the creation of new global businesses and dramatically alter the economies of nations. Hence, Governments and industry should remain alert to the reality that somewhere in the world, in a garage or a University laboratory, work is in progress that may ultimately alter the rules of business and the nature of competitive advantage that can support economic growth.

It is a reality to resolve many of the R&D problems associated with exploit-ing the opportunities shown in Table 16.1 will require more use of an approach to innovation management based on much closer, more collaborative efforts between scientists and engineers from very diverse range of different disciplines. For this outcome to occur, it will require the formation of new public–private sector partnerships. The issue of blending different technologies and exploiting the competences available across organizations requires a strategic orientation in which Governments and industry proactively collaborate to maximize the mag-nitude of new ideas being progressed through to operational viability in the shortest time possible.

Another critical issue is that the combined influence of globalization and free market access creates an even more competitive and complex world. Few organizations have the scale of internal knowledge to identify and exploit the innovation opportunities which may exist in the twenty-first century. For this reason, innovation must transcend the boundaries of the individual organization and in both the public and private sectors become integrated across all members of supply chains in order to meet users' changing needs. This is because observations of successful innovation practices in various different organizations demonstrate that successful outcomes are critically dependent upon exploiting all of the resources which exist with entire value chains (Shapiro 2001).

Managerial perspectives

In an assessment of future economic and industrial trends, Zahra (1999) concluded these will be influenced by factors which include the emergence of more entrepreneurial economies, more focus on human development, the increased importance of green economics, and leadership as the key to organizational survival and utilizing the dynamic capabilities of a knowledge-based workforce to achieve global leadership in relation to operational activities. In relation to entrepreneurship he posited that individual and corporate entrepreneurs in both the private and public sectors will assume a more powerful and significant role in society. This is because entrepreneurs recognize that survival and success in the twenty-first century will require speed, creativity, and ingenuity.

Changes in organizational behaviour can only occur where the leadership is willing to influence attitudes, behaviours, and values of both their workforce and key stakeholders. The most successful leaders are those who have sufficient vision to recognize the beginnings of strategic change in the sector in which their organization operates, predicts the future before it materializes, and move quickly to capitalize on change. Effective leaders also understand the implementation of change requires that because organizational core competences provide a unique source of superiority over other organizations, hence internal entrepreneurial capabilities must be continually evolved and updated. If an organization does not continue to invest in and develop core competencies over time, this may limit future strategic options.

Intellect and knowledge are critical factors in developing and sustaining innovative behaviour. Hence Zahra posited that investments in developing, nurturing, sustaining, and cultivating this knowledge are among the most important ways in which organizations and entire nations can sustain economic growth. He also expressed the view that successful organizations will increasingly be judged not just upon financial performance, but in relation to a broader set of variables such as customer relations, employee commitment, contribution towards society as a whole, and innovation. Hence, success in the twenty-first century will demand greater attention to building the organization's relationships with diverse stakeholder groups in ways that can lead to mutual trust and respect between organizations.

To assess the degree to which organizations shared his perspectives on the key factors influencing organizational strategies in the twenty-first century, Zahra undertook a large-scale survey of CEOs in US companies. These individuals ranked, in descending order of importance, entrepreneurship, focus on employee development, the green economy, leadership, a more balanced approach to assessing corporate performance development, and increased dynamic capabilities in relation to developing new internal competences. Subsequently, Hagen and Lodha (2004) repeated the study to determine whether these factors remained valid in the early twenty-first century. Their conclusion was that CEOs still considered all of the same factors as critically important to ensure the long-term existence of their organizations. The only difference between the two studies was in the ordering of key variables. In Hagen and Lodha's study, the ranking of factors in descending order of performance by CEOs was leadership, entrepreneurship, a focus on employee development, increased dynamic capabilities, a green economy, and a more balanced approach to measuring corporate performance. Although no researcher has undertaken a similar study of the views of CEOs in public sector organizations, it seems reasonable to conclude that their views on the factors determining long-term survival and success will be very similar to those identified by firms in the private sector.

New Technology and Process Automation

Case Aims: To illustrate how technology can lower public sector operating costs whilst sustaining current levels of service provision.

Following the need for reforms in public sector spending policies in the face of poor economic conditions and high inflation, by the 1980s Governments in most developed nations had begun to freeze or reduce the level of funds being made available to HE institutions (McPherson et al. 1989). Where this occurred, colleges and most universities responded by slowing their rates of spending, and where permitted by prevailing legislation, increased the share of costs borne by students by raising tuition fees. Such actions were insufficient to close the gap between Government funding and an ongoing rise in operating costs. In the United Kingdom, for example, the Government although aware of the adverse reaction from the electorate was forced to implement a policy of requiring UK students to pay tuition fees (Peters 1999).

By the late 1990s, UK vice chancellors were aware that operating costs were rising at a rate greater than that which could be covered by the introduction of tuition fees. Nevertheless, most institutions ignored the fact that given their labour costs represented almost 80 per cent of total operating budgets, there was an obvious need to focus on innovation and the exploitation as a way of reducing this area of expenditure. As a consequence, these institutions should have begun to invest in projects to develop their capabilities to exploit the Internet and associated advances in both communications and computers to create e-based educational delivery platforms. Instead many vice chancellors tended to focus on (a) attracting more overseas students, (b) putting pressure on the

(cont'd)

Government to increase public sector spending on Higher Education, and (c) lifting the cap on UK student tuition fees. As a result of this strategic myopia, many UK universities are now facing massive problems sustaining the viability of their operations in the face of a 25–35 per cent reduction in their budgets following the need for the Government to reduce the United Kingdom's huge public sector deficit.

There are a number of reasons why the UK university sector seems to have rejected the exploitation of e-based learning to resolve the problem of ever rising labour costs. One of the primary reasons is an apparent inability to recognize the need for change and to implement successful change management programmes. Failure to instigate change reflects the fact that most UK academics are even now highly resistant to replacing conventional, terrestrial classroom-based teaching with e-based programme delivery. In part, this reflects an aversion by some of them having to learn new IT skills as well as accepting that the 24/7 nature of distributed learning requires a different, more flexible approach to fulfilling their teaching responsibilities. Others individuals are concerned about job security because e-based learning does have the potential to reduce the number of highly educated academics required to deliver programmes. Another group holds the erroneous view that e-based learning cannot achieve the same level of quality in relation to the student learning experience. They also tend to be misinformed about operational costs and remain unaware that e-based distance learning delivery costs are lower than delivering the equivalent programme using conventional terrestrial provision.

The concerns of academic staff over their inability to learn new IT skills or worries about job security should not in reality hinder UK universities from being able to exploit e-learning to reduce labour costs, thereby ensuring the long-term survival of these institutions. In relation to the perceived weaknesses in e-based learning, the experience of academics and institutions in both the United Kingdom and elsewhere in the world is that other fundamental objections which UK lecturers continue to raise about e-based learning are totally fallacious. For example, there is growing evidence that the advent of technology such as e-mail, file downloading, online library access, video-streaming, and online conference are capable of enhancing students' perceptions of the quality of their learning experience to the point that they perceive their e-learning experience as at least equal and sometimes surpassing a terrestrial learning experience.

The success of well-structured delivery systems and adoption of a flexible 24/7 orientation towards supporting students is exemplified by Moustraining Ltd (www.moustraining.uk.com), a spin-off company from the UK's University of Plymouth. The company consistently achieves a student satisfaction rating in excess of 90 per cent. This rating is higher than virtually any of the university's terrestrial programmes. Given the perception that online learning is more

(cont'd)

expensive than an equivalent terrestrial programme, possibly the most important achievement of Moustraining is the organization's delivery cost. In recent submissions to the UK Government investigation on the need to raise student tuition fees, the second-tier colleges indicated that at best they are currently facing a break-even situation in terms of revenue versus operating costs. Assuming only 70 per cent of UK students are required to pay tuition fees, this net fee of £2303 and the Band D Government funding of £2641/student suggest that these institutions are achieving a delivery cost per student of £4944. This can be contrasted with Moustraining's delivery cost of £2353. Even if one assumes that there is a need to add an overhead cost of an additional 50 per cent to cover the costs of infrastructure and support services if Moustraining utilized the same organizational structure and operational processes as a traditional UK university, this then yields an adjusted higher cost of £3530. This delivery cost is still £1414 lower than the average delivery cost in the UK Higher Education sector. The primary reason for this difference is that most universities still rely upon using highly labour intensive administration systems. In contrast, Moustraining has invested in the development of a proprietary software system which achieves an operational cost saving of approximately 80 per cent when compared to the University of Plymouth's equivalent systems.

Assignments

Chapter 1

> ### Assignments
>
> (1) Write a report concerning the emergence of the concept of the welfare state.
>
> (2) Write a report reviewing why problems started to emerge in the ongoing expansion of the welfare state beginning in the late 1970s/early 1980s.
>
> (3) Select a Western nation and write a report summarizing actions being taken by the nation's Government to manage the size of the country's public sector deficit.
>
> ### Self-study/group discussion topics
>
> (1) Why did the events of the Great Depression and World War II act as a catalyst for the expansion of the welfare state in the second half of the twentieth century?
>
> (2) Welfare state models usually focus on seeking to offer equality of service provision to a country's entire population. Do you believe this is a viable concept in view of the scale of the public sector deficits now facing many nations?
>
> (3) The two ways of reducing public sector deficits are (i) to increase revenue flows from taxation and (ii) to reduce public sector expenditure. Which of these actions do you feel should be emphasized and why?

Chapter 2

> ### Assignments
>
> (1) Write a report describing the aims and processes associated with NPM.
>
> (2) Write a report assessing the strengths and weaknesses of returning public sector organizations to the private sector.

(cont'd)

(3) Write a report reviewing the advantages and disadvantages of using performance indicators in the management of public sector service delivery.

Self-study/group discussion topics

(1) From your experience of public sector services do you feel there is a commitment by employees to deliver a high-quality service.

(2) What is your understanding of the concept of customer orientation? Do you feel that public sector organizations' performance can be enhanced by the adoption of a customer orientation?

(3) Do you believe that the political party in power in your country is committed towards ensuring that the nation has an effective public sector and what actions are they implementing which are designed to influence the performance of public sector organizations?

Chapter 3

Assignments

(1) Prepare a report reviewing the events surrounding the recent international banking crisis.

(2) Write a report proposing your views on what actions might be taken by Governments to ensure there is no repetition of the events that caused the recent international banking crisis.

(3) Write a report reviewing the implications of population ageing on the provision and funding welfare services in the future.

Self-study/group discussion topics

(1) In what ways could have politicians implemented actions that could have avoided the onset of the recent international banking crisis?

(2) In what way do you feel globalization will influence the future delivery of welfare services in Western developed nation economies?

(3) What are the different perspectives of the various political parties in your country in relation to accepting deficit spending is an acceptable concept through which to sustain economic growth and/or support continued expansion of the welfare state?

Chapter 4

Assignments

(1) Prepare a report examining the relevance of stakeholder theory in the management and operation of PSOs.

(2) Prepare a report examining what you perceive as the embedded values of people in your country and how these are reflected in the behaviour of individuals working in the public sector.

(3) Prepare a report comparing your personal values with the values of people in your parent's generation. In what ways do these identified values influence views about (a) the importance of exhibiting a strong work ethic and (b) marriage?

Self-study/group discussion topics

(1) Compare and contrast the culture of two or more countries and identify how culture is reflected in similarities and differences in lifestyle in these countries.

(2) What are the similarities and differences in the ethics espoused by your generation versus people in your parent's generation? In what ways do the identified ethics influence differences in behaviour between these two generations?

(3) Present your perspectives on the behaviour of politicians in your country and determine how the identified traits are indicators of these individuals' ethics and personal values.

Chapter 5

Assignments

(1) Use the Internet to locate a published strategic plan for a public sector organization. Provide a critical assessment of whether you feel the proposed plan is a viable proposition in terms of optimizing the organization's provision of services.

(2) Re-assess the selected strategic plan using the spider approach proposed in Figure 5.3 for developing an entrepreneurial strategy. Do you perceive that adoption of an entrepreneurial orientation would significantly alter the organization's strategic plan?

(cont'd)

(3) Use the Internet to review the current policies of the major political parties in your country. How would these various policies influence public sector managers when seeking to define future plans based upon their expectations over the scale of financial resources that might be made available depending upon which political party is in power?

Self-study/group discussion topics

(1) Which do you consider is the more entrepreneurial business, Facebook or YouTube? What are the issues which provide the basis for your conclusion?

(2) The planning models presented in this chapter assume the user is a logical, rational decision-maker. What are the implications for entrepreneurs in the public sector who might make decisions on the basis of intuition (or 'hunches')?

(3) What are the advantages and disadvantages of the type of planning philosophies proposed by individuals such as Mintzberg which are based upon a descriptive approach to defining the strategic management process?

Chapter 6

Assignments

(1) Prepare a report defining what you believe are the attributes of an effective leader.

(2) Prepare a report examining the nature of the operational problems that leaders in public sector organizations can expect to encounter.

(3) Prepare a report assessing why transformational leaders are possibly superior to transactional leaders in the effective management of organizational change.

Self-study/group discussion topics

(1) Why do you think that the advent of NPM placed greater pressures on leaders with PSOs?

(2) What are the potential benefits of having a public sector organization being managed by an entrepreneurial leader?

(3) Why might an entrepreneurial orientation be the most effective philosophy for a public sector organization to respond to Government budget cuts?

Chapter 7

Assignments

(1) Prepare a review concerning how can the Product Life Curve be utilized as a strategic planning and analysis tool.

(2) Review how Porter's Contending Forces model can be used as a strategic planning and analysis tool.

(3) Prepare a review concerning how Value and Service Profit Chain models can be used as a strategic planning and analysis tool.

Self-study/group discussion topics

(1) Examine the relevance of the Boston Consulting Group (BCG) matrix in relation to guiding the future strategy of a public sector organization such as a university.

(2) Examine the relevance of the Product Life Curve in relation to guiding the future strategy of a public sector organization such as a university.

(3) Through the application to a public sector organization such as a university show how a SWOT analysis can assist in guiding the strategic planning process.

Chapter 8

Assignments

(1) Through application to a public sector organization such as a university prepare a report reviewing how the chosen organization could undertake an analysis of market demand for services being delivered.

(2) Prepare a report discussing the implications of population ageing on the future delivery and funding of public sector services.

(3) Prepare a report reviewing how the manifestos of political parties will influence the nature and scale of the welfare services that will be made available to a nation's citizens.

Self-study/group discussion topics

(1) How a technology be exploited as a strategy for reducing the cost of public sector service provision?

(2) How can public sector organizations' own activities be utilized to demonstrate to a nation the importance of exhibiting environmental responsibility?

(3) How can changes in a nation's economy influence the current and future provision of welfare services?

Chapter 9

Assignments

(1) Prepare a report examining why the exploitation of technology is so important in determining the ongoing economic performance of any nation.

(2) Prepare a report assessing the relevance of disruption theory in explaining success and potential adverse impact associated with the introduction of a new technology.

(3) Prepare a report reviewing the factors capable of influencing the degree of success associated with the introduction of a new technology.

Self-study/group discussion topics

(1) What areas of technology are likely to assist in either stabilizing or reducing the costs of providing health care services?

(2) Which areas of technology are most likely to improve efficiency and effectiveness of service delivery (excluding the health care sector) provision by public sector organizations?

(3) How could universities exploit new technology to reduce their educational delivery costs?

Chapter 10

Assignments

(1) Prepare a report reviewing why internal competence is a critical factor in the delivery of services.

(2) Prepare a report reviewing the concept of entrepreneurial competence.

(3) Prepare a report reviewing which internal competence can be critical in ensuring an organization is able to sustain a growth-orientated strategic plan.

Self-study/group discussion topics

(1) What are the key factors influencing organizational productivity and what actions could a public sector organization implement to improve productivity?

(2) Why are people considered a key asset within public sector organizations and how can people management strategies enhance the provision of services?

(cont'd)

(3) Why is service quality considered to be a critical issue within public sector organizations and what strategies exist for enhancing service quality?

Chapter 11

Assignments

(1) Prepare a report describing the role of an Opportunity Response Matrix in strategic planning and illustrate your answer by developing and applying this matrix to a public sector organization.

(2) Prepare a report describing the role of a Threat Response Matrix in strategic planning and illustrate your answer by developing and applying this matrix to a public sector organization.

(3) Prepare a report describing the role of Gap Analysis in strategic planning and illustrate your answer by developing and applying this concept to a public sector organization.

Self-study/group discussion topics

(1) Review the strengths and weaknesses of using a single versus multiple objectives in a strategic plan.

(2) Select a public organization, define the organization's stakeholders, and the different requirement they may have over the activities and outputs of the selected organization.

(3) Select a public organization and define what you believe should be the nature of the social responsibilities which this organization should exhibit.

Chapter 12

Assignments

(1) Prepare a review stating why you think misunderstanding can exist about what exactly is an organizational strategy,

(2) Prepare a review of what is the role of competitive advantage in determining a future organizational strategy.

(3) Prepare a report assessing the viability of RBV theory in the determination of strategy for a public sector organization.

(cont'd)

Self-study/group discussion topics

(1) Utilize the Porter competitive advantage strategy and also proposed modification to this model to determine the strategy being utilized by a public sector organization which you have selected.

(2) Select a public sector organization and assess (a) evidence of strategic defence capability and (b) strategic flexibility.

(3) Assess the benefits of using the Miles and Snow typology in the development of a future strategy for a public sector organization.

Chapter 13

Assignments

(1) Prepare a report reviewing the role of the strategic deployment phase in the strategic management process.

(2) Prepare a report reviewing why strategic alignment is critical in the successful implementation of a strategic plan.

(3) Why is customer focus an important aspect in ensuring the success of a public sector organization?

Self-study/group discussion topics

(1) Examine why process innovation is an important aspect in implementing a successful strategy in the public sector.

(2) Discuss why externalization of strategy can be an important aspect in implementing a successful strategy in the public sector.

(3) Examine why participation in networks can be an important aspect in implementing a successful strategy in the public sector.

Chapter 14

Assignments

(1) Prepare report reviewing how poor leadership can damage implementation of a successful strategy in the public sector.

(cont'd)

(2) Prepare report reviewing the nature of the abuses which leaders may exhibit and describe how these can damage implementation of a successful strategy in the public sector.

(3) Prepare report reviewing how structure and control can influence the implementation of a successful strategy in the public sector.

Self-study/group discussion topics

(1) Discuss the strengths and weaknesses associated with using PRP in the public sector.

(2) Discuss the strengths and weaknesses associated with using KPIs in the public sector.

(3) How can knowledge management be utilized to enhance the performance of public sector organizations?

Chapter 15

Assignments

(1) Prepare a report describing the evolution of governance practices in the private sector.

(2) Prepare a report describing the role of governance in public sector organizations.

(3) Prepare a report describing the obstacles confronting the implementation of governance policies in public sector organizations.

Self-study/group discussion topics

(1) Discuss the role of medical governance in the effective provision of health care services.

(2) Discuss why the leadership in public sector organizations may be ineffective in their organizations adopting a governance-orientated operational philosophy.

(3) What are the benefits of organizations exhibiting CSR?

Chapter 16

Assignments

(1) Prepare a report reviewing the economic and social implications of continued population growth on Planet Earth.

(2) Prepare a report reviewing the economic and social implications associated with the current exponential growth in the cost of health care.

(3) How could innovation provide solutions to some of the world's economic, social, and resource scarcity problems?

Self-study/group discussion topics

(1) Is global warming a major hazard for the world's peoples and what are the implications of the human race not finding an effective solution to global warming?

(2) What are the strengths and weaknesses associated with the greater use of renewable energy technologies?

(3) How might machines provide solutions for reducing the costs of future service provision in the public sector?

Bibliography

Abramov, I. (2007), Responsible business: weaving the fabric of a stable marketplace, *American Business Law Journal*, Vol. 44, No. 2, pp. 223–236.

Afuah, A. (2009a), *Strategic Innovation: New Game Strategies for Competitive Advantage*, Routledge, New York.

Afuah, A. (2009b), *Strategic Management Principles*, Routledge, London.

Albareda, L., Tencati, A., Lozano, J. M. and Perrini, F. (2006), The government's role in promoting corporate responsibility: a comparative analysis of Italy and UK from the relational state perspective, *Corporate Governance*, Vol. 6, No. 4, pp. 386–400.

Aldrick, P. and Conway, E. (2008), Toxic debt, losses now £1,800 bn. says Bank, *The Daily Telegraph*, London, 16 October, p. B1.

Allison, C., Chell, E. and Hayes, J. (2000), Intuition and entrepreneurial behaviour, *European Journal of Work and Organisational Psychology*, Vol. 9, pp. 31–42.

Amabile, T. M., Conti, R., Coon, H., Lazenby, J. and Herron, M. (1996), Assessing the work environment for creativity, *Academy of Management Journal*, Vol. 39, No. 5, pp. 1154–1185.

Anderson, A. R. and Atkins, M. H. (2001), Business strategies for entrepreneurial small firms, *Strategic Change*, Vol. 10, No. 6, pp. 311–324.

Anderson, C. R. and Zeithmal, C. P. (1984), Stage of the product life cycle, business strategy and business performance, *Academy of Management Journal*, Vol. 27, No. 1, pp. 5–24.

Anderson, M. and Sohal, M. S. (1999), A study of the relationship between quality management practices and performance in small business, *International Journal of Quality & Reliability Management*, Vol. 16, No. 9, pp. 859–872.

Anon. (2000a), Just the job, *Evening Standard*, London, 7 August 2000, p. 17.

Anon. (2000b), Private sector shake-up planned for Whitehall, *The Independent*, London, 14 January, p. 12.

Anon. (2006a), Business: the two kings get together; Google and YouTube, *The Economist*, 14 October, p. 82.

Anon. (2006b), Saving $60 billion, *Multinational Monitor*, Vol. 27, No. 1, pp. 33–36.

Anon. (2007a), Partnering for survival in pharmaceuticals: the threats facing the industry and the moves to overcome them, *Strategic Direction*, Vol. 23, No. 10, pp. 12–20.

Anon. (2007b), The Bank that failed – Britain's bank run, *The Economist*, London, 22 September, p. 1.

Anon. (2008), Our model was too dependent on wholesale funding, says Hornby, *The Daily Telegraph*, London, 19 September, p. B3.

Anon. (2009a), Americans fear health reform because they fear the reaper, *The Economist*, London, 3 September, p. 21.

Anon. (2009b), Fiscal performance and challenges, *OECD Journal on Budgeting*, Paris, Vol. 9, No. 1, pp. 23–43.

Anon. (2009c), Friends for life, *The Economist*, London, 8 August, pp. 55–56.

Anon. (2009d), Losing its magic touch, *The Economist*, London, 21 March, pp. 80–82.

Anon. (2009e), Fabless and fearless, *The Economist*, London, 8 August, p. 58.

Anon. (2009f), The rights of shareholders and the wrongs done to clients, *The Economist*, London, 8 August, p. 62.

Ansoff, H. I. (1965), *Corporate Strategy*, McGraw-Hill, New York.

Ansoff, H. I. (1991), Critique of Henry Mintzberg's 'The Design School': reconsidering the basic premises of strategic management, *Strategic Management Journal*, Vol. 12, No. 6, pp. 449–461.

Arestis, P., McCauley, K. and Sawyer, M. (2001), An alternative stability pact for the European Union, *Cambridge Journal of Economics*, Vol. 25, No. 1, pp. 131–143.

Argyris, C. and Schon, D. A. (1978), *Organizational Learning: A Theory of Action Perspective*, Addison Wesley, Reading, Massachusetts.

Aris, S. S., Raghunathan, T. S. and Kunnather, A. (2000), Factors affecting the adoption of advanced manufacturing technology in small firms, *S.A.M., Advanced Management Journal*, Vol. 65, No. 2, pp. 14–23.

Aryee, S. (1992), Public and private sector professionals: a comparative study of their perceptions, *Group & Organization Management*, Vol. 17, No. 1, pp. 72–81.

Athey, S. and Schmutzler, A. (1995), Product and process flexibility in an innovative environment, *The Rand Journal of Economics*, Vol. 26, No. 4, pp. 557–574.

Atkinson, A. A., Waterhouse, J. H. and Wells, R. B. (1997), A stakeholder approach to strategic performance measurement, *Sloan Management Review*, Vol. 38, No. 3, pp. 25–37.

Audit Commission. (1996), *Called to Account – The Role of Audit Committees in Local Government*, HMSO Publications, London.

Augier, M. and Teece, D. J. (2007), Dynamic capabilities and multinational enterprise: Penrosean insights and omissions, *Management International Review*, Vol. 47, No. 2, pp. 175–192.

Azofra, S. S., Olalla, M. G. and Olmo, B. T. (2008), Size, target performance and European bank mergers and acquisitions, *American Journal of Business*, Vol. 23, No. 1, pp. 53–63.

Babington, E. (1993), Planning in a health district: an application of computer modelling, *International Journal of Health Care Quality Assurance*, Vol. 6, No. 1, pp. 14–22.

Bak, C. A., Vogt, L. H., George, W. R. and Greentree, I. R. (1995), Management by team: an innovative tool for running a service organization through internal marketing, *Logistics Information Management*, Vol. 8, No. 4, pp. 12–19.

Baker, A. and Gill, J. (2005), Rethinking innovation in pharmaceutical R&D, *Journal of Commercial Biotechnology*, Vol. 12, No. 1, pp. 45–51.

Bakir, A. and Bakir, V. (2006), Unpacking complexity, pinning down the 'elusiveness' of strategy: a grounded theory study in leisure and cultural organisations, *Qualitative Research in Organizations and Management*, Vol. 1, No. 3, pp. 152–172.

Bass, B. M. (1996), Is there universality in the full range model of leadership? *International Journal of Public Administration*, Vol. 19, No. 6, pp. 731–761.

Bass, B. M. (1998), *Transformational Leadership*, Lawrence Erlbaum, Mahwah, New Jersey.

Bauer, C., Herz, B. and Karb, V. (2003), The other twins: currency and debt crises, *Jahrbuch für Wirtschaftswissenschaften*, Vol. 54, No. 3, pp. 248–268.

Bayraktar, E., Jothishankar, M. C., Tatoglu, E. and Wu, T. (2007), Evolution of operations management: past, present and future, *Management Research News*, Vol. 30, No. 11, pp. 843–871.

Beaver, G. (2007), The strategy payoff for smaller enterprises, *Journal of Business Strategy*, Vol. 28, No. 1, pp. 11–20.

Behn, R. D. (2003), Why performance measures? Different purposes require different measures, *Public Administration Review*, Vol. 63, No. 3, pp. 586–606.

Behnke, N. (2005), Marketing strategy: how biotechnology and speciality pharma companies can beat big pharma in marketing cancer drugs, *Journal of Medical Marketing*, Vol. 5, No. 1, pp. 10–14.

Bekefi, T. and Epstein, M. J. (2008), Transforming social and environmental risks into opportunities, *Strategic Finance*, Vol. 89, No. 9, pp. 42–47.

Bellone, C. and Goerl, G. F. (1992), Reconciling public entrepreneurship and democracy, *Public Administration Review*, Vol. 52, pp. 130–134.

Benner, M. (2004), Catching up in pharmaceuticals: government policies and the rise of genomics, *Australian Health Review*, Vol. 28, No. 2, pp. 161–171.

Berry, M. (1998), Strategic planning in small, high-tech companies, *Long Range Planning*, Vol. 31, pp. 455–456.

Bertelli, A. M. (2005), Governing the Quango: an auditing and cheating model of quasi-governmental authorities, *Journal of Public Administration Research and Theory*, Vol. 16, pp. 239–261.

Bertok, J. (1999), OECD supports the creation of sound ethics infrastructure: OECD targets both the 'supply side' and the 'demand side' of corruption, *Public Personnel Management*, Vol. 28, No. 4, pp. 673–687.

Betts, R. K. (2007), A disciplined defence: how to regain strategic solvency, *Foreign Affairs*, Vol. 86, No. 6, pp. 67–80.

Bhatia, G. K., Gay, R. C. and Honey, W. S. (2003), Windows into the future: how lessons from Hollywood will shape the music industry, *Journal of Interactive Marketing*, Vol. 17, No. 2, pp. 70–80.

Biggadike, E. R. (1979), *Corporate Diversification: Entry, Strategy and Performance*, Harvard University Press, Cambridge, Massachusetts.

Bird, B. J. (1988), Implementing entrepreneurial ideas: the case for intention, Academy of Management, *The Academy of Management Review*, Vol. 13, No. 3, pp. 442–453.

Birkinshaw, J. and Goddard, J. (2009), What is your management model? *Sloan Management Review*, Vol. 49, No. 1, pp. 81–90.

Bloomfield, P. (2006), The challenging business of long-term public–private partnerships: reflections on local experience, *Public Administration Review*, Vol. 66, No. 3, pp. 400–412.

Bonini, S. and Oppenheim, J. (2008), Cultivating the green consumer, *Stanford Innovation Review*, Vol. 6, No. 4, pp. 56–62.

Borins, S. (2000), Loose cannons and rule breakers, or enterprising leaders? Some evidence about innovative public managers, *Public Administration Review*, Vol. 60, No. 6, pp. 498–507.

Bosworth, B. and Burtless, G. (1997), Budget crunch: population aging in rich countries, *The Brookings Review*, Vol. 15, No. 3, pp. 10–15.

Bowman, J. S. and West, J. P. (2007), Lord Acton and employment doctrines: absolute power and the spread of at-will employment, *Journal of Business Ethics*, Vol. 74, pp. 119–130.

Boyd, C. (1996), Ethics and corporate governance: the issues raised by the Cadbury Report in the United Kingdom, *Journal of Business Ethics*, Vol. 15, No. 2, pp. 167–183.

Boyne, G. A. (2006), Strategies for public sector turnaround: lessons from the private sector? *Administration & Society*, Vol. 38, No. 3, pp. 365–388.

Bozeman, B. (1987), *All Organizations Are Public*, Jossey-Bass, San Francisco.

Brady, D., Beckfield, J. and Seeleib-Kaiser, M. (2005), Economic globalization and the welfare state in affluent democracies, 1975–2001, *American Sociological Review*, Vol. 37, No. 2, pp. 52–68.

Brauninger, T. (2005), A partisan model of government expenditure, *Public Choice*, Vol. 125, pp. 409–429.

Brown, A. (2006), The robot economy: brave new world or return to slavery, *The Futurist*, Vol. 40, No. 4, pp. 50–56.

Brown, L. (2003), Comparing health systems in four countries: lessons for the United States, *American Journal of Public Health*, Vol. 93, No. 1, pp. 52–61.

Brown, L. R. (2006), Rescuing a planet under stress, *The Futurist*, Vol. 40, No. 4, pp. 18–26.

Brown, R. (1992), Managing the S curves of innovation, *Journal of Business & Industrial Marketing*, Vol. 7, No. 3, pp. 41–52.

Brown-Collier, E. K. and Collier, B. E. (1995), What Keynes really said about deficit spending, *Journal of Post Keynesian Economics*, Vol. 17, No. 3, pp. 341–356.

Brunetto, Y. and Farr-Wharton, R. (2008), Service delivery by local government employees post-the implementation of NPM: a social capital perspective, *International Journal of Productivity and Performance Management*, Vol. 57, No. 1, pp. 37–48.

Bryane, M. and Gross, R. (2004), Running business like a government in the new economy: lessons for organizational design and corporate governance, *Corporate Governance*, Vol. 4, No. 3, pp. 32–46.

Bryant, W. D. and Macri, J. (2005), Does sentiment explain consumption, *Journal of Economics and Finance*, Vol. 29, No. 1, pp. 97–113.

Bryson, J. M. (1981), A perspective on planning and crises in the public sector, *Strategic Management Journal*, Vol. 2, No. 2, pp. 181–198.

Bryson, J. M. (1995), *Strategic Planning for Public and Nonprofit Organizations*, 2nd edn, Jossey-Bass, San Francisco.

Bryson, J. M., Ackermann, F. and Eden, C. (2007), Putting the resource-based view of strategy and distinctive competencies to work in public organizations, *Public Administration Review*, Vol. 67, No. 4, pp. 702–717.

Budd, L. (2007), Post-bureaucracy and reanimating public governance: a discourse and practice of continuity? *International Journal of Public Sector Management*, Vol. 20, No. 6, pp. 531–547.

Buffett, W. (2002), Who really cooks the books? *New York Times*, 24 July, p. A19.

Bunning, C. R. (1992), Effective strategic planning in the public sector: some learnings, *International Journal of Public Sector Management*, Vol. 5, No. 4, pp. 54–65.

Burke, R. J. (2006), Why leaders fail: exploring the darkside, *International Journal of Manpower*, Vol. 27, No. 1, pp. 91–100.

Burns, J. M. (1978), *Leadership*, Harper & Row, New York.

Buzzell, R. D., Gale, B. T. and Sultan, R. G. M. (1975), Market share – a key to profitability, *Harvard Business Review*, January/February, pp. 97–107.

Caldwell, J. H. (1994), Photovoltaic technology and markets, *Contemporary Economic Policy*, Vol. 12, No. 2, pp. 97–112.

Campbell, D. J. (2000), The proactive employee: managing workplace initiative, *The Academy of Management Executive*, Vol. 14, No. 3, pp. 52–66.

Carlone, D. (2001), Enablement, constraint, and *The 7 Habits of Highly Effective People*, *Management Communication Quarterly*, Vol. 14, No. 3, pp. 491–498.

Caron, D. J. and Giauque, D. (2006), Civil servant identity at the crossroads: new challenges for public administrations, *International Journal of Public Sector Management*, Vol. 19, No. 6, pp. 543–555.

Carpinetti, L. C. R. and M de Melo, A. (2002), What to benchmark? *Benchmarking*, Vol. 9, No. 3, pp. 244–255.

Carruthers, J., Rod, M. and Ashill, N. J. (2007), Purchaser–provider interaction in UK public health: improving stakeholder cooperation, *International Journal of Pharmaceutical and Healthcare Marketing*, Vol. 1, No. 1, pp. 12–26.

Carson, D. (1985), The evolution of marketing in the small firm, *European Journal of Marketing*, Vol. 9, No. 5, pp. 7–16.

Carson, D., Cromie, S., McGowan, P. and Hill, J. (1995), *Marketing and Entrepreneurship in SMEs: An Innovative Approach*, Prentice Hall, Hemel Hempstead.

Cassidy, D. (2003), Maximizing shareholder value: the risks to employees, customers and the community, *Corporate Governance*, Vol. 3, No. 2, pp. 32–39.

Cervera, A., Molla, A. and Sanchez, M. (2001), Antecedents and consequences of market orientation in public organisations, *European Journal of Marketing*, Vol. 35, No. 11/12, pp. 1259–1286.

Chaffee, E. (1985), Three models of strategy, *Academy of Management Review*, Vol. 10, No. 1, pp. 88–98.

Chaganti, R. and Chaganti, R. (1983), A profile of profitable and not-so-profitable small businesses, *Journal of Small Business Management*, Vol. 21, No. 3, pp. 43–51.

Chang, L. (2007), The NHS performance assessment framework as a balanced scorecard approach: limitations and implications, *International Journal of Public Sector Management*, Vol. 20, No. 2, pp. 101–117.

Charhi, M. (2000), Government departmental strategies: a taxonomy of strategic behaviour in the Canadian Government, *Management International*, Vol. 5, No. 1, pp. 1–14.

Chaston, I. (1996), Critical events and process gaps in the Danish Technological Institute structured networking model, *International Small Business Journal*, Vol. 14, No. 3, pp. 13–22.

Chaston, I. (2000), *Entrepreneurial Marketing*, Macmillan, London.

Chaston, I. (2004), *Knowledge-Based Marketing*, Sage, London.

Chaston, I. (2009a), *Boomer Marketing*, Routledge, London.

Chaston, I. (2009b), *Small Firm Entrepreneurship*, Sage, London.

Chaston, I. and Mangles, T. (1997), Competencies for growth in SME sector manufacturing firms, *Journal of Small Business Management*, Vol. 35, No. 1, pp. 23–35.

Chaston, I., Badger, B. and Sadler-Smith, E. (1999), Organisational learning systems in relation to innovation management in small UK manufacturing firms, *Journal of New Product Management and Innovation*, Vol. 1, No. 1, pp. 32–43.

Cheffins, B. R. (2001), History and the global corporate governance revolution: the UK perspective begins, *Business History*, Vol. 43, No. 4, pp. 87–121.

Chen, Y., Chen, H. M., Ching, R. K. H. and Huang, W. W. (2007), Electronic Government implementation: a comparison between developed and developing countries, *International Journal of Electronic Government Research*, Vol. 3, No. 2, pp. 45–59.

Child, J. and McGrath, R. G. (2001), Organizations unfettered: organizational form in an information-intensive economy, *Academy of Management Journal*, Vol. 44, pp. 1135–1148.

Cho, K. and Lee, S. (2001), Another look at public–private distinction and organizational commitment: a cultural explanation, *International Journal of Organizational Analysis*, Vol. 9, No. 1, pp. 84–102.

Christensen, C. M. (1997), *The Innovator's Dilemma*, Harvard Business School Press, Boston, Massachusetts.

Christensen, J. V. (2002), Corporate strategy and the management of innovation and technology, *Industrial and Corporate Change*, Vol. 11, No. 2, pp. 263–288.

Coates, J. F., Mahaffie, J. B. and Hines, A. (1997), The promise of genetics, *The Futurist*, Vol. 31, No. 5, pp. 18–22.

Coles, C. (2003), The growing water crisis, *The Futurist*, Vol. 37, No. 5, pp. 10–12.

Coltman, T. (2007), Can superior CRM capabilities improve performance in banking, *Journal of Financial Services Marketing*, Vol. 12, No. 2, pp. 102–114.

Conger, J. A. and Kanungo, R. N. (1998), *Charismatic Leadership in Organizations*, Sage Publications, California.

Connelly, B. (2008), Origins of the credit crisis, *The International Economy*, Vol. 22, No. 4, pp. 44–48.

Constable, G. and Somerville, B. (2003), *A Century of Innovation*, Joseph Henry Press, Washington.

Cortada, J. W. and Fraser, H. E. (2005), Mapping the future in science-intensive industries: lessons from the pharmaceutical industry, *IBM Systems Journal*, Vol. 44, No. 1, pp. 163–183.

Covey, S. R. and Gulledge, K. A. (1992), Principle-centered leadership, *Journal for Quality and Participation*, Vol. 15, No. 4, pp. 70–79.

Covin, J. G. and Slevin, D. P. (1988), The influence of organizational structure on the utility of an entrepreneurial top management style, *Journal of Management Studies*, Vol. 25, No. 1, pp. 217–237.

Covin, J. G. and Slevin, D. P. (1989), Strategic management of small firms in hostile and benign environments, *Strategic Management Journal*, Vol. 10, pp. 75–87.

Covin, J. G. and Slevin, D. P. (1991), A conceptual model of entrepreneurship as firm behavior, *Entrepreneurship Theory and Practice*, Vol. 16, No. 1, pp. 7–25.

Covin, J. G., Green, K. M. and Slevin, D. P. (2006), Strategic process effects on the entrepreneurial orientation-sales growth rate relationship, *Entrepreneurship Theory and Practice*, Vol. 30, January, pp. 57–81.

Cox, R. W. (1995), Getting past the hype: issues in starting a public sector TQM program, *Public Administration Quarterly*, Vol. 19, No. 1, pp. 89–104.

Cravens, D. W., Piercy, N. F. and Low, G. S. (2002), The innovation challenges of proactive cannibalisation and discontinuous technology, *European Business Review*, Vol. 14, No. 4, pp. 257–268.

Cray, S. (1994), Inducting non-executive directors of trust boards, *Health Manpower Management*, Vol. 20, No. 5, pp. 31–36.

Crosby, B. and Bryson, J. M. (2005), *Leadership for the Common Good: Tackling Public Problems in a Shared-Power World*, Jossey-Bass, San Francisco.

Cunha, P. M. and da Cunha, J. V. (2006), Towards a complexity theory of strategy, *Management Decision*, Vol. 44, No. 7, pp. 839–850.

Curren, J., Jarvis, R., Blackburn, R. A. and Black, D. (1993), Networks and small firms: constructs, methodological strategies and some findings, *International Small Business Journal*, Vol. 11, No. 2, pp. 13–25.

Czaplewski, A. J., Ferguson, J. M. and Milliman, J. F. (2001), Southwest Airlines: how internal marketing pilots success, *Marketing Management*, Vol. 10, No. 3, pp.14–17.

Da Silva, R. and Batista, L. (2007), Boosting government reputation through CRM, *International Journal of Public Sector Management*, Vol. 20, No. 7, pp. 548–560.

Daily, C. M. and Dalton, D. R. (2002), The problem with equity compensation, *Journal of Business Strategy*, Vol. 23, No. 4, pp. 28–31.

Dalton, D. R. and Kesner, I. F. (1985), Organizational growth: big is beautiful, *Journal of Business Strategy*, Vol. 6, No. 1, pp. 38–48.

Davies, M. (2009), Effective working relationships between audit committees and internal audit – the cornerstone of corporate governance in local authorities, a Welsh perspective, *Journal of Managing Governments*, Vol. 13, pp. 41–73.

Day, G. (2006), Aligning the organization with the market, *Sloan Management Review*, Vol. 48, No. 1, pp. 41–49.

Day, G. and Wensley, R. (1988), Assessing advantage: a framework for diagnosing competitive superiority, *Journal of Marketing*, Vol. 52, pp. 1–20.

Day, G. S. and Schoemaker, P. J. H. (2005), Scanning the periphery, *Harvard Business Review*, October/November, pp. 135–146.

De Bruijin, J. A. (2005), Management and the professionals in public service: about the risk of fruitless tension, In Veensik, M. (ed.), *Organizing Innovation: New Approaches to Cultural Changes and Interventions in Public Sector Organisations*, IOS Press, Amsterdam, pp. 48–58.

De Weaver, S., Martens, R. and Vandenbempt, K. (2005), The impact of trust on strategic resource acquisition through interorganisational networks: towards a conceptual model, *Human Relations*, Vol. 58, No. 12, pp. 1523–1543.

Demuth, L. G. (2008), A viewpoint on disruptive innovation, *Journal of the American Academy of Business*, Vol. 13, No. 1, pp. 86–94.

Denhardt, J. V. and Campbell, K. C. (2006), The role of democratic values in transformational leadership, *Administration & Society*, Vol. 38, No. 5, pp. 556–572.

Denhardt, R., Jennings, E. T. and Wildavsky, A. (1989), Image and integrity in the public service, *Public Administration Review*, Vol. 49, No. 1, pp. 74–79.

Denton, D. K. (2006), Performance improvement, *International Society for Performance Improvement*, Vol. 45, No. 3, pp. 33–37.

Dibrell, M. C., Down, J. and Bull. L. (2007), Dynamic strategic planning: achieving strategic flexibility through formalization, *Journal of Business and Management*, Vol. 13, No. 1, pp. 21–35.

Dixon, N. (1994), *The Organizational Learning Cycle: How We Can Learn Collectively*, McGraw-Hill, Maidenhead.

Donabedian, A. (1980), *The Definition of Quality and Approach to Its Assessment*, Health Administration Press, Ann Arbour, Michigan.

Dotlitch, D. L. and Cairo, P. (2003), *Why CEOs Fail: The 11 Behaviors That Can Derail Your Climb to the Top and How to Manage Them*, Jossey-Bass, San Francisco.

Dreher, A., Sturm, J. and Ursprung, H. W. (2008), The impact of globalization on the composition of government expenditures: evidence from panel data, *Public Choice*, Vol. 134, pp. 263–292.

Droege, S. B. and Dong, L. C. (2008), Strategic entrepreneurship: imitation versus substitution, *Journal of Small Business Strategy*, Vol. 19, No. 1, pp. 51–62.

Drucker, P. F. (1955), Management science and the manager, *Management Science*, Vol. 1, No. 2, pp. 115–126.

Drucker, P. F. (1985a), Entrepreneurial strategies, *California Management Review*, Vol. 27, No. 2, pp. 9–21.

Drucker, P. F. (1985b), *Innovation & Entrepreneurship: Practice and Principles*, Harper & Row, New York.

Drucker, P. F. (1994), The theory of business, *Harvard Business Review*, September/October, pp. 95–104.

DTI (2001), Business and society. Developing corporate social responsibility in the UK, *Department of Trade and Industry*, UK Government, London.

Du Gray, P. (2004), Against enterprise (but not against enterprise, for that would make no sense), *Organization*, Vol. 11, No. 1, pp. 37–57.

Dunleavy, P., Margetts, H., Bastow, S. and Tinkler, J. (2005), New Public Management is dead – long live Digital-Era Governance, *Journal of Public Administration Research and Theory*, Vol. 16, pp. 467–494.

Durand, M. (2003), French pension pickle, *The OECD Observer*, Vol. 238, pp. 11–17.

Dutton, J. E. and Jackson, S. E. (1987), Categorizing strategic issues: links to organizational action, Academy of Management, *The Academy of Management Review*, Vol. 12, No. 1, pp. 76–87.

DWP (2004), *Building on New Deal*, Department of Works and Pensions, Sheffield.

Dyson, T. (2005), On development, demography and climate change: the end of the world as we know it? *Population and Environment*, Vol. 27, No. 2, pp. 117–149.

Easterday, K. and Eaton, T. V. (2010), A looming crisis for pensions, *The CPA Journal*, Vol. 80, No. 3, pp. 56–58.

Eccles, D. and Nohria, N. (1992), Horses for courses: organizational forms for multinational corporations, *Sloan Management Review*, Vol. 33, No. 2, pp. 23–36.

Eisenbeis, R. A. (1997), Bank deposits and credit as sources of systemic risk, *Economic Review – Federal Reserve Bank of Atlanta*, Vol. 82, No. 3, pp. 4–20.

Eisenhardt, K. M. (2002), Has strategy changed? *MIT Sloan Management Review*, Winter, pp. 88–91.

Eisenhardt, K. M. and Martin, J. A. (2000), Dynamic capabilities: what are they? *Strategic Management Journal*, Vol. 21, pp. 1105–1121.

Eisner, R. (1996), The balanced budget crusade, *Public Interest*, Winter, No. 122, pp. 85–93.

Elliott, D. (1992), Renewable energy, *Environmental Management and Health*, Vol. 3, No. 2, pp. 35–39.

Ennis, R. M. (2007), What ails public pensions? *Financial Analysts Journal*, Vol. 63, No. 6, pp. 38–43.

Erikson, T. F., Magee, J. F., Roussel, P. A. and Saad, K. N. (1990), Managing technology as a business strategy, *Sloan Management Review*, Vol. 73, No. 3, pp. 73–302.

Ettlie, J. E. and Reza, E. M. (1992), Organizational integration and process innovation, *Academy of Management Journal*, Vol. 35, No. 4, pp. 795–827.

Ettlie, J. E., Bridges, W. P. and O'Kefeefe, R. D. (1984), Organizational strategy and structural differences between radical versus incremental innovation, *Management Science*, Vol. 30, No. 6, pp. 682–695.

Evans, D. M. and Smith, A. T. (2004), Augmenting the value chain, *Journal of Information Technology Theory & Practice*, Vol. 6, No. 1, pp. 61–78.

Exton, R. (2008), The entrepreneur: a new breed of health service leader? *Journal of Health Organization and Management*, Vol. 22, No. 3, pp. 208–222.

Fahy, J. and Smithee, A. (1999), Strategic marketing and the resource based view of the firm, *Academy of Marketing Science Review*, Vol. 27, pp. 1–28.

Farnham, D. and Horton, S. (eds) (1993), *Managing the New Public Services*, Macmillan, Basingstoke.

Fernald, L. W., Solomon, G. T. and Tarabishy, A. (2005), A new paradigm: entrepreneurial leadership. *Southern Business Review*, Vol. 30, No. 2, pp. 1–11.

Ferguson, G., Mathur, S. and Shah, B. (2005), Evolving from information to insight, *Sloan Management Review*, Vol. 46, No. 2, pp. 51–62.

Ferlie, E. (2007), Complex organisations and contemporary public sector organisations. *International Public Management Journal*, Vol. 10, No. 2, pp. 153–165.

Fernández-Aráoz, C. (2005), Getting the right people at the top, *Sloan Management Review*, Vol. 46, No. 4, pp. 67–72.

Finkelstein, S. (2001), Internet startups: so why can't they win? *Journal of Business Strategy*, Vol. 22, No. 4, pp. 16–21.

Finnie, W. and Early, A. (2002), Results-based leadership: an interview with Dave Ulrich, *Strategy & Leadership*, Vol. 30, No. 6, pp. 23–30.

Fisk, G. (1974), *Marketing and the Ecological Crisis*, Harper & Row, New York.

Florio, M. and Colauti, S. (2005), A logistic growth theory of public expenditures: a study of five countries over 100 years, *Public Choice*, Vol. 122, pp. 355–393.

Forbes, W. and Watson, R. (2003), Managerial remuneration and corporate governance: a review of the issues, *Accounting and Business Research*, Vol. 23, pp. 31–338.

Ford, C. W., Nonis, S. A. and Hudson, G. I. (2005), A cross-cultural comparison of value systems and consumer ethics, *Cross Cultural Management*, Vol. 12, No. 4, pp. 36–50.

Forrer, J. J., Kee, E. and Zhang, Z. (2002), Private finance initiative: a better public–private partnership? *Public Manager*, Vol. 31, No. 2, pp. 43–47.

Foster, D. and Taylor, G. (1994), Reinventing the wheel? Privatisation and the crisis of public service trade unionism, *Management Research News*, Vol. 17, No. 7/9, pp. 114–116.

Fox, J., Gann, R., Shur, A., Von Glahn, L. and Zaas, B. (1998), Process uncertainty: a new dimension for new product development, *Engineering Management Journal*, Vol. 10, No. 3, pp. 19–27.

Fredickson, G. and Smith, K. (2003), *The Public Administration Theory Primer*, Westview Press, Boulder, Colorado.

Free, C. and Radcliffe, V. (2009), Accountability in crisis: the sponsorship scandal and the Office of the Comptroller General in Canada, *Journal of Business Ethics*, Vol. 84, pp. 189–208.

Freel, M. (2006), Patterns of technological innovation in knowledge intensive business services, *Industry and Innovation*, Vol. 13, No. 3, pp. 335–359.

Freeman, R. E. and Liedtka, J. (1997), Stakeholder capitalism and the value chain, *European Management Journal*, Vol. 15, No. 3, pp. 286–295.

Freeman, T. (2002), Using performance indicators to improve health care quality in the public sector: a review of the literature, *Health Services Management Research*, Vol. 15, No. 2, pp. 126–138.

Freyens, B. (2008), Macro-, Meso- and Microeconomic considerations in the delivery of social services, *International Journal of Social Economics*, Vol. 35, No. 11, pp. 823–831.

Friedman, M. (1970), The social responsibility of business is to increase its profits, *New York Times Magazine*, Vol. 33, 30 September, pp. 122–125.

Fuchs, P. H., Mifflin, K. E., Miller, D. and Whitney, J. O. (2000), Strategic integration: competing in the age of capabilities, *California Management Review*, Vol. 42, No. 3, pp. 118–148.

Fulmer, R. M. (1993),The tools of anticipatory learning, *Journal of Management Development*, Vol. 12, No. 6, pp. 7–16.

Fulmer, R. M. and Conger, J. A. (2004), *Growing Your Company's Leaders*, AMACOM, New York.

Galbraith, J. K. (2007), What is the American model really about? Soft budgets and the Keynesian Devolution, *Industrial and Corporate Change*, Vol. 16, No. 1, pp. 1–18.

Gallagher, S. (2005), A strategic response to Friedman's critique of business ethics, *Journal of Business Strategy*, Vol. 26, No. 6, pp. 55–60.

Georgelli, Y. P., Joyce, B. and Woods, A. (2000), Entrepreneurial action, innovation, and business performance: the small independent business, *Journal of Small Business and Enterprise Development*, Vol. 7, No. 1, pp. 7–17.

Gesser, J. and Cusumano, J. A. (2005), Hydrogen and the new energy economy: why we need an Apollo Mission for clean energy, *The Futurist*, Vol. 39, No. 2, pp. 19–26.

Ghemawar, P. (1993), The risk of not investing in a recession, *Sloan Management Review*, Vol. 34, No. 2, pp. 51–59.

Ghobadian, A. and Ashworth, J. (1994), Performance measurement in local government – concept and practice, *International Journal of Operations & Production Management*, Vol. 14, No. 5, pp. 35–52.

Ghonkrokta, S. S. and Lather, A. S. (2007), Identification of role of social audit by stakeholders as accountability tool in good governance, *Journal of Management Research*, Vol. 7, No. 1, pp. 18–27.

Giddens, A. (1994), *Beyond Left and Right*, Policy Press, Cambridge.

Gilbert, N. (1990), The time trap: short-term solutions needed for long-term problems, *Management Review*, Vol. 79, No. 7, pp. 28–33.

Goldfinch, S. (2006), Pessimism, computer failure, and information systems development in the public sector, *Public Administration Review*, Vol. 67, No. 5, pp. 917–992.

Gomi, T. (2003), New AI and service robots, *Industrial Robot*, Vol. 30, No. 2, pp. 123–139.

Goodhart, C. A. E. (2006), Replacing the stability and growth pact? *Atlantic Economic Journal*, Vol. 34, pp. 243–259.

Gordon, I. (1992), A federal expression of success, *Managing Service Quality*, Vol. 3, No. 1, pp. 391–399.

Grant, G. H. (2003), The evolution of corporate governance and its impact on modern corporate America, *Management Decision*, Vol. 41, No. 9, pp. 923–934.

Greenspan, A. (2009), We need a better cushion against risk, the future of capitalism, *Financial Times*, London, 12 May, pp. 26–38.

Gronroos, C. (1990), Relationship approach to marketing in service contexts: the marketing and organizational behavior interface, *Journal of Business Research*, Vol. 29, pp. 3–11.

Guerrera, F. (2009a), Destination dustbin, *Financial Times*, London, 10th Aug, p. 5.

Guerrera, F. (2009b), A need to reconnect, *The Financial Times*, London, p. 11.

Gunasekaran, A., Folker, L. and Koby, B. (2000), Improving operations performance in a small company: a case study, Vol. 20, No. 3, pp. 316–325.

Gunasekaran, A., Tirtiroglu, E. and Wolstencroft, V. (2002), Gap between production and marketing functions: a case study, *Management Decision*, Vol. 40, No. 5/6, pp. 428–436.

Guo, C. (2002), Market orientation and business performance: a framework for service organizations, *European Journal of Marketing*, Vol. 36, No. 9/10, pp. 1154–1164.

Gupta, A. and Singhal, A. (1993), Managing human resources for innovation and creativity, *Research Technology Management*, Vol. 36, No. 3, pp. 41–49.

Hacker, M. E., Kotnour, T. and Mallak, L. A. (2001), Formalizing deployment processes in the US Government, *The International Journal of Public Sector Management*, Vol. 14, No. 3, pp. 221–240.

Hagen, A. F. and Lodha, S. S. (2004), How do CEOs perceive suggested new rules of global competitiveness in the twenty-first century? *American Business Review*, Vol. 22, No. 1, pp. 62–69.

Halal, W. E. and Nikitin, A. I. (1990), One world: the coming synthesis of a new capitalism and a new socialism, *The Futurist*, Vol. 24, No. 6, pp. 8–18.

Hales, C. (2000), Managerial work futures: new challenges in post-bureaucratic networks or old responsibilities in 'bureaucracy-lite' organisations, *Management News*, Vol. 23, No. 1, pp. 9–12.

Hales, C. (2002), Bureaucracy-lite and continuities in managerial work, *British Journal of Management*, Vol. 13, pp. 51–66.

Hall, J. D. and Sais, M. A. (1963), Strategy follows structure, *Strategic Management Journal*, Vol. 1, No. 2, pp. 149–162.

Hall, R. H. (1996), *Organizations: Structures, Processes, and Outcomes*, Prentice Hall, Englewood Cliffs, New Jersey.

Hamel, G. and Prahalad, C. K. (1993), Strategy as stretch and leverage, *Harvard Business Review*, March/April, pp. 75–84.

Hambrick, D. C. and Fredrickson, J. W. (2001), Are you sure you have a strategy? *Academy of Management Executive*, Vol. 15, No. 4, pp. 48–49.

Hamel, G. and Prahalad, C. K. (1994), *Competing for the Future*, Harvard Business School Press, Boston, Massachusetts.

Hammer, M. and Champy, J. (1993), *Reengineering the Corporations*, Harper Business, New York.

Hammond, J. B. W. (2002), Genomic discovery and the medical market: what does the future hold? *International Journal of Medical Marketing*, Vol. 2, No. 2, pp. 167–174.

Haque, N., Montiel, P. and Sheppard, S. (2000), Public sector employee productivity, *Economic Inquiry*, Vol. 38, No. 3, pp. 34–41.

Harari, O. (1992), You're not in business to make a profit, *Management Review*, Vol. 81, No. 7, pp. 53–58.

Harrinvirta, M. and Mattila, M. (2001), The hard business of balancing budgets: A study of public finances in seventies, *British Journal of Political Science*, Vol. 31, pp. 497–512.

Hatten, K. J. and Rosenthal, S. R. (1999), Managing the process-centered enterprise, *Long Range Planning*, Vol. 32, No. 3, pp. 293–310.

Hax, A. C. (1990), Redefining the concept of strategy and the strategy formation process, *Planning Review*, Vol. 18, No. 3, pp. 34–40.

Hayes, R. H. and Upton, D. M. (1998), Operations-based strategy, *California Management Review*, Vol. 40, No. 4, pp. 8–25.

Heath, J. and Norman, W. (2004), Stakeholder theory, corporate governance and public management: what can the history of state-run enterprises teach us in the post-Enron era? *Journal of Business Ethics*, Vol. 53, pp. 247–265.

Hedley, B. (1977), Strategy and the business portfolio, *Long Range Planning*, Vol. 101, pp. 9–15.

Heeks, R. (2000), *Reinventing Government in the Information Age*, Routledge, London.

Hellman, T. and Puri, M. (2000), The interaction between product market and financing strategy: the role of venture capital, *The Review of Financial Studies*, Vol. 13, No. 4, pp. 959–974.

Hemraj, M. B. (2002), Preventing corporate failure: the Cadbury Committee's governance report, *Journal of Financial Crime*, Vol. 10, No. 2, pp. 141–145.

Henderson, K. M. (2004), Characterizing American public administration: the concept of administrative culture, *The International Journal of Public Sector Management*, Vol. 17, No. 2/3, pp. 234–250.

Hendrick, R. (2003), Strategic planning environment, process, and performance in public agencies, *Journal of Public Administration Research and Theory*, Vol. 13, No. 4, pp. 491–512.

Herps, J. M., Van Johannes, H. H., Halman, I. M., Martens, H. M. and Borsboom, R. H. (2003), The process of selecting technology development projects: a practical framework, *Management Research News*, Vol. 26, No. 8, pp. 1–16.

Heskett, J., Sasser, W. and Schlesinger, L. (1997), *The Service Profit Chain: How Leading Companies Link Profit and Growth to Loyalty, Satisfaction, and Value*, The Free Press, New York.

Higgins, J. M. (1995), Innovate or evaporate, *The Futurist*, Vol. 29, No. 5, pp. 42–49.

Hills, G. E. and LaForge, R. W. (1992), Research at the marketing interface to advance entrepreneurship theory, *Entrepreneurship Theory and Practice*, Vol. 23, No. 1, pp. 33–59.

Hind, P., Wilson, A. and Lenssen, G. (2009), Developing leaders for sustainable business, *Corporate Governance*, Vol. 9, No. 1, pp. 7–20.

Hine, D. and Ryan, N. (1999), Small service firms – creating value through innovation, *Journal of Small Business and Enterprise Development*, Vol. 9, No. 6, pp. 441–456.

Hisrich, R. D. and Peters, M. P. (1992), *Entrepreneurship: Starting, Developing, and Managing a New Enterprise*, Irwin, Boston, Massachusetts.

Hitt, M. A., Keats, B. K. and DeMarie, S. M. (1998), Navigating in the new competitive landscape: building strategic flexibility and competitive advantage in the 21st century, *The Academy of Management Executive*, Vol. 12, No. 4, pp. 22–42.

Hoenig, T. M. (2008), Maintaining stability in a changing financial system: some lessons relearned again? *Economic Review – Federal Reserve Bank of Kansas City*, Vol. 93, No. 1, pp. 5–18.

Hofer, C. W. (1975), Towards a contingency theory of business strategy, *Academy of Management Journal*, Vol. 19, pp. 784–810.

Hoffman, N. P. (2000), An examination of sustainable competitive advantage concept: past, present, and future, *Academy of Marketing Science Review*, Vol. 20, pp. 1–16.

Hogarty, D. B. (1993), Beating the odds: avoid these mistakes at all costs, *Management Review*, Vol. 82, No. 1, pp. 16–22.

Holbrook, D., Cohen, W. M., Hounshell, D. A. and Klepper, S. (2000), The nature, sources, and consequences of firm differences in the early history, *Strategic Management Journal*, Vol. 21, No. 10/11, pp. 1017–1041.

Holinsworth, S. R. (2004), Case study: Henrico County, Virginia: succession management: a developmental approach, *Public Personnel Management*, Vol. 33, No. 4, pp. 475–487.

Hood, C. (1991), A public management for all seasons, *Public Administration*, Vol. 69, pp. 3–19.

Hood, C. (2006), Gaming in the Targetworld: the targets approach to managing British public services, *Public Administration Review*, July/August, pp. 515–521.

Hood, C. and Jackson, M. (1992), The New Public Management: a recipe for disaster, In Parker, D. J. and Handmer, G. A. (eds), *Hazard Management and Emergency Planning Processes – Perspectives in Britain*, James and James, London.

Hope, C. (2010), The time-wasting council workers, *The Daily Telegraph*, 20 August, p. 1.

Hoskinson, R. E., Hitt, M. A. and Hillman, C. L. (1991), Managerial risk taking in diversified firms: an evolutionary perspective, *Organisation Science*, Vol. 2, No. 3, pp. 296–314.

Huckestein, D. and Duboff, R. (1999), Hilton hotels, *Cornell Hotel and Restaurant Administration Quarterly*, Vol. 40, No. 4, pp. 28–38.

Huff, A. S. (1982), Industry influences on strategy reformulation, *Strategic Management Journal*, Vol. 3, No. 2, pp. 119–132.

Hughes, O. (2002), *Public Management and Administration*, Palgrave Macmillan, Basingstoke.

Huntington, S. P. (1993), The clash of civilizations, *Foreign Affairs*, Vol. 72, No. 3, pp. 22–50.

Hurt, M. J. (2008), Some thoughts on ethics, governance and markets, *Corporate Finance Review*, Vol. 12, No. 4, pp. 40–46.

Huys, M. and Koppenjam, J. (2010), Policy networks in practice: the debate on the future of Amsterdam Airport Schipol, In Osborne, A. P. (ed.), *New Public Governance?* Routledge, London, pp. 365–393.

Iansiti, M. (1995), Shooting the rapids: managing product development in turbulent environments, *California Management Review*, Vol. 38, No. 1, pp. 37–58.

IBM (2008), *The Enterprise of the Future*, www.ibm.com/gbs/uk/ceostudy, 12 January 2010.

Ibrahim, N. A., Angelidis, J. P. and Parsa, F. (2004), The status of planning in small business, *American Business Review*, Vol. 22, No. 2, pp. 52–61.

Ibrahim, M., Sandstrom, S., Edvardsson, B. and Kristensson, P. (2008), Value in use through service experience, *Managing Service Quality*, Vol. 18, No. 2, pp. 112–122.

Ihlen, O. (2008), Mapping the environment for corporate social responsibility: stakeholders, publics and the public sphere, *Corporate Communications*, Vol. 13, No. 2, pp. 135–143.

Jackson, I. A. and Nelson, K. (2004), Values-driven performance: seven strategies for delivering profits with principles, *Ivey Business Journal Online*, November/December, pp. B1–B8.

Jackson, P. M. (2009), The size and scope of the public sector, In Boviard, T. and Loffler, E. (eds) *Public Management and Governance*, 2nd edn, Routledge, London, pp. 27–40.

Jaffe, A. M. and Manning, R. A. (2000), The shocks of a world of cheap oil, *Foreign Affairs*, Vol. 79, No. 1, pp. 16–30.

Jansen, M. (2009), Desert sun power pulls in the big guns, *The Sunday Times*, London, 27 July, p. 11.

Javalgi, R. G., Radulovich, L. P., Pendleton, G. and Scherer, R. F. (2005), Sustainable competitive advantage of internet firms: a strategic framework and implications for global marketers, *International Marketing Review*, Vol. 22, No. 6, pp. 658–673.

Jaworski, B. J. and Kohli, A. K. (1966), Market orientation: review, refinement and roadmap, *Journal of Market Focused Management*, Vol. 1, No. 2, pp. 119–135.

Jayaraman, L., Min, L. and Byung, K. (1993), Business ethics – a developmental perspective: the evolution of the free and mature corporation, *Journal of Business Ethics*, Vol. 12, No. 9, pp. 665–676.

Jensen, S., Hougaard, E. and Nieksen, S. B. (1995), Population ageing, public debt and sustainable fiscal spending, *Fiscal Studies*, Vol. 16, No. 2, pp. 1–20.

Jerrell, T. D. (1997), A history of legally required employee benefits: 1900–1950, *Journal of Management History*, Vol. 3, No. 2, pp. 193–212.

Johnson, G. and Scholes, K. (1999), *Exploring Corporate Strategy*, Prentice Hall, Harlow.

Johnson, R. (2004), Economic policy implications of world demographic change, *Economic Review Federal Reserve Bank of Kansas City*, Vol. 89, pp. 39–65.

Johnson, R. A., Hoskisson, R. E. and Hitt, M. A. (1993), Board of director involvement in restructuring: the effects of board executives, *Strategic Management Journal*, Vol. 14, pp. 33–51.

Johnston, P. and Pongatichat, P. (2008), Managing the tension between performance measurement and strategy: coping strategies, *International Journal of Operations & Production Management*, Vol. 28, No. 10, pp. 941–967.

Jones, D. (2002), Are transformed workplaces more productively efficient? *Journal of Economic Issues*, Vol. 36, No. 3, pp. 659–671.

Jones, R. and Kriflik, G. (2006), Subordinate expectations of leadership within a cleaned-up bureaucracy: a grounded theory study, *Journal of Organizational Change Management*, Vol. 19, No. 2, pp.154–172.

Jordan, J. L., Meltzer, H., Schwartz, A. J. and Sargent, T. J. (1993), Milton, money, and mischief: symposium and articles in honor of Milton Friedman, *Economic Inquiry*, Vol. 31, No. 2, pp. 197–214.

Kahley, W. (1988), Florida's challenge: managing growth, *Economic Review – Federal Reserve Bank of Atlanta*, Vol. 73, No. 1, pp. 14–23.

Kahn, B. E. (1998), Dynamic relationships with customers: high variety strategies, *Journal of Academy of Marketing Science*, Vol. 26, No. 1, pp. 45–53.

Kalyanpur, A., Latif, F., Saini, S. and Sarnikar, S. (2007), Inter-organizational e-commerce in healthcare services: the case of global teleradiology, *Journal of Electronic Commerce in Organizations*, Vol. 5, No. 2, pp. 47–56.

Kane, E. J. (1989), The Bush plan is no cure for S&L insurance malady, *Challenge*, Vol. 32, No. 6, pp. 39–47.

Kaplan, R. S. and Norton, D. P. (1992a), *The Balanced Scorecard*, Harvard Business School Press, Boston, Massachusetts.

Kaplan, R. S. and Norton, D. P. (1992b), The balanced scorecard: measures that drive performance, *Harvard Business Review*, March/April, pp. 71–80.

Kaplan, R. S. and Norton, D. P. (1996), Strategic learning & the balanced scorecard, *Strategy & Leadership*, Vol. 24, No. 5, pp. 18–25.

Katsoulakos, T. and Katsoulakos, Y. (2007), Strategic management, corporate responsibility and stakeholder management, *Corporate Governance*, Vol. 7, No. 4, pp. 355–369.

Kaufman, G. G. and Wallinson, P. J. (2001), The new safety net, *Regulation*, Vol. 24, No. 2, pp. 28–36.

Kay, J. A. (1993), *Foundations of Corporate Success: How Business Strategies Add Value*, Oxford University Press, Oxford.

Khatri, N. and Ng. A. A. (2000), The role of intuition in strategic decision making, *Human Relations*, Vol. 53, No. 1, pp. 57–87.

Kearney, C., Hisrich, R. D. and Roche, F. (2009), Public and private sector entrepreneurship: similarities, differences or a combination? *Journal of Small Business and Enterprise Development*, Vol. 16, No. 1, pp. 26–35.

Keefer, P. and Vlaicu, R. (2007), Democracy, credibility, and clientelism, *Journal of Law, Economics, & Organization*, Vol. 24, No. 2, pp. 371–406.

Kellerman, B. (2004), *Bad Leadership*, Harvard Business School Press, Boston, Massachusetts.

Kellerman, B. (2005), How bad leadership happens, *Leader to Leader*, Vol. 35, pp. 41–46.

Kennedy, P. (2009), Read the big four to know capitalism's fate, *The Future of Capitalism, Financial Times*, London, 12 May, pp. 18–20 (www.ft.com/capitalism).

Kernaghan, K. (2000), The post-bureaucratic organization and public service, *International Review of Administrative Science*, Vol. 66, No. 1, pp. 91–104.

Kets de Vries, M. J. (1977), The entrepreneurial personality: a person at the crossroads, *Journal of Management Studies*, Vol. 14, No. 1, pp. 34–57.

Khalid, A. M. and Pearce, J. L. (1993), The influence of values on management practices, *International Studies of Management & Organization*, Vol. 23, No. 3, pp. 35–53.

Khan, A. M. and Manopichetwattan, V. (1989), Innovative and non-innovative small firms and characteristics, *Management Science*, Vol. 35, No. 5, pp. 597–606.

Khandwalla, P. J. (1977), *The Design of Organizations*, Harcourt Brace Jovanovich, New York.

Kiessling, T. E. (2004), Entrepreneurship to innovation: Austrian School of Economics to Schumpeter to Drucker to now, *Journal of Applied Management and Entrepreneurship*, Vol. 9, No. 1, pp. 80–91.

Kilbourne, W. E. (1995), Green advertising: salvation or oxymoron? *Journal of Advertising*, Vol. 24, No. 2, pp. 7–20.

Kim, S. (2002), Participative management and job satisfaction: lessons for management leadership, *Public Administration Review*, Vol. 62, No. 2, pp. 231–241.

Kim, S. (2005), Individual-level factors and organizational performance in Government organizations, *Journal of Public Administration Research and Theory*, Vol. 15, No. 2, pp. 245–253.

Kim, P. S. and Hong, K. P. (2006), Searching for effective HRM reform strategy in the public sector: critical review of WPSR 2005 and suggestions, *Public Personnel Management*, Vol. 35, No. 3, pp. 199–216.

Kirzner, I. (1979), *Perception, Opportunity and Profit*, University of Chicago Press, Chicago.

Klein, J. (2002), Beyond competitive advantage, *Strategic Change*, Vol. 11, No. 6, pp. 317–327.

Klerkx, L., De Grip, K. and Leeuwis, C. (2006), Hands off but strings attached: the contradictions of policy-induced demand-driven agricultural extension, *Agriculture and Human Values*, Vol. 23, pp. 189–204.

Kochan, A. (2005), Scalpel please, robot: Penelope's debut in the operating theatre, *The Industrial Robot*, Vol. 32, No. 6, pp. 449–452.

Koguchi, K. (1993), Financial conglomerates: how big is beautiful? *The OECD Observer, Paris*, August/September, pp. 18–26.

Kooiman, J. (1999), Social–political governance: overview, reflections and design, *Public Management Review*, Vol. 1, No. 1, pp. 67–92.

Kooinman, J. (1993), Social–political governance, In Kooiman, J. (ed.), *Modern Governance*, Sage, London.

Kopczak, L. R. and Johnson, M. C. (2003), The supply-chain management effect, *Sloan Management Review*, Vol. 44, No. 3, pp. 28–34.

Kotler, P. and Andreasen, A. (1991), *Strategic Marketing for Non-profit Organizations*, Prentice-Hall, Englewood Cliffs, New Jersey.

Kotzab, H., Grant, D. B. and Friis, A. (2006), Supply chain management and priority strategies in Danish organisations, *Journal of Business Logistics*, Vol. 27, No. 2, pp. 273–302.

Kravenuck, R. S. and Schack, R. W. (1996), Designing effective performance measurement systems under the Government Performance and Results Act of 1993, *Public Administration Review*, Vol. 56, pp. 348–358.

Kusuda, Y. (2003), A remotely controlled robot operates construction machines, *The Industrial Robot*, Vol. 30, No. 5, pp. 422–426.

Laforet, S. and Tann, J. (2006), Innovative characteristics of small manufacturing firms, *Journal of Small Business and Enterprise Development*, Vol. 13, No. 3, pp. 363–375.

Laing, A. (2003), Marketing in the public sector: towards a typology of public services, *Marketing Theory*, Vol. 3, No. 4, pp. 173–188.

Langseth, P., Bucholz, R. A. and Rosentahl, S. B. (1995), Theoretical foundations of public policy: a pragmatic perspective, *Business and Society*, Vol. 34, No. 3, pp. 261–280.

Larsan, J. (1998), RoboKent – a case study in man–machine interfaces, *The Industrial Robot*, Vol. 25, No. 2, pp. 95–101.

Larson, P. (1997), Public and private values at odds: can private sector values be transplanted, *Public Administration & Development*, Vol. 17, No. 1, pp. 131–140.

Lawrence, D. (1998), Leading discontinuous change: ten lessons from the battlefront, In Hambrick, D. C., Nadler, N. C. and Tushman, M. L. (eds), *Navigating Change*, Harvard Business School Press, Harvard, Massachusetts.

Lawton, T. C. (1999), Evaluating European competitiveness: measurements and models for a successful business environment, *European Business Journal*, Vol. 11, No. 4, pp. 195–206.

Lawton, T. C. and Michaels, K. P. (2001), Advancing to the virtual value chain: learning from the Dell model, *Irish Journal of Management*, Vol. 22, No. 1, pp. 91–112.

Learned, E. P., Christensen, C. R., Andrews, C. R and Guth, W. D. (1965), *Strategy, Policy and Cases*, Irwin, Homewood, Illinois.

Leavitt, M. (2010), Fumbled bill, *Modern Healthcare*, Vol. 40, No. 14, pp. 24–26.

Leland, S. and Smirnova, O. (2009), Reassessing privatization strategies 25 years later: revisiting Perry and Babitsky's comparative performance study of urban bus transit services, *Public Administration Review*, Vol. 69, No. 5, pp. 855–867.

Letza, S. R., Smallan, C. and Sun, X. (2004), Reframing privatisation: deconstructing the myth of efficiency, *Policy Sciences*, Vol. 37, pp. 159–183.

Leung, P. and Cooper, B. J. (2003), The mad hatter's corporate tea party, *Managerial Auditing Journal*, Vol. 18, No. 6/7, pp. 505–516.

Liedtka, J. (2000), In defence of strategy as design, *California Management Review*, Vol. 42, No. 3, pp. 8–31.

Lindbeck, A. (1995), Hazardous welfare-state dynamics, *The American Economic Review*, Vol. 85, No. 2, pp. 90–102.

Lippitt, M. B. (2003), Six priorities that make a great strategic decision, *Journal of Business Strategy*, Vol. 24, January/February, pp. 21–24.

Lorenzoni, G. and Baden-Fuller, C. (1995), Creating a strategic center to manage a web of partners, *California Management Review*, Vol. 37, No. 3, pp. 146–164.

Lumpkin, G. T. and Dess, G. G. (1996), Clarifying the entrepreneurial orientation construct and linking it to performance, *Academy of Management Review*, Vol. 21, pp. 135–172.

Lundin, M. (2007), Explaining cooperation: how resource interdependence, goal congruence, and trust affect joint actions in policy implementation, *Journal of Public Administration Research and Theory*, Vol. 17, pp. 651–672.

Lysons, A. (1999), Strategic renewal and development implications of organisational effectiveness, *Tertiary Education and Management*, Vol. 5, No. 1, pp. 47–58.

MacDonald, S. (1998), *Information for Innovation: Managing Change from an Information Perspective*, Oxford University Press, Oxford.

MacKay, R. B. and McKiernan, P. (2004), Exploring strategy context with foresight, *European Management Review*, Vol. 1, No. 1, pp. 69–78.

Madden, B. J. (2005), *Maximising Shareholder Value and the Greater Good*, www.LearningWhatWorks.com, Naperville, Illinois.

Mahoney, D. (1992), Toward a more ethical system of state and local government retirement funding, *Journal of Public Budgeting, Accounting & Financial Management*, Vol. 14, No. 2, pp. 197–125.

Mailliard, K. (1997), Linking performance to the bottom line, *HR Focus*, Vol. 74, No. 6, pp. 1–11.

Malhotra, P. and Lofgren, H. (2004), India's pharmaceutical industry: hype or high-tech take-off? *Australian Health Review*, Vol. 28, No. 2, pp. 182–194.

Manning, K., Corble, N. and Birley, S. (1992), The restructuring of the public sector in the UK, *European Business Journal*, Vol. 4, No. 4, pp. 27–37.

Markides, C. (2004), What is strategy and how do you know if you have one, *Business Strategy Review*, Vol. 15, No. 2, pp. 5–12.

Marmor, T. R. (1998), Forecasting American healthcare: how we got here and where we might be going, *Journal of Health Politics*, Vol. 23, No. 3, pp. 521–542.

Marshall, R. (2006), Broader horizons for biomass, *Chemical Engineering*, Vol. 113, No. 10, pp. 21–26.

Martel, L. (2003), Finding and keeping high performers: best practices from 25 best companies, *Employment Relations Today*, Vol. 30, No. 1, pp. 11–18.

Martin, G. (1995), Performance-related pay in nursing: theory, practice and prospect, *Health Manpower Management*, Vol. 20, No. 5, pp. 10–18.

Martin, J. (1995), Pay and performance drive human resource agendas, *Management Development Review*, Vol. 8, No. 3, pp. 6–12.

Martin, S. (2000), Implementing 'best value': local public services in transition, *Public Administration*, Vol. 78, No. 1, pp. 209–227.

Martin, S. (2010), From new public management to networked community governance? Strategic local public service networks in England, In Osborne, S. P. (ed.), *New Public Governance?*, Routledge, London, pp. 337–346.

Mascarenhas, B. and Aaker, D. A. (1989), Strategy over the business cycle, *Strategic Management Journal*, Vol. 10, No. 3, pp. 199–211.

Mason, R. B. (2007), The external environment's effect on management and strategy: a complexity theory approach, *Management Decision*, Vol. 45, No. 1, pp. 10–28.

Mattessich, P., Murray-Close, M. and Monsey, B. (2001), *Collaboration: What Makes It Work*, Amherst H. Wilder Foundation, St Paul, Minnesota.

Mayer, P. and Vambery, R. G. (2008), Aligning global strategy with planning models with accelerating change, *Journal of Global Business and Technology*, Vol. 4, No. 1, pp. 30–41.

Mayhew, K. and Neely, A. (2006), Improving productivity – opening the black box, *Oxford Review of Economic Policy*, Vol. 22, No. 4, pp. 445–461.

McAdam, R. A., Hazlett, S. and Casey, C. (2005), Performance management in the UK public sector: addressing multiple stakeholder complexity, *International Journal of Public Sector Management*, Vol. 18, No. 3, pp. 256–273.

McCarthy, B. (2003), Strategy is personality-driven, strategy is crisis-driven: insights from entrepreneurial firms, *Management Decisions*, Vol. 41, No. 4, pp. 327–340.

McCarthy, B. and Leavy, B. (1998), The entrepreneur, risk-perception and change over time: a typology approach, *Irish Business & Administration Research*, Vol. 19/20, No. 1, pp. 125–141.

McMann, S. J. H. (2009), Political conservatism, authoritarianism, and societal threat: voting for Republican Representatives in U.S. Congressional elections from 1946 to 1992, *Journal of Psychology*, Vol. 143, No. 4, pp. 341–359.

McPherson, M. S., Schapiro, M. O. and Winston, G. C. (1989), Recent trends in U.S. higher education costs and prices, *The American Economic Review*, Vol. 79, No. 2, pp. 253–258.

Meeks, C. B., Nickols, S. Y. and Sweeney, A. L. (1999), Demographic comparisons of ageing in five selected countries, *Journal of Family and Economic Issues*, Vol. 20, No. 3, pp. 223–242.

Melnyk, S. A., Calantone, R. J., Luft, J., Stewart, D. M., Zsidisin, G. A., Hanson, J. and Burns, L. (2005), An empirical investigation of the metrics alignment process, *International Journal of Productivity and Performance Management*, Vol. 54, No. 5/6, pp. 312–324.

Mendonca, M. (2001), Preparing for ethical leadership in organizations, *Canadian Journal of Administrative Sciences*, Vol. 18, No. 4, pp. 266–276.

Menzel, D. C. (1999), The morally mute manager: fact or fiction? *Public Personnel Management*, Vol. 28, No. 4, pp. 515–527.

Michael, J. P. and Taylor, W. G. (2001), Progress in electronic service delivery by English District Councils, *International Journal of Public Sector Management*, Vol. 14, No. 6/7, pp. 569–584.

Miles, R. E., Snow, C. C., Meyer, A. J. and Coleman, H. J. (1978), Organizational strategy, structure, and process, *The Academy of Management Review*, Vol. 3, No. 3, pp. 546–562.

Miller, D. (1983), The correlates of entrepreneurship in three types of firm, *Management Science*, Vol. 29, No. 1, pp. 770–791.

Miller, D. (1986), Configurations of strategy and structure: towards a synthesis, *Strategic Management Journal*, Vol. 7, pp. 223–249.

Miller, D. and Freisen, P. H. (1980), Momentum and revolution in organisational adaption, *Academy of Management Journal*, Vol. 23, pp. 591–614.

Miller, D., and Friesen, P. H. (1982), Archetypes of strategy formulation, *Management Science*, Vol. 28, No. 1, pp. 639–651.

Miller, J. G. and Warren, H. (1989), Implementing manufacturing strategic planning, *Planning Review*, Vol. 17, No. 4, pp. 22–34.

Mintzberg, H. (1979), Patterns in strategy formation, *International Studies of Management and Organisations*, Vol. 10, No. 3, pp. 67–86.

Mintzberg, H. (1990), The Design School: Reconsidering the basic premises of strategic management, *Strategic Management Journal*, Vol. 11, pp. 171–195.

Mintzberg, H. (1994a), Rethinking strategic planning part I: pitfalls and fallacies, *Long Range Planning*, Vol. 27, pp. 12–21.

Mintzberg, H. (1994b), *The Rise and Fall of Strategic Planning*, The Free Press, New York.

Mintzberg, H. (1999), Reflecting on the strategy process, *Sloan Management Review*, Vol. 40, No. 3, pp. 21–32.

Mintzberg, H. and Waters, J. A. (1982), Tracking strategy in an entrepreneurial firm, *Academy of Management Journal*, Vol. 25, No. 3, pp. 463–499.

Mishina, Y., Pollock, T. G. and Porac, J. (2004), Are more resources always better for growth: resource stickiness in market and product expansion, *Strategic Management Journal*, Vol. 25, pp. 1179–1197.

Mitchell, A. (2001), Radical innovation, *BT Technology Journal*, Vol. 19, No. 4, pp. 60–71.

Mitchell, A. and Dupre, K. (1994), The environmental movement: a status report and implications for pricing, *S.A.M. Advanced Management Journal*, Vol. 59, No. 2, pp. 35–43.

Mitchell, J. A. (1993), Poisoned chocolate: corporate governance and the Cadbury Report, *Managerial Auditing Journal*, Vol. 8, No. 3, pp. 31–35.

Molteni, M. (2006), The social-competitive innovation pyramid, *Corporate Governance*, Vol. 6, No. 4, pp. 516–526.

Montari, J. R. and Bracker, J. S. (1986), The strategic management process at the public planning unit level, *Strategic Management Journal*, Vol. 7, No. 3, pp. 251–268.

Montoya-Weiss, M. M. and Calantone, R. G. (1994), Determinants of new product performance: a review and a meta-analysis, *Journal of Product Innovation Management*, Vol. 11, No. 5, pp. 397–417.

Moon, M. J. (1999), The pursuit of managerial entrepreneurship: does organization matter? *Public Administration Review*, Vol. 59, No. 1, pp. 31–43.

Moore, G. A. (1991), *Crossing the Chasm*, The Free Press, New York.

Morash, E. A. and Clinton, S. R. (1998), Supply chain integration: Customer value through collaborative closeness, *Journal of Marketing Theory and Practice*, Vol. 6, No. 4, pp. 104–119.

Morehouse, J., O'Meara, B., Hagen, C. and Huseby, T. (2008), Hitting back: strategic responses to low-cost rivals, *Srategy & Leadership*, Vol. 36, No. 1, pp. 4–13.

Morris, M. H. and Jones, F. F. (1999), Entrepreneurship in established organizations: the case of the public sector, *Entrepreneurship Theory and Practice*, Vol. 24, No. 1, pp. 71–91.

Moullin, M. (2002), *Delivering Excellence in Health and Social Care*, Open University Press, Buckinghamshire.

Mukhopadhyay, S. K. and Gupta, A. V. (1998), Interfaces for resolving marketing, manufacturing and design conflicts: a conceptual framework, *European Journal of Marketing. Bradford*, Vol. 32, No. 1/2, pp. 101–124.

Mulgan, R. (2008), Public sector reform in New Zealand: issues of public accountability, *Public Administration Quarterly*, Vol. 32, No. 1, pp. 1–32.

Murray, S. (2009), Added value, Health Magazine, *The Financial Times*, London, Vol. 3, 16 September, pp. 36–39.

Myers, M. B. and Cheung, M. (2008), Sharing global supply chain knowledge, *Sloan Management Review*, Vol. 49, No. 4, pp. 67–73.

Nanus, B. (1992), Visionary leadership: how to re-vision the future, *The Futurist*, Vol. 26, No. 5, pp. 20–26.

National Academy for Engineering (2005), *Grand Challenges for Engineering*, National Academy for Engineering, Washington, D.C. (accessed at www.engineeringchallenges.org).

Navarro, P. (2008), Principles of the master cyclist, *Sloan Management Review*, Vol. 45, No. 2, pp. 20–24.

Navarro, P. (2009), Recession-proofing your organization, *Sloan Management Review*, Vol. 50, No. 3, pp. 45–51.

Navarro, V., Schmitt, J. and Astudillo, J. (2004), Is globalisation undermining the welfare state? *Cambridge Journal of Economics*, Vol. 28, No. 1, pp. 133–143.

Neely, A. D., Adams, C. and Crowe, P. (2001), The performance prism in practice, *Measuring Business Excellence*, Vol. 5, No. 2, pp. 6–11.

Nesvetailova, A. (2005), United in debt: towards a global crisis of debt-driven finance? *Science & Society*, Vol. 69, No. 3, pp. 396–419.

Newman, J. D., Tigwell, L. J., Warner, P. J. and Turner, F. (2001), Biosensors: boldly going into the new millennium, *Sensor Review*, Vol. 21, No. 4, pp. 268–271.

Nohria, N. and Berkley, J. D. (1994), An action perspective: the crux of the new management, *California Management Review*, Vol. 36, No. 4, pp. 70–93.

Noor, A. (2007), Re-engineering healthcare, *Mechanical Engineering*, Vol. 129, No. 11, pp. 22–27.

Norreklit, H. (2000), The balance on the balanced scorecard: a critical analysis of some of its assumptions, *Management Accounting Research*, Vol. 11, pp. 65–88.

O'Brien, F. and Meadows, M. (2001), How to develop visions: a literature review, and a revised CHOICES approach for an uncertain world, *Systemic Practice and Action Research*, Vol. 14, No. 4, pp. 495–511.

OECD (2007), Public Sector Pensions and the Challenge of an Ageing Public Service, *OECD Working Paper on Public Governance*, February, OECD, Paris.

Ogut, A., Kocabacak, A. and Demirsel, M. T. (2008), The impact of data mining on the managerial decision-making process: a strategic approach, *Journal of American Academy of Business*, Vol. 14, No. 1, pp. 137–143.

Ohmura, A. and Watanabe, C. (2006), Cross-products technology spillover in inducing a self-propagating dynamism for the shift to a service orientated economy, *Journal of Services Research*, Vol. 6, No. 2, pp. 145–178.

Oliver, R. W. (1999), Strategy in the biotech age, *Journal of Business Strategy*, Vol. 20, No. 6, pp. 7–10.

O'Looney, J. (1992), Public–private partnerships in economic development: negotiating the trade-offs, *Economic Development Review*, Vol. 10, No. 4, pp. 14–23.

Orcutt, B. L. (2003), Expenditure and deficit policy: an analysis of the William E. Simon's rules, *Atlantic Economic Journal*, Vol. 31, No. 3, pp. 219–227.

Ortt, J. R. and Schoorman, J. P. I. (2004), The patterns of development and diffusion of break-through communication technology, *European Journal of Innovation Management*, Vol. 7, No. 4, pp. 292–301.

Osborne, S. P. (2010), Introduction: The (New) Public Governance: A suitable case for treatment? In Osborne, S. P. (ed.), *The New Public Governance? Emerging Perspectives on the Theory and Practice of Public Governance*, Routledge, London, pp. 1–16.

Osborne, S. P. and Brown, K. (2005), *Managing Change and Innovation in Public Sector Organizations*, Routledge, London.

Paap, J. and Katz, R. (2004), Anticipating disruptive innovation, *Research Technology Management*, Vol. 47, No. 5, pp. 13–23.

Paarlberg, L. A. (2007), The impact of customer orientation on Government employee performance, *International Public Management Journal*, Vol. 10, No. 2, pp. 201–231.

Parasuraman, A., Zeithaml, V. and Berry, L. (1985), A conceptual model of SQ and its implications for future research, *Journal of Marketing*, Vol. 49, pp. 41–50.

Parasuraman, A., Zeithaml, V. and Berry, L. (1988), SERVQUAL: a multiple-item scale for measuring consumer perceptions of SQ, *Journal of Retailing*, Vol. 64, No. 1, pp. 12–40.

Parente, S. T. (2009), Health information technology and financing's next frontier: the potential of medical banking, *Business Economics*, Vol. 44, No. 1, pp. 41–50.

Parker, R. and Bradley, L. (2000), Organisational culture in the public sector: evidence from six organizations, *International Journal of Public Sector Management*, Vol. 13, No. 2/3, pp. 125–141.

Parks, G. M. (1977), How to climb the growth curve – eleven hurdles for the entrepreneur manager, *Journal of Small Business Management*, Vol. 15, No. 1, pp. 25–33.

Parnell, J. A., Von Bergen, C. W. and Soper, B. (2005), Profiting from past triumphs and failures: harnessing history for future success, *S.A.M. Advanced Management Journal*, Vol. 70, No. 2, pp. 36–47.

Patzek, T. D., Anti, S. M. and Campos, K. W. (2005), Ethanol from corn: clean renewable fuel for the future, or drain on our resources and pockets? *Environment, Development and Sustainability*, Vol. 7, No. 3, pp. 319–330.

Pedersen, D, and Hartley, J. (2008), The changing context of public leadership and management: implications for roles and dynamics, *International Journal of Public Sector Management*, Vol. 21, No. 4, pp. 327–339.

Pedersen, S. J. and Rendtorff, J. D. (2004), Value-based management in local public organizations: a Danish experience, *Cross Cultural Management*, Vol. 11, No. 2, pp. 71–94.

Peled, A. (2000), Politicking for success: the missing skill, *Leadership & Organization Development Journal*, Vol. 21, No. 1/2, pp. 20–29.

Persson, T. and Tabellini, G. (2000), *Political Economics: Explaining Economic Policy*, MIT Press, Cambridge, Massachusetts.

Peters, G. (1999), A systems failures view of the UK national commission into higher education report, *Systems Research and Behavioral Science*, Vol. 16, No. 2, pp. 123–131.

Peters, T. J. (1984), Strategy follows structure: developing distinctive skills, *California Management Review*, Vol. 26, No. 3, pp. 111–122.

Peters, T. J. and Waterman, R. H. (1984), *In Search of Excellence: Lessons from Americas Best Run Companies*, Harper & Row, New York.

Peterson, E. R. (2004), Seven revolutions: global strategic trends out to the year 2025, *Multinational Business Review*, Vol. 12, No. 2, pp. 111–119.

Pike, A. (1999), Commission will assess the value of partnerships, *Financial Times*, London, 18 November, p. 2.

Pilichowski, E., Arnould, E. and Turkisch, E. (2007), Ageing and the public sector: challenges for financial and human resources, *OECD Journal on Budgeting*, Vol. 7, No. 4, pp. 123–162.

Pimental, D., Bailey, O., Kim, P., Mullaney, E., Calabrese, J., Walkman, L., Nelson, F. and Yao, X. (1999), Will limits on the earth's resources control human numbers? *Environment, Development and Sustainability*, Vol. 1, pp. 19–39.

Pitt, L., Berthon, P. and Lane, N. (1998), Gaps within the IS department: barriers to service quality, *Journal of Information Technology*, Vol. 13, No. 3, pp. 191–208.

Plant, T. (2009), Strategic planning for municipalities: Ensuring progress and relevance, *Performance Improvement Journal*, Vol. 48, No. 5, pp. 26–35.

Poister, T. H. and Streib, G. (2005), Elements of strategic planning and management in Municipal Government: status after two decades, *Public Administration Review*, Vol. 65, No. 1, pp. 45–58.

Pollard, C., Young, J. and Gregg, P. (2006), Towards a simplified framework of CRM for use in public and private sectors, *Journal of Information Technology Case and Application Research*, Vol. 8, No. 2, pp. 24–35.

Pollitt, C. and Bouckaert, G. (2004), *Public Management Reform: A Comparative Analysis*, 2nd edn, Oxford University Press, Oxford.

Popovich, M. (1998), *Creating High Performance Government Organizations*, Jossey-Bass, San Francisco.

Porter, M. E. (1980), *Competitive Strategy*, The Free Press, New York.

Porter, M. E. (1985), *Competitive Advantage: Creating and Sustaining Competitive Advantage*, The Free Press, New York.

Porter, M. E. (1991), Towards a dynamic theory of strategy, *Strategic Management Journal*, Vol. 12, pp. 91–117.

Pralahad, C. K. and Hamel, G. (1990), The core competence of the corporation, *Harvard Business Review*, March/April, pp. 79–91.

Preble, J. F. (1992), Towards a comprehensive system of strategic controls, *Journal of Management Studies*, Vol. 29, No. 4, pp. 391–409.

Price, R. and Brodie, R. J. (2001), Transforming a public service organization from inside out to outside in: The case of Auckland City, New Zealand, *Journal of Service Research*, Vol. 4, No. 1, pp. 50–59.

Public Administration Select Committee (PASC) (2003), *On Target? Government by Measurement, Fifth Report of Session 2002–2003*, The Stationery Office, London.

Pullen, W. (1993), Strategic shocks: managing discontinuous change, *The International Journal of Public Sector Management*, Vol. 6, No. 1, pp. 30–40.

Quinn, J. B. (1980), *Strategies for Change: Logical Incrementalism*, Irwin, Homewood, Illinois.

Radin, B. (2006), *Challenging the Performance Movement: Accountability, Complexity and Democratic Values*, Georgetown University Press, Washington, D.C.

Radin, B. A. and Coffee, J. N. (1993), A critique of TQM: problems of implementation in the public sector, *Public Administration Quarterly*, Vol. 17, No. 1, pp. 42–59.

Radnor, Z. (2008), Muddled, massaging, manoeuvring or manipulated?: a typology of organisational gaming, *International Journal of Productivity and Performance Management*, Vol. 57, No. 4, pp. 316–328.

Radnor, Z. J. and McGuire, M. (2004), Performance management in the public sector: fact or fiction? *International Journal of Productivity and Performance Management*, Vol. 53, No. 1, pp. 23–34.

Rago, W. V. (1994), Adapting total quality management (TQM) to government: another point of view, *Public Administration Review*, Vol. 54, No. 1, pp. 61–65.

Ranky, G. N. and Ranky, P. G. (2005), Japanese prototype service robot R&D trends and examples, *The Industrial Robot*, Vol. 32, No. 6, pp. 460–465.

Ratajczak, D. (1994), What is the medical crisis, anyway, *Journal of the American Society of Chartered Life Underwriters*, Vol. 48, No. 5, pp. 22–25.

Reed, J. (2009), The future in his hands, *Financial Times Magazine*, London, 25 July, pp. 23–27.

Reich, R. (1994), Leadership and the high performance organization, *Journal for Quality and Participation*, Vol. 17, No. 2, pp. 6–12.

Reitsperger, W. D., Daniel, S. J., Tallman, S. B. and Chismar, W. G. (1993), Product quality and cost leadership: compatible strategies? *Management International Review*, Vol. 33, No. 3, pp. 7–22.

Riege, A. (2005), Three-dozen knowledge-sharing barriers managers must consider, *Journal of Knowledge Management*, Vol. 9, No. 3, pp. 18–35.

Rindova, V. and Kotha, S. (2001), Continuous 'morphing': competing through dynamic capabilities, form, and function, *Academy of Management Journal*, Vol. 44, pp. 1263–1280.

Ring, P. R. and Perry, J. L. (1985), Strategic management in public and private organizations: implications of distinctions, *The Academy of Management Review*, Vol. 10, No. 2, pp. 276–289.

Risher, H. (1995), Pay-for-performance: the keys to making it work, *Public Personnel Management*, Vol. 31, No. 3, pp. 317–332.

Ritson, M. (2007), Northern Rock has eroded its equity, *Marketing*, London, 19 September, p. 25.

Rivenbark, W. C. (2006), Evolutionary theory of routine: its role in results-based management, *Journal of Public Budgeting, Accounting & Financial Management*, Vol. 18, No. 2, pp. 223–240.

Robinson, R. B. and Pearce, J. A. (1984), Research thrusts in small firm strategic planning, *Academy of Management Review*, Vol. 10, No. 1, pp. 128–137.

Romano, C. A. (1990), Identifying factors which influence product innovation: a case study approach, *Journal of Management Studies*, Vol. 27, No. 1, pp. 75–95.

Ross, A. (2010), Trust boards accused over independence, *The Financial Times*, London, 21 August, p. 14.

Ross, B. H. (1988), Public and private sectors – the underlying differences, *Management Review*, Vol. 77, No. 5, pp. 28–36.

Rothman, H. and Kraft, A. (2006), Downstream and into deep biology: evolving business models in 'top tier' genomics companies, *Journal of Commercial Biotechnology*, Vol. 12, No. 2, pp. 86–101.

Rowe, A. J., Mason, R. O. and Dickel, K. E. (1994), *Strategic Management*, Addison Wesley, Menlo Park, California.

Rucker, M. R. (2003), Outsourcing: an ethical study in value driven management, *Journal of Applied Management and Entrepreneurship*, Vol. 8, No. 1, pp. 102–114.

Ruocco, P. and Proctor, T. (1994), Strategic planning in practice: a creative approach, *Marketing Intelligence & Planning*, Vol. 12, No. 9, pp. 24–29.

Ryan, J. (2008), The Finnish country-of-origin effect: the quest to create a distinctive identity in a crowded and competitive international marketplace, *Journal of Brand Management*, Vol. 16, No. 1/2, pp. 13–20.

Salter, B. (2007), The global politics of human embryonic stem cell science, *Global Governance*, Vol. 13, No. 2, pp. 221–232.

Salamon, L. M. and Anheier, H. K. (1998), Social origins of civil society: explaining the nonprofit sector, *Voluntas*, Vol. 9, No. 3, pp. 213–214.

Sanchez, R. (1997), Preparing for an uncertain future: managing organizations for strategic flexibility, *International Studies of Management & Organization*, Vol. 27, No. 2, pp. 71–94.

Santos, J., Doz, Y. and Williamson, P. (2004), Is your innovation process global? *Sloan Management Review*, Vol. 45, No. 4, pp. 31–37.

Sayles, L. R. (2006), The tipping point: how good executives go bad, *Corporate Finance Review*, Vol. 11, No. 1, pp. 18–25.

Schettkat, R. (2001), How bad are welfare-state institutions for economic development? *Challenge*, Vol. 44, No. 1, pp. 34–55.

Schieb, P. (1999), Feeding tomorrow's world, *The OECD Observer*, Summer, pp. 37–41.

Schofield, A. and Raynes, N. (1992), Providing a personal service in the Trent region, *International Journal of Health Care Quality Assurance*, Vol. 5, No. 5, pp. 16–19.

Schrenk, L. P. (2006), Equityholder versus stakeholder and corporate governance: developing a market for morality, *Business Renaissance Quarterly*, Vol. 1, No. 3, pp. 81–90.

Schultz, M. (1992), Postmodern picture of culture, *International Studies of Management and Organisations*, Vol. 22, No. 2, pp. 15–35.

Schumpeter, J. (1942), *Capitalism, Socialism and Democracy*, Harper Brothers, New York.

Schumpeter, J. (1950), *History of Economic Analysis*, Oxford University Press, New York.

Scott, W. T. (1985), Systems within systems: the mental health sector, *The American Behavioral Scientist*, Vol. 28, No. 5, pp. 601–612.

Sehgal, S., Sahay, B. S. and Goyal, S. K. (2006), Reengineering the supply chain in a paint company, *International Journal of Productivity and Performance Management*, Vol. 55, No. 8, pp. 655–670.

Senge, P. (1990), *The Fifth Discipline: The Art and Practice of the Learning Organisation*, Doubleday, New York.

Shapiro, S. M. (2001), *24/7 Innovation: A Blueprint for Surviving and Thriving in an Age of Change*, McGraw Hill, New York.

Sheehan, T. J. (2005), Why old tools won't work in the new knowledge economy, *Journal of Business Strategy*, Vol. 26, No. 4, pp. 53–62.

Sherman, H., Rowley, D. J. and Armandi, B. R. (2007), Developing a strategic profile: the pre-planning phase of strategic management, *Business Strategy Series*, Vol. 8, No. 3, pp. 162–171.

Shrader, C. B., Mulford, C. L. and Blackburn, V. L. (1989), Strategic and operational planning, uncertainty, and performance in small firms, *Journal of Small Business Management*, Vol. 27, No. 4, pp. 45–60.

Siebel (2003), Siebel customer success story – government, February, www.siebel.com, 14 February 2009.

Skelcher, C., Mathur, N. and Smith, M. (2005), The public governance of collaborative spaces: discourse, design and democracy, *Public Administration*, Vol. 63, No. 3, pp. 573–596.

Slater, S. F., Olson, E. M. and Venkateshwar, K. R. (1997), Strategy-based performance measurement, *Business Horizons*, July/August, pp. 37–44.

Slevin, D. P. and Covin, J. (1990), Juggling entrepreneurial style and organisational culture, *Sloan Management Review*, Vol. 31, No. 2, pp. 43–54.

Slywotzky, A. J. (1996), *Value Migration: How to Think Several Moves Ahead of Competition*, Harvard Business School Press, Harvard.

Smith, A. M. and Fischbacher, M. (2000), Stakeholder involvement in the new service design process, *Journal of Financial Services Marketing*, Vol. 5, No. 1, pp. 21–31.

Smith, G. (2004), An evaluation of the corporate culture of Southwest Airlines, *Measuring Business Excellence*, Vol. 8, No. 4, pp. 26–33.

Smith, M. (2010), BigDog to lead robot army against Taliban, *The Sunday Times*, London, 27 January, p. 14.

Smith, P. (1995), The unintended consequences of publishing performance data in the public sector, *International Journal of Public Administration*, Vol. 2, pp. 277–310.

Smith, R. (2007), Valuing defence, *Public Finance and Management*, Vol. 7, No. 3, pp. 242–259.

Stack, S. (2003), Beyond performance indicators: a case study in aged care, *Australian Bulletin of Labour*, Vol. 29, No. 2, pp. 143–161.

Steinke, C. (2008), Examining the role of service climate in health care: an empirical study of emergency departments, *International Journal of Service Industry Management*, Vol. 19, No. 2, pp. 188–209.

Steinmo, S. (1994), The end of redistribution? International pressures and domestic issues, *Challenge*, Vol. 37, No. 6, pp. 9–18.

Stern, B. B., Gould, S. J. and Benny, B. (1987), Baby boom singles: the social seekers, *The Journal of Consumer Marketing*, Vol. 4, No. 4, pp. 5–23.

Stonich, P. J. (1990), Time: the next strategic frontier, *Planning Review*, Vol. 18, No. 6, pp. 5–47.

Storey, J. and Buchanan, D. (2008), Healthcare governance and organizational barriers to learning from mistakes, *Journal of Health Organization and Management*, Vol. 22, No. 6, pp. 642–651.

Streeter, B. (2006), M&A: the deals just keep on coming, *ABA Banking Journal*, Vol. 98, No. 2, pp. 50–54.

Sundaram, A. K. and Inkpen, A. C. (2004), The corporate objective revisited, *Organization Science*, Vol. 15, No. 3, pp. 350–363.

Swank, D. and Steinmo, S. (2002), The new political economy of taxation in advanced capitalist democracies, *American Journal of Political Science*, Vol. 46, pp. 642–655.

Swiss, J. E. (1992), Adapting Total Quality Management (TQM) to government, *Public Administration Review*, Vol. 52, pp. 346–352.

Syed-Ikhsan, S. O. S. and Fytton, R. (2004), Knowledge management in a public organization: a study on the relationship between organizational elements and the performance of knowledge transfer, *Journal of Knowledge Management*, Vol. 8, No. 2, pp. 95–111.

Tan, C. W. and Pan, S. L. (2003), Managing e-transformation in the public sector: an e-government study of the Inland Revenue Authority of Singapore (IRAS), *European Journal of Information Systems*, Vol. 12, No. 4, pp. 269–281.

Tanabe, K. and Watanabe, C. (2005), Sources of small and medium enterprises excellent business performance in a service orientated economy, *Journal of Services Research*, Vol. 5, No. 1, pp. 5–21.

Tanzi, V. and Schuknecht, L. (2000), *Public Spending in the 20th Century*, Cambridge University Press, Cambridge.

Taylor, W. A. and Wright, W. A. (2004), Organizational readiness for successful knowledge sharing: challenges for public sector managers, *Information Resources Management Journal*, Vol. 17, No. 2, pp. 22–37.

Tebo, P. V. (2005), Building business value through sustainable growth, *Research Technology Management*, Vol. 48, No. 5, pp. 28–32.

Terwiersch, C. and Ulrich, K. (2008), Managing the opportunity portfolio, *Research Technology Management*, Vol. 51, No. 5, pp. 27–38.

Thietart, R. A. and Vivas, R. (1984), An investigation of success strategies, *Management Science*, Vol. 30, No. 12, pp. 1405–1424.

Thompson, J. D. (1967), *Organizations in Action*, McGraw Hill, New York.

Thompson, S. (1999), Takeover stories drive Footsie back above 6,000, *Financial Times*, London, 28 September, p. 54.

Thompson, S., Teo, H. and Pian, Y. (2003), A contingency perspective on Internet adoption and competitive advantage, *European Journal of Information Systems*, Vol. 12, No. 2, pp. 78–89.

Treacy, F. and Wiersema, F. (1995), *The Discipline of Market Leaders*, Harper Collins, New York.

Tridimas, G. (2001), The economics and politics of public expenditure, *Public Choice*, Vol. 106, No. 3/4, pp. 299–321.

Trott, P. (1998), Growing businesses by generating genuine business opportunities: a review of recent thinking, *Journal of Applied Management*, Vol. 7, No. 2, pp. 211–223.

Turner, J. (2007), Developing executive leadership in the public sector, *Public Manager*, Vol. 36, No. 4, pp. 50–55.

Ulla, P. (2006), Assessing fiscal risks through long-term budget projections, *OECD Journal on Budgeting*, Vol. 6, No. 1, pp. 127–187.

Ulwick, W. A. and Bettencourt, L. A. (2008), Giving customers a fair hearing, *Sloan Management Review*, Vol. 49, No. 3, pp. 62–68.

UN/DESA (2005), *World Public Sector Report 2005: Unlocking the Human Potential for Public Sector Performance*, United Nations, New York.

Urry, M. (2003), Young leader holds on to his dream: mortgage lender's chief executive is happy in his job – but he knows it may not last for ever, *Financial Times*, London, 10 February, p. 22.

Utting, K. (2009), Assessing the impact of Fair Trade coffee: towards an integrative framework, *Journal of Business Ethics*, Vol. 86, pp. 127–149.

Vaitheeswaran, V. J. (2007), Oil, *Foreign Policy*, Vol. 163, pp. 24–29.

Valentin, E. K. (2001), SWOT analysis from a resource-based view, *Journal of Marketing Theory and Practice*, Vol. 9, No. 2, pp. 54–70.

Van Dooren, W., Bouckert, G. and Halligan, J. (2010), *Performance Management in the Public Sector*, Routledge, London.

Van Peursem, K. A., Pratt, M. J. and Lawrence, S. R. (1995), Health management performance: a review of measures and indicators, *Accounting, Auditing & Accountability Journal*, Vol. 8, No. 5, pp. 34–71.

Vanger, S. and Huxham, C. (2010), Introducing the theory of collaborative advantage, In Osborne, S. P. (ed.), *New Public Governance?* Routledge, London, pp. 163–184.

Veenswjik, M. (2005), Cultural change in the public sector: innovating the frontstage and backstage, In Veenswjik, M. (ed.), *Organizing Innovation: New Approaches to Cultural Change and Interventions in Public Sector Organisations*, JOS Press, Amsterdam, pp. 3–14.

Vijayaraghavan, T. A. S. (1995), Strategic options for state road transport undertakings in India, *International Journal of Public Sector Management*, Vol. 8, No. 1, pp. 48–59.

Vinten, G. (2001), Corporate governance and the sons of Cadbury, *Corporate Governance*, Vol. 1, No. 4, pp. 4–8.

Vredenburgh, D. and Brender, Y. (1998), The hierarchical abuse of power in work organizations, *Journal of Business Ethics*, Vol. 17, No. 12, pp. 1337–1347.

Wagner, E. R. and Hansen, E. N. (2005), Innovation in large versus small companies: insights from the US wood products industry, *Management Decision*, Vol. 43, No. 5/6, pp. 837–851.

Wagstyl, S. (2010), A change in gear, *Financial Times*, London, 12 May, p. 13.

Walker, D. M. (2005), Our nation's financial condition and fiscal outlook, *Public Manager*, Vol. 34, No. 1, pp. 29–33.

Walker, H. and Brammer, S. (2009), Sustainable procurement in the United Kingdom public sector, *Supply Chain Management*, Vol. 14, No. 2, pp. 128–136.

Wallop, H. (2010), 1920s panic that led to a war on waste, *The Daily Telegraph*, London, 28 April, p. 4.

Wasserman, T. (2006), YouTube, *Brandweek*, 9 October, pp. M16–M18.

Webster, E. (1992), The changing role of marketing in the corporation, *Journal of Marketing*, Vol. 56, No. 3, pp. 1–17.

Weihrich, H. (1982), The TOWS matrix: tool for situational analysis, *Long Range Planning*, Vol. 15, No. 2, pp. 54–66.

Weiner, S. E. (1995), Budget deficits and debt: a summary of the bank's 1995 symposium, *Economic Review – Federal Reserve Bank of Kansas City*, Kansas City, Vol. 80, No. 4, pp. 5–18.

Wells, J. T. (2006), Will history repeat itself? *The Internal Auditor*, Vol. 63, No. 3, pp. 38–44.

Wensley, R. (1982), PIMS and BCG: new horizons or false dawn? *Strategic Management Journal*, Vol. 3, No. 2, pp. 147–159.

Weymes, E. (2004), Management theory: balancing individual freedom with organisational needs, *The Journal of Corporate Citizenship*, Vol. 16, pp. 85–98.

Whalen, C. (2008), The Rubin–Greenspan legacy, *The International Economy*, Vol. 22, No. 4, pp. 54–58.

Wheen, F. (1999), The great passport rip-off: the £120m contract that caused chaos, *The Guardian*, Manchester, 30 June, p. T.5.

White, L. H. (1989), Public management in a pluralistic arena, *Public Administration Review*, Vol. 49, No. 6, pp. 522–531.

Wilkinson, D. (1997), Whole system development – rethinking public service management, *International Journal of Public Sector Management*, Vol. 10, No. 7, pp. 505–533.

Wilkinson, T. J., McAlister, A. and Widmier, S. (2007), Reaching the international consumer: an assessment of the international direct marketing environment, *Direct Marketing*, Vol. 1, No. 1, pp. 17–37.

Williams, G. (1998), Biotechnology market development in Ireland: issues of strategy, risk and partnership, *Irish Marketing Review*, Vol. 11, No. 2, pp. 39–48.

Willman, P., Coen, D., Currie, D. and Siner, M. (2003), The evolution of regulatory relationships: regulatory institutions and firm behaviour in privatized industries, *Industrial and Corporate Change*, Vol. 12, No. 1, pp. 69–78.

Wilson, I. (2000), The new rules: ethics, social responsibility and strategy, *Strategy & Leadership*, Vol. 28, No. 3, pp. 12–21.

Wisniewski, M. and Stewart, D. (2004), Performance measurement for stakeholders: the case of Scottish local authorities, *International Journal of Public Sector Management*, Vol. 17, No. 3, pp. 222–233.

Wonglimpiyarat, J. (2004), The use of strategies in managing technological innovation, *European Journal of Innovation Management*, Vol. 7, No. 3, pp. 229–250.

Wootton, C. and Roszkowski, C. L. (1999), Legal aspects of corporate governance in early American railroads, *Business and Economic History*, Vol. 28, No. 2, pp. 325–326.

World Bank (1997), *Helping Countries Curb Corruption*, The World Bank, Washington, D.C.

Wray, L. R. (1993), Money, interest rates, and monetarist policy: some more unpleasant monetarist arithmetic? *Journal of Post Keynesian Economics*, Vol. 15, No. 4, pp. 541–570.

Yakita, A. (2001), Uncertain lifetime, fertility and social security, *Journal of Population Economics*, Vol. 14, No. 4, pp. 635–651.

Yoon, S. and Kuchinke, P. (2005), Systems theory and technology: lenses to analyze an organization, *Performance Improvement*, Vol. 44, No. 4, pp. 15–20.

Young, B. S., Worchel, S. and Woehr, D. J. (1998), Organizational commitment among public service employees, *Public Personnel Management*, Vol. 27, No. 3, pp. 339–347.

Yukl, G. and Falbe, C. (1990), Influence tactics and objectives in upward, downward and lateral influence attempts, *Journal of Applied Psychology*, Vol. 75, pp. 132–140.

Yusoff, W. Z., Ismail, M. and Newell, G. (2008), FM-SERVQUAL: a new approach of service quality measurement framework in local authorities, *Journal of Corporate Real Estate*, Vol. 10, No. 2, pp. 130–147.

Zahra, S. A. (1999), The changing roles of global competitiveness in the 21st century, *Academy of Management Executive*, Vol. 14, pp. 36–42.

Zahra, S. A. and Pearce, J. A. (1990), Research evidence on the Miles–Snow typology, *Journal of Management*, Vol. 16, No. 4, pp. 751–767.

Zanra, S. A. and Nielsen, A. P. (2002), Sources of capabilities, integration and technology commercialization, *Strategic Management Journal*, Vol. 23, No. 5, pp. 377–398.

Zineldin, M. (2005), Quality and customer relationship management (CRM) as competitive strategy in the Swedish banking industry, *The TQM Magazine*, Vol. 17, No. 4, pp. 329–344.

Index